38 Basic Speech Experiences

Perfection Learning®

Editorial Director Julie A. Schumacher

Picture Research Emily J. Greazel, Lisa Lorimor, Mark Hagenberg

Writer Lisa Dillman, Educational Specialist, Chicago, Illinois

Design Emily J. Greazel, Mark Hagenberg

Acknowledgments

Photo Credits

Associated Press: pp. 148–149, 164–165, 172, 192, 196–197, 210–211, 218–219, 222, 226–227, 230, 268–269, 350–351, 356–357; © Bettmann/CORBIS: pp. 254–255; © Douglas Kirkland/CORBIS: pp. 280–281; © John Springer Collection/CORBIS: p. 70; PARAMOUNT TELEVISION/THE KOBAL COLLECTION/COSTA, TONY: p. 341; © FOUGERE ERIC/CORBIS SYGMA: pp. 346–347; © Mark Peterson/CORBIS: p. 177; © Reuters/CORBIS: pp. 328–329

(*Credits continued on page 433*)

Copyright © 2005 by Perfection Learning® Corporation
1000 North Second Avenue
Box 500
Logan, Iowa 51546-0500
Tel: 1-800-831-4190 • Fax: 1-800-543-2745
perfectionlearning.com

      7 8 9 RRD 12 11

[hardcover] ISBN-13: 978-0-7569-3494-1
[hardcover] ISBN-10: 0-7569-3494-x

[softcover] ISBN-13: 978-0-7891-6434-6
[softcover] ISBN-10: 0-7891-6434-5

Printed in the United States of America

38

Basic Speech

11th Edition

Speech

Experiences

Clark S. Carlile, *Professor Emeritus, Idaho State University*

Dana V. Hensley, *Wichita Collegiate School*

Perfection Learning®

Contents

UNIT 1 Getting Started

UNIT 2 Personal Speeches

Contents

3 UNIT Speeches to Share Information

UNIT 4 Speaking Persuasively

Contents

UNIT 5 Social Speeches

Contents

UNIT 6 Speeches for Special Occasions

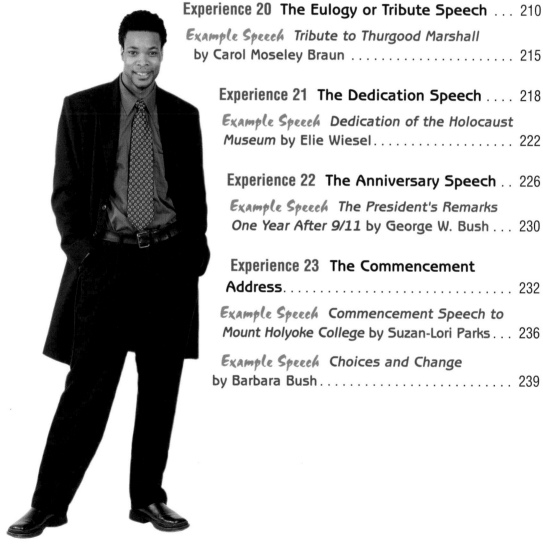

UNIT 7 Contest Speaking

Contents

UNIT 8 Business and Career Speaking

The Mass Media

Contents

UNIT 1 Getting Started

To do anything well takes preparation and practice. Learning how to be an effective public speaker is no exception. This unit will take you through some of the basics of preparing and presenting a speech for an audience. These fundamentals form the backbone of public speaking. They are also skills that will come in handy in the future—no matter where you go or what you do in your life.

How Communication Works

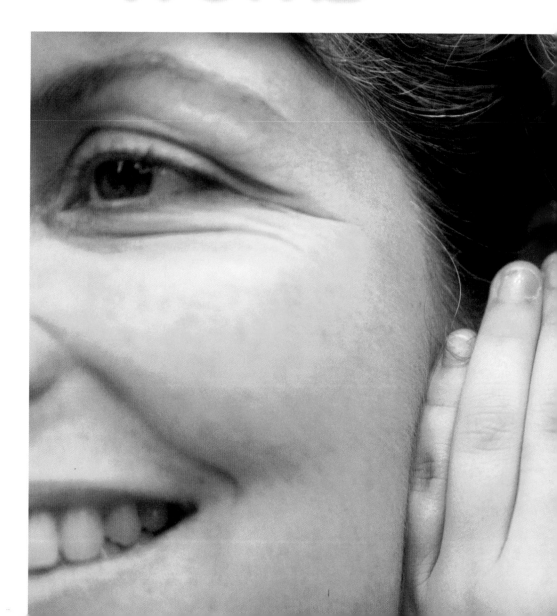

In This Chapter . . .

What is communication? Most people think they know. Yet many wrongly assume that communication happens only when a person is speaking. Imagine that you have just come home from school. You open the door and your dog bounds over to greet you. She wags her tail and wriggles as you smile and bend down to pet her. Not one word has been exchanged, yet you and your dog have just communicated.

Listening to a speaker means paying attention to both verbal and nonverbal forms of communication. So what is communication? **Communication** is an exchange of information that occurs anytime someone else sees and/or hears you. As you make your way through this chapter, you'll find out how communication happens. You'll also get some pointers on becoming a better speaker—and a better listener.

Speak Up!

Write your own definition of the word *communication*. When you're finished, exchange definitions with a classmate. Read the definitions aloud. Note the similarities and differences in the two. Then work together to combine your definitions into one that you both can agree upon.

Encoding and Decoding Meanings

When you were a small child just beginning to talk, every word you learned had a special meaning for you. You had a personal association with each new word. For example, the word *kitten* meant *your kitten* because to you there was no other. You invested each word with the meaning you had given it. You are older now and you no doubt attach broader meanings to your words. You have learned that there are many kinds of kittens in the world, yet you still attach *your* meaning to your words. The problem with communicating your ideas to someone else is that the other person will have his or her own associations and meanings for your words—and those meanings may be different from yours. If so, the person may not fully understand you. You will have communicated *something*, but it might not be what you intended.

The process of putting words together in phrases and sentences to represent feelings and ideas is called **encoding**. Listeners interpret your words by sorting out ideas they create in their own minds, a process known as **decoding**. It sounds a bit like working with secret codes, doesn't it? To some extent, that's exactly what it is. Yet you do it without even thinking every single day.

Other factors in your communication include how loudly and quickly you speak, and how high or low your voice is. These factors communicate things that you're feeling for which you have no specific words. Your friends can usually tell by your voice whether you are happy, sad, tired, or angry. A simple "good morning" can tell others that something is bothering you or that you're having a great day. Most people communicate their feelings whether they intend to or not.

Your appearance is another important part of what and how you communicate. Your clothes, hair, and personal hygiene tell others who you are. Consider what these factors are saying to others about you.

Activity

Think about a recent encounter you've had with a friend or family member. Try to recall specific details about what the person communicated to you verbally and nonverbally. What did the person's posture, facial expressions, voice, and overall manner tell you? How did these factors reflect what the person was saying to you? Share your impressions.

Encoding and Decoding as Precisely as Possible

The best way to bridge the gap between what you say and what the other person hears is to use accurate and specific words. For example, instead of describing an object as "brightly colored," you might state what those colors are: "orange and red." Instead of saying, "He was a big man," you might say, "He was six feet three inches tall and weighed 250 pounds."

Avoid general words such as *pretty, nice, fast, slow, beautiful,* and *bad.* The more specific you can be, the better your chances of communicating effectively will be. Use correct grammar and pronunciation. Remember to articulate clearly. And, finally, use as few words as possible. Don't make a listener decode fifty words when you can say the same thing with twenty-five.

Considering Your Audience

When you prepare a speech for a class assignment, it's important to remember that the underlying purpose of *all* public speaking is to communicate with an audience. To communicate as effectively as possible, you'll need to keep your audience in mind through every step of your preparation.

Communication requires you to send and receive messages. When you are speaking, your audience is receiving and sending messages to you by nonverbal means. **Messages** are thoughts and feelings we express through commonly agreed-upon **codes**, or language and behaviors. Effective communication depends on each communicator's ability to encode and decode messages as accurately as possible. But there are other factors that can get in the way of communication.

- **Noise** is anything that interferes with communication. Noise can be physical—for example, an air conditioner turning on and off or a truck roaring by outside the room where you are speaking. Noise can also be psychological, as when audience members are bored or distracted by something unrelated to your speech. And, finally, noise can be physiological, as in the situation where the room is too hot or cold, or your voice is too loud or soft, which can distract the listener from what you're saying. A speaker must anticipate the noise potential and do whatever is necessary to minimize it.

- Your **field of experience** provides reference points that allow you to decode messages and take meaning from them. Every person's experience is unique. No two communicators have exactly the same field of experience. That's why it is so important for communicators to evaluate the fields of experience of the potential audience; they

must anticipate as well as possible what knowledge and attitudes the audience might have about the topic. For example, if you are speaking to residents of a retirement community, you might safely assume that the audience will not be familiar with the songs of your favorite band. Therefore, using song lyrics from that band to illustrate a point will likely lead to audience confusion. The song will be outside their fields of experience. It would be more appropriate to use a song or poem they might be familiar with—one that illustrates the same point in your speech.

- The **context** of a given communication exchange includes the wide range of environmental and chronological factors. The context of a given transaction includes the historical, seasonal, and temporal setting in which the communication takes place; the geographical location and the culture(s) in which you are speaking; recent news events; and so on.

Informal and Formal Communication

You communicate with many different audiences on any given day. Most of these encounters probably take the form of **informal communication**. This type of communication is spontaneous. You don't prepare in advance; you improvise. Examples of informal communication include

- making introductions,
- talking on the phone,
- answering a question in class, and
- chatting with your friends and family.

Formal communication is more structured. In most cases this type of communication takes preparation. Examples include

- being interviewed for a job,
- giving a speech,
- taking part in a debate, and
- doing a dramatic reading from literature.

Activities

A. List five informal communication situations you have experienced in the past week.

B. List three instances of formal communication you have had.

Nonverbal Communication

Take a moment to think about all the elements that can add layers of meaning to a speaker's words. Here are some examples:

- Facial expressions
- Hand gestures
- Eye movements
- Head and body movements (nodding, shrugging, etc.)
- Posture
- Smiling or frowning

These are nonverbal expressions. Interpreting them correctly may tell you more than the speaker's words.

Every effective communication takes place on two levels: verbal and nonverbal. Using both levels allows communicators more opportunities to understand one another. Sometimes a speaker's words may contradict his or her nonverbal messages. Very often speakers send out unintentional physical messages. For example, a speaker might claim to be confident while nonverbally expressing embarrassment or fear by blushing, trembling, and avoiding eye contact. A speaker who uses vivid, exciting language but delivers it in a flat monotone without many gestures isn't communicating effectively. Studies show that when an audience has to choose whether they believe the verbals or the nonverbals of a speaker's presentation, they tend to go with the nonverbals. That's why it's important to pay attention to your movements and your vocal rate, volume, and inflection. (For more on this important aspect of public speaking, see Experience 5, "The Speech to Develop Body Language," on page 88.)

Activity

With a partner, act out these statements nonverbally.

- I'm glad to be here.
- I'm very excited.
- I'm exhausted.
- Thank you.
- Be careful.
- That's a relief.

Listening with Intention

Even if you follow all the rules of good communication, you'll sometimes find yourself talking to people who don't listen well enough to understand you. These people are listening in order to argue or to talk about their own ideas. They hear only a part of what you say, so they only partially decode the message you are sending.

Activity

With a partner, improvise a scene in which one of you tells the other a personal anecdote of one or two minutes' duration. After the speaker tells the story, the listener restates the story exactly as he or she heard it. The storyteller corrects any wrong information or mistaken impressions. Then switch roles. Afterward, discuss which of you listened most effectively.

Communication was once viewed as a simple process of speakers trying to hit a target (the audience) with their ideas. We now know that communication is a much more complex process. For more on developing your listening skills, see Chapter 6.

Talking Points
Aristotle's Legacy

More than 2,300 years ago, the Greek philosopher Aristotle (384 B.C.–322 B.C.) laid the groundwork for modern public speaking. Aristotle's mentor was the brilliant thinker Plato. In Plato's opinion most public speakers were fast-talking politicians who manipulated their audiences with lies and half-truths. Mere *rhetoric* (one person speaking to many), Plato claimed, was worthless. Aristotle disagreed. He viewed public speaking as an art. He was the first person ever to suggest that the audience was a key factor in the communication process.

Aristotle (right) teaches Alexander the Great.

These days, no public speaker would make a presentation without first considering the audience. But that trend began way back in fourth-century Greece when Aristotle had a new and revolutionary idea. Aristotle claimed that all public presentations were a balance of ethics (a set of beliefs about what is right and wrong), emotion, and logic.

- The *ethical* part of public speaking is what the communication reveals to the audience about the speaker's character. The main idea here is that telling a truth is ethical; telling a lie or obscuring the truth is unethical.
- The audience experiences an *emotional* reaction to the communication.
- The actual words the audience hears make up the *logical* aspect of the communication.

Activity

Think about a speech you recently heard on the news, at school, or elsewhere. Write two or three sentences about each area of the speech's presentation: ethical, emotional, and logical. How would you rate the speech according to Aristotle's criteria?

Building a Speech:
Topic, Audience, and Purpose

In This Chapter . . .

The first rule of good public speaking is adequate preparation. Preparing a speech is like getting ready to run a marathon. Both require many trial runs before the event actually takes place. To attempt a speech without adequate preparation is just as foolhardy as attempting a marathon without training. In this chapter you'll learn preparation techniques that will help you make a special occasion of every public speaking experience.

Speak Up!

Tell your classmates about an activity at which you excel. You might choose a sport, music, dancing, drawing, or debate, for example. How did you become good at this activity? When you take part in it, what do you do to prepare yourself?

Choosing a Topic

For the audience, a well-prepared speaker makes a speech seem easy. But it's *not* easy. Hours of intense preparation go into an excellent performance. It all begins with choosing the right topic.

Let's imagine that your teacher has given you a speech assignment. You have two weeks to prepare a presentation. What should you talk about? Where should you start? To begin your preparation, use the following guidelines.

1. **Choose a topic that interests you.** If you're not interested in the topic of your speech, no one else will be either. Think about your hobbies or special interests. For example, you may be interested in sports, theater, or coin collecting. Any one of these topics could form the basis of a speech. Alternatively, you might consider writing about a political issue or event. Whatever topic you choose, make sure that it is something you want to explore further.

2. **Be sure you can find sufficient material on your subject.** Otherwise your speech might come up short in terms of both quantity and quality. Your five-minute speech might dwindle down to a minute and a half. So first consider what you already know about the subject. Then begin your search for information from respected sources on your topic. Be on the lookout for quotations, statistics, anecdotes, visual aids, and any other materials you might be able to use to illustrate your ideas and hold your audience's attention. (For a list of references and information sources, see Chapter 3.) If you can't find enough information on a topic, don't choose it.

3. **Be sure your topic is appropriate to you, your audience, and the occasion.** Any topic that is not adjusted to these three factors will be inadequate. If you're talking to a general audience, it probably wouldn't be appropriate to launch into a speech on the complexities of honors algebra equations. If you have any doubts about the appropriateness of a given topic, either find a new topic or check with your instructor. And remember that offensive language—including profanity and ethnic or racist slurs—is never appropriate.

4. **Be sure you have enough time to research the topic and that it can be covered in the time available for the speech.** Having too much information to cover can be just as problematic as having too little. Suppose you tried to encapsulate the entire American Revolution in one five-minute speech. Your speech would not be specific enough to gain an audience's attention.

Activities

A. List five potential speech topics. Choose subjects that interest you and/or subjects you would like to learn more about.

B. Choose three topics from the previous activity. For each topic, list at least three possible sources of information you could explore.

C. Choose three of the five topics that follow and suggest at least one occasion for which each would make a suitable basis for a speech.

  • The history of the atomic bomb

- Basics of the American justice system
- Protecting our natural resources
- What you should know when deciding on a college
- The problem of peer group pressure

D. Choose three of the five occasions below and suggest at least one suitable speech topic for each.

- student government meeting
- sales meeting
- book club presentation
- graduation
- tour group

E. Choose three speech topics or titles from the activities above and estimate how many minutes you would need to give each speech. Explain your reasoning.

F. Which of the following topics would require the most research? The least? Why?

- The human digestive system
- The early history of television
- Why more students are choosing business colleges
- Federal funding for the arts
- Reality TV

Narrowing Your Topic

If you have chosen a broad topic, it often helps to focus on a single aspect of it. For example, using the example of the five-minute speech about the American Revolution, you might choose to talk about the harsh conditions of the American soldiers at Valley Forge during the winter of 1778.

Here's how one student narrowed her topic for a successful speech. Being a dog lover, she began with the broad general topic "dogs." From there she narrowed the topic to "dog breeds." She made a list of all the breeds she knew. From that list, she chose golden retrievers. Her speech was eventually titled "Why Golden Retrievers Make Good Pets."

Activities

A. In your opinion, which of the following topics could be covered adequately in a five-minute speech?

- Football
- The health benefits of citrus fruits
- School policies
- Health care
- Habits of the redheaded woodpecker
- Three great places to visit in Washington, D.C.

B. Reorder this list of topics from the broadest to the narrowest.

- American tourist attractions
- Aspen, Colorado
- Colorado
- Mountain getaways
- Rocky Mountains
- Skiing in Aspen
- Aspen's Running Bear Lodge
- Vacation destinations

C. Narrow each of the following broad topics into a topic suitable for a five-minute speech.

- Oceans
- Government
- Movies
- Trees
- Junk food
- Music

Analyzing Your Audience

To deliver a speech, you'll find it's very helpful to know something about your audience members. When you prepare to make a formal presentation, you should ask yourself questions about your audience. For example, what is their average age, gender, ethnic background, income level, occupation, or level of education?

For now, you'll probably deliver most of your speeches to other students in your class. You'll have a good idea of age and gender. But you should also have some idea of how much they already know about your topic. Think about how much background information you will need to provide. The object here is to provide enough, but not too much, information to get your point across.

Above all you'll want to generate interest and keep them focused on what you have to say. Often it helps to have a "hook," a piece of information or a question that a large portion of the audience is likely to relate to. For example, in a speech about the nutritional content of a sandwich from a popular fast-food restaurant, you might start out with the question, "Has anyone in this room ever eaten fast food?" Immediately you will connect with your audience and a wide variety of feelings and beliefs about fast food.

Credibility

It is up to listeners to decide whether or not they believe what a speaker is saying. But you the speaker have an obligation to use as many tools as possible to gain their trust. **Credibility** is the perception that a speaker is knowledgeable, trustworthy, and dynamic. Listeners want to know that you thoroughly understand the topic,

that you have the audience's best interests at heart, and that you feel strongly about the speech's content.

Sometimes a speaker has credibility with the audience even before the speech begins. If the audience is familiar with the speaker or the speaker's reputation, credibility might be based on past experience. If the speaker is formally introduced, what is said about him or her may increase credibility, particularly if the introduction mentions the speaker's past accomplishments.

In many public speaking situations, however, the speaker is neither known by nor formally introduced to the audience. Your speech should establish your credibility as early as possible. One way to do this is to state your experience with, your research on, or your interest in the topic you are about to address. Referring to shared experience or history with the audience can serve to establish common ground with your listeners.

Activities

A. For each topic listed below, describe an audience that would likely be very receptive to a speech on the subject and one that would most likely *not* be receptive.

- Choosing the right career in business
- Stage makeup
- Brief history of rock-and-roll music
- Nutritional properties of beef
- Computer literacy in the workplace
- Ballet dancer Mikhail Baryshnikov

B. Look at your answers for Activity A. Choose one of the topics and its potentially disinterested audience. Discuss with a classmate what you could do to generate interest in your presentation.

Determining Your Purpose

Public speaking takes more than simply choosing an interesting topic. Every time you make a public speaking presentation you should do so with a purpose in mind. Your **purpose** is your overall intention, the reason you are making the speech. Most speeches fall into one of three general categories. They **inform**, **entertain**, or **persuade**. To determine your purpose, ask yourself what reaction you want from the people who hear you. Do you want them to understand an idea better? To become stirred up or aroused about something? To perform an act, such as voting for or against a candidate or contributing money or joining an organization? Here are some examples of speeches and their purposes:

Speech Title
"An Organization for One and All"

Purpose
To *persuade* students to vote and to take part in student government

Speech Title
"Laughing Can Cure What Ails You"

Purpose
To *inform* audience members of the health benefits of laughter

Speech Title
"This Dog's Life"

Purpose
To *entertain* listeners with the story of a local firehouse dog

It's important to know what you want the audience to do as a result of your speech. If you don't have this point settled, then you don't really know why you organized the speech the way you did. You don't know what you want and neither does your audience. You can't very well expect an audience to get anything from your speech if you yourself don't know what you want them to get. Not having a clear purpose is one of the most common causes of poor public speaking. So decide on a purpose and then direct all your efforts toward achieving it.

Activities

A. Although most speeches serve more than one purpose, decide what the main purpose might be for each of the following speech titles.

- The Lonely Battle of the Class Clown
- Listen Up! The Secret of Becoming a Better Listener
- You Can Save Kellogg Forest
- How to Deal with Test Anxiety
- Confessions of a Vegetarian
- Volunteering Builds Character

B. Which kind of speech do you think would be the most difficult to prepare? Why?

C. Besides informing, entertaining, and persuading, what other purposes for speaking might there be?

Talking Points

Adapting to Your Audience

Whether you're talking to one person or a whole roomful, speaking effectively means adapting to your audience. Maintaining an open mind and some sense of spontaneity allows you to anticipate and analyze audience response as you are speaking. That way you will be more likely to interpret audience feedback accurately and respond appropriately.

In formal speaking situations you may have the time and opportunity to learn about your audience before you make your speech. In most cases, however, what you learn about the audience will come to you as you are in the process of speaking. It pays to be able to gauge your audience's response from moment to moment.

Audience Feedback

An audience will provide you with a lot of information, most of it nonverbal. Imagine that you are speaking to a large group of people. Consider these two audience reactions.

- Audience members are leaning forward listening. Their eyes are on you. Occasionally you see heads nodding.
- Audience members are leaning back in their chairs. Many of them are looking at the floor, shifting in their seats, and checking their watches. Occasionally someone yawns.

It's clear which response is preferable. But even if people seem not to be paying close attention to your speech, it's important for you to stay focused. There are a few things you can do to change the dynamic.

- Pick up the pace. Sometimes speakers lapse into a monotone or a rhythmic speech pattern without being aware of it. Check in with yourself. If you feel that you're slipping into a pattern, try to speak more quickly and inject a bit more personality into your voice and tone.
- Maintain eye contact with the audience. American audiences tend to feel a speaker is more credible if he or she can look them in the eye.

- Make sure your movements and gestures are natural and that they relate directly to what you're staying. Wild or unfocused gestures tell the audience that you are not in control. Using no gestures at all will make you seem stiff and uncomfortable.
- Above all, be sincere. If you are not sincere, your audience will sense it.

Never Blame the Audience

It's a great feeling to look out at your audience and know that they are "with you." But often audiences may come across as neutral. They're waiting to hear what you have to say so they can decide what they think about it. They're taking a wait-and-see position. It's important that you do not take this the wrong way. Avoid blaming the audience if they seem less than enthusiastic. Keep in mind that they are there to listen to you. If you begin your speech with a lighthearted comment and they fail to laugh, move on. Your job is to communicate with them. Do your best and make it your responsibility to win their interest and support.

Activity

With a small group of classmates, model speaker and audience behavior. One person stands before the others and tells a brief anecdote of his or her choice. The others listen quietly and then tell the speaker what was memorable and/or entertaining, as well as physical or vocal elements that the speaker might improve. Take turns so that everyone gets a turn to speak.

What You Should Know About Your Audience

Ask yourself these questions and then find the answers either through actual interviews, or, if that isn't possible, make an educated guess.

1. Who will be in your audience? (Classmates? Adults? Children?)
2. What are the interests or the past experiences of the audience members? How do they relate to your topic?
3. What do they already know about your topic?
4. Will they have any preconceived notions about your topic?
5. How can you adapt your speech to make it more interesting to your audience?

Building a Speech:
The Body

In This Chapter . . .

Once you have established your topic and purpose, you can move on to develop the body of your speech. From shaping your main idea and details to finding sources and avoiding plagiarism, this chapter will guide you through the process. For now you need not worry about an introduction or a conclusion. We'll discuss those speech elements in Chapter 4. As discussed in the previous chapter, keep your audience in mind as you proceed through the steps of building your speech.

Speak Up!

Write the word *hobby* at the top of a sheet of paper. Think about what this word means to you. Do you have more than one hobby? If so, which hobby is more important to you? What do you enjoy most about it? Write a paragraph about it. Read your paragraph aloud to the class. Do you think the topic has potential to become a larger speech? Why or why not?

Deciding on Your Thesis and Main Ideas

Once you have decided on a purpose, determine which aspect of your topic will best embody that purpose. For example, if the purpose of your speech is to inform, which elements of the topic do you want your audience to understand? Identify the main ideas you think must be communicated. Narrow your focus until you have between two to five main points. A typical audience will remember no more than that.

Once you have selected your main ideas, it's time to craft the thesis of your speech. The **thesis** is a one-sentence statement that clearly and concisely explains what you're going to talk about in your speech. For many speeches, the thesis tells the listener exactly what your position is on the topic you will be discussing. Here are some sample thesis statements:

- The city council must take action on the dangerous traffic situation on West Main Road.
- Learning to play the piano can build skills in many areas of a person's life.
- Brushing your teeth too often can damage your gums.

A strong thesis statement can provide a blueprint for your entire speech, which will make it much easier to fill out the rest of the speech as you go. Do not rush the development of this important part of your preparation.

Tips for Testing the Strength of Your Thesis

- Make sure your thesis is a complete sentence, not a fragment.
- Form your thesis as a declarative sentence, not a question.
- Be sure your thesis does not imply that you will discuss more than you can cover in your allotted time.
- Make sure your thesis has enough substance to distinguish your presentation of the topic from anyone else's.

Activity

Write a thesis statement for each of the following topics. Use the tips above to test each one.

- Preservatives used in breakfast cereals
- Effects of insomnia on daily life
- Acupuncture and allergies
- Study habits of high school sophomores
- Falling attendance at local sports events

Gathering Supporting Materials

Your next step is to gather material and information for your speech. Once you have determined your main ideas and your thesis, you'll need to provide a variety of supporting materials to help explain your ideas to the audience, and to back up those ideas with evidence. This part of your preparation will take you on a search for information from respected sources on your topic. While you are gathering basic information, you will also want to look for

- appropriate quotations,
- statistics,
- examples,
- anecdotes,
- visual aids, and
- models.

Be on the lookout for anything that will help illustrate your ideas and hold your audience's attention. By planning ahead you can determine the kinds of supporting materials that will be ideal for your speech. Then all you need do is conduct a search for those specific materials.

Quotations

A strong quotation can give your idea the authority of an expert. This is important; you want the audience to know that you're not alone in your thinking. For example, using Abraham Lincoln's famous line from the Gettysburg Address—"[G]overnment of the people, by the people, and for the people ..."—in a speech that argues in favor of allowing a particular rule to be voted on by the whole school, lends Lincoln's reputation as a statesman and one of the greatest American presidents in support of your point. Quotes can come from history, the media, local experts in a particular field, and even your own family members.

Statistics

Statistics, including charts and graphs that put numerical concepts into a visual format, help the audience to understand an idea and make comparisons. Many listeners feel that thinking about concepts in numerical form helps them to understand the range and depth of the topic you are presenting. Instead of saying that a particular company expects "a lot of layoffs soon," the audience gets a clearer idea of the impact of lost jobs when they hear statistics, such as "100 layoffs" or "25 percent of the staff." Although statistics can help your speech a great deal, it's important not to depend too much on them. After all, you don't want your point to get lost in a sea of numbers! Use statistics to illustrate your point, not to replace it.

Examples and Anecdotes

Examples or anecdotes are brief stories that personalize your topic for the audience. Good examples and anecdotes make the information more vivid and spur the audience's imagination. For instance, a statement that "Drunk driving kills innocent people" will make more of an impression on the audience if the example is about a specific person who lost his or her life to a drunk driver. Giving a face and a name to the victim will make the same point more immediate for an audience.

Visual Aids

Many people learn best when they can visualize the idea a speaker is trying to convey. Selecting visual aids for your speech can really pay off in terms of connecting with your audience.

Types of Visual Aids

Photographs. These can be enlarged for maximum visibility or placed on a transparency projector.

Video segments. These can be very effective provided that they are cued up properly and presented as efficiently as possible. There's nothing that makes an audience drift off quicker than a speaker having trouble starting or stopping the VCR or DVD player.

Computer-generated graphics.

Selected objects. This can be equipment that you intend to demonstrate.

Assistants. Your assistants can help you model a process or movement.

Scale model. These are visual aids that are used to help explain objects and ideas that are either too large or too small to be displayed at the presentation. For example, a speaker might illustrate his or her point by using a scale model of a space shuttle or a blowup of a human skin cell. Models allow the audience to get an instructive view of things they might otherwise be unable to see.

The keys to using visual aids successfully are good planning so that the visuals actually add to what you're saying, and practice in presenting so you can anticipate any problems that might arise regarding placement of the visuals or operation of the display equipment.

Other Supporting Materials

Other materials that can add depth to your speech include definitions, which can come from dictionaries or from experts on the topic. Song lyrics, poetry, and lines from plays or films can help an audience feel the emotions involved in a particular issue.

Activities

A. Name three sources where you might find quotes to use for the following topics.

- Popular sports equipment
- Police crackdown on speeding motorists
- Budget increases for state government
- Annual music festival in the park
- Holiday customs in Poland

B. Name three statistics that you might try to find for each of the following topics.

- Ethnic diversity at Ridgeland Elementary School
- Pie consumption in the United States
- Stock market activities during the early 1990s
- AIDS in America
- Veterans of the Vietnam War

Locating Reference Sources

When preparing a speech, finding source materials can be one of the biggest obstacles students face. However, this doesn't have to be a problem. You just have to be willing to look around a bit. Don't believe that you can't find enough material on your chosen topic. Instead, check all the sources available to you.

Where will you find these sources? The best place, the single greatest resource, is the library or media center. There you will find just about any information you desire, provided you have the patience to find it.

Wouldn't it be nice if everything you needed for your speech were located inside a single book? Unfortunately, that's not usually how it works. You may have to look in several books, magazines, newspapers, pamphlets, encyclopedias, and so on. You might have to surf the Web. Some information will be easy to find; some you might have to dig for. To find little-known sources, you can always ask the librarian for help. Usually, a librarian can provide more useful materials in ten minutes than a student can digest in several hours. Most libraries also have Internet- and CD-ROM-based resources.

Besides going to the librarian for assistance, try using the following research tools to find the information you need.

1. **Card catalog** Although many libraries are phasing out card catalogs in favor of computer-based catalogs, your library may still use this system. Check here for the title and/or author of materials located within the library.

2. **Computer catalog** These catalogs often have easy-to-follow on-screen instructions for finding everything you need.

3. **Encyclopedias** Many encyclopedias are now available on CD-ROM. General-information encyclopedias include *Encyclopaedia Britannica, Encyclopedia Americana,* and *Collier's Encyclopedia.* Special-interest encyclopedias include the following:

   Afro-American Encyclopedia (history, great personalities, literature, art, music, dance, athletic accomplishments of black people from ancient to modern times)

   Cambridge History of Latin America

   Encyclopedia of Asian History

   The Encyclopedia of Education (history and philosophy of education)

   Encyclopedia of Latin American History and Culture

   The Encyclopedia of Religion (articles concerning all world religions)

   Grzmek's Animal Life Encyclopedia (information on lower animals, insects, fish, mammals, and birds)

   International Encyclopedia of the Social Sciences

   McGraw Hill Encyclopedia of Science and Technology (information on all branches of sciences, agriculture, and technology)

   Mythology of All Races (myths and folklore from around the world)

4. **Yearbooks** These reference texts are put out annually, so they often contain more up-to-date information than a regular encyclopedia. Here is a list of some of the more useful yearbooks:

   Americana Annual (source of current events)

Britannica Book of the Year (annual record of events that was first published in 1937)

The Cousteau Almanac (an inventory of life on our watery planet)

Statesman's Yearbook (statistical and historical information of the states of the world)

World Almanac and Book of Facts (a wealth of mostly statistical information on hundreds of subjects)

5. **Indexes** An index is a registry of publication information relating to literature and periodicals. Some worthwhile indexes are:

New York Times Index (lists information that can be found in copies of the *New York Times*)

Poole's Index to Periodical Literature (covers years up to 1906; very useful for finding old historical material on hundreds of topics)

Readers' Guide to Periodical Literature (covers the years since 1900; lists sources of information in practically every field)

6. **Biographical dictionaries** These references contain brief biographical sketches of famous or newsworthy individuals. Good examples are:

Contemporary Authors (a listing of current writers of fiction, nonfiction, poetry, journalism, drama, film, and television)

Current Biography (short biographies of people in the news)

Dictionary of American Biography (a collection of biographical information about people who have died; kept up to date with supplements)

National Cyclopedia of American Biography (the most comprehensive list of famous Americans living or dead available in one source)

Newsmakers (published three times a year with information about politicians, business leaders, and entertainment personalities in the current media)

Who's Who in America (brief biographies of notable living persons of the United States)

7. **Special dictionaries** There are times when you may need a specialty dictionary. For example, if you are looking for information and definitions of slang terms, you can check Partridge's *Dictionary of Slang and Unconventional English*. If you need to know about foreign words and terms, look for Mawson's *Dictionary of Foreign Terms*. Check with the librarian about other specialized dictionaries.

8. **Quotations** Most libraries have a number of good sources for quotations. You can also use an Internet search engine (Google, Yahoo, etc.) to identify or find quote material. Examples of text editions include:

Bartlett's Familiar Quotations (traces quotes to their sources in ancient and modern literature)

The Oxford Dictionary of Quotations

Stevenson's *The Home Book of Quotations* (approximately 50,000 quotations, arranged alphabetically by subject)

9. **Government publications** These materials cover an almost limitless array of subjects. Ask the librarian or media specialist about them.

10. **Computer-assisted research** You can access huge amounts of research material using a library or home computer system. Using a powerful search engine such as Google or Yahoo you can access just about any kind of information you seek by typing in keywords. For example, if you were doing research on the history of your hometown, you could go to google.com and type the name of the town and your state in the search box. You would then click "Go" and within seconds you would be guided to a variety of links, possible Web pages where you might locate the necessary information.

You can find other great sources on the Internet by checking the archives at major media sites. For example, you can find plenty of information about current events and past history at CNN Interactive (www.cnn.com).

Remember that not all of the information available on the Internet is credible. Be sure that the site you choose is a reliable one. In general, Web sites that are administered by organizations are more reliable than those run by individuals. Always try to double-check specific facts and statistics in more than one source. (For more about determining the credibility of sources, see Talking Points on page 29.)

11. **Interviews** Many students overlook the firsthand interview as a source of information. Remember that interviewing an expert can give your speech a valuable edge.

Activities

A. In which type of encyclopedia would you expect to find information on the following subjects?

- Dietary habits of koalas
- Latest developments in cancer research
- Ancient tales from Ethiopia
- Computer viruses
- Gross national product of Nicaragua
- Taiwan's economic outlook

B. In what type of reference guide might you find information on the following subjects?

- Arnold Schwarzenegger
- Hubble telescope
- Size of the Atlantic Ocean (in square miles)
- Top ten colleges in the United States
- Former president Bill Clinton
- Current U.S. population
- Adolf Hitler

Organizing Your Materials

Once you've gathered the basic information and supporting materials, you must put the information together in an order that your audience will be able to follow with ease, and perhaps even anticipating where the speech will go next.

There are several ways to organize material in an orderly and logical sequence. Main points ordered **chronologically** follow a time sequence pattern such as past, present, and future or one, two, three. For example, if you were speaking about the steps involved in the process of baking a cake, you would not put dry ingredients in the oven before you have gathered and mixed them. Telling a story to the audience follows a chronological sequence of beginning, middle, and end.

Ordering your speech **spatially** means organizing ideas in such a way that each main point occupies a specific physical space in relation to the others. For example, you might describe the effect of a disease on the human body from the head, down to the shoulders, through the torso, and down the legs. Or you might discuss a current U.S. trend by looking at the ways it manifests on the West Coast, through the western states, on through the middle of the country, and over to the East Coast.

Using the **problem/solution** method of organizing your ideas you begin by presenting the materials that define and illustrate a particular problem; then you follow with information regarding a possible solution. An example of this organizational pattern would be a speech that begins by discussing the problems of the small number of organs donated for transplants and then presents the solutions currently under consideration to alleviate this problem—for instance, consent signatures on the backs of driver's licenses.

Organizing your material in a **cause/effect** pattern means that you identify the cause of a particular problem and then go on to identify the effects resulting from it. For instance, you might begin by discussing the terrorist attacks

of September 11, 2001, and then report what effects the attacks had in terms of subsequent U.S. government policies.

A **topical** organization pattern is one that speakers use when there is no logical relationship between the speech's ideas. It is the organization of ideas in the order of topics you wish to cover. For example, an informative speech on breeds of dogs might group the dogs in categories based on what the breeds were designed to do—for example, hunting breeds, working breeds, and companion breeds. Each of these categories is important but they do not naturally connect to each other in a particular order. So as a speaker, when you use the topical pattern of organization you shouldn't assume that your audience will be able to anticipate your next main point. Instead, you help them along by providing parallel language. For example, you would start your description of each category of dog with similar language: "Hunting dogs provide their owners with tracking and retrieving skills…. Working dogs provide their owners with assistance in tasks that require strength and/or perseverance…. Companion dogs provide their owners with friendship and loyalty." The repetition signals the audience that you're shifting to another key piece of information.

Outlining Your Ideas

You can make your organization process easier by outlining the main components and points of your speech. In the most in-depth type of outline, you write a complete sentence for each point you want to make. You then use the outline to memorize the logical progression of your speech. Here is an example of a complete sentence outline for a speech about body language.

Type of speech Informative

Name (Speaker's Name)

Purpose of this speech (Briefly discuss what you want your audience to learn, to think, to believe, to feel, or to do because of the speech. For example, "I want my audience to have a better understanding of body language.")

Title: BODY LANGUAGE

Introduction

I. Your physical movements talk for you.

> A. They tell secrets about you.

> B. They tell what kind of person you are.

> C. I will discuss the behavior we call body language.

Body

I. Everyone uses movements with spoken words.

> A. They are a natural part of human behavior.

> B. People are unaware of their movements.

>> 1. Posture reflects inner thoughts.

>> 2. Eyes, hands, and feet speak eloquently.

II. Body language can be helpful.

> A. It can make a person attractive to others.

>> 1. Movements can reflect honesty.

>> 2. Appearance can bring favorable responses.

>> 3. Behavior patterns can make friends.

> B. Employers observe body language.

>> 1. They make judgments from what they see.

>> 2. They hire or reject an applicant by watching movements and posture.

III. Body language can be improved.

> A. A person can enhance personal appearance.

> B. Anyone can strive for better posture and walking habits.

Conclusion

I. People are born with body language.

> A. It influences life.

> B. It speaks louder than words.

The complete sentence outline is just one way of outlining material. There are many others. If your instructor prefers a specific type of outlining, find out what it is. The most important thing is that it must make logical sense so that you can easily follow it. It takes time and effort to construct a complete sentence outline, but it is time well spent.

If your speech works well enough, your audience will have no idea that you are leading them through a very tightly structured presentation. Be concise. Use clear transitions when moving from one point to the next. As you move through your points, internal summaries of the information you have stated will help the audience keep up.

Avoiding Plagiarism

Talking Points at the end of Chapter 1 presented Aristotle's idea that sound ethics is a crucial part of public speaking. In general, communicating the truth is ethical; lying or obscuring the truth is unethical. Listeners judge a speaker based on whether they believe he or she is trying to reveal, or to cover up, the truth.

Plagiarism is the unethical practice of representing the work or words of others as one's own. By passing off another's words or ideas as one's own, a speaker is in effect lying. As a speaker, you must take careful notes when you do your research. Make sure you attribute any quoted material to its original author or source. It is not enough to change a few words to make it sound a little different. If you use someone else's material or ideas, say so. Avoiding mention of the original source is plagiarism. The penalties for plagiarism can be very high. One instance can have a long-term effect on a student's reputation and future academic standing. Don't do it.

Talking Points

Evaluating the Credibility of Internet Sources

When you are locating source material for your speech, try to be aware of the *quality* of the information, not just the *quantity*. Avoid quoted material if the speaker or writer is obviously biased. If you feel the source contains questionable facts, don't use it. Double-check historical information in at least two other sources. If the sources disagree, you will have to check further. Write down all the sources you look up to make sure you can cite them accurately.

As you locate the information you need, it's important to make sure that your sources are credible and unbiased. This is a factor in all research, but it is a particularly complex question when it comes to Internet sources.

There is a massive amount of information available on the World Wide Web. But the Web itself is largely unregulated, which means anyone can list any information there, whether it is true or not. Sites associated with universities, libraries, and professional associations are generally more credible than those created by individuals. Some guidelines for making sure that the Internet information you use is credible can be found in the box at the right.

Guidelines for Source Credibility

- If the source is a person, try to find his or her biographical information.

- If the source is an organization, try to find more information about it. Many Web sites include a description of the organization's goals, concerns, and practices.

- Make sure the information is current. Many Web sites include the date the site was last updated. If the information is out of date, don't use it.

- Make sure the Web site is providing information, not advertising a product or advocating a particular cause.

- Is the information clearly stated? If you can't follow it, it's not a good source for your speech!

Activities

A. Go to the Web and find examples of each of the points listed in the box at right. Be prepared to share your examples with the class.

B. Choose a topic and find three sites that you would use for credible source material. Then, find three cites that might not be as trustworthy. Explain your choices.

Building a Speech:
The Introduction and Conclusion

In This Chapter . . .

Now that you've completed the body of your speech, it may be easier to add the introduction and the conclusion—two more important pieces of the public speaking puzzle. The introduction is your one chance to make a first impression. The conclusion leaves the audience with the final thoughts that pull your speech together.

Speak Up!

Consider a speech topic such as "improving study habits." Think of an attention-getting statement you might use to open your remarks on this subject. Write it down. Then, remembering to use eye contact and good posture, deliver your introductory statement to the class.

Crafting Your Introduction

Though your introduction obviously will be delivered at the beginning of your speech, you should prepare it as one of the last steps in the process. This is practical because you need to have the body of the speech outlined and the ideas developed before you can determine how they should be introduced. The length of an introduction may vary considerably from one speech to the next; however, it should not comprise more than one-fourth of the entire speech. It may comprise much less.

It has been said that every public speaker has the audience's attention upon rising to speak. That's perhaps the only moment in public speaking where audience attention is a sure thing. If the audience's attention begins to wander, it is usually *after* the speaker begins to talk. A good introduction can make use of the initial moments between the speaker's rise and his or her presentation of the speech. It can grab the audience's attention and hang on to it while the speech gets under way.

Defining the Purpose of Your Introduction

Your introduction will probably have one of three main purposes. We will take a look at each of them.

1. Perhaps the most common purpose of an introduction is to gain attention, arouse interest, and excite the curiosity of the listeners. You can accomplish this in several different ways:

   - You can **refer to the purpose** of the gathering with a few brief remarks explaining and commenting on the occasion. You may refer to the audience's special interests and show how the subject is connected to those interests. (Note: Never apologize for the speech you are about to make.)

   - You may **pay the audience a genuine compliment** regarding their hospitality, their interest in your topic, or the outstanding leadership qualities of the sponsoring organization. Make sure that you are sincere about what you say, as the audience's judgment of your speech will be strongly influenced by your opening statements.

   - You might **open with a story** (humorous, human interest, exciting, etc.) that arouses the audience's curiosity. The story should be linked to the subject. Never tell a story that is not related to your point.

   - You may **refer to a recent incident** that is familiar to the audience. For example:

     "Last week three people were burned to death because their school building had improper fire escape exits."

     This paves the way for the main thrust of the speech—the need for a new school building.

   - You may **use a quotation** to open your remarks and set the stage for the ideas your speech will reveal. Make sure the quotation is relevant to your subject. Tie it in with a brief explanation.

   - You might choose to **open with a novel idea** or a striking statement to arouse your audience's curiosity. Be careful not to overdo it, however. You won't be able to sustain sensationalism throughout the whole speech. An example of an introduction that uses a novel idea or a striking statement is:

"The other night I sat by and watched as an older man walking down the street was attacked and beaten almost to death by a vicious group of thugs. That horrible image has stuck with me for days now. (Pause.) Of course, it was only a movie. But that's the problem with graphic violence. Real or fictional, it stays inside your head."

- You may also **refer to a preceding speaker** or communication event to secure interest and attention. For example, the great speaker Anna Howard Shaw opened her famous speech on 'God's Women' this way:

"The subject, 'God's Women,' was suggested to me by reading an article in a Chicago newspaper, in which a gentleman defined God's Women. It has always seemed to me very remarkable how clear the definitions of men are in regard to women, their duties, their privileges, their responsibilities, their relations with each other, to men, to government, and now to God; and while they have been elucidating them for years, we have been patiently listening."

- You might **ask pertinent and challenging questions** to arouse audience curiosity. These questions should have a direct bearing on the material that is to follow. Questions can be phrased in this type of structure: "Did you know that...? Do you want this to happen to you?"

- You can also **combine two or more of these techniques**. How you combine your introduction techniques will depend on the audience, the occasion, the type of speech, and the environment.

2. **You may open your speech with the intention to prepare and open the minds of the audience for the thoughts to come.** This is particularly necessary if the audience is hostile. It's best accomplished by giving background and historical information so that the audience will be able to understand the subject completely. You can often accomplish this purpose by quickly establishing your right to speak. You can recount the research you've done on the subject, name prominent people associated with the endeavor, and/or modestly tell about certain honors, offices, and awards you have received as a result of your accomplishments in areas that are closely related to the topic.

3. **A third objective you may have for your speech's introduction is to indicate the direction and purpose of the speech and to illuminate what end it will serve.** You can do this by stating the subject in general terms and announcing and explaining the thesis of the talk. It's not enough to give a simple topic statement. Most topic statements don't inspire attentiveness from an audience. Here's an example of an introduction that forecasts the speech to follow:

"Ladies and gentlemen: I have chosen to speak with you today on the subject of crime, which is costing our nation untold billions of dollars each year. I intend to explain to you what I see as the causes of crime as well as some forms of prevention. It is only by *understanding* crime that we can hope to combat it."

A Few More Things to Think About

Dullness, cliché ideas or language, extraneous length, false leads, and fillers have no place in a good introduction. Avoid simply stating your topic. False modesty and/or self-deprecating remarks having to do with the presentation or content of your speech should definitely be left out. To grab your audience's attention and maintain their goodwill, try for a fresh and original approach to the top of your speech.

There's one more important thing to keep in mind. Your public presentation actually begins before you speak. It starts with your behavior as you wait to take the platform and immediately after you get there. Speakers who are onstage in full view of the audience should remain comfortably and calmly alert, yet politely seated. Audience members will be appraising you as they wait to hear what you have to say. When you are introduced, rise quietly and move to the place where you will speak. After you get there, take a few moments and deliberately survey the scene. Then after addressing the person presiding and anyone else who should be acknowledged, you are ready to begin your introductory remarks.

Activities

A. Find a quote for one of the following thesis statements:

-   Living alone in the woods can be very therapeutic.
-   Reading can broaden a person's horizons.
-   Travel is definitely worth the time and trouble.

B. Use any of the techniques previously described to craft a combination introduction.

C. Select one of the introductions you created in the activities above. Read it over several times until you are very familiar with it. Read the introduction aloud to your classmates. Try to present it with some spontaneity. Remember to make eye contact with your listeners.

D. Use a pen to circle or highlight the most important words in your introduction. Read the introduction silently several times. Then deliver your introduction to the class again. This time use the written version as you would note cards. Present your introduction just as you would for a complete speech.

Crafting Your Conclusion

A speech must have an ending, and in order to be successful, that ending should be one of the speech's most impressive elements.

Your speech's conclusion brings together all the thoughts, emotions, discussions, arguments, and feelings that you have tried to communicate to the audience. Your closing words should make a powerful emotional impression on the audience. Logic alone is usually insufficient to move an audience to act or to think in the way a speaker suggests. The conclusion is the last opportunity to emphasize the point of the speech. It should be a natural culmination of all that you have said before. It should contain no weak remarks.

The conclusion should be one of the most carefully prepared parts of your speech. Some authorities believe that speakers should craft the conclusion first. Starting your preparation with the conclusion will certainly give you a way to aim your speech toward a predetermined end. But other authorities recommend crafting the conclusion near the end of your speech-preparation process so that you can draw your final remarks from the complete draft of the speech. A third approach is to prepare the conclusion and the introduction at the same time after the body of the speech is complete. That way the introduction and the conclusion can work together to serve an overall purpose.

Regardless of when you craft your conclusion, there is one point on which all authorities agree: the conclusion must be carefully worded, carefully organized, carefully rehearsed, and, in most cases, committed to memory. It should represent no more than 10 percent of your total speech. Depending on the nature of the speech, the speaker, the audience, the occasion, and the speech environment, it can be quite a bit shorter than that.

Never use your conclusion to bring up new material, as that would mean you'd have to prolong the speech unnecessarily. Also, introducing new material late in the speech may make the ending seem anticlimactic, which can be irritating for the audience.

When you have stated the conclusion of your speech, thank the audience for their attention. Hold the floor for a few moments before leaving the podium. It's important not to scurry away from the podium or make any silly gestures or remarks. That type of behavior can quickly diminish your audience's favorable impression. It is the audience's job to decide what they think of your speech. Don't give them any reason to feel that listening to you was not worth their time.

To deliver a great conclusion, your mind, body, and spirit must work together in harmony. Use direct eye contact, appropriate gestures and actions, alert posture, and your most sincere voice. The effort to deliver your conclusion can be compared to a runner who uses a final surge of power to lunge over the finish line to victory.

Now that you know what should go into your conclusion, how do you go about reaching the goal? What methods should you use? The answer is complicated. There are many ways to develop a conclusion. Below are some of the most effective ones.

1. A **summary** is a popular method for closing a speech. In a summary you can restate the speech title, the purpose, a particular phrase that you've used throughout the speech, a quotation from literature that succinctly says what your speech has been aiming toward, or use any other means that brings the main point of the speech into final focus for the audience. Here's an example:

   "As you can see, interviewing for a job can be much easier if you prepare yourself well in advance by learning about the company, knowing your own strengths and weaknesses for the job, and building up your self-confidence before you go in."

2. For some longer formal speeches, you can use **recapitulation** to restate points in a one-two-three order. The danger of this method is that it may become monotonous. Done well, though, it can be highly effective. Here's an example:

   "To be sure that you all understand my reasons for believing as I do, let me restate my main points. First, a global federation is the only type of government that will keep the world from destroying itself. Second a global federation is the only type of government that is acceptable to a number of nations, and third, a global federation is the most democratic form of world government yet conceived by human beings. For these reasons, I favor the establishment of a global federation."

In general, it's not a good idea to use recapitulation for the conclusion of a very short speech because the audience can easily remember your main points. Sometimes you can close a very short speech with the final main point, provided the point is strong enough. Usually, though, more is needed to close even a short speech.

3. Your conclusion might also employ a **striking anecdote, analogy,** or **simile.** You can use these elements separately or combine them and weave them into a summary or a recapitulation conclusion. One strong conclusion used this analogy for a speech about children in crisis:

   "Just as a wind snuffs out the light from a candle, the winds of turmoil and discontent in our cities are snuffing out the lives and potential light of too many innocent youth. It is time to act to save our children."

4. An **emotionally charged or idealized statement** of the thesis may serve as a useful conclusion. If the title of the speech were "Our Country's Future," a fitting conclusion might be:

   "I want the legacy of this generation of Americans to be one of viewing progress as a never-ending process. I want us to be able

to show that we recognized those things that must remain unchanged, and we preserved them. And that we had the foresight to determine what needed to be altered, and we did it. Let us take our place among other generations of Americans who made decisions not just for today, but also for tomorrow. And not just for themselves, but for all Americans."

5. Your conclusion may center on a **powerful restatement of your thesis**. If the subject were, for example, "Volunteerism can change your life," the final words might be "Volunteerism, giving of your talents to improve someone else's condition, can change a life. In fact, it can change yours as well as the those of the people you help."

6. You can use a **vivid illustration of the central idea** to conclude your speech. For example:

   "Millions of Americans once worshiped basketball star Michael Jordan. They were mesmerized by his talent, agility, and record-shattering perseverance. Yet with all the money he made, the fame he received, the charities he supported, and the advances he made for his sport, it's important to remember that he built his career on a solid foundation of a college education."

7. A **call for action from the audience** may clinch your speech. This type of conclusion must of course pertain to the ideas you've stated earlier. For a speech titled "Building Good Government," the conclusion might read:

   "Let us not sit by and do nothing while professional politicians corrupt our government and squander our money. Let's go out one by one, by twos and threes, or by hundreds and vote for better, more representative government! Tomorrow's Election Day. Vote your conscience. It's our only hope!"

No matter what style of conclusion your choose, remember that your presentation isn't over just because you stop talking. So don't jump the gun when it comes to returning to your seat. Edging away from the podium while you are still speaking will leave the audience with a negative impression of you and your speech.

Activities

A. Summarize a news story or a recent event in your life.

B. Write a summary of a simple multi-step process such as making a bed, raking leaves, or washing and drying dishes.

C. Write an analogy or a striking anecdote to illustrate one of these speech topics:

  • A flood in a southern town
  • A transportation strike
  • Decorating committee for the senior prom
  • The acting career of Abraham Lincoln's assassin, John Wilkes Booth
  • Organizing a neighborhood garage sale

D. Write an emotional or idealized statement about your school or about an organization you belong to.

E. Write a conclusion using either a powerful restatement of a thesis or a vivid illustration of a central idea for a speech.

F. Write a conclusion to a speech to get your audience to take action on an issue of your choice. Make sure it is something you believe in.

G. Rehearse and edit a conclusion from one of the activities above and present it to the class. Remember to stand up straight and to look your audience in the eye. When you have finished, take the time to acknowledge your audience and then walk back to your seat.

Titling Your Speech

The title of your speech should be provocative, brief, relevant to your subject, and interesting. The title is one of the first things your audience will read about in the paper or hear before you speak. Though a mediocre title won't ruin a presentation, a good one can spark a great deal of initial interest in the speech to come.

Activity

Write a possible title for each of these thesis statements:

  • America's health-care system is in crisis.
  • Massage therapy can help sports injuries.
  • The Grant Park High School gymnasium needs a renovation.
  • Come to the Sundance Film Festival.
  • Local car dealer Omar Abadin has won an award from the Better Business Bureau.

Delivering Your Speech

In This Chapter . . .

In any public speaking presentation, what you have to say is important—and so is how you say it. Now that you understand the basic speech components, you can move on to the actual wording of your speech. In this chapter you will learn what goes into the actual physical presentation of a speech: wording the speech, making notes, rehearsing, and using visual aids. You'll even get some pointers on how to control stage fright.

Speak Up!

Your view of the world is unique to you. Your public speaking should reflect this. Even when you speak about an everyday event or situation, your perception of it will be different from anyone else's. As an example, write a five-sentence description of your classroom. Include plenty of details about how the room looks, sounds, smells, and feels to you. Read your description aloud.

Wording Your Speech for Presentation

How you word your speech is up to you. Your speech should reflect both your point of view and your personality. In this section, we'll discuss two reliable options for wording your presentation.

1. The first method for wording your speech is to rehearse aloud from a complete sentence outline (or other type of outline) until you have attained a definite mastery of the words you plan to use. It is wise to memorize the introduction and conclusion although you should not memorize the entire speech word for word. If you commit the whole speech to memory, you will leave yourself little room for spontaneity. As a consequence your speech might come off as overly stiff. You should of course memorize the sequence of your main points regardless of how much you practice. In any case, if you plan to use notes during your speech, be sure to use the final copy of your speaking notes during the last few rehearsals. (For more on using notes, see "Preparing Speaker's Notes.") You might also consider tape-recording your first or second rehearsal to determine what wording changes you might need to make.

2. Another method for wording your speech is to write it out in full, then read the manuscript aloud several times to master the general ideas and necessary details. After doing this, construct a set of very brief notes containing only the main ideas of your speech. Rehearse aloud from them until you master the general wording and the order of the main points. A tape recorder is a good tool with this method as well. Hearing yourself on tape allows you to make adjustments and to become aware of mumbling or monotonous delivery.

Activities

A. Which method of preparation do you think you would find more helpful? Why?

B. Use one of the methods described on this page to create the basis of a five-minute speech on a topic of your choice.

Preparing Speaker's Notes

There are two common ways to prepare your speaker's notes. You can put a few words on a card or sheet of paper, or you can prepare a complete sentence outline. In Chapter 3 you read a complete sentence outline for a speech about body language (see page 27). Here is a sample copy of notes a speaker might use in presenting a five- to six-minute speech on the same topic.

BODY LANGUAGE

1. MOVEMENTS TALK
2. EVERYONE USES
3. HELPFUL
4. CAN IMPROVE
5. BORN WITH

Each word stands for an idea. You should write each word in large capital letters so that you can take it in at a glance. The actual size of a note card is three-by-five inches, about the size of a postcard. Bear in mind that speaking notes should serve only as a guide, not a crutch. You should have the speech clearly in your mind, not in a pile of note cards.

When you give your speech, hold your note card by the lower right-hand corner between your thumb and forefinger.

Activity

Using the notes for "Body Language" as a model and the basis of a speech from the previous activity, write a five-item set of speaker's notes on your topic.

Rehearsing Your Speech

No matter whether you use an outline or speaker's notes, it's important to rehearse your speech aloud. The number of oral rehearsals you will need depends entirely on you. Most speakers require at least four to six rehearsals.

One of the best ways to rehearse a speech is to stand in front of a mirror so that you can observe your posture and other body language. Some students are uncomfortable with the idea of using a mirror because they claim it bothers them to observe themselves. This is a flimsy excuse. A few trial runs in front of the mirror will vastly improve most speeches and speakers. And if you want to take it one step further, a videotape of your practice session is one of the best forms of self-evaluation.

Activities

A. Using your speaker's notes, rehearse your speech with a partner. Afterward ask questions about how well you communicated. Try to incorporate changes as you go through the speech a second and third time.

B. Present your speech to the class, using your speaker's notes and your visual aid.

C. Write a self-evaluation to rate your performance.

Improving Your Vocal Quality

When you speak to an audience your voice is your main physical tool. It doesn't matter how well worded and beautifully structured your speech is if no one can hear it. You have no doubt heard people speak in squeaky, shrill voices or in dull, bland monotones. Speakers with good vocal quality make the audience want to listen to them. Speakers with poor vocal quality make the audience want to stop listening.

Proper Breathing

Many vocal problems are the result of improper breathing. Nervous speakers often breathe too shallowly to support the volume they need for a public forum. When you **project** your voice to speak to an audience, you should breathe using the muscles of your lower chest and abdomen, rather than those of your neck and upper chest. Using your lower chest will give you stronger breath support. It will also take pressure off your throat. Breathing the wrong way can strain your throat, which can lead to hoarseness. A steady habit of this can cause long-term damage to your vocal cords. (For more on voice projection, see the Talking Points on page 47.)

Activities

A. To ensure proper breathing, stand up straight and put one hand on your abdomen at the space between the two sides of your rib cage. As you take a deep breath in, try to fill up that space with air. The part of your body that rises as you fill it with air is called your *diaphragm*. When you breathe out, your diaphragm should contract. Do this several times.

B. Open one of your textbooks to a random page. Breathing normally, read aloud until you run out of breath. Have a classmate time how long you are able to read normally before you to need another breath. (Note: Do not try to go beyond your capacity. When you feel you need to take a breath, do so.) Then time your partner. Next, place your hand on your diaphragm and take a deep breath. Read aloud the same portion of the textbook that you read previously. Have your partner time you. Then time your partner. Was there a difference between your times?

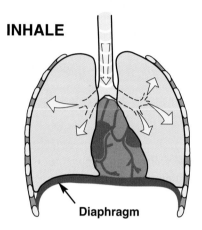

INHALE

Diaphragm

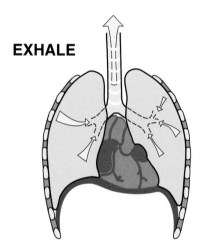

EXHALE

Articulation Problems

Have you ever heard a speaker who sounded as if his or her mouth were full of oatmeal? **Articulation** problems—problems speaking clearly—are common for beginning speakers. Mumbling and/or dropping the ends of words can make your speech nearly unintelligible for your listeners. You can use a tape recorder to help identify any articulation problems. Sometimes it's also helpful to ask your instructor or a trusted friend or classmate for feedback about your articulation. In most cases, becoming aware of the problem will help you to solve it. If you come across words that you consistently stumble over or mispronounce, take extra time with those words. Repeat them over and over again until you can say them clearly each time.

Activity

Tongue twisters can help you to articulate more clearly. Choose two of the following and practice them until you can repeat each three times in a row without stumbling or sounding as if your mouth were full of oatmeal.

- Unique New York

- She stood on the balcony, inexplicably mimicking him hiccoughing, and amicably welcoming him home.

- Imagine an imaginary menagerie manager imagining managing an imaginary menagerie.

- How much wood would a woodchuck chuck if a woodchuck could chuck wood?

- Theophilus Thistle, the successful thistle sifter, in shifting a sieve full of unsifted thistles, thrust three thousand thistles through the thick of his thumb.

Pacing Your Presentation

If you feel nervous about public speaking, you're not alone. Many people list public speaking as one of their greatest fears. In fact, it is common to have a few butterflies in the pit of your stomach when you first get up in front of an audience. But it's important to recognize that this nervousness is natural. You can use it to your advantage if you keep breathing and stay focused on presenting your ideas. In many cases, the adrenaline you feel when you approach the podium can add energy to your presentation. The flipside of this is that nervousness can cause you to speak at far too rapid a rate. Blasting through your introduction as if you can't wait to finish the speech is not a solution. You must resist the temptation to get the speech over with in a hurry. Instead, when you walk to the podium or the front of the classroom, take some deep breaths. This should make you feel calmer. When you reach the podium, take a moment to survey your audience. Keep breathing.

Even if you're nervous throughout your speech, it's important to keep your speaking rate steady. It's just as bad to lapse into a monotone as to speak too quickly. Either of these pacing problems is likely to make your audience stop listening. Stay focused on the ideas you want to get across.

The main thing is to use your voice normally and conversationally. Speak earnestly and loudly enough to be heard by everyone in the room. If you are truly interested in getting the audience to understand you, it's likely that your articulation, vocal variety, pitch, volume, and pacing will take care of themselves.

Activity

Talk to someone you believe is a good public speaker. You might choose a friend, a teacher, a relative, or a coworker. Interview that person as to what he or she does to prepare for speaking.

Understanding Body Language

Speaking is a whole-body activity. To be an effective speaker, you will have to use your feet, legs, hands and arms, trunk, head, and even your eyebrows. **Body language** consists of movements, facial expressions, postures, and gestures. Shrugging, nodding, rubbing your eyes, or slumping are all parts of body language. Body language can be conscious or unconscious. For example, you might wink at a friend consciously, but you might also blink unconsciously when you are surprised or anxious.

It is nearly impossible to speak without *some* body language. Just because you're not aware of all that goes on while you speak doesn't mean that you aren't using some actions. As you become a stronger public speaker, you will develop techniques to reinforce your words with appropriate body language. For more on this topic, see Experience 5, "The Speech to Develop Body Language," on page 88.

Activities

A. Make a list of body language movements. You should be able to come up with at least twenty. Circle those movements that you are aware of making yourself. Put a check by those that you are aware of in other people.

B. Bring in pictures from a magazine or newspaper that illustrate some of the movements you listed for Activity A.

C. With a partner improvise a conversation. You can talk about anything, but try to make it as natural as possible. Then repeat the improvisation. This time try not to make any gestures. Tell each other whenever body language takes place—whether it's voluntary or involuntary.

Using Visual Aids

When you create a **visual aid** (a poster, graph, map, photo collage, etc.), try to make sure that it serves your purpose by illuminating one or more of your speech's main points. Use color to emphasize details and to compare and contrast ideas.

Whenever you use a visual aid, you should practice with it so that you know you can handle it smoothly during your speech. Make sure that every member of your audience will be able to see it. Lettering and images should be visible even at a distance.

It's a good idea to keep your visual aid out of sight until you are ready to use it. Face the audience and not the visual aid when you are presenting. When you are finished with it, place it out of view again.

Activity

Brainstorm with classmates about the kinds of visual aids you might create for the following topics:

- World hunger
- The pet adoption process
- Current clothing fashions
- The Academy Awards
- Magic tricks
- Genetic engineering
- Nuclear testing

Conquering Stage Fright

Preparing for a quality speech involves developing a positive attitude about the entire speaking situation. Yes, you will be nervous the first few times you give a speech. You will most likely experience some degree of stage fright. Understand, though, that while stage fright will usually disappear after a while, nervousness just before speaking will not. Use the surge of energy you feel to launch your speech more vigorously. You will gain self-confidence and poise as you make more speeches, but do not expect a miracle. Your mental attitude should allow you to recognize your own strengths and weaknesses, but you should not be morbidly disturbed if you aren't the world's greatest speaker on your first few attempts.

Be willing to take advice from your instructor and, sometimes, from your classmates. The people who watch and listen to you will notice things about your performance that you are not able to see.

Make an honest effort to prepare adequately. Preparation is the key to quality public speaking. As you progress you should take pride in your improvement. Maintaining a healthy positive attitude will ensure that you reach your speaking goals.

Activity

Talk to students who participate in school plays, debate, or forensics or who have made speeches during school assemblies. Ask them for tips about dealing with stage fright or nervousness before and during speaking. Take notes and be ready to share what you learn with your classmates.

Talking Points
Can You Hear Me Now?

You may remember a television commercial in which a cellular phone technician repeatedly asked, "Can you hear me now?" Whether walking in a jungle or strolling down a city street, the young technician repeated the question after every few steps. This catch phrase, intended to show consumers the cellular service's vast network, provides a valuable lesson about communication: If your audience can't hear you, you can't communicate with them.

In some formal speaking situations you will use a microphone. But for most public speaking you will have to depend on the power of your own voice. For this reason, it's a good idea to warm up your voice a bit before a speech.

Keep in mind that even if you are speaking in what you consider to be a very loud voice, there may be a problem with the room's **acoustics**, or its ability to conduct sound. So watch the audience carefully for signs that they are able to hear your speech. If you feel some people are unable to hear you, it's all right to ask a question such as, "Can you hear me in the back?"

Activities

A. Stand at your desk and whisper a short sentence of your choice. Speak as softly as you can. Your classmates will raise their hands when they can hear you. Raise your voice by degrees until all of your classmates have raised their hands. You will have to speak at least this loudly during a speech.

B. Take a deep breath from your diaphragm. Let your breath out slowly as you vocalize the word *oh*. When you reach the end of the breath, take another one and vocalize the word *ah*. Gradually increase your volume. Try to keep the tone steady. Don't strain. Feel the vibration in your throat.

C. Use the tongue twisters on page 43 as a vocal and articulation warm-up. Gradually increase your vocal pace and volume.

Listening
and Evaluating

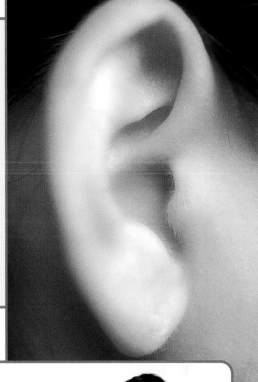

In This Chapter . . .

Public speaking takes a lot of work. As a speaker, you must try to engage your audience and hold their attention from start to finish. But listeners have a responsibility to the public speaking process as well. They owe it to the speaker to listen carefully and to evaluate what they hear. In this chapter we'll look at these skills in more depth.

Speak Up!

Share a recent experience you had as a member of an audience. It might have been at a school assembly, a class presentation, or a dramatic performance. What was the experience like? Was the audience engaged? Were *you?* Describe why the experience did or did not hold your attention.

Listening

For any public speaking presentation to be effective, the speaker must make a competent presentation to an audience that takes the trouble to listen. As a listener you should abide by the rules of audience etiquette. Following these rules will allow you and your fellow audience members to get the most from a speaker's presentation.

Audience Dos and Don'ts

DO arrive on time for the presentation and take your seat quietly. Arriving late can inconvenience the speaker and your fellow audience members.

DO turn off your cell phone, pager, chiming watch, or anything that makes noise of any kind for the duration of the presentation.

DO remain attentive.

DON'T roll your eyes or make faces.

DON'T sigh or yawn loudly.

DON'T shuffle or fidget during the speech. This includes tapping your foot, cracking your knuckles, drumming your fingers on your desk or chair, and so on.

DON'T speak during the presentation—not even in a whisper.

DO take notes when appropriate.

DO applaud the speaker once the presentation is finished.

What makes a person a good listener? The ability to listen might strike you as a common skill, one that everyone possesses. But being a good listener means more than simply hearing what is said. Many people assume they are good listeners when in reality their listening skills need work.

Listening Actively

Good listeners actively seek meaning from what they hear. They listen for key information, evaluate it, and respond to it. Are *you* a good listener? Use the following checklist to analyze your listening skills.

Traits of a Good Listener

As a listener …

Do you relate what you hear to your own experience?

Do you use prior knowledge to understand new ideas or information?

Do you think of questions you would like the speaker to answer?

Do you make associations and create vivid mental images to help you remember the information?

Do you take notes?

Do you use eye contact and good posture to show the speaker that you're paying attention?

Do you ask questions when it's appropriate to do so?

Do you analyze your response to the presentation afterward?

Listening Critically

To listen critically means going beyond merely understanding the meaning of what you hear. It means analyzing the ideas for their strengths and weaknesses. A critical listener is not a passive observer. He or she is fully engaged in listening to find the answers to certain questions or to understand which questions are truly important.

A good public speaker has a purpose for speaking. Likewise, a good listener attempts to identify the speaker's purpose and to evaluate how well the speaker accomplishes that purpose. Sometimes a speaker identifies his or her purpose at the beginning of the speech. At other times a speaker will build toward the purpose and illuminate it at the end of the speech. Either way, listening for the purpose and identifying the main ideas are important aspects of critical listening.

Activities

A. Think about the list of *dos* and *don'ts* on the facing page. How would you rate yourself and the people in the audience you described in the Speak Up! activity on page 49? What could you or your fellow audience members have done to be a better audience?

B. To assess your listening skills, interview a classmate about his or her life. Take notes on the person's responses to the following questions:

What is your full name?

Where were you born?

How old are you?

Do you have a job? If so, what is it?

Are you a member of any clubs or organizations? If so, which ones?

Do you play a musical instrument? If so, what?

Do you speak more than one language? If so, which ones?

Do you play a particular sport? If so, which one?

Where do you live now?

What are your hobbies?

What do you most enjoy doing?

C. Using your notes from Activity B, introduce your classmate to the rest of the class. Then check with the classmate you interviewed to see whether you got all the information right.

Barriers to Listening

If you're like most people, there are times when you listen well—actively and/or critically—and times when you don't. Recognizing the things that stand in the way of active listening is the first step toward becoming a better listener.

Physical and Mental Barriers

Imagine that you are sitting in your last class before the lunch hour. You forgot to eat breakfast this morning and your stomach is grumbling. Also you stayed up pretty late last night talking on the phone with a friend. At the front of the room, your instructor is speaking to the class. She says, "Did everyone get that?" You realize suddenly that you have no idea what she's talking about.

There are a couple of things going on here. First, active listening takes energy. If you're hungry and you didn't get enough sleep last night, you're not going to be very energetic or focused. Hunger and fatigue can distract even the best listeners. Your physical and mental states are key factors in your ability to listen.

Environmental Barriers

Imagine that you have now eaten lunch and it's time to go to your next class. It's cold outside, but inside it's nice and warm—so warm, in fact, that you begin to feel a little sleepy. Ten minutes later, your instructor suddenly calls on you to answer a question. Again, you realize you haven't been paying attention—you've heard the instructor's words, but you haven't been listening. So what's the problem now? In this case, your environment is working against you. Because the room is very warm, the energy you might have had after lunch begins to dissipate. Other environmental barriers to good listening might include noise inside or outside the room, light that is too bright or too dim, and overcrowded conditions in the room.

Of course it's important to eat properly and get enough rest. Ideally, a warm, crowded room won't act as a sedative. But even if you feel overly warm or cool, even if you are very hungry or too full, and even if you are sleepy, you still have an obligation as a listener. Sometimes it is simply a matter of concentrating harder despite the obstacles.

Activity

List three other possible physical, mental, or environmental barriers to active listening.

Listener Bias

Like most people, you no doubt have opinions and deeply held beliefs about all kinds of subjects. But good listeners know that it's important to pay attention with an open mind. If you come into a presentation already knowing you're going to disagree with the speaker, you leave him or her no room for persuasion. You shut yourself off from learning something new—something that might even have succeeded in changing your mind.

Pay attention to your reaction if you find yourself responding very negatively or positively to a speaker at the very beginning of a speech. Sometimes a person's way of speaking or physical appearance can trigger an emotional response. For example, if a speaker looks vaguely like your favorite cousin you might find that you're biased in favor of what that speaker will say. Try to remain as objective as possible about the speaker and his or her presentation.

Activities

A. Which of the following are biased statements?

All babies are cute.

Nobody really enjoys cleaning up.

I love science and math, but history is boring.

I'm voting for Dale Rivera because he's a better person than the other candidate.

Being an artist is fine, but you can't make a living at it.

Artists are more interesting than most other people.

The smell in here is sickening.

Abraham Lincoln was America's most honest president.

Red meat is terrible for you.

Sometimes you win and sometimes you lose.

I believe in justice for all who deserve it.

B. Look for print or television advertisements that use a celebrity spokesperson. Have any of these ads ever influenced how you feel about a particular product? Discuss your impressions with a small group of classmates.

Taking Notes

Whether you're jotting things down for your own speech or writing down the main ideas of someone else's, taking effective notes can make all the difference.

As a listener, you are trying to understand a speech's main idea and supporting details. When you take notes on a speech, you should pay special attention to the speaker's use of repetition and emphasis. If a speaker mentions something more than once, the chances are good that it is one of the main ideas of the speech.

When you take notes, you don't have to write in complete sentences. There usually isn't time for that anyway. By the time you finished writing a complete sentence the speaker would likely have moved on to the next point. Instead, just write key words and phrases. Write only enough to ensure that you'll understand your notes later. If you think of a question you want to ask the speaker, jot down a phrase to remind you of that as well.

Activity

Read through the following paragraphs from the opening of President Franklin D. Roosevelt's "Infamy" speech. Then reread the passage and take notes.

"Yesterday, December 7, 1941—a date which will live in infamy—the United States of America was suddenly and deliberately attacked by naval and air forces of the Empire of Japan.

The United States was at peace with that nation and, at the solicitation of Japan, was still in conversation with its Government and its Emperor looking toward the maintenance of peace in the Pacific. Indeed, one hour after Japanese air squadrons had commenced bombing in Oahu, the Japanese Ambassador to the United States and his colleague delivered to the Secretary of State a formal reply to a recent American message. While this reply stated that it seemed useless to continue the existing diplomatic negotiations, it contained no threat or hint of war or armed attack.

Franklin Delano Roosevelt

It will be recorded that the distance of Hawaii from Japan makes it obvious that the attack was deliberately planned many days or even weeks ago. During the intervening time the Japanese Government has deliberately sought to deceive the United States by false statements and expressions of hope for continued peace.

The attack yesterday on the Hawaiian Islands has caused severe damage to American naval and military forces. Very many American lives have been lost. In addition American ships have been reported torpedoed on the high seas between San Francisco and Honolulu...."

Evaluating

As you progress through this book, you will be asked to make evaluations of your classmates' speeches. You will also receive such evaluations from your classmates about your own work.

Evaluating Your Peers

When you listen to another person speak you form all sorts of impressions. When it comes time to evaluate the person's presentation, you must organize these impressions into a coherent response that points out what the speaker did and did not do well.

1. **Oral evaluations** are given aloud in front of the class. This type of evaluation can benefit both the speaker and the listeners. Everyone makes mistakes. Oral evaluations allow everyone to learn from their own mistakes and successes as well as the mistakes and successes of others.

   For oral evaluations to function most effectively, each student must work to develop and maintain an atmosphere of trust in the classroom. That means everyone must do his or her best to provide **constructive feedback**. Making fun of anyone for any reason during an evaluation is destructive behavior. So is making overly negative comments. When you are asked to provide an oral evaluation, use the following guidelines to form your response:

   - Begin by saying something positive. Tell the speaker what he or she did well. That will give the speaker the confidence to hear any not-so-positive feedback that follows. It will also give the speaker confidence for the next presentation.

   - When you give negative feedback, don't point out every little thing the speaker failed to do well. Instead, choose one or two points that might be improved. Otherwise the speaker might become embarrassed or overwhelmed.

   - If you feel you know what the speaker could do to improve the speech, make a suggestion.

   - Always try to make your feedback as specific as possible. Avoid general statements such as, "I just didn't like the way you did that" or "Maybe this isn't a good topic for you." Instead, use specific examples from the speech to illustrate your points.

   Remember that each speaker should have a purpose—to entertain, inform, or persuade. The criteria for evaluating each type of speech may vary a bit. For example, if the goal of a speech is to persuade, the speech naturally will contain some elements that would not be part of, say, a speech to entertain. It's up to you to listen actively and critically to evaluate whether or not a speaker achieved his or her purpose.

2. **Written evaluations** are usually more detailed than oral evaluations. Whereas in an oral evaluation you take part in a group discussion of a classmate's work, in a written evaluation you must analyze all aspects of the presentation in written form. You can do this in any number of ways, but one of the most effective is to use a **rubric**, or set of standard criteria, with which you can rate each speech. On page 55 is an example of a rubric for evaluating a presentation. (Note that each of the 38 speech experiences in this book ends with a specific evaluation rubric.)

Organization

- What organization method did the speaker use? (spatial, chronological, etc.)
- Did the introduction lead the audience into the speech and present the speaker's goal? Was the body of the speech logical and easy to follow?
- Did the conclusion summarize the main points of the speech and close with a memorable statement?
- What could the speaker do to improve in this area next time?

Content

- What was the speaker's purpose?
- Did the speaker achieve the purpose?
- Did the speech offer sufficient examples and details?
- What techniques did the speaker use to help the audience remember important information?
- What could the speaker do to improve in this area next time?

Delivery

- Describe the speaker's appearance, voice, and attitude.
- Did the speaker use language that was appropriate for the audience?
- If the speaker used technical terms or unfamiliar words, did he or she define them?
- What could the speaker do to improve his or her delivery next time?

Being Evaluated by Your Peers

Just after delivering a speech, you may not feel much like being evaluated. At that particular moment, even the most constructive feedback can sometimes seem harsh. So it's good to realize in advance that these feelings can come up. But it's also very important that you listen with an open mind to any and all feedback.

If you feel yourself becoming defensive, take a deep breath. Realize that your classmate is trying to help you, not hurt you. If you don't understand a particular comment, ask for clarification. Make sure that your evaluators tell you specifically what they saw and heard. Only through honest, specific feedback can you all grow and learn together.

Evaluating Yourself

There are several methods you can use to evaluate your own public speaking presentations. One is to create a rubric to rate yourself on each speech.

When you evaluate your own public speaking, you should look at two main factors: the content of your speech and your delivery. Use the following guidelines to evaluate your speech's content:

- Check to see that you used as many sources as possible and that you have cited them properly to avoid plagiarizing. (For more about avoiding plagiarism, see Chapter 3.)
- Make sure the organization of your speech is clear and easy to follow.
- Your introduction should be attention-getting and logical.

- Your conclusion should summarize your main ideas and provide a memorable final thought.

It's a bit more difficult to evaluate your delivery. After all, you can't see yourself as you're presenting your speech. One of the best methods is to tape-record or videotape yourself giving a speech. Listening to a tape-recording can reveal problems in pitch, articulation, inflection, rate, and volume. Watching yourself on videotape can reveal strengths and weaknesses in your voice, posture, gestures, grooming, facial expressions, and body language. When you watch or listen to yourself on cassette or videotape, use these guidelines to evaluate your delivery:

- Listen for positive vocal qualities, such as fluency, variety in pitch and inflection, clear articulation, adequate volume, and a good pace.

- Listen for negative vocal qualities, such as harshness; nasality; monotone; shrillness; articulation problems; and fillers such as "okay," "ya know," and "um."

- Look for positive physical qualities, such as good posture and appropriate facial expressions and gestures.

- Notice negative physical aspects of your performance, such as stiffness, a frozen expression, slumped posture, and wild or unconnected gestures.

Some people find it embarrassing to watch or listen to themselves on tape. But remember that as a public speaker, you are asking an audience to pay attention to you. Knowing exactly what they're seeing and hearing can help you to develop speaking techniques that will not only get their attention, but win their good opinion as well.

Activities

A. Tape-record yourself giving a speech or telling a story. Listen to the tape several times. Think about what you might do to improve your performance. Then tape the speech again. Do you notice any improvement?

B. Have a partner videotape you as you give a speech or tell a story. Ask your partner to give you feedback about your presentation. Then watch the videotape together.

Talking Points
Self and Peer Evaluation

It's important to stay open to feedback when you're first learning to speak in front of an audience. And, not surprisingly, the need for feedback doesn't go away. Bad habits can crop up in even the most experienced speakers. Successful speakers seek feedback about their public speaking. You can do this too. Rehearse your speech for a parent or a trusted friend. Make sure the person knows you are looking for honest feedback. Once the person gives you feedback, make sure you understand it. Then remember to accept the feedback gracefully and thank the person who gave it.

When you evaluate a peer, try to give the kind of feedback that you yourself would find helpful. That doesn't mean you should say only positive things or things that aren't true. But there are a number of ways to provide respectful, constructive feedback that informs the speaker about elements he or she might be able to improve. For example, which of these comments would you find more helpful?

1. "Your posture was just awful."

2. "I think you might be able to control your breathing better if you stand up a little straighter."

Which of the comments below is the most constructive?

1. "Your gestures need to be toned down. You looked like you were directing traffic at a busy intersection."

2. "Swinging your arms like that really took your speech downhill. You should try not to move at all."

3. "I swing my arms when I get nervous. I noticed you did that too. I find it helps to use fewer gestures."

Number 1 might be construed as teasing. Number 2 contains a negative comment followed by a bad suggestion. Number 3 is designed to make the recipient feel better about his or her chances for the next speech. By comparing the speaker to himself or herself, the evaluator created a connection.

Activities

A. Rewrite these negative statements to reflect more constructive feedback.

"Your voice is really squeaky and shrill. It was bugging me to listen to it."

"Your speech was boring."

"You don't know anything about that topic. Why did you pick it?"

"You must've said the word 'um' a hundred times!"

"You were shifting from one foot to the other so you looked like you were doing some kind of weird dance."

"Your visual aids were no good."

"How much time did you spend preparing for this speech—three minutes?"

"Your speech wasn't as good as Andrea's speech on the same topic."

B. Rewrite the following general statements to make them more specific.

"I liked your introduction."

"One of your visual aids was great."

"I stopped paying attention about halfway through your speech."

"I wish you would've ended the speech better."

"I got a lot out of your speech."

UNIT 2 Personal Speeches

"I am SO afraid to give a speech!" Any time a public speaking class is required at a high school or university, the teacher is bound to hear this statement every semester. Even more students probably experience the fear without saying so aloud.

If such a statement resonates with you to any degree, you will find that this unit will help you begin to overcome those concerns.

Speech Experiences in This Unit

The Introductory Speech

Specs for the Introductory Speech

Time limit

1–2 minutes.

Speaker's notes

See the questions in the Preparing and Organizing segment of this chapter.

Sources of information

This speech uses information from your own life, so you will not have to do any research.

Outline

This assignment is quite short. If you'd like, you can write a brief outline of the information you plan to present.

Speak Up!

Share an experience you have had speaking in front of a group. It need not have been a formal speech event. You might have spoken during a meeting or at a team practice. Try to recall your reaction to being in the spotlight. Was it a good experience? Why or why not?

Purpose and Expectations of This Assignment

In completing this assignment, you will

- organize familiar material in a format to present to others;

- experience speaking in front of an audience to become aware of aspects of effective delivery such as eye contact, volume, gestures, and vocal variety; and

- get a feel for presenting ideas in front of a group.

This will be the first speech you present in this course. You will find out what it's like to get on your feet and tell a group of people something about yourself. You don't have to give a long biographical account of your life. But you do have to provide a structure for your speech, one that allows you to present yourself in the most interesting way possible. When it comes to public speaking, everyone has to start somewhere. This experience will give you a positive beginning.

Defining the Introductory Speech

An **introductory speech** is a public speaking event in which you introduce yourself to a group of people. You will probably make many introductory speeches during your lifetime. Some situations in which you might be called upon to make this type of speech are

- club and organizational meetings,

- board meetings,

- teaching and learning situations,

- panel discussions, or

- rallies.

One reason that your first assignment is to make an introductory speech is to let the audience get acquainted with you. Another reason is to give you an opportunity to learn what it's like to stand in front of a group of people who are waiting to hear what you have to say. Unlike many other kinds of public speaking, in an introductory speech you don't have to worry about doing research on your subject; after all, your subject is *you*. Clearly there is no one in the world that knows more about you than you do.

Preparing and Organizing

Some people thrive on the rush of energy they get from public speaking. But if you're like most people, you might feel a little nervous about giving this first speech. That's natural, and it reinforces the importance of being prepared for each presentation. So what do you need to do to be better prepared? An introductory speech is all about making a great first impression. You'll want to present the best possible version of yourself.

First it's important to understand that you will very likely be anxious prior to a speech—and that you can control that nervous reaction. To be scared, nervous, and tense is normal. These thoughts and feelings are often referred to collectively as **stage fright**. It would be strange if you *didn't* experience some feelings of stage fright the first time you speak in front of an audience.

From a scientific point of view, stage fright or anxiety is the result of your adrenal glands functioning more than they usually do. Athletes and actors have these same anxious moments prior to a game or a performance. Nervousness is the high-octane fuel that injects extra life into their performances. In the right amount, nervousness can be very useful. As you give more speeches

throughout this course, you will feel yourself gaining more command over your nerves. So don't try to rid yourself of this energy. All you need to do is control it.

This speech will be short; nevertheless, you should plan and organize it very carefully.

Although this speech will be about you, there are still some choices to make. You must decide which elements of your life you will be sharing. Like everyone else, you have many facets to your personality and history. Perhaps you are a musician, a pet owner, the world's best baby-sitter, a shopper with an attitude, or a sports nut. As you mentally flip through your life and times, think about areas that your audience might find interesting.

1. Answer the questions below on a note card or sheet of paper. Use a few brief words or phrases for each answer. You can use these answers as the basis of your presentation.

Or you can substitute your own questions for some of those listed.

- What is your full name?
- Where and how did you spend your childhood?
- Tell about your hometown or neighborhood.
- How do you spend your spare time?
- Who are your favorite movie actor and actress? Why?
- What is your favorite sport? Why?

2. Decide the order in which you want to present the answers to these questions. What information do you think needs the most emphasis? Which elements will give the audience the clearest idea of exactly who you are? Reorder the questions to fit your purpose.

3. Start off with a friendly introduction. Keep it conversational, but avoid being overly chatty. You have only a couple of minutes, so you can't afford to waste any time.

4. Present each point listed on your note card. Spend the majority of your time on your most important points.

5. When you are ready to close your remarks, conclude with a brief summarizing statement.

6. It will help you to practice aloud several times. Stand in front of a mirror while you speak or present your speech to a parent or friend. Do not memorize your answers word for word, since this could make your remarks sound like a recitation.

Presenting

When your name is called, walk quietly to the front of the room. Do not do anything to draw unnecessary attention. When you get there, stand politely. If you feel overly nervous, take a couple of deep breaths. Keep your weight on both feet or on your slightly forward foot. Try not to lock your knees.

Let your hands hang loosely at your sides unless you need to look at your notes. When you refer to your note card, raise it high enough that you do not need to lower your head. Grasp your note card lightly between your thumb and index finger. Do not roll, crumple, twist, or disfigure it in any way. It is permissible to place your other hand on a tabletop or a chair back if you can do so without drawing attention.

When you begin your speech, speak in a normal conversational tone—just as you would if you were telling a story about yourself to a group of good friends. Your voice might be a little shaky at first, but it will probably level out as you continue speaking.

Show interest in your remarks. Good speaking is good conversation. If you feel yourself slipping into a monotone, change your rhythm and pace. Be sure that everyone can hear you.

When you look at different members of your audience—and you should do this often—focus on their foreheads just above their eyes. By focusing on a person's forehead, you will not be distracted from your thoughts by his or her eye movements or by a blank stare. Avoid shifting your eyes too often. Above all, don't flit your eyes to the point where they never rest anywhere. Instead, select focal points within your audience and move your eyes to these points as you speak. Each time you focus on a member of your audience, you make a connection with him or her. Your eye contact can make each audience member feel as if you are speaking directly to him or her.

If you feel like moving around a few paces, do so naturally, without shuffling or scraping your feet. Don't pace. When you are not changing positions, stand still.

Pause at least two seconds after your final words; then go calmly and politely to your chair. Do not rush or crumple your notes into a wad and shove them in your pocket. Upon reaching your chair, avoid slouching, sprawling, heaving a big sigh, and any other behavior that says, "Whew, I'm glad that's over!" You may feel that way; however, try to keep in mind that your speech isn't over until the audience stops paying attention to you.

Evaluating

Evaluate a classmate's introductory speech. Rate the following criteria on a scale from 1 to 5 with 1 being "needs much improvement" and 5 being "outstanding."

- Was the talk well organized?
- Was the speaker's introduction smooth?
- Did you feel you learned something about the speaker's life and personality?

- Were there smooth transitions between points?
- Did the speaker use his or her notes effectively?
- Did the speaker provide an effective conclusion?

Give an overall score to the speech and be ready to explain it.

A Speech on Communication Apprehension

Specs for a Speech on Communication Apprehension

Time limit
   None.

Speaker's notes
   25–50 words for the interview report.

Sources
   The person or persons interviewed.

Outline
   Prepare a 75- to 150-word complete sentence outline.

Speak Up!

Share an anecdote about a time when you have been nervous or afraid. What physical symptoms did you notice? Did you feel any other emotions beyond the anxiety? What did you do to change the situation?

Purpose and Expectations of This Assignment

In completing this assignment, you will

- identify common feelings associated with performance anxiety,

- interview a seasoned public speaker about his or her experiences of stage fright, and

- organize and present speech material that may be associated with some of your own anxieties.

As you learned in Experience 1, most people regularly experience some level of performance anxiety even if they speak in public frequently. In fact, you'll recall that many speakers claim their nervousness actually has a positive effect because it keeps them alert and animated. The best way to make sure that speech anxiety helps rather than hurts you is to be thoroughly prepared. However, it can also be very helpful to discuss feelings of nervousness with people who may actually deal with it on a regular basis. The speech on communication apprehension will help you learn from others and take the opportunity to identify your own concerns and possible solutions.

Defining the Speech on Communication Apprehension

The **speech on communication apprehension** is designed to help you identify and confront the stage fright you may experience during public speaking. You will see that nearly all speakers suffer some similar fears and physical reactions, including apathy, speechlessness, shortness of breath, dry mouth, weak knees, pain in the stomach, or trembling hands and/or knees. This speech, however, is unique; it is not designed for presentation in a public setting beyond the classroom.

Preparing

For this speech you will interview up to three people who have a variety of speaking experiences, for example, a teacher, pastor, performer, or other professional. You might also interview someone who has had more limited experience in public address such as a student leader or classmate.

Take notes as you go through the following questions with each person you interview.

- How often do you speak in public?

- Do you get nervous? If so, what are the symptoms you feel?

- How do you deal with stage fright?

- What would you recommend to a beginning speaker for dealing with stage fright?

- Has your level of nervousness changed with more experiences in public speaking? If so, how?

Be sure you ask your subjects to explain further any ideas that you do not fully understand. This will be your only opportunity to clarify their meanings and to understand their experiences before you present your speech.

Take very careful notes during your interview(s). If you wish to record an interview on audiocassette, be sure to ask the person's permission before you begin.

After the interview, compare the experiences of those you interviewed with your own experiences and thoughts about performance anxiety. Identify the intensity of your thoughts and symptoms. Write them down as you do. Review the tips and suggestions you received from the people you interviewed and see if there are any you feel might work for you.

Ask your teacher about other methods of addressing communication apprehension that you may not have encountered in your interviews. Review those possibilities for yourself as well. Select one or two ideas to try before presenting this speech.

Organizing

Organize your speech carefully. Remember that the order in which you present information is one of the keys to a successful presentation. Here is one effective plan you might use.

1. Begin with an anecdote about stage fright. If you heard a funny story from one of your interviewees—or if you have one of your own—plan to open the speech with that. Sometimes humor can be a very handy public speaking tool. It can loosen up both you and your audience. Try not to laugh at the story unless your audience does.

2. Tell the audience about the people you interviewed and their experiences and advice about dealing with communication apprehension.

3. Your speaking notes should cover each interviewee separately, but after you describe each one you may draw some common conclusions about performance anxiety in general.

4. Your final point should tell about your own anticipation of or experience with communication anxiety, and about the one

or two suggestions you tried before presenting this speech.

5. Conclude your speech with a reference back to your opening story, perhaps imagining how one of the suggestions you tried could have changed the outcome.

Presenting

This should be a simple, non-dramatic, and sincere discussion straight from the heart. Keep the tone casual. Deliver the speech as if you were talking with a group of friends. Try to keep your gestures and facial expressions as natural as possible. When you have completed your presentation, simply return to your seat.

Evaluating

Evaluate a classmate's speech on communication apprehension. Rate the following criteria on a scale from 1 to 5 with 1 being "needs much improvement" and 5 being "outstanding."

- Was the speech well organized and easy to follow?
- Did the speaker choose interesting subjects to interview?
- Did the speaker provide examples?
- Was the speaker able to use experiences from his or her own life?
- Was the speaker's delivery natural and conversational?
- Were the speaker's gestures appropriate to the material?

Give an overall score to the speech. Then choose one area where you think the presentation could be improved. Make suggestions for how the speaker might present that element next time.

Talking Points

Dealing with Stage Fright

Who experiences stage fright? Ninety percent of all public speakers, that's who!

- Sir Laurence Olivier, a renowned English actor whose career spanned six decades, claimed he experienced stage fright before nearly every performance.

- For powerhouse singer-actor Barbra Streisand, known for her roles as a feisty go-getter in such films as *The Way We Were* and *Funny Girl*, stage fright is just part of her pre-performance tradition.

But as most performers and athletes know, the audience actually *wants* them to be great. You should keep this in mind as well—your audience isn't sitting out there waiting for you to fail. They want you to succeed. They want to be interested, persuaded, informed, or entertained by what you have to say.

One thing that might surprise you about stage fright is that even if you experience severe symptoms, your audience isn't likely to notice. Many beginning speakers admit to friends that they were nervous during a speech only to hear their friends say, "Really? I couldn't tell at all!"

When you allow yourself to feel vulnerable because you believe everyone can see your red face or your trembling hands, the

Barbara Streisand as "Baby Snooks"

chances are that you will compound the problem by adding unconnected and uncomfortable gestures or making strange facial expressions. Understanding that no one else is as aware of your nerves as you are can help you gain control of the situation.

Public speaking is the same as most other skills in that the more you practice, the more you will improve. So get used to it! Take advantage of every opportunity you have to speak in front of an audience. You will feel your confidence growing each time. In the meanwhile, here's a list of tips to help you control performance anxiety:

1. **Make sure you are completely prepared.** If you know your material well, you're less likely to feel tongue-tied.

2. **Take care with your appearance.** When you look your best, you feel more confident.

3. **Relax those tight muscles.** Nervousness can cause you to constrict your muscles. This makes you look and feel even more tense. Before you speak, take some deep breaths and try to relax all your major muscle groups. This will really pay off when you step in front of the audience.

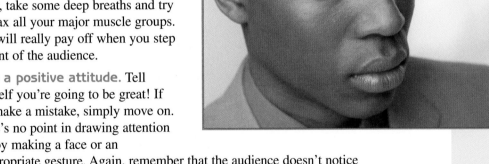

4. **Keep a positive attitude.** Tell yourself you're going to be great! If you make a mistake, simply move on. There's no point in drawing attention to it by making a face or an inappropriate gesture. Again, remember that the audience doesn't notice your mistakes or your nervousness the way you do.

When you begin your speech, you will very likely feel butterflies in your stomach. You may experience a sinking feeling, sweaty palms, or trembling hands and knees. These symptoms usually diminish once you're past the speech's introduction. But even if they continue, remember that they don't have to affect your ability to speak. Focus on delivering your ideas as effectively as possible.

A Speech About a
Personal Experience

Specs for the Speech About a Personal Experience

Time limit

3–4 minutes.

Speaker's notes

10-word maximum.

Source of information

Your own personal experience.

Outline

Prepare a 50- to 100-word complete sentence outline to be handed to your instructor when you rise to speak. Your instructor may wish to write comments on it regarding your speech.

Speak Up!

Share an experience you've had that was special to you in some way. It might be a personal triumph, a surprising event, or a time when you realized something for the very first time. Try to remember the details of the experience. What made it special? Why do you remember it?

Purpose and Expectations of This Assignment

In completing this assignment, you will

- determine the purpose of the presentation to be created,
- analyze the occasion for the presentation,
- select an appropriate topic,
- adapt the speech material to the occasion,
- outline the speech,
- identify and rehearse appropriate gestures to enhance the message, and
- determine and rehearse the appropriate level of enthusiasm for the topic.

Creating and presenting a speech about a personal experience will help your public speaking skills take a big leap forward. Although the speech will be about you, it nonetheless requires thorough preparation. You will develop your topic by speaking about something you have experienced that will be interesting to your listeners. You should feel increased confidence and poise as a result of this speech experience. Your ease before the group should improve noticeably.

Defining the Speech About a Personal Experience

A speech about a **personal experience** may have any one of the three basic purposes: (1) **to inform,** (2) **to persuade**, or (3) **to entertain**. The subject and occasion of your remarks will determine which purpose is appropriate. If you want to tell a funny or amusing personal story, you plan to entertain your listeners. If you wish to tell about your stamp collection, your purpose will be to inform. And if you want the audience to take action based on your speech, then your purpose will be to persuade. For this speech experience, confine your efforts to one of these three types of speeches.

There are unlimited occasions for a speech about a personal experience. Speakers present this type of speech at all kinds of gatherings— for example, school assemblies, club meetings, business meetings, and religious services. You have probably heard such a speech on television or radio. It may have come from a news reporter, a missionary, an athlete, a celebrity, or a member of the general public.

Choosing a Topic

If you have had an exciting experience, select it for your speech. Whatever you decide to talk about should be vivid in your memory. As you think about it you may feel prickly chills race up your spine, you may laugh, or you may feel sad. No matter what, the experience should be personal. It should tug at one or more of your emotions.

There is no limit to the topics that can be adapted for this type of speech. A presentation on the subject of swimming could be presented in many different ways. It might be informative (a discussion of the different strokes), persuasive (a call to action about the importance of teaching children how to swim), or entertaining (a description of your experience as a lifeguard).

Study the following list to spur ideas about a personal experience you might like to present to the class.

- Moving
- Flying

- Sports
- Summertime activities
- Parental separation
- Friends
- Youth programs
- Embarrassing experience
- Family outing
- Driving
- Movies
- Travel

Do not fall back on the old excuse that you can't think of anything interesting to talk about. The topic you choose may not be all that interesting

in and of itself. It is your responsibility to plan to tell about your personal experience in an interesting way. You can do this. All it takes is a little effort. Choose a topic without delay, and then read the rest of this assignment to find out how to prepare and present a speech on the topic you have chosen.

Preparing

Your attitude about yourself and your audience will play a big part in the success or failure of this speech. You should not sabotage yourself into thinking that what you have to say is uninteresting. Consider for a moment the child who runs to you eagerly, grabs your hand, and excitedly tells you about a big dog two doors down the street. The story captivates you; yet there is nothing inherently fascinating about a big dog you have seen many times. Why then are you interested? The answer lies in the extreme desire of the child to tell you the story. The child wants you to understand and is excited about the event. That is the secret to getting an audience to listen attentively. You must have that same desire to make your audience understand you and/or enjoy what you are saying.

To prepare for this speech you first need to decide what kind of presentation you want to make. Do you want to inform your listeners about something, or to persuade them to think as you do, or to take a specific action? Perhaps you simply want to entertain them. No matter what your purpose may be, now is the time to figure it out. For general information on figuring out a purpose for your speech, reread the section in Chapter 2 entitled "Determining Your Purpose" (page 15). Consider what elements and ideas concerning the experience will most interest your audience. If you would like to find out more about speeches that inform, skim through Experience 8; for speeches to persuade, see Experience 10; and for speeches to entertain, see Experience 13.

Once you have determined the type of speech you want to present, prepare an outline (see "Organizing" below. Once that's done, ask yourself these questions.

1. *Does your speech merely list people, places, things, and times without providing details?* Vitalize the people, places, and things in your speech by describing what happened; quoting; and pointing out unusual, humorous, or exciting incidents.

2. *Is your speech only about you?* If so, you can improve it by talking about what was happening around you. For example, if your speech is about how you rescued a drowning person, do not be satisfied by saying, "I jumped in and pulled my brother out of the water." Tell what the drowning person was doing. Describe his struggles. Tell how deep the water was and how far he was from shore. Recount your fears and other thoughts as you pulled him toward shore. Maybe the current almost took you under. Or perhaps you had to pull him along by his hair. Emphasize such factors as your exhaustion while you fought to stay afloat. Here is an example of a suspenseful recounting of such an incident:

   My brother John and I were at the ocean for the very first time. I guess we'd been swimming for about an hour. Suddenly I heard John screaming for help. He was way out there thrashing around in the deep water.

He yelled to me that he had a cramp. Then he went under. I swam out, paddling as hard as I could, and pulled him up. He almost took me under with him once, but I got him out onto the sand and gave him artificial respiration. I learned how to do that when I was a kid. I was really scared John wouldn't make it, but after a second he coughed up a little water and started breathing normally.

Next, rehearse your speech aloud for friends or in front of a mirror. Do this until you have memorized the speech's sequence of events. *Do not memorize the actual wording.* Every time you rehearse you will cover essentially the same things, but never with exactly the same words. Each rehearsal will set the pattern of your speech more firmly in your mind. The number of times you rehearse will depend on your own comfort level. After several practices you should be able to present the speech with confidence.

Organizing

To help you organize the speech, you should create a detailed outline. This means that you must set up the events of the speech in the order in which you want to talk about them.

1. Make sure that you have a curiosity-arousing introduction, one that will grab the audience's attention. Check this point carefully.

2. For the body of your speech, consider your own personal thoughts and reactions, the activities and statements of others who played a part in the event or situation, and

any objects that made the experience thrilling, exciting, upsetting, sad, or funny.

3. Do you have a strong conclusion? A speech is never complete without one.

4. Make a final evaluation of your outline before you decide that it's ready for presentation. Ask yourself if you would be interested in this speech if you were listening to it in the audience. By putting yourself in the listener's place you might be able to go back in and add more vivid details. Write your notes in large letters so you can read them easily. Use note cards that are at least three by five inches in size.

Presenting

When you hear your name, hand your outline to your instructor, and move calmly to the front of the room. Take a moment to focus your thoughts.

Let your arms and hands gesture whenever you need to emphasize what you are saying; otherwise your hands should hang comfortably at your sides or rest easily on a speaker's stand or chair back. Make your movements deliberate. Use body language to demonstrate any points you can.

Use your voice normally and conversationally. Talk loudly enough to be heard by the person sitting farthest from you. If you are truly interested in gaining your audience's attention and understanding, your vocal variety and force will very likely take care of themselves.

Do not fiddle with your notes or roll them into a tube. Hold the notes calmly between your thumb and forefinger in either hand. When referring to your notes, raise them to a level that permits you to glance at them without bowing your head. Do not try to hide them; using notes is nothing to be ashamed of. They can serve as a map for your speech. Treat them as casually, and with as much respect, as you would a road map during a trip.

Speak with authority. Audiences generally do not like to listen to speakers who babble on about topics they really know nothing or very little about. In formal public speaking, it is important to learn to tell your audience as directly as possible how you come to know what you know. One of the easiest ways to speak with authority is to deliver a speech about a personal experience.

Evaluating

Choose a classmate's speech to evaluate. Rate the following criteria on a scale from 1 to 5 with 1 being "needs much improvement" and 5 being "outstanding."

- Was the speaker enthusiastic about the subject?
- Did the speaker structure the speech with a logical order?
- Did the speaker deliver the speech with authority?
- Was the speaker's delivery natural and conversational?
- Were the speaker's gestures and facial expressions appropriate to the material?
- Did the speaker handle his or her notes well?

Give an overall score to the speech. Then choose one area where the speaker's performance may have given you new ideas about your own public speaking.

Example Speech

The Earth Trembled

by Gail Anderson

For Christians, Good Friday holds a point in history unequaled since the dawning of all mankind. March 27, 1964, another Good Friday, holds a memorable position in the stream of my life as the day of the Alaska earthquake.

I was 13 at the time, living in Anchorage, Alaska. The fact was that a "Good Friday suppertime" sort of atmosphere was beginning to creep into the minds of each of the members of my family. We might even have been bored had it not been for the anticipation of the evening meal that was almost ready.

The day was calm. My father, as usual, was absorbed in his newspaper. "Kitchen-puttering" occupied my mother. My brother was engaged in some nonsensical activity. Snow was falling. The quiet, peaceful cover it gave the earth could only be viewed as ironic now, in the face of what was to come.

The snow was still falling when the hanging light fixtures began to swing and the rattle of furniture could be heard on the tile floor. At first, our reaction was amusement. But our amusement quickly turned to terror. As we stumbled down stairs and through doors, trying to avoid falling objects, we heard and felt the rumble of the earth. As the front door forcibly flung us into the mounds of snow in the front yard, the earth continued to roll and groan. And then, as we lay sprawled on the sidewalk, the ground cracked open. All around me the snow was forming rifts as great expanses of the frozen earth were separating.

The noise was deafening. Hysterical cries of neighbors blended with the rumble of the earth and the creaking of houses. Our station wagon bounced like a rubber ball. Trees on the mountains in the distance were waving like a wheat field in a breeze.

Finally the earth became still. And as night fell, we were left to our own thoughts. The only radio station we could muster faded in and out, but from it we learned of the scope of this earthquake. It spared my family and our home, but took the lives and homes of many, many others.

In Anchorage, homes, schools, and businesses lay in ruins, paradoxically powdered with snow. But the people joined together to help one another. The homes left standing were crowded, but a unity of spirit made these conditions bearable.

Immediately, work began to rebuild and restore. Radio announcers neglected their families to keep people informed, as television and newspapers were not to be lines of communication for some time. People were living without heat, water, mail service, and many other things. Essentials were the essence of a united survival.

And so, as on the original Good Friday, man experienced one of the most vivid and dramatic events of a lifetime. The tragedy of the earthquake, while it caused much pain and destruction, actually brought people closer together, made them more understanding, and brought them closer to God.

The Pet Peeve or Opinion Speech

Specs for the Pet Peeve or Opinion Speech

Time limit
None.

Speaker's notes
Optional. Your speech may be
more effective without them.

Source of information
You.

Outline
Optional.

Speak Up!

Share with classmates an experience or
situation that bothers you. It need not
be anything earth-shattering. You
might sound off about your Friday
night curfew or chores and
obligations at home. Explore your
feelings about the issue.

Purpose and Expectations of This Assignment

In completing this assignment, you will

- concentrate on establishing and maintaining eye contact with the audience while presenting a speech,

- identify your point of view on a topic, and

- experience body movements, feelings, and vocal qualities associated with dynamic speech delivery.

Thus far in your speeches you may have felt varying degrees of nervousness and tension. As a result you may have taken the stage fearfully, spoken in hushed or weak tones, and used few if any gestures. Perhaps you have not made eye contact with your audience, or you may have lacked sufficient enthusiasm. Such self-consciousness is probably caused by worries over how you're coming across to the audience. If you focus less on how you look to the audience and more on what you're trying to communicate to them, you will feel much more confident.

One way to overcome self-consciousness and tension is by talking about something that really interests you. This speech is designed to give you the feeling of real-live speaking in which you cast aside all inhibitions, fears, and thoughts of yourself. See what you can do with it.

Defining the Pet Peeve or Opinion Speech

The pet peeve speech focuses on a subject about which you have strong thoughts and opinions— something that causes you anger, disturbance, or concern. Your pet peeve can be about an action that you find objectionable or an event that you believe infringes on your rights. It may be about a recent occurrence, or it may concern an event that happened some time ago. The subject must, however, be vivid in your memory. It must be something that still bothers you in the present.

Choosing a Topic

No one enjoys listening to a speech by a person who sounds bored with his or her subject. In fact, studies show that speakers who are not dynamic suffer a loss of credibility with their listeners. One way to begin to experience being a dynamic speaker is to select a topic that you already know gets your energies flowing—and a speech about a pet peeve offers you a perfect opportunity. If you're like most people, you can think of plenty of things that bother you. However, if you're stumped, check out these fertile sources of potential pet peeves. Find a topic within one of these broad general categories or make up one of your own.

- Bad drivers
- Student rights
- Personality traits
- Internet
- Homework
- Stereotypes
- Curfew
- Testing
- School regulations
- Waiting in line
- Poor sportsmanship

Preparing

Once you choose your pet peeve, consider all of your thoughts and feelings about it. Make up your mind to use this speech to blow off some steam to your audience.

Open your introduction with a specific example of your pet peeve. Then state in one sentence what you believe about your pet peeve. This statement should be the thesis of your speech. Follow it up with several key points about the issue. These points should lead you to a memorable conclusion. Try to end your speech on a high note.

Rehearse several times before the presentation. Prepare your opening sentence and practice it aloud for a family member or in front of the mirror. Go over the key points in your mind. Rehearse them aloud, but don't memorize them. Your preparation will be relatively simple for this speech; after all, it's your personal reaction to something that bothers you. If your point of view is strong enough, you will very likely be secure in your delivery with relatively little rehearsal. This does not mean you shouldn't prepare at all. But the main thing here is your point of view. The stronger it is, the more the audience will appreciate your presentation.

When you rehearse this speech, be sure to speak with enthusiasm. Some students are self-conscious when it comes to rehearsing. They think they don't have to speak up, make appropriate gestures, and so on until they're in front of an audience. But this speech is about your unique take on a personal pet peeve. Don't save it for the audience. Rehearse with energy each time. You will notice a distinct difference in the way you present a speech topic you feel strongly about versus the way you present one about which you're unsure.

Presenting

If you want to deliver a truly effective speech about a pet peeve, you will have to put your whole body and mind into it. Mean every word. Show your personality in every moment. Use dynamic and colorfully appropriate language. Let a slow fire that has been smoldering within you suddenly explode. Pour hot verbal oil on the blaze and let it roar and burn! In short, really let yourself go. Be strong and show it. If you feel like waving your arms, do it. If you feel like scowling in disgust, go ahead and scowl. If you feel like shouting, by all means shout. Whatever you do, just be sure you go all out. If you do, you'll probably be surprised at the power you're able to unleash.

After your speech, the instructor and class will comment orally on your effectiveness. They should be able to tell whether or not you really meant what you said. Listen carefully to their comments and suggestions. If any comments seem general, ask for a specific example. Be courteous. Feedback is one of the best tools you have for improving your public speaking.

Evaluating

Evaluate a classmate's speech about a personal experience. Be prepared to give oral feedback to the speaker on the following questions.

- Was the speaker enthusiastic about the subject?
- Did the speaker use eye contact to connect with the audience?
- Did the speaker deliver the speech with authority?
- Were the speaker's gestures and facial expressions appropriate to the material?

When you share your thoughts with the speaker, remember to avoid being overly negative. Begin your comment by citing something the speaker did well. Try to be specific and give examples whenever you can.

Example Speech

Cell Phone Rudeness

by Matthew Arnold Stern

This speech is from the advanced Toastmasters manual, Humorously Speaking. *It was first delivered in May 2000.*

Cell phones: For many, an indispensable communications tool. For others, just another way to be rude. I'm sure that many of you have experienced cell phone rudeness. Perhaps some of you are guilty of cell phone rudeness. I've found that there are three main ways to be rude with cell phones.

We all know what number one is: It's using your cell phone when driving! When I got my cell phone, I got not just one, but two full-color brochures about why you should not use your cell phone while driving. People still do it. You see those fools on the road with their cell phone in one hand and their Starbucks cappuccino in the other. How are they steering the car!? (Yes, I know. Not very well.)

But, this isn't the only way people are rude with cell phones. There are those who believe that when they press the little button to take or place a call, they are immediately enveloped with an Invisible Cone of Privacy. They believe that this enables them to stand in the middle of any public place and talk about any subject they want—no matter how personal or how embarrassing—and no one else can hear them.

I saw this the other day at the post office. I was in the lobby with about 20 other people waiting to mail a package, and this guy was chatting on his cell phone, "Hey, Martha. I'm at the post office right now . . . " Like, duh. This guy probably spent $269 for his Motorola flip-phone, and then probably got one of those top-of-the-line $90 a month one-rate plans, just to tell Martha that he's at the post office. For a mere 33-cent stamp, he could mail Martha a letter and prove he was at the post office!

What made things worse is that he apparently believed that the louder he spoke, the more effective his Invisible Cone of Privacy became. So, he spoke at the top of his lungs, "I went to my proctologist appointment this morning. Do you wanna hear all about it?" And, all of us in that lobby shouted, "NO!" I guess he then realized that his Invisible Cone of Privacy wasn't working very well at that time.

Third, we all know that it's rude to interrupt a meeting by taking a cell-phone call. What's worse is when people bring their cell phones to meetings in hopes of being interrupted. You can tell who these people are: When they sit down, they take their cell phone out of its holster and put it on the table directly in front of them. They then take out their Palm VII and put it on the table right next to their phone. You know that they are just waiting for something to beep at them. They are begging, hoping, pleading for something to beep at them. It's their not-so-subtle way of saying, "There are things I'd rather do than be at this meeting with you."

In fact, I recently changed jobs partially because of a meeting with a person like that. At a previous employer, I had a meeting with the vice president *du jour* to find out what he planned to do with our documentation department. This was a meeting I had tried to set up for weeks. When I finally came into his office, he had his cell phone on the desk in front of him, right directly in the line of sight between him and me. He said to me, "Matt, I want to express to you how important I feel you are to this organization. I want to show you how important I think documentation is to our products."

Of course, at this point, his cell phone rang. When people interrupt a meeting to take a cell-phone call, they always say the same thing: "Excuse me, but I must take this." He went on, "Hello? . . . That's okay. You're not interrupting me . . . I'm in a meeting, but it's not anything important." As it turned out, documentation wasn't really that important to him.

So, if you are a cell-phone user, please practice courtesy when using your cell phone. Don't use your cell phone while driving. Don't use your cell phone to show everyone you have a cell phone. And one other thing . . . oh, my cell phone is ringing. Excuse me, but I must take this.

Example Speech

The Arrogance of Power

by Senator Robert C. Byrd
Senate Remarks, March 19, 2003

I believe in this beautiful country. I have studied its roots and gloried in the wisdom of its magnificent Constitution. I have marveled at the wisdom of its founders and framers. Generation after generation of Americans have understood the lofty ideals that underlie our great Republic. I have been inspired by the story of their sacrifice and their strength.

But today I weep for my country. I have watched the events of recent months with a heavy, heavy heart. No more is the image of America one of strong, yet benevolent peacekeeper. The image of America has changed. Around the globe, our friends mistrust us, our word is disputed, our intentions are questioned.

Instead of reasoning with those with whom we disagree, we demand obedience or threaten recrimination. Instead of isolating Saddam Hussein, we seem to have isolated ourselves. We proclaim a new doctrine of preemption which is understood by few and feared by many. We say that the United States has the right to turn its firepower on any corner of the globe which might be suspect in the war on terrorism. We assert that right without the sanction of any international body. As a result, the world has become a much more dangerous place.

We flaunt our superpower status with arrogance. We treat UN Security Council

members like ingrates who offend our princely dignity by lifting their heads from the carpet. Valuable alliances are split. After war we will have to rebuild America's image around the globe.

The case this Administration tries to make to justify its fixation with war is tainted by charges of falsified documents and circumstantial evidence. We cannot convince the world of the necessity of this war for one simple reason. This is a war of choice.

There is no credible information to connect Saddam Hussein to 9/11. The twin towers fell because a worldwide terrorist group, Al Quaeda, with cells in over 60 nations, struck at our wealth and our influence by turning our own planes into missiles, one of which would likely have slammed into the dome of this beautiful Capitol except for the brave sacrifice of the passengers on board.

The brutality seen on September 11th and in other terrorist attacks we have witnessed around the globe are the violent and desperate efforts by extremists to stop the daily encroachment of western values upon their cultures. That is what we fight. It is a force not confined to borders. It is a shadowy entity with many faces, many names, and many addresses.

But this Administration has directed all of the anger, fear, and grief which emerged from the ashes of the Twin Towers and the twisted metal of the Pentagon towards a tangible villain, one we can see and hate and attack. And villain he is. But, he is the wrong villain. And this is the wrong war. If we attack Saddam Hussein, we will probably drive him from power. But, the zeal of our friends to assist our global war on terrorism may have already taken flight.

The general unease surrounding this war is not just due to "orange alert." There is a pervasive sense of rush and risk and too many questions unanswered. How long will we be in Iraq? What will be the cost? What is the ultimate mission? How great is the danger at home? A pall has fallen over the Senate Chamber. We avoid our solemn duty to debate the one topic on the minds of all Americans, even while scores of thousands of our sons and daughters faithfully do their duty in Iraq.

What is happening to this country? When did we become a nation which ignores and berates our friends? When did we decide to risk undermining international order by adopting a radical and doctrinaire approach to using our awesome military might? How can we abandon diplomatic efforts when the turmoil in the world cries out for diplomacy?

Why can this President not seem to see that America's true power lies not in its will to intimidate, but in its ability to inspire?

War appears inevitable. But, I continue to hope that the cloud will lift. Perhaps Saddam will yet turn tail and run. Perhaps reason will somehow prevail. I along with millions of

Americans will pray for the safety of our troops, for the innocent civilians in Iraq, and for the security of our homeland. May God continue to bless the United States of America in the troubled days ahead, and may we somehow recapture the vision which for the present eludes us.

The Speech to Develop
Body Language

Specs for the Speech to Develop Body Language

Time limit

4–5 minutes.

Speaker's notes

10-word maximum.

Sources of information

Two are required, preferably three. For each source make sure you list the specific magazine, book, or Internet site; title of the article; author's full name; date of publication; and the chapter or pages where you found the material. For Internet sites, include the address (URL). If a source is a person, identify the person by title, position, and occupation. Attach your source list to your outline.

Outline

Prepare a 75- to 150-word complete sentence outline.

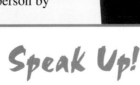

Speak Up!

Have various class members try pantomiming these emotions: fear, anger, sadness, joy, boredom, surprise. Watch carefully and take notes on the body language used to convey these feelings. As a class, talk about the movements and gestures used for each feeling as well as what can and cannot be shown through body language.

Purpose and Expectations of This Assignment

In completing this assignment, you will

- understand the use of bodily actions and gestures in public speaking,

- identify appropriate and meaningful body language for a given speech,

- determine the relationship between body language and sincere communication, and

- listen to constructive criticism and determine necessary adaptations.

Many beginning speakers do not realize that public speaking is a whole-body activity. But consider the way you communicate each day. When you are telling a story to a friend, you don't stand stiffly with a frozen expression on your face as you speak. You use your arms, you smile, you shrug, you raise your eyebrows, and you gesture with your hands. Yet when you get up in front of the class to give a speech you may find that every muscle in your body is rigid. If you move only your vocal cords, tongue, and jaws, you make use of only half of your communication tools. If you put all of your communication skills into action, you will use gestures and body movements as well. This speech experience is designed to develop your body language skills so that you can use your whole body to improve the quality of your speech.

Defining the Speech to Develop Body Language

You can choose any type of **speech to illustrate body language**, as all public speaking should feature some degree of bodily action and gestures. Body language will assist you in communicating your purpose, regardless of what that purpose might be.

Bodily actions may be defined as the movements of the body as it changes places. **Gestures** are movements of individual parts of the body, such as raising an eyebrow, shrugging the shoulders, smiling, or using hand motions. All movements are body language.

Every body movement has a meaning of its own. It is nearly impossible to speak without using some body language. You may not be completely aware of every movement and gesture while you speak, but that in no sense means that you are not using body language. The point to bear in mind is that all speech communication should be accompanied by appropriate and meaningful body language.

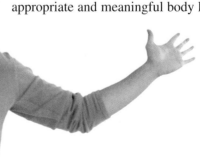

Choosing a Topic

Select a subject that you can demonstrate as you talk about it. The purpose of the speech itself will be to inform the listeners. As always, it's best to choose a topic that interests you. Make sure you can find adequate source materials. You must also keep your audience in mind; the speech must be suitable to them as well as to you.

To help you decide on a topic, think about sports and hobbies in which you have participated. Ask yourself what you know how to do that others may not. Because this speech will require considerable planning, you should select your topic without delay. After you make your choice, stick to it even if you discover that it is more difficult to prepare than you had anticipated. Do not change topics just because you misjudged the amount of effort it would take you to prepare.

Preparing

Find appropriate source materials for this speech by visiting the library, the Internet, or people you wish to interview. Take notes on what you learn and remember to keep track of each source.

When you have outlined the structure of your speech (see Organizing on page 92), you can begin your rehearsal process.

In rehearsal, as you earnestly present your ideas, try to make them clearer by demonstrating what you have to say. Do this by acting out certain parts as you talk. If you tell the audience that it is best to mount a horse a certain way, show them how to do it. If you say a baseball should be thrown a certain way, demonstrate it with all the force and energy you would use if you were actually pitching. Alternatively, you might do it in slow motion to show the position of your fingers on the ball and your arm in motion.

In rehearsing this speech, use both bodily actions and gestures, as these will constitute a large part of the speech. Don't memorize the physical actions in rigid detail. If you do, you run the risk of a mechanical performance. Instead, stand before a mirror while you rehearse. If possible, use a mirror large enough that you can see your whole body rather than just the upper half of it. Get a friend to watch and give you helpful feedback. You might also videotape your speech and critique your own performance by watching the tape.

While you rehearse, strive to create a well-organized set of spontaneous actions. Rather than memorizing the actions, you must try to generate them through the earnestness of your desire to communicate with your listeners. You should feel compelled to use your body and hands to express yourself. These actions need not reflect anyone else's movements or gestures—they are your own, just as your walk and style of speaking are your own. All you need to do is observe yourself in action to eliminate awkwardness, undesirable posture and foot positions, and distracting mannerisms.

The idea is that if you are willing to undergo a little self-inflicted critique, you can develop your own style of gesture and bodily action. You might find it helpful to do a bit of research on body language. However, do not adopt gestures that look or feel unnatural. It's important to remember that gestures and movements should be large and deliberate enough for the audience to see. Your posture should be one of alertness. Stand tall. Keep your weight on the balls of your feet and on the forward foot.

Bodily action should be relaxed and easy, vigorous and coordinated. There should be no hint of nervous tension, which is characterized by shuffling feet and restless pacing. In moving to the left, lead with the left foot; in moving to the right, lead with the right foot. Move quietly without clomping your heels or scraping your soles. Be sure that any movement is motivated and acts as a transition between ideas, an emphasis, or a device for releasing bodily tension and holding audience attention. Use bodily action deliberately until you develop the habit to make it a part of every speech.

You may also want to exhibit pictures, charts, diagrams, or other visual aids. Or you might want to write or draw on the blackboard. If you use any of these communication aids, be sure that your equipment is all set up before you begin.

Organizing

When you have gathered your source materials, organize the information into a main idea and details. Present these in a logical order by creating a complete sentence outline. After all, if the audience can't follow your logic, they won't understand you. If they don't understand you, then you won't really have communicated.

Your introduction should open with a quote or an entertaining example of the process you are about to demonstrate. Use the introduction to launch yourself into the body of the speech. Then write down each major point that you will use to make the audience understand the process that you're communicating. Follow up the main body of your speech with supportive information that leads to a logical and well-worded conclusion. The conclusion should rephrase or enlarge upon the information or example in the introduction.

Presenting

When you present this speech, approach the speaker's stand with the attitude of a person determined to win. Take pride in the fact that

you are going to use your entire body to present a speech that will really interest your listeners. With a winning attitude, you can't lose.

If your demonstration is so vigorous that it makes you a little short of breath, so much the better. It will mean that you were truly trying to *show* as well as *tell* the audience about your topic.

If you feel yourself slipping into unconnected or superfluous gestures, take a moment or two to calm down and regroup. Some speakers report that nervousness can make them feel as if they are not in their own bodies. If you catch yourself feeling that way, it is up to you to find your way back.

Evaluating

Choose a classmate's body language speech to evaluate. Consider the following questions as you do the evaluation.

- Did the speaker's gestures match the content of the presentation?

- Were the gestures and body language natural or did they seem stiff and forced?

- Did the speaker's body language enhance the presentation or distract from it?

Give the speech a number rating from 1 to 5 with 5 being "outstanding."

3 UNIT
Speeches to Share Information

In Unit Two you learned how to make speeches dealing with your own personal experience. In this unit, you'll move on to speeches that are designed to share specific information with a particular audience. You'll get the chance to try your skills at demonstrating a process, speaking to inform, and giving an oral book review. Together these speeches will build your public speaking skills— and your confidence.

Speech Experiences in This Unit

The Demonstration Speech

Specs for the Demonstration Speech

Time limit
4–5 minutes.

Speaker's notes
10-word maximum.

Sources of information
Two are required, preferably three. For each source, give the specific magazine, book, or Internet site from which it was taken; the title of the article; the author's full name; the date of publication; and the chapter or page number. If the source is a person, identify the person completely by title, position, and occupation. List these on the outline form. For Internet sites, list the address (URL).

Outline
Prepare a 75- to 150-word complete sentence outline.

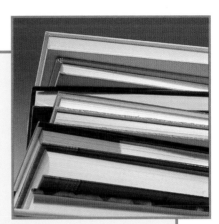

Speak Up!

Your teacher will give a drawing or diagram to one student. Without showing the diagram, this person will give the class step-by-step instructions on how to draw the same diagram on their papers. When all students are finished, they will compare their drawings to the original. Were the instructions clear enough to create an identical drawing? Were any steps missed?

Purpose and Expectations of This Assignment

One of the most important purposes for public speaking is to share information. Sharing information and ideas is such a valuable part of a well-functioning society that the right to do so is protected by the U.S. Constitution. Sharing information publicly—whether with an individual or a group—can be done in several ways. One of the most common is the demonstration speech, in which the information is visually illustrated in several sequential steps that build on one another. In such a situation you the speaker will likely demonstrate and explain the topic to someone who has little or no experience with it. For this reason you must make sure you begin at the beginning of the process and include every step.

In completing this assignment, you will

- identify essential steps in a topic to be demonstrated,
- organize a speech chronologically,
- explain a process to others in a clear manner,
- prepare and use visual aids, and
- identify the best means of fitting available material into a limited time frame.

Defining the Demonstration Speech

A demonstration speech is a type of informative speech. It is designed to impart to the audience information they can use to replicate a process or understand a process-oriented idea. A successful demonstration speech teaches the essential steps in completing a task or process. Also, most demonstration speeches require **visual aids** of some kind to illustrate parts of the process.

Choosing a Topic

Because your purpose is to show your audience how to do something or how something works, you should select a topic that allows you to present information to them and also to demonstrate it. Avoid obvious or trivial topics such as how to make a sandwich.

When considering what types of things you can demonstrate, keep in mind the room in which you will be making your presentation. Depending on such factors as space, noise, lighting, and so on, you may need to narrow your topic. For example, instead of demonstrating how to play tennis, the size of the classroom where you will be speaking may require you to limit your topic to a demonstration of different positions for holding the racket and various swings and stances to take when facing an opponent. Be sure you can demonstrate the topic in such a way that all audience members will be able to see you. Additionally, narrow your topic to fit the time limit given by your instructor. Here is a list of topics that might make the basis of a good demonstration speech.

- How to program a videocassette recorder (VCR)
- How to take good photographs
- How to play the flute
- How to organize a party
- How to play soccer
- How to organize a neighborhood watch program
- How to give CPR or first aid

Preparing and Organizing

Because the demonstration speech must provide each step of the process in the order in which it occurs, the most frequently used method of organization for these speeches is **chronological order**. Begin by jotting down each of the steps in the process as you recall it. Try your organization out on a friend to see if he or she can complete the process according to the steps you have identified. If your friend can't do this successfully, you may need to add additional steps.

When you are satisfied that you have figured out all the necessary steps for the topic you have selected, develop each step into a complete idea, explaining its necessary ingredients and/or processes. Identify any visual aids you might need to make each step as clear as possible. Before you present it to your audience, practice the complete demonstration, including the necessary visual aids, several times. This will help you locate any problems or glitches that may arise with the space, your visual aids, or the audience's ability to see as you demonstrate.

Presenting

When you present this speech, begin by taking the necessary time to set up the visual aids. You will already have practiced your setup, so you should be able to get yourself ready within a very short time. Place your notes strategically so that you can see them without looking down. Make sure that handling your notes does not interfere with using your visual aids.

Present the speech with the full confidence of one who knows the material very well. Remember, you have selected a topic that is likely to be new to the audience but is familiar to you; therefore, you are the expert. Complete each step as you have prepared it, referring to your notes to ensure that you do not skip any necessary steps.

Conclude your speech with a brief summary/review, then remove all visual aids as quickly, efficiently, and quietly as possible.

Evaluating

Evaluate a classmate's demonstration speech. Rate the following criteria on a scale from 1 to 5 with 1 being "needs much improvement" and 5 being "outstanding."

- Was the speaker able to set up quickly and efficiently?
- Did the speaker structure the speech with a logical progression?
- Did the speaker deliver the speech with authority?
- Were you able to follow the demonstration well enough to feel comfortable doing the process or explaining it to someone else?

Give an overall score to the speech. Then choose one area of the speaker's performance that may have given you new ideas about your own demonstration speech. Write a short paragraph to explain.

Talking Points

Where Are All the Great Topics?

As you know by now, it's not always the subject matter that sells a speech. Most of the time it's the speaker. That said, there are a few methods you can use to make sure you snag the most interesting topic possible for each public speaking presentation you make.

The next time you're asked to prepare a speech, read over the following list of possibilities.

1. Make a list of everything you know more about than other people might. Perhaps you have an unusual hobby. If so, think about using it as an informative speech assignment. If your hobby is something you can demonstrate to the audience, so much the better.

2. Perhaps you have lived in several different cities. If so, you might prepare a speech about the special features of a city or compare the various cities with one another.

3. You have a great resource in your family, friends, and neighbors. You might ask an elderly neighbor about a historical event she or he remembers. Then use those comments as the basis for research on that topic.

4. What are you curious about? You can use a speech assignment as a way to learn about anything that interests you.

5. What makes you feel sad, happy, thrilled, scared, or frustrated? What public controversies have stirred you lately? You can write a speech that supports your viewpoint.

6. What does your audience (in this case, your classmates) need to know about? Your speech can serve as a community service by giving your audience information about such subjects as job opportunities; careers available to those who are not planning to go to college; how to resolve differences of opinion without violence; or how to better understand individuals with different racial, religious, economic, or ethnic backgrounds.

Topics are everywhere. The topic that interests you is the one to choose. Your fascination with your topic will help the audience to become fascinated as well.

Example Speech

Start Canoeing and Enjoy Your Weekends

by Joann Bopp

[*The speaker's props were canoe paddles, an armless chair, and a small rug.*]

Wouldn't you like to get more fun and relaxation out of your leisure time? Those two-day weekends could be spent away from the busy, hurried city life that most of us lead. Just put a canoe on top of your car and head for water. A canoe can float on as little as four inches of water. A quiet lake, stream, or pond may hold more fascination than you ever imagined. A canoe could also bring the thrills of shooting rapids of a swift running river, but that is for the experienced boatman.

I would like to give you a few rules and demonstrations to show you the basics of how to canoe. The number one rule is getting in and out of the boat correctly. Canoeing is often thought of as being very dangerous, but the danger usually occurs when getting in or out of the canoe. To get in, you step first to the center, lengthwise, and place the other foot behind [*demonstrate on rug*]. Then lower yourself to a kneeling position, which is the correct canoeing position [*demonstrate by kneeling on rug*]. There are braces across the canoe to lean against. Once you have established this low center of gravity, the canoe has great stability. Getting out is just the reverse. Keep your weight to the center as much as possible [*demonstrate by getting off the rug*].

These are the paddles [*show paddles*]. They are made of fir, a soft wood that holds up well in water and is lightweight. To select the paddle, measure it to your height. It should come to about your chin [*demonstrate*]. To hold the paddle, grip the end with one hand and with the other hand grasp it a little above the blade [*sit in the chair to demonstrate paddling strokes*].

The basic stroke is called the cruising stroke, or the bow stroke. Extend the paddle in front of you [*demonstrations follow*], close to the canoe, and dip into the water, bringing it straight back to the hip by pushing with the top hand and pulling with the lower hand. Now bring the paddle back to repeat. The paddling is usually done by a two-person team; this is known as *tandem paddling*. In tandem paddling the person in front is the steersman who steers the boat. The person in the rear is the bowman and provides the power. The bowman uses the bow stroke most of the time [*demonstrations follow*]. The steersman uses the bow stroke also but often makes a hook outward on the end of the stroke to keep the canoe on course. This version of the bow stroke is called the *J-stroke*. The steersman also uses the sweep stroke for turning. It is a wide, sweeping, arclike stroke made close to the water's surface [*demonstrate*]. To stop or go backwards, the backwater stroke is used. Simply place the paddle into the water at a right angle to the canoe and hold it firmly to stop [*demonstrate*]. To go backwards, reverse the bow stroke [*demonstrate*]. [*Rise to a standing position with paddles in hand.*]

This is by no means all there is to know about canoeing, but if you can accomplish these things you will be able to have fun. So to enjoy the outdoors and take a break from a humdrum routine. I hope you will try canoeing.

The Speech to
Inform

Specs for the Speech to Inform

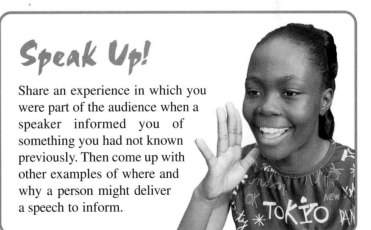

Time limit

4–5 minutes.

Speaker's notes

10-word maximum.

Sources of information

Two are required, preferably three. For each source, give the specific magazine, book, or Internet site it was taken from; the title of the article or work; the author's full name; the date of publication; and the chapter or pages on which you found the material. If a source is a person, identify him or her completely by title, position, occupation, etc. List your sources on the outline form. For Internet sites, list the address (URL).

Outline

Prepare a 75- to 150-word complete sentence outline.

Speak Up!

Share an experience in which you were part of the audience when a speaker informed you of something you had not known previously. Then come up with other examples of where and why a person might deliver a speech to inform.

Purpose and Expectations of This Assignment

Of the millions and millions of talks given each year, a large percentage are specifically designed to inform the audience—to tell people something that will benefit them in some way. While no one can foretell accurately what kind of speeches you may be called upon to present in the future, it is safe to assume that you will speak many times to inform other people. This speaking assignment offers insights into the informative speaking process.

In completing this assignment, you will

- demonstrate knowledge of material that is largely unfamiliar to others;
- analyze an audience's interest in, and knowledge of, a particular topic;
- relate new material directly to a particular audience;
- understand the fundamentals of informative-speech preparation; and
- create a complete sentence outline of the speech material.

Defining the Speech to Inform

A **speech to inform** provides a clear understanding of the speaker's ideas about a subject. It also arouses the listeners' interest because the material presented is relevant to their lives.

There are many occasions for an informative speech. Speakers give informative talks from the lecture platform, in the pulpit, in the classroom, and at business meetings. Informative speeches take place any time reports are made, instructions are given, or other ideas are presented by means of lectures and discussions.

The point to bear in mind is that an occasion for an informative speech arises any time information is disseminated.

Choosing a Topic

To select a subject for an informative speech, it can be very helpful to do **an analysis of the audience**—in this case your classmates. It is important for the speaker to analyze the intended audience as thoroughly as possible in order to avoid presenting material they already know. If a speaker does not take such care in planning, at best the listeners will be bored, and at worst they will be angry that their listening energies have been wasted on "old news."

You the speaker are responsible for knowing more about your subject than anyone in your audience might. Select a topic that interests you, one that is appropriate to the audience you will address. It helps to select a topic that you are curious about. Think about something that you read or heard on television that left you wanting to know more. Be sure that you can find information about the topic you select.

Don't put off choosing a topic. Study the list below for some possible informative speaking topics.

- Jobs of the future
- Space exploration
- Major world religions
- Costs of college education
- Robots
- Movie special effects
- Baseball card collecting
- Juvenile crime
- Homelessness
- Best vacation spots in the world
- Living wills

Preparing and Organizing

To prepare for this speech—or any speech—you must know and follow certain fundamentals of preparation. You have worked with all of these elements in other speeches. Here are the steps to follow.

1. Choose your subject.
2. Analyze the occasion.
3. Analyze the audience.
4. Gather your source materials.
5. Organize and support your main points with evidence.
6. Word your speech by creating a complete sentence outline.
7. Rehearse your speech aloud.

The information you present must be accurate. To ensure that it is, you must find acceptable sources of information written by reliable and competent authorities. Your audience should know where you got your material. For an informative speech, you don't simply give information—you also offer your conclusions and views and evaluations of the information. All this entails the neat assimilation of all you have pulled together—that is, your entire speech. For this reason, you must study no fewer than two information sources. Under no circumstances should you be satisfied to glance hurriedly through an article in a popular magazine and jot down a few notes. That's a sloppy job of acquiring knowledge; it wouldn't enable you to give an effective informative speech.

If you wish to organize your thoughts logically, you should decide on your objective early. Ask yourself what reaction you want from this particular audience. Next, divide your speech into three conventional parts: the introduction, the body, and the conclusion. To be even more effective, some speakers break down their talks by using various combinations of the following steps.

1. Gain attention.
2. Make your audience want to hear your ideas.
3. Present your ideas.
4. Tell why this material is important to your listeners and how it affects them.
5. Ask your audience to study the topic further or to take some action on it.

The time required for any one division of a speech varies greatly; however, you should spend more time on presenting your ideas than on any other step.

To create **coherence, unity,** and a **logical order** for the material, outlining your speech is a must. Without these rhetorical qualities, your thoughts may turn into a jumbled mass of words with little direction. An outline is to the speaker what a road map is to a person taking a car trip—it shows you where you are going and how to get there.

Although you will work from a very detailed outline and you may use speaking notes, by the time you get in front of your audience, you should have rehearsed the speech a number of times. You should be very familiar with the speech's ideas and organization. So rehearse in front of a mirror or with a tape recorder as many times as necessary (usually about four) to fix the proper steps and the order of their presentation. Practice the speech for a friend or family member and get reactions. Do not memorize every single word.

How to use notes for informative speaking is a matter of opinion. If you are adequately prepared, you will probably not need notes. If you must refer to notes, they should be short sentences, phrases, or single words that have a particular meaning to you. The notes you hold in your hands should be brief, concise, and entirely familiar. A quick glance should be sufficient for you to gather their full meaning so that you can speak fluently yet logically. Write your notes on index cards.

Your speech should have only two or three main points. Support these with examples, illustrations, analogies, and facts. Don't be afraid to inject humor and anecdotes to add interest. Always be sure that these additions are suited to your subject and audience. Be sure your speech moves forward at a good pace. Don't allow the speech to drag or become stalled. And finally, put plenty of effort into creating an interesting introduction and an equally effective conclusion.

Presenting

Hand your outline to your instructor when you rise to speak. Your instructor may want to follow along while listening to your speech, and he or she may write suggestions for improvement on the outline. Remember that this outline is not to be used while you are speaking. State two or three sources of information within your speech presentation.

An informative speech should be an easy, energetic presentation. Be enthusiastic and original in what you have to say. Use your whole body. You can draw pictures, exhibit charts, and do whatever else is necessary to get your ideas across. As always, take the stage with confidence, utilize expressive bodily action, maintain eye contact, and stay within the time limit. Your conclusion should be as strong, appropriate, and well prepared as your opening remarks.

Evaluating

Evaluate a classmate's speech to inform. Rate the following criteria on a scale from 1 to 5 with 1 being "needs much improvement" and 5 being "outstanding."

- Did the speaker structure the speech with a logical progression?
- Did the speaker deliver the speech with authority?
- Were the speaker's information sources current and/or credible?
- Was the speaker enthusiastic and energetic?
- Did the speaker seem well informed about the topic?
- Were you able to learn something new or gain fresh insights from the speech?

Give an overall score to the presentation. Be prepared to comment about what you learned, or discuss areas of particular interest within the speech.

Example Speech

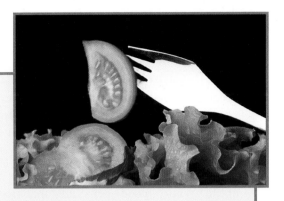

The Heart Attack Bug

by Christina Foust

For most people worried about heart attacks, the salad bar is an island of serenity. Nearly every choice makes the heart rest easy: low fat, low cholesterol, low calories, and low carb. But without one stunning safety feature, the salad bar could make your heart stop: the sneeze guard.

It could protect you from the heart attack bug: *chlamydia pneumoniae*. This tiny bacteria, according to the June 7, 1997, *New Scientist* "is now 'overwhelmingly' " linked to heart disease. The August 1997 *World Press Review* estimates that over half of the population is infected and probably has no idea of it or the damage it can do.

Thanks to the discovery of the heart attack bug, however, the April 28, 1997, *Newsweek* says, "cardiology is in for a revolution." This is one revolution we can't afford to miss. Therefore, we will first unravel the mystery of the heart attack; second, become familiar with the bug's place in it; and finally, discuss some implications that this finding has for the future of hearts everywhere.

First, let's unravel some of the mysteries of heart attacks. Any red-blooded American knows that high cholesterol can lead to heart problems. Doctors thought so, too, until evidence pointed to the contrary. As *Science News* of June 4, 1997, points out, most victims have normal cholesterol counts.

This is not to say that people with high cholesterol never get heart attacks. But many of us will testify that our sinful Uncle Jerry, who's smoked a pack a day and eaten red meat for dessert on a regular basis, is alive and kicking at 80. Meanwhile, some of the healthiest among us suffer from heart disease.

As the *World Press Review* explains, this last incongruity intrigued scientists in Sweden nine years ago. While training, eight athletes suddenly died of cardiac arrest. All were on low-fat diets, were nonsmokers, and had the heart attack bug.

But how could bacteria causing simple flu-like symptoms shut down something as resilient as the human heart? Obviously, doctors needed a better explanation of the heart attack.

The major cause of heart attacks, if you paid attention in health class, is atherosclerosis, or clogging of the arteries. When we eat a diet high in fat and cholesterol, it accumulates in our heart's vessels, plugging the flow of blood. Without blood, the heart stops.

However, as Michael Gimbrone, Harvard Medical School pathologist, tells the April 3, 1997, *Washington Post*, atherosclerosis is much more than a simple "clogged pipe." Atherosclerosis is now thought to be a result of inflammation.

continued

Example Speech cont.

Science News explains. First, the vessel wall becomes injured and inflamed. Picture when you cut your finger. Remember the swelling and excess heat on the injury? That's inflammation, like in the blood vessel.

Now instead of a clogged pipe, imagine a car crash. White blood cells are the first emergency crew on the scene, doing protective duty for your body. But, as in a real-life accident, curious onlookers soon pile up on the scene. In your heart's case, these are more fat molecules.

Soon, the body sends a police crew to stop damage done by this fat accumulation. These smooth muscle cells cover the layers of cells and fat. With so many bodies in the street, traffic comes to a standstill. Though the process is much, much slower in your arteries, the same principles apply. Your body's own defenses actually clog its vessels.

But how does a common bug fit into this picture? Now that we've unraveled the mysteries of the heart attack with the inflammation hypothesis, let's see how the heart attack bug relates.

As *Newsweek* explains, *chlamydia pneumoniae*, known as CP, is a bacteria that spreads as a microdrop infection to the lungs. Coughs and sneezes spread the bug, leading to flulike symptoms that can escalate into pneumonia.

Scientists in Europe linked this infection to the inflammation hypothesis by American doctors. The June 21, 1997, *British Medical Journal* explains that British doctors found CP in 79 percent of coronary artery samples from patients with atherosclerosis; but only 4 percent of non-atherosclerotic samples contained the bacteria.

Frankfurt professor of infectious diseases Wulfgang Stille tells *Der Spiegel* of April 21, 1997, 60 to 80 percent of atherosclerosis cases "are evidently caused by an infection with the CP bacterium."

That's right; CP is as serious as a heart attack. The *New York Times* of July 15, 1997, reports that high CP levels created a four times greater risk for cardiac arrest. Scientists are even more convinced because antibiotic treatment practically eliminated the chance for another heart attack.

The July 15, 1997, American Heart Association journal, *Circulation*, explains the theory. Remember our first white blood cells, or monocytes, on the scene of the injury of the vessel? According to vessel inflammation expert Valentin Fuster, these cells are also designed to "root out blood-borne infection at early stages." CP has found out how to cheat our hearts, as *Circulation* states, by turning "a monocyte into live 'ammunition' for clot formation."

The helpful white blood cell becomes a Trojan horse. It arrives at the damage with CP as an unwanted passenger, which deposits itself along with the monocyte. The body senses more trauma from the bacteria's presence. So, it sends more monocytes to help. The cells build up, plugging the flow of blood over time, leading to a heart attack.

As R. Wayne Alexander, chief cardiologist at Emory University, told the *Washington Post,* "It's really a major shift in the way we think about heart attacks." Thanks to the link of the heart attack bug, we can now understand how a marathon runner can die of a couch potato disease.

Finally, let's view some of the implications this finding has for the future of hearts everywhere. We will see that the discovery will help in early detection and treatment, but we will also note that there is still more to be done in the war against heart disease.

Initially, the CP/heart attack relationship will help doctors detect the possibility of a heart attack, sometimes years in advance. As the *Doctor's Guide* Web site reported on December 10, 1996, a new test with "over 90 percent reliability" in diagnosing CP is being marketed. This is especially important, according to the August 11, 1997, *Newsweek,* because "arterial disease may kill you in a minute, but it usually develops over a lifetime."

Because it is bacteria, treatment with antibiotics after early detection could reduce the risk of a heart attack. However, as one doctor told the *World Press Review,* "nothing could be more dangerous than ... handing out antibiotics blindly." An antibiotic-resistant strain of CP could have worse consequences than mere heart attacks. Because the bug also causes respiratory problems, scientists need to be especially careful in antibiotic treatment.

The key, then, may be an anti-inflammation drug instead: perhaps one that doctors already have—aspirin. As the *Wall Street Journal* of April 3, 1997, explains, anti-inflammatory drugs more fine-tuned and powerful than aspirin may be developed to stop inflammation caused by CP. If we know the bacteria's there, we can work to stop our body's reaction to it.

Another thing to keep in mind, though, as heart researcher Dr. Sandeep Gupta admits in the January 1997 *Heart,* "the atherosclerosis link between *chlamydia* and heart disease has yet to be verified." To do so, Gupta recommends "prospective vaccination and antibiotic" trials. Sometimes, these trials take considerable time.

So, if you think that protecting yourself from sneezes is all you need for a healthy heart, think again. CP may be a risk factor, like smoking or a sedentary lifestyle. But risk factors are extremely complex and intertwined. As *Newsweek* of August 11, 1997, suggests, we all need to limit fat, cholesterol, smoking, and become more physically active.

Heart disease is like a dangerous lottery—we don't know the combination that will guarantee the deadly prize. However, with the information we have gained today, we can take our health into our own hands. We have unraveled the mysteries of heart attacks, became more familiar with the heart attack bug and its place in the heart attack, and discussed some implications this finding has for the future of hearts everywhere.

Many people valiantly graze through the twigs and grass of the salad bar for its health benefits, no matter how it tastes. But with the awareness of *chlamydia pneumoniae* and its relation to heart attacks, we know there's really only one good reason to avoid the low-fat oasis—if it doesn't have a sneeze guard.

The Book Review

Specs for the Book Review

Time limit
  10–15 minutes.

Speaker's notes
  50-word limit.

Source of information
  The book you select for review; sources of information about the author.

Outline
  Prepare a 75- to 100-word complete sentence outline.

Speak Up!

Think about a time you read a book, bought a CD, or saw a movie because someone recommended it. Why did you follow this person's suggestion? What did he or she do or say that aroused your interest? Would you be just as likely to read, buy, or view it if the recommendation came from a teacher? A sibling? Someone that you didn't know very well? Why or why not?

Purpose and Expectations of This Assignment

An oral book review is a unique occasion for a speech because the topic is clearly determined by the text in question. Still, it is not appropriate on such occasions to read large portions of the text to the audience. They have assembled to hear a concise, complete summary of the text, as well as the speaker's personal evaluation. This chapter will help you experience the making of such an evaluation and summary. You might enjoy presenting your opinions to the class in a creative and interesting way. You'll gain plenty of valuable information and enjoyment from the book you are reviewing. Also, as a class member, your review will add to the growing body of knowledge of all of your classmates. Because each class member will review a different book, many authors' ideas will be presented. This will provide a general fund of information that would otherwise be difficult and time-consuming to attain.

In completing this assignment, you will

- analyze and evaluate a text;
- understand methods of preparing a review; and
- present the review from minimal speaking notes.

Defining the Book Review

An **oral book review** is an orderly talk about a book and its author. As a speaker you must provide pertinent information about the author as well as the book. Generally speaking, you should include an evaluation of the work relative to composition and ideas. The end of your talk will be to inform, to stimulate, to entertain, and, possibly, to persuade listeners to read (or to avoid) the book. The book reviewer is expected to know the material well, to be familiar with the process and methods of giving a review, and to be able to present the information in an organized and interesting manner. These requirements demand an unusually thorough preparation.

Occasions for an oral book report can occur almost anywhere. They are common in scholastic, civic, religious, and other organizations. In just about any kind of club or society, school, or church, book reports are often an integral part of the program.

Choosing a Book to Review

For this particular experience, each student in the class should select a different book. It is easier if it is fiction as compared to nonfiction or a textbook. You may want to use a book you are reading for another class or a book you have recently read. You probably won't have time to read a new novel before you give your report. Whatever the book, it should be approved by the instructor before you start to prepare your speech.

First of all, follow your instructor's assignment. If you are asked to report on a specific type of book, such as science fiction, go to the library and find a book of that genre. If your instructor leaves the selection completely up to you, select a book that you enjoyed reading—one you couldn't put down. If you have time to read a book before the assignment is due, check the *New York Times Review of Books* and the list of best sellers. Finally, go to a bookstore or library and peruse the latest titles.

Preparing and Organizing

As you know, every speech must have a purpose. The book report is no exception. For every book report you should determine whether your purpose is to inform, to entertain, or to persuade. To organize your material, tell about the author's age, family background, and education; when the author first published; anecdotes about the author; quotations about the author; hometown; prizes won for writing; and/or why the book was written.

Then consider the specific book. Why did you choose it? When was it written? Why was it written? Is it biographical, historical, fictional, or what? What do the professional reviewers say about it? Ask your librarian to show you book reviews such as those from the *New York Times, Christian Century, Saturday Review of Literature, New Republic, The Nation*, and others. What is your opinion? Formulate your own. Do not plagiarize someone else's evaluation of the book. Create your own evaluation methodology based on the elements of a short story. (Exposition, complication, conflict, crises, climax, falling action, resolution, character, setting, and plot.)

Give examples and comments in answering the following questions.

1. Are the plot and organization well constructed?

2. Is the writer's style interesting?

3. How are situations and characters portrayed?

4. Do the characters seem real and alive?

5. Does the story move forward to a climax?

6. Is the information interesting and useful? Do you recommend the book? Why?

One of the best ways to master these questions is to read the entire book—or the sections that you are preparing to review—several times. First, read the text through for enjoyment. Read it through a second and third time for information you plan to use in your report. As for getting your material in mind, use whatever method works best for you. It is a good idea to make a careful and detailed outline, after which you rehearse aloud until your sequence of thoughts has been firmly fixed in mind. Use quotations sparingly and limit them to 150 words each.

vivid and descriptive language, a neat appearance, poise, and confidence.

1. Do you have an excellent introduction and conclusion?

2. Are you sure your speech is logically organized all the way through?

3. Does your report contain an evaluation of the book?

4. Have you reported on selected segments of the book that represent the author's objective?

5. Did you include information about the author?

Evaluating

Evaluate someone else's book report. Rate the following criteria on a scale from 1 to 5 with 5 being "outstanding."

- Was the speaker knowledgeable about the various aspects of the book?

- Did the speaker structure the speech with a logical progression?

- Did the speaker deliver the speech with authority?

- Was the speaker's purpose clear?

Give an overall score to the speech. Then decide how your classmate's presentation compared to yours. Write a paragraph explaining your decision and the reasons you came to this conclusion.

Presenting

First of all, have the report in your head. Do not have the book in your hands so that you use it as a crutch while you give your report. Following previously marked pages or taking up time by reading is not reviewing. Use the book only for your quotations. If you use notes, limit yourself to three words or fewer for each minute that you speak.

Utilize all of the aspects of good speech—a friendly manner, animation, vigor, communicative attitude, bodily action and appropriate gestures, a well-modulated voice that is easily heard, correct pronunciation, clear articulation,

Speaking Persuasively

Try to count how many times a day someone tries to persuade you to do something, or believe something, or change something! Persuasion happens nearly every time we communicate with others. It is particularly important for public address in a democratic society, as we all strive to work together for the protection and advancement of our communities and nation. In this unit you will work on three persuasive speaking assignments. The skills you gain in persuading, motivating, and creating goodwill will be useful in many other areas of your life.

Speech Experiences in This Unit

The Speech to
Persuade

Specs for the Speech to Persuade

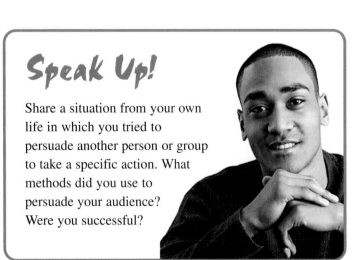

Time limit

5–6 minutes.

Speaker's notes

75-word maximum.

Sources of information

Two are required, preferably three. For each source list the specific magazine, book, or Internet site it was taken from; the title of the article; the author's full name; the date of publication; and the chapter or page numbers where the material was found. If a source is a person, identify him or her by title, position, and occupation. List these on the outline form. For Internet sites, give the address (URL).

Outline

Prepare a 75- to 150-word complete sentence outline.

Speak Up!

Share a situation from your own life in which you tried to persuade another person or group to take a specific action. What methods did you use to persuade your audience? Were you successful?

Purpose and Expectations of This Assignment

The techniques used to bring others around to a specific point of view are referred to collectively as the "art of persuasion." You will have many encounters in business, political, and social life in which you are either being persuaded or you are trying to persuade someone else. Listening well and communicating your thoughts effectively will enhance your persuasive skills. For a speech to persuade, the challenge will be to build reasons and evidence into arguments that will compel listeners to agree or even act on their convictions in support of your position. This assignment will introduce you to this public speaking purpose. As you craft a persuasive speech, you will discover techniques that will improve your overall communication.

In completing this assignment, you will

- identify a debatable proposition and adopt a position on it;

- understand the use of evidence, reasoning, and emotion to convince another; and

- organize arguments for clarity and maximum impact on listeners.

Defining the Speech to Persuade

Think about the last time you asked your parents for a special type of clothing. Did you give a persuasive argument containing logic, evidence, and emotion by stating why you had to have it?

Speeches to persuade are so common that you may be unaware of them as a specific public speaking experience. In fact, you use your powers of persuasion every day without even thinking about it. But as a persuasive public speaker you will have to use certain techniques to gain the audience's conviction. The speech to persuade is one that causes the audience to change, adopt, modify, or continue a belief or action. You must present sufficient logic and evidence to swing the audience to your position on a debatable proposition. This usually entails asking them to take the action that you suggest. Often it is not only wise but also necessary to appeal to the audience's emotions on such issues as fear, aging, health, wealth, love of country, self-preservation, desire for recognition, desire for adventure, loyalty, political beliefs, religion, and so on. In order to ignite the audience's emotions, you must thoroughly analyze your listeners so that you can base your appeal on their beliefs and attitudes. You also must present your logic and evidence in such a way that it directs the audience's thinking through channels they can readily follow.

In every debate—be it between two rival schools, within the membership of a legislative body, among friends, or in court proceedings—the speakers' statements involve persuasion through logic, evidence, and emotion.

Choosing a Topic

Be very careful in choosing a topic for your speech to persuade. You'll need to think carefully about the way you word your topic. Remember that you must reveal the idea or action you would like your audience to adopt. For example, let's imagine that you decide to persuade your listeners that "All schoolbooks should be free." Notice the word *should*. By putting that word into your topic, you show that your purpose is to persuade your audience to believe this is a sound idea that would be beneficial if it were carried out. You are not asking them to carry out the plan by standing behind book counters and handing out free textbooks.

Your topic must be a specific proposition that offers a debatable solution to a controversial problem. Simply stating the obvious—for example, "We should all drive more carefully"—is not enough. Everyone already agrees on this point. Suggest a definite and debatable *solution*, such as: "The legislature should pass a law limiting speed on the highways to 60 miles per hour," or "Anyone who is convicted of traffic violations should be required to attend driver's school for two weeks." These are proposals about which people disagree. We can readily say "yes" or "no" to them. We can debate these proposals, but we cannot debate the overall idea that "We should all drive more carefully," because we all agree on it to begin with.

A sales talk is not appropriate for this assignment because the purpose of a sale is to make your listeners reach into their pockets, pull out money, and give it to you. A sales talk requires them to *do* something. Naturally, a certain amount of persuasion will precede the request for money, but the actual purpose of a sales talk is to get people to hand over the cash. This type of speech is discussed in Experience 28. We may conclude then that a speech to persuade is not a sales talk, as it is not primarily to motivate action; instead it is designed to change a person's mind about something on which there is definite disagreement or controversy.

Examine your topic closely to be certain that it's something on which you can base your speech to persuade. If you are in any doubt, consult your instructor. Here are some sample topics.

- Child abuse
- Rally for a political candidate or cause
- Juvenile crime

- Affirmative Action
- Drug education
- American values
- National debt
- Ethics in government
- Campaign finance reform
- Immigration
- TV and movie violence
- Population control
- AIDS education
- Internet controls and regulation
- Multilingual education

Preparing and Organizing

In preparing the speech to persuade, remember that your purpose is to bring people over to your way of thinking. This is obviously not an easy task; however, there are a number of methods you can use to smooth the way for an effective presentation.

To achieve a convincing effect, you need to organize your speech carefully. Following is one example of a workable structure.

1. **Present a history of the problem.**
   Discuss the events leading up to the present time that make the topic important. Tell why it is significant for the audience to hear the discussion you are about to present. (Do not spend too much time on the history—you have other points to cover.)

2. **Discuss the present-day effects of the problem.** Use examples, illustrations, facts, and statements from authorities that clearly demonstrate the situation. These are musts if you wish to be convincing.

3. **Discuss the causes of the effects you listed in point two.** Here again you must present examples, illustrations, facts, and statements from authorities to prove your points. Be sure you show how the causes are bringing about the effects you mentioned. For example, if you say that a community's air quality has gotten 30 percent worse (effect) because of emissions from a certain manufacturing company (cause), you must definitely establish this cause rather than permit your audience to believe that the air *might* be worse because of the company's toxic emissions.

4. **List possible solutions to the problem.** Discuss briefly the various alternatives that could be followed, but illustrate that they are not effective enough to solve the problem. Give evidence for your statements by using examples, illustrations, authorities' views, facts, and analogies.

5. **Give your solution to the problem.** Show why your solution is the best answer to the problem. Present your evidence and the reason for believing as you do. This must not be simply your opinion. It must be logical reasoning backed up by evidence.

6. **Show how your proposal will benefit your audience.** This is the real meat of your entire speech if you have thoroughly fulfilled each step up to this point. This is where you must convince the audience. Benefits might include more money, safer streets, longer life, more happiness, better roads, better schools, lower taxes, or cheaper cost of living. In other words, your listeners must see clearly and vividly that your proposal will benefit them.

If the preceding speech structure doesn't work for your topic, here is another plan that works well.

1. **State your proposition** in the introduction.

2. **Present a history of the problem** that led to the proposal you are asking your audience to adopt.

3. **Show that your proposal is *necessary*.** Offer evidence that establishes a need for your proposal. Assure the audience that no other proposal (solution) will do.

4. **Show that your proposition is practical.** Give evidence to prove that it will do what you say it will do. In other words, show that it will solve the problem.

5. **Show that your proposition is *desirable*.** This means providing evidence showing that it will be beneficial rather than neutral or harmful.

6. **Conclude with a final statement in support of your proposal.**

On the other hand, if you are *opposed to* a certain proposal, you may establish your point of view by offering arguments that show any one of the following.

1. **The proposition is not needed.** Give evidence.

2. **The proposition is not practical.** Give evidence.

3. **The proposition is not desirable.** Give evidence.

Of course, if you can establish all three of these points, you will be more convincing than if you prove only one.

If you fail to have the body of your speech properly organized and all of your points supported by evidence, you will have trouble persuading an audience to adopt your point of view. As with most types of public speaking, the best guarantee of success is careful preparation.

In addition to an organized speech with points supported by evidence, you must have a well-constructed introduction and a powerful conclusion. Once you have crafted these elements, rehearsal will determine whether or not you are actually prepared to present a convincing speech. Even though you possess volumes of evidence, a clear structure, and vivid language, you must still deliver the speech confidently, without excessive use of notes, if you want to be convincing to your audience. Make sure that you rehearse your speech accordingly.

You'll find source materials on the Internet and at the library. Encyclopedias, magazines, newspapers, Web sites, and readers' guides all offer excellent sources. Check with your instructor and librarian for further assistance.

Presenting

Naturally, your presentation will vary according to your audience, the occasion, and the size and acoustics of the room. You would not speak to a small group of businesspeople in the same manner that you would address a large political gathering. In general, aim for a frank, enthusiastic, and energetic presentation. Use a reasonable amount of emotion; however, don't overdo it. Your bodily action should match your words in terms of vigor and intensity.

You must show that *you* are convinced of what you say. Your voice and actions should reflect a sincere belief in your views and through inflections and modulations, carry the ring of truth and personal conviction. Make sure you speak forcefully enough to be heard by everyone in the room.

If you use notes, be thoroughly familiar with them. Do not try to hide them. Hold them high enough that when you look at them you don't have to bow your head. If you want to keep your hands free, you can place your notes on the podium. After the conclusion of your speech, remain standing for two or three seconds before you return to your seat. Check with your instructor to see if there will be time to take questions.

Evaluating

Evaluate a classmate's speech to persuade. Rate the following criteria on a scale from 1 to 5 with 1 being "needs much improvement" and 5 being "outstanding."

- Was the speaker warm and friendly?
- Did the speaker seem genuinely convinced of his or her proposal?
- Were the speaker's posture and body language appropriate?
- Did the speaker use examples, quotes, and other materials?
- Was the speech well structured?
- Did the speaker use credible sources to support each point in the speech?
- Were the speaker's words audible and clear?

Give an overall score to the speech. Then write down one thing that the speaker did exceptionally well and one thing that could be improved.

Talking Points
The Language of Persuasion

While every public speaking situation calls for well-chosen, appropriate language, the art of persuasion calls for a closer look at the words a speaker or writer chooses.

In trying to persuade an audience to adopt your point of view, you may use both emotional and logical appeals.

Emotional Appeals

Of course, you feel strongly about your topic and you are eager to present your ideas to an audience. So it is normal, even desirable to use emotion-filled words and phrases. Your audience should see your enthusiasm and passion for your subject.

Just be careful not to get carried away with over-the-top positive or negative appeals. Such language used carelessly can cause an audience backlash. If one statement seems too good or bad to be true, the audience may decide that nothing you say can be believed.

Often **loaded language** can be found in overly emotional appeals. The dictionary definition of a word is its **denotative** meaning. The strong emotional appeal suggested by a word is its **connotative** meaning. For example, the word *steed* brings to mind a great, beautiful horse, perhaps ridden by a knight or princess. On the other hand, *nag* makes us think of a broken-down, spiritless horse. Look at the examples in the chart below.

Neutral	Positive	Negative
speech	oration	harangue
large	colossal	monstrous
thin	slim	gaunt
talk	chat	prate

Illogical Fallacies

Getting emotional about your subject matter can also lead to false arguments or fallacies. No matter how much you want to persuade your audience, you must guard against these logic traps as you prepare your speech.

1. **Overgeneralization** When we generalize, we make statements that apply to many people, things, or situations.

   > *Generalization*: Good grades are an important factor in college admission.

   > *Overgeneralization:* Only straight-A students will get into college.

2. **Circular Reasoning** This happens when the speaker tries to prove a point by simply repeating the same idea with different words.

   > Students at Kennedy High School are extremely intelligent because only smart students go there.

3. **Cause-and-Effect Fallacy** This fallacy occurs when a writer or speaker makes a cause-and-effect connection where none exists.

   > I tripped and fell just after I walked under a ladder. Therefore, walking under a ladder causes bad luck.

   > I got sick while riding on the bus. Therefore, all bus rides will make me sick.

4. **Either/Or** This type of faulty logic happens when a speaker or writer implies that there is only one solution to a problem when, in fact, there may be several possible alternatives.

   > Either we raise taxes or we close the public library.

   > Either we have a fundraiser or there will be no senior prom.

5. **Ad Hominem (Against the Man)** This fallacy occurs when a speaker attacks a person, rather than an action. For example, if someone writes a book with which you disagree, argue against the ideas, but don't call the author an idiot.

6. **Bandwagon** This approach is often used in advertising. It goes something like this: Everyone else is doing (buying) it, so you should too.

Example Speech

A Whisper of AIDS

by Mary Fisher
Houston, Texas
Republican National Convention,
August 19, 1992

Thank you. Thank you. Less than three months ago at platform hearings in Salt Lake City, I asked the Republican Party to lift the shroud of silence which has been draped over the issue of HIV and AIDS. I have come tonight to bring our silence to an end. I bear a message of challenge, not self-congratulation. I want your attention, not your applause.

I would never have asked to be HIV positive, but I believe that in all things there is a purpose; and I stand before you and before the nation gladly. The reality of AIDS is brutally clear. Two hundred thousand Americans are dead or dying. A million more are infected. Worldwide, forty million, sixty million, or one hundred million infections will be counted in the coming few years. But despite science and research, White House meetings, and congressional hearings; despite good intention and bold initiatives, campaign slogans, and hopeful promises, it is—despite it all—the epidemic which is winning tonight.

In the context of an election year, I ask you, here in this great hall, or listening in the quiet of your home, to recognize that the AIDS virus is not a political creature. It does not care whether you are Democrat or Republican; it does not ask whether you are black or white, male or female, gay or straight, young or old.

Tonight I represent an AIDS community whose members have been reluctantly drafted from every segment of American society. Though I am white and a mother, I am one with a black infant struggling with tubes in a Philadelphia hospital.

Though I am female and contracted this disease in marriage and enjoy the warm support of my family, I am one with the lonely gay man sheltering a flickering candle from the cold wind of his family's rejection.

This is not a distant threat. It is a present danger. The rate of infection is increasing fastest among women and children. Largely unknown a decade ago, AIDS is the third leading killer of young adult Americans today. But it won't be third for long, because unlike other diseases, this one travels. Adolescents don't give each other cancer or heart disease because they believe they are in love, but HIV is different; and we have helped it along. We have killed each other with our ignorance, our prejudice, and our silence.

We may take refuge in our stereotypes, but we cannot hide there long, because HIV asks only one thing of those it attacks. Are you human? And this is the right question. Are you human? Because people with HIV have not entered some alien state of being. They are human. They have not earned cruelty, and they do not deserve meanness. They don't benefit from being isolated or treated as outcasts. Each of them is exactly what God made—a person, not evil, deserving of our judgment; not victims, longing for our pity—people, ready for support and worthy of compassion.

My call to you, my Party, is to take a public stand, no less compassionate than that of the President and Mrs. Bush. They have embraced me and my family in memorable ways. In the place of judgment, they have shown affection. In difficult moments, they have raised our spirits. In the darkest hours, I have seen them reaching not only to me, but also to my parents, armed with that stunning grief and special grace that comes only to parents who have themselves leaned too long over the bedside of a dying child.

With the president's leadership, much good has been done. Much of the good has gone unheralded, and as the president has insisted, much remains to be done. But we do the president's cause no good if we praise the American family but ignore a virus that destroys it.

We must be consistent if we are to be believed. We cannot love justice and ignore prejudice, love our children and fear to teach them. Whatever our role as parent or policymaker, we must act as eloquently as we speak—else we have no integrity. My call to the nation is a plea for awareness. If you believe you are safe, you are in danger. Because I was not a hemophiliac, I was not at risk. Because I was not gay, I was not at risk. Because I did not inject drugs, I was not at risk.

My father has devoted much of his lifetime guarding against another holocaust. He is part of the generation who heard Pastor Nemoellor come out of the Nazi death camps to say, "They came after the Jews, and I was not a Jew, so I did not protest. They came after the trade unionists, and I was not a trade unionist, so I did not protest. Then they came after the Roman Catholics, and I was not a Roman Catholic, so I did not protest. Then they came after me, and there was no one left to protest."

The lesson history teaches is this: If you believe you are safe, you are at risk. If you do not see this killer stalking your children, look again. There is not family or community, no race or religion, no place left in America that is safe. Until we genuinely embrace this message, we are a nation at risk. Tonight, HIV marches resolutely to AIDS in more than a million American homes. Littering its pathway with the bodies of young men, young women, young parents, and young children.

One of those families is mine. If it is true that HIV inevitably turns to AIDS, then my children will inevitably turn to orphans. My family has been a rock of support. My 84-year-old father, who has pursued the healing of nations, will not accept the premise that he cannot heal his daughter. My mother refuses to be broken. She still calls at midnight

continued

Example Speech cont.

to tell wonderful jokes that make me laugh. Sisters and friends, and my brother Phillip, whose birthday is today, all have helped carry me over the hardest places. I am blessed, richly and deeply blessed, to have such a family.

But not all of you have been so blessed. You are HIV positive, but dare not say it. You have lost loved ones, but you dare not whisper the word AIDS—you weep silently. You grieve alone. I have a message for you. It is not you who should feel shame. It is we, we who tolerate ignorance and practice prejudice, we who have taught you to fear. We must lift our shroud of silence, making it safe for you to reach out for compassion. It is our task to seek safety for our children, not in quiet denial, but in effective action.

Someday our children will be grown. My son Max, now four, will take the measure of his mother. My son Zachary, now two, will sort through his memories. I may not be here to hear their judgments, but I know already what I hope they are. I want my children to know that their mother was not a victim. She was a messenger. I do not want them to think, as I once did, that courage is the absence of fear. I want them to know that courage is the strength to act wisely when we are most afraid. I want them to have the courage to step forward when called by their nation or their Party and give leadership, no matter what the personal cost. I ask no more of you than I ask of myself or of my children. To the millions of you who are grieving, who are frightened, who have suffered the ravage of AIDS firsthand—have courage, and you will find support. To the millions who are strong, I issue this plea—set aside prejudice and politics to make room for compassion and sound policy.

To my children, I make this pledge: I will not give in, Zachary, because I draw my courage from you. Your silly giggle gives me hope; your gentle prayers give me strength; and you, my child, give me the reason to say to America, 'You are at risk.' And I will not rest, Max, until I have done all I can to make your world safe. I will seek a place where intimacy is not the prelude to suffering. I will not hurry to leave you, my children, but when I go, I pray that you will not suffer shame on my account."

To all within the sound of my voice, I appeal: "Learn with me the lessons of history and of grace, so my children will not be afraid to say the word AIDS when I am gone. Then, their children and yours may not need to whisper it at all." God bless the children, and God bless us all, good night.

Example Speech

We Need a Bereavement Center

by Meghan Ortega

Dan McFeeley, writing for the *Indianapolis Business Journal*, stated, "Thousands of kids across the country are forced every year to deal with the untimely death of a father, mother, sister, or even a close friend."

At Baker University, many students and faculty members have lost a loved one and have had nowhere to turn for comfort. A support group is very much needed to help individuals cope with loss. With the implementation of a bereavement program, faculty members and students would have such a support system.

Less than three months ago, my father unexpectedly passed away, and I am currently enrolled in a bereavement program called the Solace House. Today I am going to show you the need for a bereavement program at Baker and a proposed solution.

First of all, how many of you know the definition of *bereavement*? I have said this word many times and yet many people don't know what it is. Bereavement is the loss of a loved one, whether it is through divorce or death.

While at college and away from your ultimate support system, your family, it is harder for students to cope with death. Having a campus support system would give students and faculty a place to turn.

You would not believe how many of us are affected by death: My father recently passed away. Another student, Nicole, also had her father pass away a few weeks ago. Dr. Emel told us today that she has a funeral to attend after this class. And I'm sure all of you remember Bree who passed away this last fall. In some way, we are all affected by death.

I contacted Head Quarters, which is a 24-hour crisis hot line, to see where the closest bereavement center is. The closest center is 20 minutes away in Lawrence. I strongly feel the need for a facility here in Baldwin where students will have easier access.

Bereavement counseling is a positive process. It is meant to help the individual cope with death, accept it, and keep on living. It is a healing process.

If the bereavement process is not supported, the individual can become depressed. The *Solace House Quarterly* newsletter states that

continued

when individuals don't have a source of support, they turn toward "self-destructive forms of expressing their grief, which lead to depression, antisocial behaviors, physical complications, and lack of family communication." In other words, they shut themselves off and become dysfunctional to society.

Now that I've told you how important this need is, let's look at a solution to the problem. My idea of a bereavement center here at Baker is modeled after the Solace House. Meetings would be one day every other week, and trained volunteers would help individuals in a group setting. They would not be there to tell individuals what to do or how to do it, but rather to guide and listen.

When you have lost someone, the most comforting thing is just to have a person listen to you. Volunteers at the bereavement center help you go through problems you are experiencing now and prepare you for future obstacles that you will have to face. They help you accept death and not to be angry and deny it.

Speaking with students on campus, I have found that many see the need for a bereavement program. Reghan, who was a cheerleader with Bree, stated that, "Finding support and having someone understand what you are going through always makes it easier to cope and share feelings." I believe that it is very important for the individual to feel comfortable.

You may be wondering why a bereavement program is needed when our campus already makes a counselor

available to us. I honestly would not get the same benefits from one-on-one counseling as I do from group counseling. With group sessions an individual is able to interact with others who have had the same experiences. This allows individuals to see that they are not alone.

[*Show a picture of Bree, a Baker student who passed away, and a picture of my siblings.*] In closing, I want to note that Bree used to watch my siblings over the summer. Mallory, my younger sister, was really attached to her. So not only did she lose her favorite babysitter, but a father as well [*Show picture of Dad.*] I want to share with you an excerpt from a story my younger sister wrote shortly after my father's death, entitled "My Father's Ending":

"When we were at the hospital all I was thinking was is he going to die? Will he be hooked up to machines all the rest of his life?

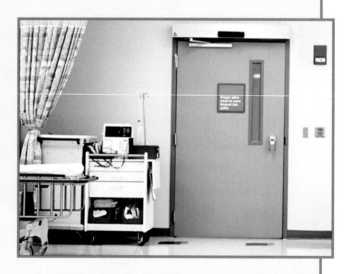

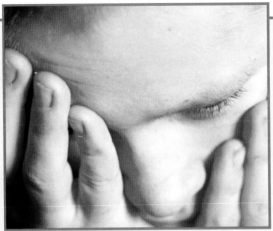

Will he still be athletic? Those were all of the questions that were running through my head. Later during the night around 8:50 my sister and I went to go see my dad. We were almost to the door and then all of a sudden over the intercom we hear "CODE BLUE," which means someone's heart has stopped. When we heard that, me and my sister started crying so hard and hugging my mom and crying on her shoulder. They told us to wait. So we did. We waited about 20 minutes and then one of the doctors came in and said, 'Well, Terri, I'm sorry, but he died.' We all started crying because everyone in that room loved him in a different way."

Losing a loved one is unavoidable, but how we treat the bereavement process can be changed. A support group is needed to help individuals cope with loss. After speaking to individuals on campus that have lost loved ones, the majority agreed that a support group is needed. Faculty, such as Reverend Ira DeSpain, would be "pleased to facilitate" such a group.

The first step would be an initial meeting with Student Senate to present a petition requesting the program. Your support in signing the petition and attending such a meeting would be greatly appreciated. Thank you.

The Speech to Motivate

Specs for the Speech to Motivate

Time limit

4–5 minutes.

Speaker's notes

50-word maximum.

Sources of information

Two are required, preferably three. For each source give the specific magazine, book, or Internet site from which it was taken; the title of the article; the author's full name; the date of publication; and the chapter or page numbers where the material was found. If a source is a person, identify him or her by title, position, and occupation. List these on the outline form. For Internet sites, give the address (URL).

Outline

Prepare a 75- to 150-word complete sentence outline.

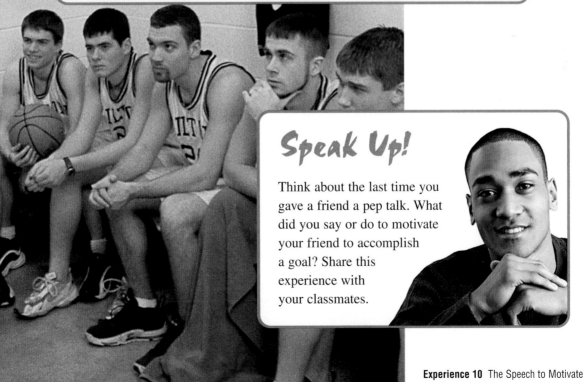

Speak Up!

Think about the last time you gave a friend a pep talk. What did you say or do to motivate your friend to accomplish a goal? Share this experience with your classmates.

Purpose and Expectations of This Assignment

Oftentimes people need to be stimulated to be concerned about a proposition or problem. When a speaker appeals to the audience to *do* something but fails to stir them sufficiently, the audience is generally only mildly interested. As a speaker, it is to your advantage to learn the speaking methods and approaches that stimulate audiences. This assignment will provide an experience for the speech to motivate. Using the methods you learn here, you will be able to incite an audience to take action based on your words.

In completing this assignment, you will

- identify speaking strategies that move listeners to action,
- understand the role of emotional appeals in motivation,
- select appropriate language for vividness to motivate the audience, and
- organize ideas in a manner that builds enthusiasm in listeners.

Defining the Speech to Motivate

The **speech to motivate** an audience is similar to the speech to persuade except that **motivation implies action**. If presented successfully, a speech to motivate makes audience members want to *do* something. If its purpose is fulfilled, it touches the audience on both an emotional and an intellectual level. Consequently audience members may feel impelled to adopt new attitudes and/or take the speaker's suggested action.

The basic features of the speech to motivate are vivid language, obvious sincerity, and enthusiasm on the part of the speaker, as well as appeals to the audience's basic emotions. Catchy slogans, specific examples, illustrations, and facts help the speaker in the motivation process. The speaker may also use emotional cues such as the big guy against the little guy, the bad against the good, and the money that can be earned against that which will go unearned.

Common occasions for motivational speeches are anniversary memorials, dedications, commencement exercises, religious gatherings, conventions, political rallies, pep meetings, sales promotions, and half-time sessions in which a coach arouses the team's will to win.

The motivational speech demands a vigorous presentation. It calls for enthusiasm, energy, force, power, and spirit. The quantity of each will depend upon the response the speaker is seeking from the audience. But most of all, like so many other types of speeches, the speech to motivate requires sincerity.

Choosing a Topic

Of the many variations on public speaking none demands more sincerity from the speaker than the speech to motivate. Therefore, when choosing a topic from the following list or when looking for your own topic, make sure it is something you believe in. Try to avoid subjects that are suitable for the national congress or for presentation over National Public Radio. Find a discussion suitable for your audience—in this case, your classmates. It does not have to be startling or overwhelming. The occasion calls for a speech that is appropriate to your situation; it should be well within the scope of your own experience. Here are some possible topics.

- Volunteer your time
- Term limits for elected officials
- Wetlands protected with taxpayer money
- Sex education for all public schools
- Change your eating habits
- Local programs to assist the homeless
- Exercise to be healthy
- Lowering teen pregnancy rates
- Learn a foreign language
- Cell phone use should be prohibited while driving

Preparing

You will prepare this speech according to the same steps you followed in the speech to inform and the speech to persuade. However, it's very important that you give some attention to your purpose, which is to stimulate the audience to take *action*. This purpose should underlie every statement you utter.

After you select your topic and purpose, do your research carefully. As usual, there is no better source of materials for a speech than the library and/or media center. The librarian and your instructor will assist you in locating materials. There may be people on the faculty or friends you know who have special knowledge. Do not overlook interviews with them.

When you feel you have located enough information, begin your organization. In the speech to motivate, a key five-point strategy of organization developed by Professor Alan Monroe is a popular format. Monroe's Motivated Sequence is detailed for you in the section that follows. The steps are: attention, need, satisfaction, visualization, and action.

Organizing

Use the following format to organize a strong motivational speech.

1. First, look through your research materials for an attention-grabbing story or statistic and use this to create an introduction that gets your audience's **attention** as well as reveals the topic.

2. Next, develop a sense of **need** by explaining why there is a problem or why something needs to be done. Use examples to help your audience understand the full scope of the situation at hand.

3. Then provide **satisfaction** for the audience by offering a solution that will eliminate the problem you have outlined. Give enough details about the solution so that the audience can clearly see how it will be applied and how it will stop the problem.

4. Next, help the audience envision what it would be like if they were to do what you ask. **Visualization** is the art of painting a verbal picture in the audience's mind—you can use it to show how things will be better if they take the action you recommend, or how things will be much worse if they do not.

5. Finally, explain to the audience what specific **action** they can take to solve the problem. Be as specific as possible. Give your audience any information you have that will make it easier to take the action you have described. Conclude by reviewing the problem and the solution and directly calling upon the audience to take action. Your speech will have **psychological unity** if you can tie your closing lines to the attention-getter you used in the introduction.

In arranging and organizing the main body of your remarks, try to create vivid phraseology, word pictures, and graphic illustrations to create associations in your listeners' minds. You may also offer slogans and catchy phrases to make your ideas stick with your listeners. Be specific by naming certain persons and definite places within your speech. If you want to stimulate people to action, you need to tell them who's involved and where they should go to respond to the facts you present. Avoid abstract or intangible examples, illustrations, and facts.

Remember that your ideas must hit their mark and make a strong impact.

The last step in preparing this speech will be rehearsal. Be sure you practice enough that you know from memory the sequence of ideas that you plan to present. Avoid memorizing the speech word for word. Practice in front of a mirror and/or your friends until you feel competent to speak to a larger audience.

Presenting

As always, make sure you are properly dressed and groomed. When you reach the podium, take a few moments to orient yourself before you begin speaking.

Unless you are speaking on a solemn occasion involving reverence, devotion, or extremely deep feeling, try to create a forceful, dynamic, and energetic vocal presentation. Your voice and manner should be animated and sincere. Emphasize your ideas with appropriate bodily action and gestures. Remember that your audience will reflect your presentation. They will be just as lively or solemn as you stimulate them to be.

Evaluating

Evaluate a classmate's speech to motivate based on the following questions.

- Was the speaker enthusiastic?
- Did the speaker seem well informed?
- Did the speaker use Alan Monroe's organizational format?
- Did the speaker deliver the speech with authority?
- Did the speaker's presentation motivate you toward a certain action?

Example Speech

Three Lies

J. C. Watts, Congressman, 1994–2002
This speech was delivered to students in Altus, Oklahoma.

There are three lies in America today that I want every one of you to be aware of.

The first lie is this: "I am entitled to one mistake." Young people, that lie will trip you up every time if you believe you are entitled to mistakes. We all make mistakes, but we are not entitled to mistakes. If you live your life believing that you are entitled to mistakes, you will bounce from wall to wall, never having any substance, never having any direction in your life.

Now, you all might be too young to remember a story about a man named Len Bias. Len Bias was a power forward for the University of Maryland. He had just been drafted by the Boston Celtics. He was going to be the guy, along with Larry Bird, Kevin McHale, and Robert Parrish, that was going to get the Celtics back to the NBA championships. Six foot nine inches tall, 220 pounds . . . he was a Michael Jordan kind of a guy. He could handle the ball well, shoot the ball well, jump well, and dribble the ball well. I mean six foot nine inches tall, 220 pounds and he was cat-quick! Len Bias was the first player taken out of the NBA draft picks about eight years ago. Len Bias had some friends, so-called friends, come by. They were going to celebrate him being the first player taken in the NBA draft. They'd brought by a little crack cocaine. Len Bias tried this crack cocaine, his heart didn't respond to it, and it killed him in a matter of minutes. Now, I don't know if Len Bias was a regular drug user or not. I can't say that as a matter of fact. But I can't help but think—in the back of my mind—that Len Bias thought—in the back of his mind—"Hey, no big deal. I'm only human. I'm entitled to mistakes. So what if I get caught, so what if I get busted, so what if something bad happens. So what, I'm only human. I'm entitled to celebrate." Len Bias was saying "I'm entitled to one mistake." Young people, that one mistake cost him his life. You see, that is why we should not live our lives believing that "I'm entitled to mistakes"—we make mistakes, but we are not entitled to them.

The second lie is this, and this one is the one that really gets many junior high and high school students. It got me just as it does many junior high and high school students.

The second lie is "it will never happen to me."

Young people, we believe that. We believe that all those bad things that happen in life happen to other people and will never happen to me. We tell ourselves that—it will never happen to me. There's an incident that I experienced about six years ago that if I live to be 150 years old I will never forget. I am a big National Basketball Association fan.

continued

Example Speech cont.

The L.A. Lakers have been and are still my favorite basketball team. I used to love to see the Lakers play when they had Kareem Abdul-Jabbar, Magic Johnson, James Worthy, Michael Cooper, all those guys. I used to love to see them play!

Magic Johnson was my favorite basketball player. I loved to see Magic Johnson come down the court. He'd whip that ball between his legs dribbling, he'd flip it behind his back to the left, he'd flip it to the right. He would dish out those marvelous assists to James Worthy or Michael Cooper coming down the wing and man, they'd make those fast breaks, and slam dunk the ball. Magic would dish out those marvelous assists and he would turn around to the crowd and he would flash that big billion dollar smile. Man, I used to love to see that, to see him perform. My favorite basketball player. I remember coming home one evening from work, it was about five or six years ago. I remember throwing my coat over the back of the couch and watching this press conference with my favorite basketball player, Magic Johnson . . . six foot nine inches tall, 215 pounds, point guard for the L.A. Lakers, huge billion dollar smile, this guy I loved to see play. Do you know what he said to all of the youth of America? I'll never forget it; it still rings in my ears today. Magic Johnson was having a press conference and he said this: "I guess I was naive; I never thought it would happen to me." Do you know what Magic was talking about? What he said he thought would never happen to him? Magic Johnson had been tested positive for HIV. He said, "I guess I was naive—I never thought it would happen to me." And that rings in my ears to this day. Magic talked about it. I heard him say it time and time again. "I was naive, I never thought it would happen to me."

Young people, we do things that we know aren't right and that we shouldn't be doing, and do you know what we tell ourselves? "Ah, it'll never happen to me; I'll never get caught." I remember about five years ago I had my truck stolen—in broad daylight. I remember when I called the police to come do a written report on this. I remember standing there leaning on that desk thinking "I can't believe this is happening to me." That happened to other people. I saw it on the news, I read about it in the paper, but I never thought it would happen to me . . . but it did. Everybody knows Pete Rose. Pete Rose, no question, should be in Major League Baseball, but Pete Rose got kicked out of Major League Baseball because he was gambling on baseball—that's against the rules. I can't help but think—in the back of my mind—that Pete thought—in the back of his mind—when he was placing those bets, he was saying, "Ah, that'll never happen to me; I'll never get caught." Young people, what if someone would have come to us when we made some of those bad decisions, someone of some influence could have gotten to me when I made some of those bad decisions in my life, or someone could have gotten to the teachers when they were making bad decisions in their lives, or if someone could have gotten to Pete Rose or Magic Johnson. Consider if some person of influence could have gotten there and said "Hey, Magic, hey Pete, is it worth the rest of your life? Is it worth losing your reputation, losing your career over, the rest of your life, what you've done?" Young people it can happen to you.

The third lie is this, and be careful that you understand this one. "I've got plenty of time."

Young people, do you know what we tell ourselves? We think, "Man, I'm going to be a professional baseball player; I'm going to be a professional basketball player; I don't have to worry about that math stuff, that reading stuff, that English stuff, and that science stuff; I don't have to worry about that stuff, I've got plenty of time for that!" Young people, you don't have plenty of time. You are in an institution today and you should thank God for those people you see standing around the walls. They call them teachers. You should thank God that you've got those teachers that will push you and force you to do what you know, and they know, you are capable of doing. We get so interested in so many other things that are totally irrelevant to our abilities to compete in a global marketplace for jobs and to take care of our families and to get the things we want to have, like a car for transportation, and a home to live in. Hey, that math, science, reading, and English, all those things are very important in that effort. We cheat ourselves so badly because we don't spend the time that we should making sure that we know how to read and write and do the arithmetic and the science and the English, that we have the computer skills that we need. We think, "Man, I've got plenty of time for that." No you don't have plenty of time. Today is the day you start preparing for the rest of your life. Today is the first day of the rest of your life, and I hope that you will start preparing today.

In summary, the three lies are: "I'm entitled to one mistake"—no, you're not. We make mistakes, but we are not entitled to them. The second lie is—"It will never happen to me." Yes, young people, it can happen to you. And the third lie is this—"I've got plenty of time"—you don't have plenty of time. Understand reading, writing, arithmetic, and have the computer skills to compete in the age of technology and computers. Today is the day you start preparing for the rest of your life. I don't know how many of you believe that going to college is important. Some of you may go to vocational school; some of you may go to work right after high school. I don't know what you are going to do, but I hope that you will understand this—that good things happen to people that will work hard, pay the price, understand sacrifice and commitment, will take pride in getting an education, and will have enough faith to believe that "I can do." If you believe that doesn't work—I hope that you will take a good look at the gentleman standing here before you.

I hope that you will decide that America really is a great country. That it is a place that I want to be, to raise my family, to work, to contribute to society. Because if a little kid from Eufala, Oklahoma, who grew up in a poor black neighborhood on the east side of the railroad tracks can some day grow up and end up in the U.S. House of Representatives, that tells you that we live in a pretty good country.

A Speech to
Gain Goodwill
from a Disagreeing Audience

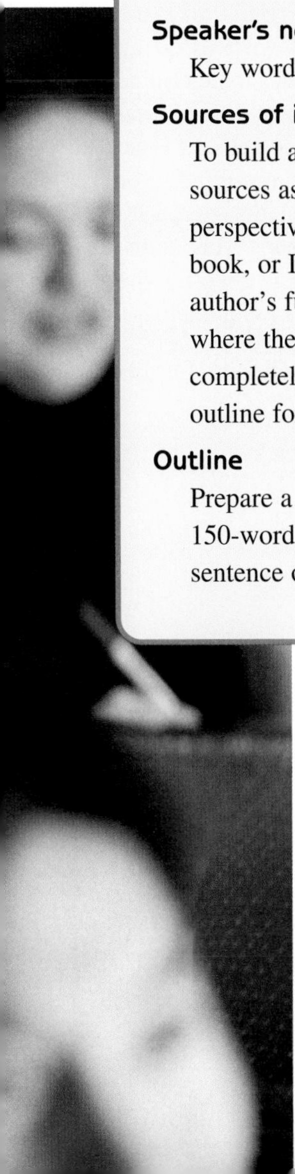

Specs for the Speech to Gain Goodwill from a Disagreeing Audience

Time limit

6–7 minutes.

Speaker's notes

Key words only.

Sources of information

To build and maintain credibility for this speech, use as many outside sources as possible. But remember that you must still present your perspective on the issue. For each source, provide the specific magazine, book, or Internet site from which it was taken; the title of the article; the author's full name; the date of publication; and the chapter or pages telling where the material appeared. If the source is a person, identify him or her completely by full name, title or position, and occupation. List these on the outline form. For Internet sites give the address (URL).

Outline

Prepare a 75- to 150-word complete sentence outline.

Speak Up!

With another student, improvise a situation between you and your parents or guardians. You want a raise in your allowance. You already know that this will be a tough battle because your folks think you are getting too much already. How will you begin to win them over? What will you do to establish goodwill and open the way for a future discussion of the issue?

Purpose and Expectations of This Assignment

Facing an audience that does not agree with your position on a particular issue can be a daunting task. If an audience feels strongly enough against your ideas or proposal, building good-will may be the sole purpose of your first attempt to address them. The objective in giving this type of speech is to pave the way for future possibilities. This assignment will help you find the best ways to build audience support for a controversial idea. It is designed to give you an opportunity to try your hand at such a challenge.

In completing this assignment, you will

- present ideas to a disagreeing audience in a clear manner,

- understand the role of shared values in developing goodwill with an audience,

- anticipate and refute counterarguments, and

- determine a respectful approach to speaking to disagreeing audiences.

Defining the Speech to Gain Goodwill

By making a **speech to gain goodwill** you attempt to secure the audience's favorable attitude toward yourself (and the topic, if possible). If you were to present the speech to an agreeing or neutral audience, it would be a persuasive speech. However, with a disagreeing audience, using too much persuasiveness often serves only to strengthen the listeners' defensive tendencies.

You should approach the speech to gain good-will from the perspective of the informative speech. You will want to inform the disagreeing audience of values you share with them as well as explain how you have drawn a conclusion on the issue that differs from theirs.

Choosing a Topic

For this assignment you should select a topic about which you feel strongly. But don't choose a topic about which everyone you know agrees with you. Instead make it a controversial topic—one on which many people could take the opposite perspective. You may wish to do an informal survey of your classmates to determine their perspectives on particular issues that interest you. Or you may wish to select a topic with a particular audience in mind—for instance, a topic on which you disagree with parents, teachers, or other groups you know. Consult with your instructor before choosing the topic you will work with for this assignment.

Some examples of topics and audiences for this speech might include

- The disadvantages of curfews (audience: parents);

- The disadvantages of assigning grades (audience: teachers and other school personnel);

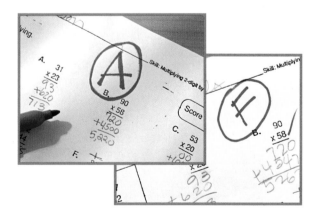

- The advantages of legalizing marijuana for medical purposes (audience: doctors); and
- The advantages of physician-assisted suicide (audience: medical personnel).

Preparing and Organizing

As you prepare for this speech, remember that your purpose is to gain goodwill and that you will best accomplish this through an informational approach. As soon as you have selected your topic, begin to gather materials that support your position on the issue. These supporting materials must come from sources your disagreeing audience will respect—for example, people who are widely regarded as experts in the field, institutions that do not have a financial interest in the issue one way or the other, and news outlets that are known for their objectivity.

After you have gathered your materials, organize the information in a clear progression for the audience. Look for particularly vivid examples, stories, or statistics that illustrate your points. Narrow the issue to the two or three main points you most want to make to your audience. Organize them in much the same way that you would for any informative speech. You want the audience to be able to anticipate the flow of your ideas.

Plan to begin the speech by finding something everyone can agree on. By establishing common values with your listeners, you can gain their sympathies. After all, they can't help but support the values they already hold. In this way you will begin the speech in accord with your listeners and it will set the tone for them to follow you through the rest of the ideas you present. However, this strategy will most likely have no effect if the audience believes you are insincere. In fact, an insincere attempt will probably cause you to lose credibility.

A disagreeing audience is likely to be pondering counterarguments to your position as you speak. If such objections are well known and available in advance, it may be prudent to acknowledge them in your speech and take the opportunity to refute them or tell why you disagree. However, if you have not thought

through and researched the opposing arguments in advance, it may be unwise to toss them in at the last minute. If you do choose to address the counterarguments you are aware of, support them with outside sources as much as possible to indicate that you are not the only one holding this position.

Do not expect to convert your audience. Set a goal to establish goodwill so that the dialogue on this topic may continue in any way possible. Above all, your audience must have the feeling that you are sincere and that you ultimately have their best interest at heart. Creating a sense of goodwill means that you seek a friendly, positive relationship with the audience even if you continue to disagree on this particular topic.

Conclude your speech with a review of the values you share with them and a brief statement of your position. Show your audience how those shared values can be most fully realized through the position you have taken.

Presenting

Deliver your speech with confidence, friendliness, good humor, and modesty. Do not take on an air of superiority in any way. Your audience must believe you will respect their views even if they are not willing to shift their position on the issue.

Dress respectfully. Pay attention to your posture. Be alert and eager to communicate.

Avoid unnecessary formality. Speak clearly and loudly enough that everyone in the room can hear you. Body language and gestures, as always, should be appropriate to the subject matter, the audience, and the occasion.

Evaluating

Evaluate a classmate's speech to gain goodwill. Rate the following criteria on a scale from 1 to 5 with 1 being "needs much improvement" and 5 being "outstanding."

- Did the speaker avoid being confrontational?
- Did the speaker try to find common ground with the audience?
- Did the speaker structure the speech with a logical progression?
- Did the speaker seem enthusiastic and open?
- Did the speaker use vivid examples and illustrations?
- Was the speaker's body language appropriate?

Give an overall score to the speech. Then choose one area of the speaker's performance that may have given you new ideas about your own public speaking. Write a short paragraph to explain.

Example Speech

On Gun Control

by Charlton Heston
National Press Club, February 11, 1997

Today I want to talk to you about guns: Why we have them, why the Bill of Rights guarantees that we can have them, and why my right to have a gun is more important than your right to rail against it in the press.

I believe every good journalist needs to know why the Second Amendment must be considered more essential than the First Amendment. This may be a bitter pill to swallow, but the right to keep and bear arms is not archaic. It's not an outdated, dusty idea some old dead white guys dreamed up in fear of the Redcoats. No, it is just as essential to liberty today as it was in 1776. These words may not play well at the Press Club, but it's still the gospel down at the corner bar and grill.

And your efforts to undermine the Second Amendment, to deride it and degrade it, to readily accept diluting it and eagerly promote redefining it, threaten not only the physical well-being of millions of Americans but also the core concept of individual liberty our founding fathers struggled to perfect and protect.

So now you know what doubtless does not surprise you. I believe strongly in the right of every law-abiding citizen to keep and bear arms, for what I think are good reasons.

The original amendments we refer to as the Bill of Rights contain ten of what the constitutional framers termed unalienable rights. These rights are ranked in random order and are linked by their essential equality. The Bill of Rights came to us with blinders on. It doesn't recognize color, or class or wealth. It protects not just the rights of actors, or editors, or reporters, but extends even to those we love to hate. That's why the most heinous criminals have rights until they are convicted of a crime.

The beauty of the Constitution can be found in the way it takes human nature into consideration. We are not a docile species capable of co-existing within a perfect society under everlasting benevolent rule.

We are what we are. Egotistical, corruptible, vengeful, sometimes even a bit power-mad. The Bill of Rights recognizes this and builds the barricades that need to be in place to protect the individual.

You, of course, remain zealous in your belief that a free nation must have a free press and free speech to battle injustice, unmask corruption and provide a voice for those in need of a fair and impartial forum.

I agree wholeheartedly—a free press is vital to a free society. But I wonder: How many of you will agree with me that the right to keep and bear arms is not just equally vital, but the most vital to protect all the other rights we enjoy?

I say that the Second Amendment is, in order of importance, the first amendment. It is America's First Freedom, the one right that protects all the others. Among freedom of

continued

Example Speech cont.

speech, of the press, of religion, of assembly, of redress, of grievances, it is the first among equals. It alone offers the absolute capacity to live without fear. The right to keep and bear arms is the one right that allows "rights" to exist at all.

Either you believe that, or you don't, and you must decide.

Because there is no such thing as a free nation where police and military are allowed the force of arms but individual citizens are not. That's a "big brother knows best" theater of the absurd that has never bode well for the peasant class, the working class or even for reporters.

Yes, our Constitution provides the doorway for your news and commentary to pass through free and unfettered. But that doorway to freedom is framed by the muskets that stood between a vision of liberty and absolute anarchy at a place called Concord Bridge. Our revolution began when the British sent Redcoats door to door to confiscate the people's guns. They didn't succeed: The muskets went out the back door with their owners.

Emerson said it best:

By the rude bridge that arched the flood,
Their flag to April's breeze unfurled,
Here once the embattled farmers stood,
And fired the shot heard round the world.

King George called us "rabble in arms." But with God's grace, George Washington and many brave men gave us our country. Soon after, God's grace and a few great men gave

us our Constitution. It's been said that the creation of the United States is the greatest political act in history. I'll sign that.

In the next two centuries, though, freedom did not flourish. The next revolution, the French, collapsed in bloody Terror, then Napoleon's tyranny. There's been no shortage of dictators since, in many countries. Hitler, Mussolini, Stalin, Mao, Idi Amin, Castro, Pol Pot. All these monsters began by confiscating private arms, then literally soaking the earth with the blood of ten and tens of millions of their people. Ah, the joys of gun control.

Now, I doubt any of you would prefer a rolled up newspaper as a weapon against a dictator or a criminal intruder. Yet in essence that is what you have asked our loved ones to do, through the ill-contrived and totally naive campaign against the Second Amendment.

Besides, how can we entrust to you the Second Amendment when you are so stingy with your own First Amendment?

I say this because of the way, in recent days, you have treated your own—those journalists you consider the least among you. How quick you've been to finger the paparazzi with blame and to eye the tabloids with disdain. How eager you've been to draw a line where there is none, to demand some distinction within the First Amendment that sneers "they are not one of us." How readily you let your lesser brethren take the fall, as if their rights were not as worthy, and their purpose not as pure, and their freedom not as sacred as yours.

So now, as politicians consider new laws to shackle and gag paprazzi, who among you will speak up? Who here will stand and defend them? If you won't, I will. Because you do not define the First Amendment. It defines you. And it is bigger than you—big enough to embrace all of you, plus all those you would exclude. That's how freedom works.

It also demands you do your homework. Again and again I hear gun owners say, how can we believe anything that anti-gun media says when they cannot even get the facts right? For too long you have swallowed manufactured statistics and fabricated technical support from anti-gun organizations that wouldn't know a semi-auto from a sharp stick. And it shows. You fall for it every time.

Thats why you have very little credibility among 70 million gun owners and 20 million hunters and millions of veterans who learned the hard way which end the bullet comes out. And while you attacked the amendment that defends your homes and protects your spouses and children, you have denied those of us who defend all the Bill of Rights a fair hearing or the courtesy of an honest debate.

If the NRA attempts to challenge your assertions, we are ignored. And if we try to buy advertising time or space to answer your charges, more often than not we are denied. How's that for First Amendment freedom?

Clearly, too many have used freedom of the press as a weapon not only to strangle our free speech, but to erode and ultimately destroy the right to keep and bear arms as well. In doing so you promoted your profession to that of constitutional judge and jury, more powerful even than our Supreme Court, more prejudiced than the Inquisition's tribunals. It is a frightening misuse of constitutional right, and

I pray that you will come to your senses and see that these abuses are curbed.

As a veteran of World War II, as a freedom marcher who stood with Dr. Martin Luther King long before it was fashionable, and as a grandfather who wants the coming century to be free and full of promise for my grandchildren, I am troubled.

The right to keep and bear arms is threatened by political theatrics, piecemeal lawmaking, talk-show psychology, extreme bad taste in the entertainment industry, an ever-widening educational chasm in our schools, and a conniving media, that all add up to cultural warfare against the idea that guns ever had, or should now have, an honorable and proud place in our society.

But all our rights must be delivered into the 21st century as pure and complete as they came to us at the beginning of this century. Traditionally the passing of that torch is from a gnarled old hand down to an eager young one. So now, at 72, I offer my gnarled old hand.

I have accepted a call from the National Rifle Association of America to help protect the Second Amendment. I feel it is my duty to do that. My mission and vision can be summarized in three simple parts.

First, before we enter the next century, I expect to see a pro-Second Amendment president in the White House.

Secondly, I expect to build an NRA with the political muscle and clout to keep a pro-Second Amendment congress in place.

Third is a promise to the next generation of free Americans. I hope to help raise a hundred million dollars for NRA programs

continued

Example Speech cont.

and education before the year 2000. At least half of that sum will go to teach American kids what the right to keep and bear arms really means to their culture and country.

We have raised a generation of young people who think that the Bill of Rights comes with their cable TV. Leave them to their channel surfing and they'll remain oblivious to history and heritage that truly matter.

Think about it—what else must young Americans think when the White House proclaims, as it did, that "a firearm in the hands of youth is a crime or an accident waiting to happen"? No—it is time they learned that firearm ownership is constitutional, not criminal. In fact, few pursuits can teach a young person more about responsibility, safety, conservation, their history, and their heritage, all at once.

It is time they found out that the politically correct doctrine of today has misled them. And that when they reach legal age, if they do not break our laws, they have a right to choose to own a gun—a handgun, a long gun, a small gun, a large gun, a black gun, a purple gun, a pretty gun, an ugly gun—and to use that gun to defend themselves and their loved ones or to engage in any lawful purpose they desire without apology or explanation to anyone, ever.

This is their first freedom. If you say it's outdated, then you haven't read your own headlines. If you say guns create only carnage, I would answer that you know better. Declining morals, disintegrating families, vacillating political leadership, an eroding criminal justice system, and social morals that blur right and wrong are more to blame—certainly more than any legally owned firearm.

I want to rescue the Second Amendment from an opportunistic president, and from a press that apparently can't comprehend that attacks on the Second Amendment set the stage for assaults on the First.

I want to save the Second Amendment from all these nitpicking little wars of attrition—fights over alleged Saturday night specials, plastic guns, cop killer bullets, and so many other made-for-prime-time non-issues invented by some press agent over at gun control headquarters—that you guys buy time and again.

I simply cannot stand by and watch a right guaranteed by the Constitution of the United States come under attack from those who either can't understand it, don't like the sound of it, or find themselves too philosophically squeamish to see why it remains the first among equals: Because it is the right we turn to when all else fails.

That's why the Second Amendment is America's first freedom.

Please, go forth and tell the truth. There can be no free speech, no freedom of the press, no freedom to protest, no freedom to worship your god, no freedom to speak your mind, no freedom from fear, no freedom for your children and for theirs, for anybody, anywhere without the Second Amendment freedom to fight for it.

If you don't believe me, just turn on the news tonight. Civilization's veneer is wearing thinner all the time.

Thank you.

UNIT 5

Social Speeches

Chances are, at some point you will be called upon to present a speech at a social event. Whether you present an award to the honoree at a banquet; receive an award yourself; say a public good-bye to colleagues, fellow students, or coworkers; or introduce a famous speaker to an excited group of fans, the ability to find the right words—and to create a great moment—will serve you well. This unit will introduce you to a variety of social speeches.

Speech Experiences in This Unit

The Speech to
Entertain

Bill Cosby delivers the commencement address at Fordham University.

Specs for the Speech to Entertain

Time limit
5–6 minutes.

Speaker's notes
10- to 15-word maximum.

Sources of information
Two are required, preferably three. For each source, give the specific magazine, book, or Internet site it was taken from; the title of the article; the author's full name; the date of publication; and the chapter or page numbers where the material was found. If a source is a person, identify him or her by title, position, and occupation. List all sources on the outline form. For Internet sites, provide the address (URL).

Outline
Prepare a 75- to 150-word complete sentence outline.

Speak Up!

In small groups come up with a definition of humor. What makes something funny? Are there different kinds of humor? What do you personally find humorous? What do others in your group think is funny? When your definition is complete, have someone from your group read it to the class.

Purpose and Expectations of This Assignment

There is a common misconception about presenting a speech to entertain; many people assume that it's easy, or that a series of jokes or unstructured chatter is all it takes to speak effectively. This is far from the truth. A humorous speech to entertain can be one of the most difficult to pull off. When attempting an entertaining speech, some people succeed—and others do not.

Everyone likes to be entertained. But individuals may differ in terms of what they find entertaining. For the speaker who seeks to amuse or delight his or her audience, there are several strategies to consider.

This assignment is designed to help you explore the ways humor can be applied to a message to make the new information or persuasive argument more appealing and fun for the listeners. An example of a specific purpose statement for a speech to entertain might be to introduce the audience to the latest in technological advances, but it could also provide them with humorous examples of how that technology came to be, or how it might be used in the future.

In completing this assignment, you will

- understand the complexity of using humor in a speech,
- identify several strategies for making a speech humorous, and
- plan and deliver a speech that both entertains and enlightens an audience.

Defining the Speech to Entertain

A **speech to entertain** is a high-energy presentation that requires focus on your audience as well as concentration on your subject, appearance, and actions. It can rely on words, anecdotes, bodily actions, gestures, voice, speech construction, special devices, demonstrations, unusual situations, pantomime, or any combination of these. Occasions for humorous speeches are dinners, club meetings, special assemblies, parties, and other social gatherings.

Advanced preparation and practice are critical to the success of this type of speech. You must tailor the content to fit the audience and the occasion. Outline your speech and make sure you have a captivating introduction—one that grabs and holds the audience's attention.

The body of the speech must be appropriate to the occasion and fit your style of delivery and sense of humor. Your comic timing, gestures, and facial expressions will be important to the effectiveness of your delivery.

Your conclusion should leave your audience wanting more of your speech. However, it's also important for the conclusion to sum up the key points that you want the audience to remember.

Some speeches make listeners laugh uproariously; others produce only chuckles and snickers; and still others bring forth only small smiles. It is important to understand that a humorous speech does not necessarily have to be hilarious to be entertaining.

The special feature of a humorous speech is that it builds humorous situations that develop a line of thought or an idea. The speaker is not required to ask the audience to take any action or to make the audience feel closely related to the subject. That said, a humorous speech *might* do more than simply entertain. There is nothing to prevent a humorous speech from being informative, stimulating, or convincing, provided none of these goals become the chief aim of the speech, which is to entertain. The thought or ideas presented are the core of the speech around which the humor is built.

Choosing a Topic

Keep in mind the five elements that govern the selection of any speech topic: (1) the audience, (2) the occasion, (3) the speaker, (4) the speech itself, and (5) the surroundings in which the speech will be given. Your choice of a topic must be keyed to these controlling factors. Of course, since you will be the speaker, the subject that you choose must be one you can present with confidence.

Other factors to keep in mind when choosing a topic are the time allowed for preparation, the availability of materials from which to build the speech, your own personality, your ability to present certain kinds of material and ideas, and your type of presentation. You should make your choice of topic with all of these considerations in mind. The following ideas should stimulate your thinking.

- Why people laugh
- Embarrassing moments
- School-related moments
- Learning to cook
- Getting a pet to the vet
- Finding an old diary
- Parents really *are* people
- Superstitions
- Learning to drive

Preparing

As in the preparation of any good speech, pay particular attention to the organization of your main points, the arrangement of materials, and your rehearsals. Keep your purpose, to entertain, clearly in mind. Along with the basics of good speech preparation, there is one other ingredient to this speech—humor. Unless you are a natural-born comedian, the need to be funny can put even more pressure than normal on a novice speaker. There are, however, some time-tested approaches. To achieve humor, try the following.

1. Tell a joke on yourself.

2. Tell a joke on someone in the group (but don't embarrass the person) or some well-known person.

3. Make reference to the speech situation, or a local, state, or national issue.

4. Make reference to the occasion or other similar occasions.

5. Associate a speech with past incidents.

6. Imitate members of the group, or local, state, national, or world figures. (You should never be insulting. Keep the comments light.)

7. Use exaggeration.

8. Use deliberate underestimation.

9. Allow yourself some sudden changes of thought.

10. Share with the audience some surprising thoughts.

11. Use a humorous afterthought tacked to the end of an otherwise serious statement.

12. Twist some of your own ideas or the ideas of others. (Do not overdo this.)

13. Deliberately misinterpret facts or figures for effect.

14. Make intentional errors for effect. (This must be done very skillfully.)

15. Intentionally place yourself in a humorous situation.

16. Deliberately misquote someone present or a well-known authority. (Be discreet—you want to be funny, not insulting.)

20. Give examples that are entertaining or that make an amusing point.

21. Impersonate a character (but do not make your whole speech an impersonation).

22. Demonstrate or overly dramatize a point.

23. Concoct new words, apply certain words to new situations, or give them new meanings. Join two or more words together with hyphens; then apply them to your speech.

24. Be quick to adapt your opening remarks to include the slips of the tongue of other speakers. Do not overwork this device or it will become tiresome; be appropriate.

25. Talk about people in public life, international situations, and recent happenings in the news in an entertaining way.

26. Think about and implement the strategies talk show hosts employ in their opening monologues.

27. Shakespeare said, "Brevity is the soul of wit." Don't let your speech go on past the point of the audience's interest.

28. Cue the audience to your speech's special moments by changing the tone of your voice slightly, then segue into the next sequence.

17. Restate a well-known quotation to give it a humorous twist.

18. Use humorous facial expressions and/or grimaces.

19. Use anecdotes.

To practice your comic timing, you may need to study comedy material and be prepared to practice with your instructor. And it goes without saying that ample rehearsal is absolutely vital. What could be worse than a speaker attempting to be funny while searching for cues from notes?

Your humorous speech should not degenerate into a series of unrelated funny stories, nor should it consist of merely telling a single story. If you use anecdotes as illustrations, they must apply to the theme of the speech or in some way assist you in making your point.

After you construct a clever and interesting introduction, develop your remarks in a logical order. Bolster these points with examples, illustrations, facts, quotations from authorities, and analogies. Finally, create a conclusion to your speech that is the appropriate cap for everything you said in the speech.

How will you know that your speech is entertaining? The answer is that you won't—not until you get in front of your audience. The only insurance you have is your preparation. Your own ingenuity and intelligence are your best assets when it comes to preparing a humorous speech. Use these inherent personal resources well and you will have little to worry about.

Presenting

The speech to entertain is characterized by a generally lively presentation. The speech should proceed with a smooth flow. Use pauses and hesitations for effect. If you get laughs, stop speaking until the moment when the laughter crests. As it is waning, begin speaking again. Try not to laugh at your own jokes.

It is necessary, however, that you enjoy the audience and the occasion. Try to hit each punch line at the right moment and then move on to the next one.

And finally, always try to leave your audience wanting more.

Evaluating

Evaluate a classmate's speech to entertain. Be prepared to give oral feedback to the speaker on the following questions.

- Was the speaker enthusiastic about the subject?
- Did the speaker use eye contact to connect with the audience?
- Did the speaker use some of the methods listed on pages 152–153 of this lesson?
- Did the speaker deliver the speech with authority?
- Did the speaker hold for laughs?
- Were the speaker's gestures and facial expressions appropriate to the material?

When you share your thoughts with the speaker, remember to avoid being overly negative. Begin your comments by citing something the speaker did well. Tell him or her about what entertained, amused, and interested you. Try to be specific and cite examples whenever you can. Confine your more negative comments to two or three constructive examples.

Example Speech

The Plight of the Onion

by John E. Koch

Ordinarily, ladies and gentlemen, I am a very peaceful individual. It requires an event of great importance to stir my peaceful nature. Lately, such an event has come to pass. I must speak out in defense of my convictions, for silence would prove me a traitor not only to my own generation, but also to generations to come. I cannot display indifference when the issue demands enthusiasm.

Just what is this issue that stirs the hearts of men to take arms against that sea of troubles and by opposing, end them? I do not feel that I am unique in being affected by this onslaught on human liberty. You, ladies and gentlemen, have also been touched by this debasement of our customs and traditions. What is this menace of which I speak that poses such a threat to all that we hold so dear? Is it a green-eyed fire-spouting monster from Mars, or a creature from the moon? No, it is not. It is one of our own kind. It is referred to as a scientist.

It will suffice to mention no names since we must judge them by their works. The intrusion of these people on our liberties has caused many to sound the call to arms; for when we are enveloped by that sea of troubles, we must fight back or swim.

The scene of attack is Idaho State University. There, a group of scientists, as they call themselves, have been secretly experimenting, unbelievable as it may seem, to deprive the onion of its cooking odor. In some secret cache are hidden away thousands of odorless onions, the first line of odor-free American vegetables.

Picture the onion without its smell, and you deprive millions of Americans of a familiar fragrance that signals the secrets of the coming meal. To remove its odor is to destroy all that is dear to it—its personality. The thought is enough to bring tears to one's eyes.

Although this is bad enough, the scientists will not stop here. They will not remain content with having removed the odor from the onion, but with their long tentacles they will reach out farther into the realm of life. What will be next—the smell of cooking cabbage, the grit of spinach, the hot of peppers, and soon the removal of color and taste? Will our diet become a mass of odorless, tasteless, colorless nourishment? It might, if we do not arise and take arms to prevent this calamity. I beg you to rally defenders to the cause of the onion.

As Americans, we must demand the onion with its odor, the spinach with its grit, the pepper with its hot. Let us not sit here idly any longer. Arise and carry that plea to all Americans. Keep the scientist out of the kitchen; keep the onion out of the college.

The After-dinner Speech

Specs for the After-dinner Speech

Time limit

5 minutes.

Speaker's notes

None.

Sources of information

Two are required. For each source, give the specific magazine, book, news story, or Internet site from which it was taken. If a source is a person, identify him or her by title, position, and occupation. List these on the outline form. For Internet sources, give the address (URL).

Outline

Prepare a 75- to 150-word complete sentence outline.

Speak Up!

Either think of a speech given after a dinner or banquet you attended or ask an adult to tell you about an after-dinner speech he or she has experienced. In small groups or as a class, list the kinds of topics that seem to be most common for this type of speaking. Then decide which topics would be interesting and which would be boring. How could the boring topics be made more appealing?

Purpose and Expectations of This Assignment

One of the best ways to learn anything is to experience it. From the experience of preparing this speech assignment, you will gain firsthand knowledge of after-dinner speaking. You will see how a program is arranged, how the serving of food and drink is coordinated with the speeches, and how the toastmaster or master of ceremonies keeps events moving along.

In completing this assignment, you will

- understand how an after-dinner program is arranged,
- identify the duties of a toastmaster or master of ceremonies,
- determine an appropriate purpose for an after-dinner speech, and
- adapt a speech topic to a specific setting.

Defining the After-dinner Speech

An **after-dinner speech** is a talk following a meal at which a group has gathered. The speech may have a serious purpose or it may be designed to give entertainment and pleasure. The type of speech that you present depends on your purpose. The speech is also governed by the occasion, its objective, and the reason for your remarks. There are all kinds of different occasions for the after-dinner speech. It may be a business luncheon, club dinner, committee meeting, special breakfast, promotional gathering, campaign inauguration, social celebration, anniversary, or any one of a dozen other occasions.

Choosing a Topic

Decide on the purpose of your speech. Be sure you can develop your topic to fulfill that purpose. Select something suitable and interesting to you that is easily adapted to both the occasion and the audience. As with any other speech, plan your topic well in advance. Here are some ideas.

- Best friends
- Gender communication
- A success story
- Of all the sad words
- Ten years from now
- A better world for all
- Raising parents

Preparing

You will need to study this assignment carefully to learn the requirements of successful after-dinner speaking. You will use information you have studied previously relative to speech organization, wording, and practice. Plan to use no notes. If you are a **toastmaster** or **master of ceremonies**, knowledge of and preparation for your task will be the only insurance you need for a successful performance.

After-dinner speaking takes place, of course, within the context of a meal being served. Keep in mind that most people listen less well just after eating, so after-dinner speeches do not generally include critically important information. More frequently, after-dinner speeches are designed to entertain and celebrate the occasion for the dinner or the special guests present. That said, an after-dinner speech certainly *can* impart information or persuasion, but those are secondary purposes in most cases. This chapter will provide you with the opportunity to design appropriate remarks for such an occasion, as well as understand the complexities of planning the event.

Having figured out your subject and the manner in which you will treat it, complete the preparation of your speech carefully. Before you consider yourself fully prepared, find out all you can about the program at which you will speak, the estimated time at which you will speak, who will precede you, and who will follow you. Use all this information to ensure that your speech is in line with the occasion.

It is not necessary and certainly not always advisable to tell a joke on the toastmaster or master of ceremonies, regardless of what he or she may say during your introduction. If the occasion calls for humor, you should be ready to meet it. If you're in doubt as to how to respond, play it safe. Good taste never offends. As far as risqué stories go, leave them at home. Do not tell jokes about race or religion.

The conclusion is an extremely important part of an after-dinner speech. You want to leave the audience with a strong impression and a feeling of enjoyment and satisfaction. Summaries are the most common type of conclusion. If you use

a summary conclusion, be brief and recap only the main points. Attention-getting materials or anecdotes also make effective conclusions.

Review your introduction and see if there is a way to tie the conclusion to it. For instance, if you quote a famous person in the introduction, refer back to the quotation to summarize or quote a similar thought from the same or a different person.

Always keep in mind the purpose of the speech as you develop your conclusion. If the purpose is to persuade, an appeal at the end may be effective. If the purpose is to entertain, an amusing story may be the most effective.

To complete the preparation of the after-dinner speech, you should practice aloud several times in front of a mirror or use a tape recorder. It's sometimes a good idea to solicit a friend or family member to watch you give your speech. Then you must be willing to listen to advice or criticism, but make sure that such feedback is valid before you incorporate it into your speaking.

It is the obligation of the toastmaster or master of ceremonies to see that everything is ready to go, to open the proceedings, to keep them on schedule, and to close the meeting.

First, to arrange everything, the toastmaster should arrive at the meeting place at least an hour early. Then he or she should perform the following duties.

1. Advise the servers in detail as to how the meal is to be served.

2. Note the arrangement of the banquet room and suggest any changes you think appropriate.

3. Inquire about a checkroom or other space for coats, and then make certain it is available and ready for use.

4. Locate restrooms and be ready to direct people to them.

5. Shortly before serving time, personally check place cards on the tables to be sure that there are enough.

6. Keep careful track of the guests as they enter so that you will know when everyone has arrived.

7. If the group must initially wait in the lobby, indicate when they are to go into the dining hall. If everyone has previously gathered in the dining room, be the first to seat yourself. That will signal to the others that they should follow your example.

8. Your general duty will be to welcome your guests (or assign someone else to do so), introduce them, advise them on what to do with their coats, and put them at ease.

9. During the banquet, remain alert to make sure everything goes well.

10. See that the committee pays for the banquet or makes definite arrangements to settle the account later. Also see that a tip is left for the servers. Of course, when there are several toastmasters, these duties may be divided among them. Everyone should know the specifics of what they are to do. That way they can carry out each obligation conscientiously.

With regard to introducing the speakers, you and your fellow toastmasters must gather considerable information several days in advance. This includes the names of the speakers, their topics, biographical information for introducing each speaker, and the order of the speakers.

All of this information must be drawn together at a toastmasters' meeting and mutually agreed upon. The act of introducing the speakers requires ingenuity and planning. A toastmaster should *not* make a speech. This pleasure belongs to the after-dinner speakers. The toastmaster merely presents each speaker by giving a short introduction. Thirty seconds usually suffices—sometimes less—but never more than a minute or two. The introduction may include the speaker's name and topic and perhaps a clever statement or two about him or her. Depending on the occasions, a brief anecdote may be in order. After the speaker concludes, the toastmaster should thank the speaker and the guests for attending.

Presenting

As an after-dinner speaker, your presentation should reflect the type of speech you deliver. In general, a simple organization, graphic word pictures, sufficient humor, lively and animated delivery, and a forward progression of ideas characterize after-dinner speeches.

Dress, voice, and body language should be in harmony with the occasion and environment. Speak loudly to be heard by every person in the room. Be careful not to scrape your chair across the floor when you rise to speak. To prevent this, see that your chair is far enough from the table so that you may rise freely without moving it. When the chairperson, toastmaster, or master of ceremonies introduces you, rise and address him or her according to position and gender—for example, "Thank you, Mr. Toastmaster," or "Thank you, Madam President."

Evaluating

Critique a classmate's after-dinner speech. Use the following criteria:

- Was the purpose(s) of the speech clear?

- Was the speech appropriate for the occasion?

- Was the speech preparation based on good standards learned in previous lessons?

- Did the speaker use appropriate tone and body language?

- Did the conclusion of the speech leave the audience with a strong impression and a feeling of satisfaction?

Example Speech

What Is Most Important?

by Tim Borchers

I was walking down the street one day when this weird-looking bearded guy wearing a toga approached me. "You may be just the person I am looking for to carry out my quest." I walked faster, but he chased after me. "You are to tell the world of terrible destruction. The citizens of the world don't know how to think anymore." He looked real intense and kind of sad, so I let him continue. "The citizens believe everything told to them by bad people. There is only one way to save the world from pending doom. Someone must teach the world how to think again." I was wary. "Can I do that?" I asked. He replied, "You must at least try."

My buddy Plato once theorized people would blindly accept society's versions of importance, truth, and reality without critically evaluating these ideas. Unfortunately, we do. Now we must begin to examine what we often take for granted. We must understand, first, how we allow capitalists to tell us what is important; second, how we permit society to tell us what is true; and finally, how we rely on the media to tell us what is happening in the world.

I was sitting in my civics class one day and, in between naps, I caught the teacher asking, "Anyone, anyone? Who can tell me the implications of the Supreme Court case *Mapp vs. Ohio*?" The guy sitting next to me, wearing a "Property of the Football Team" sweatshirt, raised his huge hand and said,

"Uh . . . 15 yards and a loss of down?" I thought, "Football player; he's dumb." Then I thought for a minute. "In six years, he will have been drafted by the pros, making a million dollars a year. I'll be graduating from college, $50,000 in debt. *I'm dumb!*" Then I started to question our society. "Why do Madonna, Bill Cosby, and Donald Trump all make more money than our teachers?"

In the beginning of time, or when TV was first invented, same difference, these people became famous by appearing on the tube. As soon as they became famous, they started advertising products for capitalists. Advertising for capitalists made these people rich and consequently important. Let's face it, since teachers are never on TV or in the movies, they don't get corporate endorsements, and voila!—they aren't important. Could you imagine? "Hi! I'm Tim Borchers, former student, now I'm a teacher. When it comes to shoes, I wear Nike Wing Tips. When it comes to education, just do it!"

By now you're thinking, "I can't play football and I'm not a money-grubbing unethical capitalist swine. So how do I know what's important?" First, we need to write our representatives and senators. Tell them to support legislation abolishing capitalism!

I don't suppose that will work, so let's make it simple: **think**! Don't accept the societal hierarchy created by capitalists. Stand up and say "Teachers are more important than football players." Establish for yourself what is important.

But knowing what's important is not enough. We must also see how society is full of stereotypes—society's statements of truth. I asked Plato when stereotypes started. He said he didn't know. So I turned to Dr. Seuss. Dr. Seuss said,

> "Once there were two kinds of people in the world. The star-bellied sneetches had bellies with stars. The plain-bellied sneetches had none upon thars. When the star-bellied sneetches went out to play ball, could a plain belly get in the game? Not at all!"

We haven't advanced very far from the days of the sneetches. Television and movies perpetuate stereotypes until we don't know what's true.

Fortunately, there is a solution. Critically evaluate what society says. That's right, we have to think. Don't start stereotypes. Don't repeat stereotypes. And if you hear someone repeating a stereotype, tell them to knock it off. Tell them to solve the greenhouse effect, make world peace, or go read a book.

You're asking, "What's the final thing we do without thinking?" It is this: we accept the media's perspective of what's happening in the world. Doris Graber, in her book *Mass Media and American Politics,* argues that the press indicates how much importance we should attach to public issues. This is called the media's agenda-setting function.

You won't know what's going on in the world by reading news magazines, so you must determine what's important based on what *you* think and not the amount of press an issue gets. A social studies instructor of mine once said, "Develop your perception of reality based on information-gathering from a cross-section of media." Sorry, spending five minutes reading *USA Today* won't work.

We've reached a point where we don't know what's important, "true," or "really" happening in the world. Rather depressing, but here's some advice: Don't let the Donald Trumps of the world think for you. Cognate, muse, ponder, meditate, create, don't watch so much TV, read a book, don't eat sweets, wear your seatbelt. And above all, remember the ideals that make our country great—knowledge, discipline, and individuality.

Nomination to Office and Acceptance Speeches

John F. Kennedy accepts the Democratic party's nomination for president, 1960.

Specs for Nomination to Office and Acceptance Speeches

Time limit
2–3 minutes. Keep your speech within the allotted time.

Speaker's notes
Do not use notes for this assignment.

Sources of information
To nominate someone else, simply be accurate in your statements regarding the person's qualifications. To accept a nomination, you are the only source needed.

Outline
Prepare a 50- to 100-word complete sentence outline.

Speak Up!

As a class, brainstorm some humorous "positions" that need filling around your school such as "Spitball Bowl Chairperson" or "Vice-President of the Chronically Tardy." Then have individual students give a brief speech nominating classmates to one of the offices. (Be funny, not mean or insulting.) Next, the person nominated must give his or her acceptance speech.

Purpose and Expectations of This Assignment

Nominating an individual for a leadership position sometimes requires remarks that inspire confidence in voters. For this assignment, you will have a chance both to nominate someone to an office with appropriate efforts to establish the candidate's credibility, and to accept a nomination or election with sincerity, assuring voters that they have made a good choice.

In completing this assignment, you will

- determine an appropriate candidate for a particular office;

- generate arguments that will establish confidence in the candidate;

- organize and present the speech in a clear, concise, and confident manner; and

- identify the necessary elements for a speech of acceptance.

Defining Nominating and Acceptance Speeches

A **nominating speech** is one in which a speaker places the name of another person before an assembly as a candidate for office. Before you can make a nomination, the chairperson of the assembly must announce that nominations are in order, and you the nominator must be formally recognized to speak. Once you have been recognized, your speech should be limited to just a few minutes.

In presenting a candidate to the audience, you should provide a brief background and tell why the candidate is especially suited for the office in question. Be sure to say you are nominating

"[name of the person]" to the position. Do not leave the audience guessing who the nominee might be or to which position you are nominating him or her.

An **acceptance speech** in which you accept a nomination for an office is one in which you publicly recognize your own nomination. Your purpose is to give the audience confidence in you. An occasion of this sort is potentially important; anything you say may be used for or against you. If you are surprised by the nomination, it is wise not to say anything about your lack of preparation for you could easily say the wrong thing.

Choosing a Topic

For a nominating speech, think about organizations to which you belong and decide on a person you would like to nominate as an officer. Another possible choice is to nominate a person for a political office. You can research campaign literature to help you. You must have confidence in the ability of the person you nominate. Be sure that he or she is acceptable as a candidate. Choose someone reasonably well known with a good record.

For an acceptance speech, base your remarks on your own interest in the topic/organization and in the suitability to your audience. Think about the clubs and organizations to which you and your classmates belong. If you hold an office or have held one, re-create that situation.

Preparing

When you speak at a special occasion, there is usually a particular context that frames the speaking experience. Each situation comes with particular traditions and social etiquette that creates a unique atmosphere for both presenter and audience.

Proper etiquette at a special occasion dictates good manners and a willingness to engage in conversation. Definitely be a few minutes early and be prepared to follow the schedule set by the chairperson even if it changes at the last possible second.

Be positive about the occasion in your conversation and in your formal speech. You can introduce appropriate humor along with historical facts; however, most of these occasions will be semiformal events that are steeped in tradition.

You must be very careful to follow the tradition of the event and not violate its inherent rules of order.

In the nominating speech, all of the elements should point in one direction: Elect this candidate! Organize the speech carefully. Name the office and set forth its specific requirements and needs. Then show that your candidate has exceptional qualifications to satisfy the needs and demands of the office. Be specific. Mention training, experience, leadership abilities, and outstanding character traits. Clinch your point by summarizing and stating that these issues are the issues to consider when choosing a candidate.

When you make an acceptance speech, be sure to adhere to all the usual rules for preparing a speech. Since the purpose of this speech is to establish yourself as a leader, speak in well-chosen words of appreciation for the honor conferred on you by the nomination or election. Do not talk about yourself; rather, speak of the organization and its importance. Commend its history, its achievements, and its principles. Explain how these have made it grow and will continue to operate in the future. You may refer to the names of great people of past fame in the organization and promise to uphold their ideals. Finally, pledge your loyalty and support to the organization.

State frankly that you accept the nomination or office with a complete realization of its responsibilities, which you fully intend to carry out. It would be appropriate to make a concluding remark repeating your appreciation of the honor. Be brief. Going on too long might make your audience feel they have made a mistake!

Assuming that you know ahead of time that you will be nominated, rehearse your speech aloud until you have the sequence of ideas well in mind. Give particular attention to the introduction and conclusion.

Presenting

You must have confidence in yourself. Your attitude should be one of dignity, friendliness, sincerity, and enthusiasm. Pay attention to your appearance. Make sure it is appropriate to the occasion and the audience.

The words of your speech must be vivid, descriptive, and meaningful. Talk loudly enough to be heard by everyone in the room. Speak clearly and at a pace that is neither too fast nor too slow. Aim for a fluency and readiness of speech. This will help the audience to have confidence in you.

Your entire body must manifest your emphasis, spontaneity, and sincerity. Your appearance, actions, and manner must work together to persuade the audience that you are worthy of the honor. Naturally you should avoid giving the appearance of being overly confident, overbearing, or conceited. Have a lively, energetic, unhesitant manner, as well as a pleasant confident voice and a sincere desire to communicate.

Evaluating

Rate a classmate's nomination or acceptance speech. Use the questions below to guide your review.

Nomination

- Did the speaker explain why the candidate is especially suited for the position?
- Was the speaker's tone and body language appropriate for the occasion?
- Was the speech well-organized?
- Did the speaker give you enough information about the nominee?

Acceptance

- Did the speaker exhibit self-confidence?
- Did the speaker express appreciation for the honor of being nominated?
- Did he/she talk about the organization rather than herself/himself?
- Could the speaker be heard by all audience members?

Example Speech

Nominating Speech

by John R. Knorr

In the past years, the Medical Practice Board of Missouri has made many innovative moves, a few of which have been nationwide firsts. These moves have often been spearheaded by a single person. Tonight I am pleased to nominate Nell Healy, R.N., to be chairperson of the Allied Health Advisory Committee. Ms. Healy, through her work as Head of Nursing at Washington University Hospital, has seen the health-care field from many sides. She not only has the foresight the chairmanship demands, but also the experience to convert the future into the present. Ms. Healy was at the head of the lobby for the Nurse Training Act that was adopted by the Missouri Legislature last month.

Ms. Healy has shown the board that there is more to the health-care field than patient care in understaffed hospitals. There are dedicated people today who would go into the nursing field if only given the chance. This is because the most vital programs of Nursing Education can't presently give them that chance.

As chairman of the Allied Health Advisory Committee, Ms. Healy will be an advisor to the Missouri Legislature on health-care matters. She will be at the head of a branch of the Medical Practice Board that everyone will be proud to represent.

Ms. Healy has shown through her expressed views that the patient and the patient's health are our highest priorities. This post needs a chair with this outlook. For these reasons I am proud to put before the board Ms. Nell Healy for nomination to be chairperson of the Allied Health Advisory Committee.

Example Speech

Accepting a Nomination

by Tom J. Mayer

Mr. President, officers, and fellow members of FFA, all of you are dedicated to a purpose which can be realized: The purpose of strengthening the agricultural backbone of our country and restoring the farm family to its rightful position. We have seen our parents and grandparents toil long hours to nurture life in once fallow tracts of land. The recognition they deserve still lies fallow, but the Future Farmers of America are seeking more than the vision of our parents—we are seeking the culmination of world events that must place the fruits of our labor in utmost demand.

The heritage of the farmer in this country is rich. Cities, towns, even countries have been fed, and they receive the fruit of our greatest office, that of provider. Each one of us stands in the gap as provider for the world. Let us stand boldly in recognition of the office handed us by our parents, and make them as proud to be called our parents as we are to be called their children.

The nomination to the office of national president of Future Farmers of America is a special privilege, and one I accept with much pride and appreciation. The challenge demanded by this position is great, not only because of the decisions concerning future operations, but because of the standards realized by all of you. I accept this nomination with confidence in the foundation of our heritage and the progressive attitude of our membership.

Example Speech

Accepting an Office

by Mary-Alice Shaw

President Ugaki, members of the board, and delegates: Three years ago I was attracted to the Intermountain Hospice Support Group for personal reasons. I admired the unique combination of compassion and profession-alism evident within the organization, and I appreciated the fact that your support existed for those of us left to deal with terminal ill-ness at some level in our lives.

As I look around at those of you here today, I see the past three years reflected back at me. I see the tears shared, the small joys experienced, and the patience and under-standing given so readily and so often. I see a concept that has grown and flourished and gained validity and worldwide recognition.

I have endeavored to contribute as much of my abilities and talents and time as I could toward our common goals, and I have been proud to be a part of the whole. The challenges have been difficult, the failures few but palpable, and the satisfactions many. But the people involved have impressed me the most.

I've come to respect each of you with whom I've worked for your cooperative spirit, extensive knowledge, and extreme caring. Your willingness to teach me what you could was gratifying. Your criticisms were valid and offered in a constructive manner. You supported my ideas and projects, and you gave me that important pat on the back for encouragement when I needed it most. This

has all provided me with one of the most positive work environments imaginable, and I thank you for that.

Just when I thought I had the best of situations, you topped it by asking me to accept the position of Regional Coordinator. I'm pleased and humbled by the realization that you think I can do this most important job for you and do it well.

We have difficult decisions ahead of us. There are many questions on controversial subjects to be answered. There are sensitive ethical and moral realities to be faced. I appreciate your confidence in my ability to make those decisions wisely.

I willingly accept that challenge. I am excited by the responsibilities that await us, and I know that together we can accomplish so much in the field of terminal care giving. I am honored to be able to represent you as your Regional Coordinator. Thank you.

The
Introduction Speech

First Lady Hillary Clinton is introduced by Soha Arafat, wife of Palestinian leader Yasser Arafat.

Specs for the Introduction Speech

Time limit

1–2 minutes.

Speaker's notes

Use key ideas, dates, events, or quotations only.

Sources of information

For this assignment, you may use a real person or a fictitious one. If you choose a real person, be sure to check your facts and ascertain the pronunciation of the person's name.

Outline

Prepare a 50- to 100-word complete sentence outline.

Speak Up!

Ask a classmate the following three questions:

1. What is your full name?
2. What is your favorite leisure activity?
3. Name one thing you believe in.

Take notes on your classmate's answers. Then introduce your classmate to the rest of the class. Try to make the information sound as interesting and positive as possible.

Purpose and Expectations of This Assignment

At some point in their lives, most people will be asked to give an introduction speech. An untrained speaker can sometimes pull this off and present a decent introduction. But too often, an introduction speech can be haphazard and embarrassing. This not only makes the introducer look bad, it also weakens programs that feature lecturers. Of all the types of speeches you may make in the future, it is likely that at least one will be the introduction of a featured speaker. This assignment will provide an introduction speech experience to get you started.

In completing this assignment, you will

- understand how to set the tone of a speaking event for another speaker;

- be able to establish the credibility of another speaker with the audience; and

- identify and locate the information that may be required in an introduction.

Defining the Introduction Speech

An **introduction speech** is one in which a chairperson or someone else introduces a speaker to an audience. The purpose is to bring audience and speaker together in the proper spirit. The introduction should provide the speaker's name and build the audience's interest in the subject. The introduction should be just long enough to make the audience and speaker feel comfortably acquainted. And finally, it should put the speaker at ease.

As an introducer, you should avoid attempts at being humorous. Never embarrass the speaker by heaping on too much praise or by belittling

him or her in any way. In introducing a speaker, you should not call attention to yourself. You should never say or do anything that might detract from what the speaker will say. There is an old adage in public speaking that states "Get up, speak up, shut up." An introducer can hardly go wrong in following this advice.

Choosing a Topic

For this assignment you will have to decide what type of imaginary audience and occasion you want to use. You will also have to decide the identity of the specific person you plan to introduce. Be sure that your speaker is a suitable fit with your chosen occasion. You may choose someone you know, someone whose work or career is familiar to you, or an imaginary person. Some possible situations for a speech of introduction include

- a college president to a high school audience,

- the mayor to a public gathering,

- a war hero to a school assembly,

- a Hollywood celebrity to your school, and

- a sports star to an athletic awards banquet.

Preparing

In preparing this speech, you may draw your information from four sources: the speaker, the subject, the audience, or the occasion. Not all of these may be necessary in every speech; however, in many cases each is a suitable, if not a required, source. The material must be accurate and pertinent.

You will construct your introduction speech from the four sources just mentioned and a fifth, yourself. Short though this speech is, you must make it count. So organize and arrange it carefully by selecting only the most important bits of information.

First of all, know how to pronounce the speaker's name correctly. Find out about the speaker's background to decide what you might share with the audience during the introduction. This may concern the speaker's education, special training, travel experience, honors and awards, membership in organizations, important positions, books written, or any other achievements. You should know the topic of the speaker's speech. As with the speaker's name, you must get it right. But you should say nothing about the speech that might "steal the thunder" of the remarks. Be familiar with the dynamic of the audience and the event.

Before you set your ideas, confer with the person you are going to introduce if possible, and, in conference, arrive at a definite understanding regarding what you plan to say in your introduction. Once this has been resolved, rehearse aloud until you are confident that you are thoroughly prepared.

Presenting

When the moment arrives for you to introduce the speaker of the event, rise calmly, take your place on the platform, pause until the assembly grows quiet, and then deliberately address the audience loudly enough for all to hear. Don't strain; keep your voice natural, and make sure you have enough breath to support your words. You may say, "Ladies and gentlemen," or use some other **salutation** or form of introduction appropriate to the audience and the occasion. Your body language and gestures should be limited.

Keep in mind your role in the occasion. People did not come to hear you or see you. You are a small but necessary cog in the wheel of events surrounding the speaker. Your poise, confidence, and appropriate but brief remarks are all that will be expected or wanted from you. You may greet the audience and mention the occasion. Do not make any remarks about the audience.

At the moment you present the speaker, announce his or her name and subject as follows: "I am happy to present (full name), who will address you (or speak to you) today on (subject)." Then turn to the speaker and say his or her name. You may bow slightly or nod and take your seat when the speaker rises and approaches the front of the platform.

If you are chairperson of the assembly, it will be appropriate for you to express publicly the audience's appreciation of the speaker at the conclusion of the address.

Evaluating

Evaluate a classmate's introduction speech. Rate the following criteria on a scale from 1 to 5 with 1 being "needs much improvement" and 5 being "outstanding."

- Did the introducer use appropriate vocal tone and volume?
- Did the introducer limit gestures and bodily actions?
- Did the introducer keep the speech succinct?
- Was the introducer able to provide a few interesting details about the speaker?
- Did the introducer structure the speech with a logical progression?
- Did the introducer deliver the speech with authority?

Example Speech

Introduction of Bill Gates, Chairman, Microsoft Corporation

by James Stukel, President, University of Illinois

February 24, 2004

One of the pleasures of being president of a great university is the opportunity to meet extraordinary men and women who come to our campus to inform, to entertain, to provoke, and to instruct our community of scholars and students learning to be scholars. It is my guess, Bill Gates will do all of these.

We at the University of Illinois are very proud to be the first stop on Bill Gates' Five Campus Tour. The other schools are Harvard, MIT, Carnegie-Mellon, and Cornell. I think the students there, your counterparts in Cambridge, and Pittsburgh, and Ithaca, are as excited as we are to hear Bill Gates share his perspective on issues and computing, and perhaps give us a glimpse into the future.

Before I introduce him, I would like to remind you that computing is deeply embedded in the culture of this campus, and we are proud to say we have maintained our edge. Our students, faculty and staff enjoy more than 47,000 network connections by which we connect to the world, and people connect to us. More than 1 million times a week, people log on to the online catalogue of the University of Illinois Library, which is the third, only to Harvard and Yale, in size of its collection. And this campus is a giant in research and development in science and engineering. We have more than 80 centers,

labs, and institutes where important, life-altering work is under way. Among them is the widely known National Center for Supercomputing Applications, which is helping to build the future of high performance cyber infrastructure. And this new office here at the far edge of the campus is the Beckman Institute for Science and Technology where 600 researchers collaborate. And finally I would be remiss not to mention the investments in R&D that brought us to the happy place of having two of our faculty members win Nobel Prizes.

As you know, they are Paul Lauterbur, who was awarded the Nobel Prize in Medicine for his groundbreaking work on the MRI, and Tony Leggett, Nobel Prize winner for pioneering theoretical work in understanding super fluid.

But that's enough about us; it's time that we move on to our guest this evening. You are here to see Bill Gates, the Chairman and Chief Software Architect of Microsoft Corporation. As you know, Microsoft is the worldwide leader in software, services, and Internet technology for personal and business computing. Last year's revenues topped $32 billion, and the company employed 55,000 people in 85 countries. And Mr. Gates is an iconic figure in contemporary computing.

While attending Harvard, Bill Gates and his childhood friend Paul Allen started Microsoft and launched a revolution. The fledgling company was more interesting than the classroom for Bill Gates, so he dropped out in his junior year. In his case, it was clearly a great decision. He not only built a company, but more importantly he built a vision. Both were built on the idea that the computer would be a valuable tool on every office desk, in every home, and that software was key. The penetration of personal computing in our businesses, our offices, our public libraries, on the train or on the plane, and in our home is astonishing and truly reflects the Bill Gates view that if the software is right, they will come.

Bill Gates also is an author of two books. One of them, *Business at the Speed of Thought*, is available in 60 nations and 25 languages. It shows how computer technology can solve business problems in fundamentally new ways. By the way, the proceeds of both books are donated to nonprofits that support the use of technology in education and skill development.

Since he is a man on the edge, it makes sense that Bill Gates also has invested in biotechnology, one of the most exciting frontiers in science, and you probably have heard that he and his wife Melinda have endowed a foundation with $24 billion. Their generosity extends to global health, technology for public libraries that serve low-income neighborhoods in the U.S. and Canada, and a variety of other community and special projects. He's an avid reader, a golfer, and a bridge player. He is a household name, a visionary, a philanthropist, and tonight he is our guest. So please join me in giving an Illinois welcome to William H. "Bill" Gates.

Welcoming
and Response Speeches

Specs for Welcoming and Response Speeches

Time limit

1–3 minutes.

Speaker's notes

You won't really need notes for this assignment. If you decide to use them, stick with key ideas only.

Sources of information

None required. If you include sources, they may be real or fictitious.

Outline

Prepare a 50- to 100-word complete sentence outline.

Speak Up!

Share an experience in which you welcomed someone into your home, workplace, organization, or club. What did you say? How did you want the other person to feel? If you had to write a speech to welcome that person, what might you say?

Purpose and Expectations of This Assignment

The speech of welcome and its response occupy a place of importance in public speaking. They make up an integral part of public relations among groups that convene daily throughout the country. You will almost certainly be asked to give or respond to a speech of welcome at some time. This assignment will help you to be ready to promote goodwill when the opportunity arises.

In completing this assignment, you will

- learn how to promote friendship through a public speech,
- understand the importance of a response to a welcome, and
- identify common interests and values of hosts and guests.

Defining Welcoming and Response Speeches

A **speech of welcome** is one made publicly for the purpose of extending greetings and promoting friendship with an invited guest. The person being welcomed should feel sincerely wanted and believe that the hosts are delighted to have him or her there. Brevity, sincerity, geniality, and simplicity characterize this type of speech.

A **speech in response** to a welcome is simply a reply to the sentiments expressed by the host. Its purpose is to cement goodwill and friendship by expressing mutual feelings. It is short, courteous, and friendly. Often the response speech is impromptu in nature and as such places a burden of doing fast thinking and uttering logical thoughts on the person who presents it. It also demands sincerity and a respectful manner from the speaker. Practice in speech fundamentals will serve you well on such occasions as these.

Choosing a Topic

Select an occasion that interests you. Decide what organization you will represent and what position you hold within that group. Select one you know something about or one about which you can easily find information. Recall situations in which you have heard a speech of welcome and response, or select one of the following.

- A native son or daughter returns home to visit
- A newly elected school superintendent arrives in your community
- A banquet is held for new teachers
- The governor visits on state business
- New officers join the student council
- A sister city from another country sends a delegation to visit
- An organization holds a convention in your city

Preparing

First, keep clearly in mind the purpose of the occasion and the speech. If you are welcoming others, your purpose is to make guests feel comfortable, honored, and glad to be there. If you are responding to the welcome, your purpose is to express your appreciation of the hospitality that has been extended.

To welcome others, mention the organization you represent, its character, the work it is doing, and a few points of interest about it. Pay tribute to your guests for their work and tell of advantages they will gain by their visit. Note who the guests are, where they are from, and whom they represent. Comment briefly on interests your organization holds in common with them. Express anticipation of pleasant associations and mutual benefits. Invite your guests to feel at home and to participate fully in your community.

To respond to a welcome, address the hosts and those associated with them. Acknowledge the greeting of welcome and the hospitality of the organization. Express sincere thanks for the courtesies offered. Extend greetings from your own organization and mention that the occasion is mutually advantageous. Predict future, pleasant associations with the host organization. Mention that you have been made to feel most welcome and at home. Finally, thank your hosts again for their hospitality, extend best wishes, and be seated.

Presenting

Let the occasion govern your presentation. If it is formal, act and speak appropriately. If it is informal, adjust your remarks appropriately. In either case, be genuine. Feel what you say. Your attitude and demeanor must be a combination of appreciation and friendliness. Extend the same geniality you would to welcome people into your home or to be received in someone else's home.

Speak loudly enough to be heard. Use your normal voice as much as possible. Speak clearly. Pronounce all names distinctly and correctly. Smile pleasantly. Build your poise by maintaining an alert posture. Your language should be simple, vivid, appropriate, and devoid of slang or repetition. Be brief but complete.

Here are a few additional suggestions.

- Have a few serious thoughts in your speech even though the general atmosphere may be carefree.

- Do not resort to telling a series of anecdotes.

- Do not apologize. Accept your responsibility and meet it as a mature person by having something worthwhile to say.

Evaluating

Evaluate a classmate's speech of welcome or response. Rate the following criteria on a scale from 1 to 5.

- Was the speaker warm and friendly?

- Did the speaker seem genuine?

- Were the speaker's posture and body language appropriate?

- Were the speaker's words audible and clear?

Give an overall score to the speech. Then tell the speaker one element of the speech that you feel needs improvement. There may be several, but choose the element that you believe was weakest.

Example Speech

Welcome to Western America High

by Setits Raclile

Principal Rogers and delegates to the Seventh Regional Government Conference, it is my pleasure as senior class president to welcome you to our school, where we hope you will learn a lot and have a good time doing it. This is the first time you have honored Western America High School by selecting us as your host, and we are both proud and happy to have you here today.

Our achievements and our problems are no doubt similar to yours, and they make us either joyous or perplexed, depending on whether we are doing something notable or having trouble. I do believe, however, that every achievement by schools represented here today should be shared so that we may all benefit from each other's successes. And I believe just as strongly that we should discuss the problems we all face every year. By doing this, we can learn from each other how to improve our individual governments and thus improve our schools in this region.

I told you Western America High is pleased to have you as our guests—and to show you we really mean it, our school governing council has arranged free bus tours over Exhibition Scenic Drive during our afternoon recess. Just climb on a bus in the parking lot and you'll get the ride of your life with more hairpin curves and thrilling views than you ever dreamed of. Then tonight at eight o'clock in this building, there will be a delegates' dance with an outstanding band, which our students will attend to help make your evening more enjoyable.

Once again I want to tell you how glad we are that you are here. We will do our best to help you have a successful conference and a pleasant visit. Thus we will all profit greatly from this wonderful experience. When you leave tomorrow, we want you to take our friendship and best wishes with you, but until then have a good time and thank you for joining us.

Example Speech

Response to a Speech of Welcome

by Yenan Noscaasi

Fellow delegates and Principal Rogers, I want to thank Mr. Raclile for his most friendly remarks and tell him we do feel the sincere welcome he speaks of. Already there seems to be present among us a spirit of cooperation and strong desire to exchange information helpful to every school represented at this conference. I truly believe that if each of us can gain only one new idea from our various group meetings and the guest speakers, we will all return home with the satisfaction of having attained something worthwhile.

We all trust that our presence here will in a sense express the esteem we hold for Western America High School. It's a privilege to come here to share our experiences and thoughts with Western's students and delegates in their outstanding facilities. We can all see how much preparation they have made for us. Clearly they are doing everything possible to make this conference a success.

As representative-at-large from all schools present, I want to thank Western America High for arranging our housing and meals; also for the bus tour coming up this afternoon and the big dance tonight. I'm sure everyone will enjoy these events. By having a good time together and exchanging ideas, we will have a conference second to none. So to our hosts I want to say on behalf of all of us "thanks for everything."

Presenting
and Accepting Gifts
or Awards

Specs for Presenting and Accepting Gifts or Awards

Time limit
1–3 minutes.

Speaker's notes
For presenting, use key words only; do not use notes for accepting.

Sources of information
None required. If used, they may be real or fictitious.

Outline
Prepare a 50- to 75-word complete sentence outline.

Speak Up!

Share an experience when you had to thank someone for a gift or an honor. What did you say? Did you prepare your thoughts in advance? Alternately, think about a time when you were thanked for something. Did the speaker seem sincere? How could you tell?

Purpose and Expectations of This Assignment

Societies have used the ritual of publicly presenting gifts and awards for centuries. Every time such an occasion occurs, the person giving the honor must make a presentation speech. This in turn sets up the situation in which the recipient must say a few words of acceptance.

It isn't easy to make a public presentation or acceptance, to handle the situation with confidence, and to utter thoughts that reflect the spirit of the event. Yet over the course of your life, you will probably be asked to fulfill one or both of these duties at various times. This assignment is designed to help you know what to do on either occasion.

In completing this assignment, you will

- identify the appropriate elements in a speech to present or accept an award,
- understand the role of modesty and gratitude in accepting an award or gift, and
- recognize different types of occasions for acceptance or presentation speeches.

Defining Presentation and Acceptance Speeches

The Presentation Speech

An effective **presentation speech** is short, sincere, and complimentary toward the recipient. It often requires tact and good taste as an audience may be divided in its attitude toward the recipient—especially if others in the crowd are deserving of the same honor. There may have been intense rivalry between those seeking to win the award. Feelings and emotions might have been running high. Your objective with this type of speech is to understand the audience, to avoid embarrassing the winner, and to use language that will be appreciated by everyone present. This requires being simple, yet gracious.

Occasions for this type of speech vary. One common occasion is the presentation of an award. This may be formal; the winner may or may not have been selected in advance of the award ceremony. Speakers in these situations focus on the general interest generated by the award, the careful consideration of the judges, the worthiness of all the nominees, and the delicate position of everyone involved.

Another occasion is when an organization such as a school, church, society, or group receives an award or gift. This situation is likely to be formal, though there will be no surprise. Speakers generally emphasize the symbolism or utility of the gift.

A third occasion commemorates the recognition of service. For the recipient there may or may not be an element of surprise. However, the sentiments and emotions of the recipient may be very sensitive. The presentation speech should consist of the person who is being honored.

A fourth kind of presentation also revolves around recognition of service, but the occasion is more lighthearted. This type of award often comes as a surprise to the recipient. There is no rivalry, but rather good fellowship that is possibly linked to a farewell. Examples of this kind of occasion include retirement or a move away from a community. These occasions focus on the happy side of fellowship, and express some regret for the departure but also hope for the future of the recipient.

The Acceptance Speech

An **acceptance speech** is a recipient's sincere expression of appreciation for a gift or award. It should establish the person as a friendly, modest individual to whom the people may rightfully pay tribute. Its purpose should be to impress the donors with the worthiness of the recipient and to make them happy in their choice. Shallow or fatuous remarks are completely inappropriate in this situation.

In some instances no acceptance speech is necessary. In this case, a pleasant "thank you" accompanied by an appreciative smile are all that is necessary. To do more than this can be awkward. The recipient must decide on each occasion whether or not a speech is wanted or needed.

Occasions for acceptance speeches take place, potentially, any time an award or gift is presented. The possibilities for presentations and their accompanying speeches are unlimited.

Choosing a Topic

You have undoubtedly been to an award presentation and acceptance or have observed one on television (the Tonys, the Emmys, the Oscars, or the Miss America pageant, for example). You may wish to select an occasion with which you are familiar. If no experiences immediately come to mind, consider one of the following possibilities.

- Scholarship
- Cash prize for winning a sales contest
- Prize for writing poetry or creating a work of art
- Donation of funds for a new park
- Award for outstanding community service
- Environmental award for a school or group
- Championship award to a team
- Eagle Scout award

Preparing

The Presentation Speech

Make certain you are fully aware of the occasion and any particular requirements governing the presentation. Keep in mind that you are speaking on behalf of those who have sponsored the award or gift. Consider this an honor, *not* an opportunity to speak out about your favorite subject.

It is your responsibility to say things the sponsors would want you to say on their behalf. By all means incorporate the fundamentals of the basic speech organization. Use appropriate language and keep in mind the audience and the occasion.

As you prepare your presentation, keep the following things in mind. First, avoid over-praising the recipient; pay tribute with wise restraint. Second, pay appropriate homage to the audience; refer to the occasion that brought them together, a brief history of the event, and the purpose and symbolic value of the award or gift being presented. Third, do not overemphasize the gift itself or its value. Instead, stress the work or merit the award represents. Finally, recount how worthy the recipient is and tell how this worth was recognized or discovered. If you know the honoree personally, it would be good to mention that you are intimately aware of his or her service or merit.

Rehearse your ideas aloud until you have them thoroughly in mind. Do not memorize your speech (which would hinder your fluency in delivery), but be sure to know the overall progression of ideas.

The Acceptance Speech

Frequently recipients are not told in advance that they will be honored; this can prove embarrassing if they do not know how to respond with simple sincerity.

As this type of speech is often impromptu, there isn't much you can do in the way of preparation beyond formulating a standard pattern of ideas about which you will speak. If you are informed in advance that you are to receive a gift or award, then, of course, you should prepare a speech. In this case, simply follow the usual principles of good speech construction.

Whether speaking impromptu or delivering a well-rehearsed speech, you should use simple language. Begin by expressing a true sense of gratitude for the gift or award. If you are truly surprised, you may say so; however, the surprise must be genuine. Be polite. Graciously disclaim total credit for the award. Give credit to those who assisted you in any way. Praise their cooperation and support.

Do not apologize for winning or disclaim your worthiness, as this would be insulting to your audience and, in particular, to those who selected you for the tribute. Accept the award or gift sincerely.

The nature of the award will determine what you say next. You may express appreciation for its beauty or significance, but do not over-praise or overvalue the gift itself. Be grateful that an honor has been bestowed on you. Do not express disappointment in any way.

Conclude your remarks by speaking of your plans for the future, especially as they may relate to the gift or award or the work associated with it. As a final sentiment you may repeat your thanks for the recognition.

Presenting

When presenting or accepting an award or honor, your attitude and manner must reflect the occasion. There must be no ostentation, flamboyancy, or showiness in your speech or actions. Dress appropriately and be respectful.

As a presenter you will call the recipient to the platform. As a recipient, you will move forward

politely and alertly, neither hurrying nor loitering.

As a recipient, when you reach the stage or podium, be sure you stand so that the audience can see and hear you. Do not obscure the gift. Let the audience see it.

Be sure to speak loudly enough to be heard by everyone present, especially if you are turned partially away from the audience to present or receive the award. Observe all the elements of dynamic stage presence. If, as a recipient, you are to return to the audience after the presentation, carry the award or gift in your hand. Do not stuff it into a pocket.

Evaluating

Evaluate a classmate's presentation or acceptance speech. Be prepared to give oral feedback to the speaker on the following questions.

- Did the presenter use appropriate language and gestures?

- Was the presenter appropriately restrained but complimentary about the recipient?

- Did the presenter speak clearly and follow a clear progression of ideas?

- Was the recipient appropriately modest?

- Did the recipient thank others who may have helped him or her to achieve the award?

- Did the recipient speak clearly?

- Did the speaker deliver the speech with sincerity?

- Were the speaker's gestures and facial expressions appropriate to the occasion?

When you share your thoughts with the speaker, avoid being overly negative. Begin your comment by citing something the speaker did well. Try to be specific and cite examples whenever you can.

Example Speech

A Speech Presenting a Gift or Award

by Valerie Ritter

Fellow parents and athletes: This awards banquet has been an annual event for several years. Some of you here tonight will look forward to many more banquets such as this, while others will reminisce about the banquets of the past. These are special nights for athletes and parents, for it is because of you that these banquets are held. As president of the scholarship selection committee, it is with great pleasure that I am able to present this award.

This evening there is a student present who has earned recognition by means of his outstanding performance as an athlete. This recognition presented by the university is to provide financial assistance for students with athletic ability.

The recipient is a transfer student from the College of DuPage located in Glen Ellen, Illinois. He has been active as an athlete throughout his school years. Tonight I wish to present Mr. Rich Kielczewski with a scholarship recognizing his ability in the game of tennis.

Rich is honest and hardworking and is dedicated to the sport of tennis. He always seems to put forth more effort than is originally necessary. He is also a qualified and very competent tennis instructor.

Rich has entered many amateur tournaments. Among those in which he has captured the crown are the Chicago District Tournament and six consecutive conference titles. He has also received recognition of the people of Illinois by being ranked sixteenth in the state.

I have known Rich for a long time and have many times witnessed his stunning ability to overcome his opponent. I personally know of no other person more deserving of this tennis scholarship. In view of these outstanding qualities and accomplishments, I am very pleased to present Rich Kielczewski with this scholarship on behalf of Northwest Missouri State University.

Example Speech

A Speech Accepting an Award

by Ed Ashcraft

(The recipient was completely surprised to receive this award.)

Thank you, Dr. Ellis; thank you ladies and gentlemen. I really don't know what to say; I am at a complete loss for words.

My principal called me this evening to the phone and told me he would be at the school board meeting this evening, to give the board some input on our needs in the Science Department. He asked if I could be there in case he needed some off-hand information about our department. Of course, I said I would be happy to attend, since we had discussed these needs many times.

As you have heard, Mr. Soderquist gave us quite an in-depth list of our needs, plus some methods for improving our department. When he finished his presentation, I assumed he managed to get through it without my help. But I felt good about being there, just in case I was needed.

But I certainly did not expect this. The Golden Apple Award for the most outstanding teacher? Me?

I've held so many differing types of job in my life, but I knew the first day I walked into a classroom that this would be where I would spend the rest of my life. I look forward to Monday morning, getting back to my kids. To receive such a prestigious award for something I enjoy doing so much, well, as my students would say, "This is too much, man!"

I certainly want to thank my principal for recommending me for this award. Also, all of my fellow teachers, who voted for me. I can't thank the school board enough for this great honor.

I will keep my Golden Apple on my desk. Each morning I will take a minute to remind myself of the great trust that's been placed in me. I will do the best that I can to honor that trust. Thank you again.

Example Speech

Accepting the Congressional Gold Medal (excerpt)

by Tony Blair, Prime Minister of Great Britain

July 18, 2003

Thank you. Mr. Speaker and Mr. Vice-President, honorable members of Congress, I'm deeply touched by that warm and generous welcome. That's more than I deserve and more than I'm used to, quite frankly.

And let me begin by thanking you most sincerely for voting to award me the Congressional Gold Medal. But you, like me, know who the real heroes are: those brave service men and women, yours and ours, who fought the war and risk their lives still. And our tribute to them should be measured in this way, by showing them and their families that they did not strive or die in vain, but that through their sacrifice future generations can live in greater peace, prosperity, and hope.

Tony Blair addresses Congress as Vice-President Dick Cheney and House Leader Dennis Hastert look on.

Let me also express my gratitude to President Bush. Through the troubled times since September the 11th changed our world, we have been allies and friends. Thank you, Mr. President, for your leadership.

Mr. Speaker, sir, my thrill on receiving this award was only a little diminished on being told that the first Congressional Gold Medal was awarded to George Washington for what Congress called his "wise and spirited conduct" in getting rid of the British out of Boston. On our way down here, Senator Frist was kind enough to show me the fireplace where, in 1814, the British had burnt the Congress Library. I know this is kind of late, but sorry.

Actually, you know, my middle son was studying 18th-century history and the American War of Independence, and he said to me the other day, "You know Lord North Dad? He was the British prime minister who lost us America. So just think, however many mistakes you'll make, you'll never make one that bad."

Members of Congress, I feel a most urgent sense of mission about today's world. September the 11th was not an isolated event, but a tragic prologue, Iraq another act, and many further struggles will be set upon this stage before it's over.

There never has been a time when the power of America was so necessary or so misunderstood, or when, except in the most general sense, a study of history provides so little instruction for our present day.

We were all reared on battles between great warriors, between great nations, between powerful forces and ideologies that dominated entire continents. And these were struggles for conquest, for land, or money, and the wars were fought by massed armies. And the leaders were openly acknowledged, the outcomes decisive.

Today, none of us expect our soldiers to fight a war on our own territory. The immediate threat is not conflict between the world's most powerful nations. And why? Because we all have too much to lose. Because technology, communication, trade, and travel are bringing us ever closer together. Because in the last 50 years, countries like yours and mine have tripled their growth and standard of living. Because even those powers like Russia or China or India can see the horizon, the future wealth, clearly and know they are on a steady road toward it. And because all nations that are free value that freedom, will defend it absolutely, but have no wish to trample on the freedom of others.

We are bound together as never before. And this coming together provides us with unprecedented opportunity but also makes us uniquely vulnerable. And the threat comes because in another part of our globe there is shadow and darkness, where not all the world is free, where many millions suffer under brutal dictatorship, where a third of our planet lives in a poverty beyond anything even the poorest in our societies can imagine, and where a fanatical strain of religious extremism has arisen, that is a mutation of the true and peaceful faith of Islam.

And because in the combination of these afflictions a new and deadly virus has emerged. The virus is terrorism whose intent to inflict destruction is unconstrained by

continued

Example Speech cont.

human feeling and whose capacity to inflict it is enlarged by technology.

This is a battle that can't be fought or won only by armies. We are so much more powerful in all conventional ways than the terrorists, yet even in all our might, we are taught humility. In the end, it is not our power alone that will defeat this evil. Our ultimate weapon is not our guns, but our beliefs.

There is a myth that though we love freedom, others don't; that our attachment to freedom is a product of our culture; that freedom, democracy, human rights, the rule of law are American values, or Western values; that Afghan women were content under the lash of the Taliban; that Saddam was somehow beloved by his people; that Milosevic was Serbia's savior.

Members of Congress, ours are not Western values, they are the universal values of the human spirit. And anywhere, any time ordinary people are given the chance to choose, the choice is the same: freedom, not tyranny; democracy, not dictatorship; the rule of law, not the rule of the secret police.

The spread of freedom is the best security for the free. It is our last line of defense and our first line of attack. And just as the terrorist seeks to divide humanity in hate, so we have to unify it around an idea. And that idea is liberty. We must find the strength to fight for this idea and the compassion to make it universal. Abraham Lincoln said, 'Those that deny freedom to others deserve it not for themselves." And it is this sense of justice that makes moral the love of liberty.

In some cases where our security is under direct threat, we will have recourse to arms. In others, it will be by force of reason. But in all cases, to the same end: that the liberty we seek is not for some but for all, for that is the only true path to victory in this struggle. But first we must explain the danger.

Our new world rests on order. The danger is disorder. And in today's world, it can now spread like contagion. The terrorists and the states that support them don't have large armies or precision weapons; they don't need them. Their weapon is chaos.

The purpose of terrorism is not the single act of wanton destruction. It is the reaction it seeks to provoke: economic collapse, the backlash, the hatred, the division, the elimination of tolerance, until societies cease to reconcile their differences and become defined by them. Kashmir, the Middle East, Chechnya, Indonesia, Africa—barely a continent or nation is unscathed.

The risk is that terrorism and states developing weapons of mass destruction come together. And when people say, 'That risk is fanciful,' I say we know the Taliban supported al-Qaeda. We know Iraq under Saddam gave haven to and supported terrorists. We know there are states in the Middle East now actively funding and helping people, who regard it as God's will in the act of suicide to take as many innocent lives with them on their way to God's judgment.

Some of these states are desperately trying to acquire nuclear weapons. We know that companies and individuals with expertise sell it to the highest bidder, and we know that at least one state, North Korea, lets its people starve while spending billions of dollars on developing nuclear weapons and exporting the technology abroad.

This isn't fantasy, it is 21st-century reality, and it confronts us now. Can we be sure that terrorism and weapons of mass destruction will join together? Let us say one thing: If we are wrong, we will have destroyed a threat that at its least is responsible for inhuman carnage and suffering. That is something I am confident history will forgive.

But if our critics are wrong, if we are right, as I believe with every fiber of instinct and conviction I have that we are, and we do not act, then we will have hesitated in the face of this menace when we should have given leadership. That is something history will not forgive.

But precisely because the threat is new, it isn't obvious. It turns upside-down our concepts of how we should act and when, and it crosses the frontiers of many nations. So just as it redefines our notions of security, so it must refine our notions of diplomacy.

There is no more dangerous theory in international politics than that we need to balance the power of America with other competitive powers, different poles around which nations gather.

Such a theory may have made sense in 19th-century Europe. It was perforce the position in the Cold War. Today, it is an anachronism to be discarded like traditional theories of security. And it is dangerous because it is not rivalry but partnership we need; a common will and a shared purpose in the face of a common threat.

• • •

And I know it's hard on America, and in some small corner of this vast country, out in Nevada or Idaho or these places I've never been to, but always wanted to go. I know out there there's a guy getting on with his life, perfectly happily, minding his own business, saying to you, the political leaders of this country, "Why me? And why us? And why America?"

And the only answer is, "Because destiny put you in this place in history, in this moment in time, and the task is yours to do."

And our job, my nation that watched you grow, that you fought alongside and now fights alongside you, that takes enormous pride in our alliance and great affection in our common bond, our job is to be there with you. You are not going to be alone. We will be with you in this fight for liberty. We will be with you in this fight for liberty. And if our spirit is right and our courage firm, the world will be with us.

Thank you.

The Farewell Speech

Specs for the Farewell Speech

Time limit
4–5 minutes.

Speaker's notes
Do not use notes for this speech.

Sources of information
None required. The information may be real or fictitious.

Outline
Prepare a 75- to 100-word complete sentence outline.

Speak Up!

What three things would you say to a classmate or neighbor who was moving away? Now reverse roles. What would you say if you were the one who was leaving?

Purpose and Expectations of This Assignment

Another public-speaking situation you may someday encounter occurs when you are the guest of honor at a farewell party. As the person of the hour you invariably will be asked to say a few words before taking your leave. Will you be ready for such an honor?

The fact is that too often the guest of honor's farewell speech may be only a mumbling of incoherent remarks. That's usually because the person has never had a previous experience of this kind and does not know the appropriate thing to say. This speech assignment will give you some training that will come in handy in the future whenever you are called upon to make a speech of farewell.

In completing this chapter you will

- identify the necessary elements of a speech of leave-taking,

- analyze the emotions present in a farewell situation and determine how to adapt a speech to the audience, and

- organize and present a speech of leave-taking.

Defining the Farewell Speech

A **farewell speech** is one in which a person publicly says good-bye to a group of friends or colleagues. It should express the speaker's appreciation for what the colleagues have helped him or her to accomplish and for the happiness and camaraderie they have shared. Farewell speeches are common at both formal and informal gatherings. One common informal farewell party situation occurs at a meeting following the day's work. At that point the person

who is leaving receives commendation, favorable testimonials, and sometimes a gift. He or she, too, will be expected to say a few words. The formal occasion is, of course, much more elaborate and as such it features many formalities.

Occasions for the farewell speech always have to do with someone leaving. Situations may vary greatly; however, a few of the usual ones are

- retiring after years of service or employment,

- leaving to take a new job,

- being promoted to a position that demands a relocation,

- concluding service in a civic or religious organization,

- graduating and leaving school,

- moving to another community for any reason whatsoever.

The occasion, whatever its purpose, usually is not treated with undue sadness, although a successful farewell ceremony elicits true sincerity from the person who is leaving and from those who will stay behind. In presenting a farewell speech, the speaker may have feelings of deep emotion, but these should be expressed in a manner in keeping with the occasion.

Choosing a Topic

Think about situations that involve leaving to go to a new place or to take advantage of a new opportunity. Have you ever moved from one community or school to another? Was there something you wanted to say to those you were leaving behind? Select a situation that has meaning for you as a result of your own experiences or observations. If you are having difficulty coming up with your own topic, consider the following.

- Going home after living in a foreign country
- Moving to a new school
- Going back home after a summer job
- Leaving for South America to study rain forests
- Going to New York to become an actor
- Leaving for college on an athletic scholarship

Preparing

Remember that this is a special occasion and that old friends and associates are honoring you. The atmosphere may be highly emotional. There may be some sadness or a mood of intense gaiety and goodwill. When speaking in a situation such as this, carefully analyze the probable mood of your audience. If you are likely to receive a gift, plan your remarks so that you may accept it graciously. Sincerity must dominate your words whatever they may be.

Farewell speeches usually follow a well-defined pattern with appropriate variations, which the speaker deems necessary. Begin your talk by referring to the past—perhaps the time when you first arrived and your reasons for coming to the community. A bit of humor and a few brief, interesting anecdotes may be in good taste. Continue your thoughts by pointing out how your ideals and those of the audience, though perhaps not completely attained, inspired you to do what you did, and that you realize there is still work to be done.

Express appreciation for the audience's support of your efforts, which made your achievements possible. Commend the harmony and the cooperation that prevailed. If you can do so with sincerity, tell them that you will always remember your association with this group as one of the outstanding times in your life. Speak next of your future work; speak briefly but sincerely. Explain why you are leaving, and what compelled you to transfer to a new field or location. Show that your work just completed will act as a background and inspiration to that which lies ahead. Continue by encouraging those who remain, and predict greater achievements for them. If you know who is to succeed you, praise that person. Conclude with a genuine expression of your appreciation for your audience and a continued interest in their future. If you received a gift, give a final word of thanks for it.

Omit any reference or allusion to unpleasantness or friction that may have existed. Do not make any part of this occasion bitter or sad. Be happy and leave others with the same feeling. Smile and make sure that a good impression will follow you.

Presenting

In this speech, match your manner to the mood of the occasion and audience. Do not go overboard in terms of your emotion. Remember that your aim is to be neither too solemn nor too buoyant. Use a friendly and sincere approach throughout. Speak loudly enough to be heard by everyone in the room. Use body language and gestures suitable to the audience, the occasion, the speech, the environment, and yourself.

Avoid ponderous phrases, overemotional wording or tone, redundancy, and flowery or florid attempts at oratory. Let everything you do and say, coupled with a good appearance and alert posture, be the evidence that you are genuinely and sincerely mindful of the audience's appreciation of you at this, the time of your departure.

Evaluating

Evaluate a classmate's farewell speech. Rate the following criteria on a scale from 1 to 5 with 1 being "needs much improvement" and 5 being "outstanding."

- Was the speaker warm and friendly?
- Did the speaker seem to have a strong sense of the occasion?
- Were the speaker's posture and body language appropriate?
- Did the speaker give credit to members of the audience?
- Did the speaker express his or her thoughts sincerely?

Give an overall score to the speech. Formulate one comment that you think might help the speaker to do better next time and share it with him or her.

Example Speech

Farewell to Baseball

by Lou Gehrig

In 1939 Hall-of-Famer Gehrig was diagnosed with Amyotrophic Lateral Sclerosis, a fatal neuromuscular disorder now called Lou Gehrig's disease. His farewell address was delivered on July 4, 1939, in New York City.

Fans, for the past two weeks you have been reading about the bad break I got. Yet today I consider myself the luckiest man on the face of the earth.

I have been in ballparks for seventeen years and have never received anything but kindness and encouragement from you fans. Look at these grand men. Which of you wouldn't consider it the highlight of his career just to associate with them for even one day?

Sure I'm lucky.

Who wouldn't consider it an honor to have known Jacob Ruppert? Also, the builder of baseball's greatest empire, Ed Barrow? To have spent six years with that wonderful little fellow, Miller Huggins? Then to have spent the next nine years with that outstanding leader, that smart student of psychology, the best manager in baseball today, Joe McCarthy?

Sure I'm lucky.

When the New York Giants, a team you would give your right arm to beat, and vice versa, sends you a gift—that's something.

When everybody down to the groundskeepers and those boys in white coats remember you with trophies—that's something.

When you have a wonderful mother-in-law who takes sides with you in squabbles with her own daughter—that's something.

When you have a father and a mother who work all their lives so you can have an education and build your body—it's a blessing.

When you have a wife who has been a tower of strength and shown more courage than you dreamed existed—that's the finest I know.

So, I close in saying that I might have been given a bad break, but I've got an awful lot to live for.

Example Speech

Farewell Speech

by Reed Adams

Fellow faculty members, students, parents, and guests, I am greatly honored by your presence tonight. I always had to live by a rule when leaving a place to move on in the world, which was to just leave and try to forget the people left behind as soon as possible. However, that will not be possible for me to do with you.

For the last eight years you have shared in my joys and my sorrows; we have shared in change but have learned that change just for change does not work. You people as the community have brought my family and me from vagabonds of the educational system to actual professionals in that field. Your ideals and your school have made this change in me. Without this change I would not have the opportunity that has now availed itself to me.

I remember my first day at this school well. I had such high hopes of how I was going to change the whole education system, but my first day at school changed that. The students entered the room and took their seats, but it seemed my techniques of teaching would not work. It seemed that the harder I tried the more the students seemed

to resent me and what I was trying to teach them. Then one of the students came up to me at the end of the day and said that he really would have enjoyed my class if he had not had so much on his mind.

I asked him if it was something I could help him with, and he said he wished that I could, but I was a little bit too old to be on the football team. I had been so wrapped up in changing the system that I had forgotten to

listen and learn what was happening in the school. The biggest game of the season was the first one with us playing Western High. The whole student body was more interested in that than what I was trying to teach, so that's how the idea for our ten-minute rap sessions at the first of every class began.

We have had good times, bad times, broken hearts, and romance, but the most important thing we have learned is that we are people and we all make mistakes. That is why we accept other people and their mistakes, as well as our imperfect selves. I am indebted to you all for the wonderful example you have set for me—and for my family—in this area.

Next fall you will continue in your education. Some of you will become doctors and lawyers and others will find jobs right out of high school. But whatever you do, I hope you will remember, as I will, the wonderful experiences and academic achievements as well as the sports of Highland High School.

The new house we have purchased in Mississippi has a large mantel in the center of the room, and this plaque you have given me tonight will go there beautifully. We had been wondering what we were going to put there. Thank you very much, and may whatever you believe in bless and keep you happy.

Impromptu Speaking

Specs for Impromptu Speaking

Time limit

2–5 minutes.

Speaker's notes

During your first two impromptu speech experiences, you may use notes to remind you of your organizational method. After that, memorize the method and apply it as you speak.

Sources of Information

Your own background and reading.

Outline

None necessary.

Speak Up!

Each student should write a speech topic (serious or humorous) on a piece of paper. The topics are collected and put in a container. When your name is called, you must pull out a topic and begin speaking on it. Add as much structure as possible to your impromptu speech. (If you don't know anything about the topic, use your imagination and make things up!) Keep talking until your instructor tells you to stop. How successful were you? What difficulties did you experience?

Purpose and Expectations of This Assignment

This speech experience is designed to expose you to impromptu speaking and to prepare you for the difficulties and rewards of off-the-cuff discourse. Many students assume that impromptu speakers are unprepared. In reality, while the speech itself may be unprepared, an effective impromptu speaker is well prepared to speak. There are a number of methods that, when used properly, will enable a speaker to perform well on the spur of the moment every time. This assignment will help you to master those methods.

In completing this assignment, you will

- experience the challenges of off-the-cuff discourse,

- prepare a strategy for dealing with the need to speak on the spur of the moment,

- practice organizing ideas quickly for clear communication, and

- develop composure for speaking in a challenging setting.

Defining Impromptu Speaking

Impromptu speaking is a talk for which a speaker has done no formal preparation. He or she simply takes the floor, selects a subject, and begins. Various techniques are used for impromptu expression. A common procedure is one in which the speaker takes the floor after being asked to talk on a subject the speaker may or may not know anything about. In another method each of several persons in the audience suggests a topic; the speaker has a few seconds to choose the topic on which she or he feels best suited to address; then the speaker begins to talk.

There are many variations as to topic selection; however, the fundamental principle is that the ideas the speaker voices are unrehearsed and unprepared.

The purpose of presenting this kind of speech is the same as that for any other type of speaking: to communicate with the audience. The distinctive feature of an impromptu presentation is the unprepared delivery and the suddenness with which a person is confronted with a speech situation. Impromptu speaking takes place when a person is called upon without warning to say a few words at a luncheon, special meeting, social gathering, or other occasion.

Suggested Topics for Impromptu Speaking

Now you will work on a variation of the Speak Up activity on page 205. Write three topic suggestions on a paper. Each one should be general enough that any member of the class can use it as the basis of an impromptu speech. That means you should avoid topics such as "The Joys of Tap Dancing" or "A Trip to Yellowstone Park." Your instructor will ask you to supply a topic for another student from time to time as needed during the class, so keep your three topics handy. Examples of suitable topics for impromptu speaking are

- dancing,
- movies,
- school events,
- vacation,
- jobs,
- traffic laws,
- music videos, and
- sports.

In many impromptu-speaking situations you won't get to choose a topic. However, if you are given a choice of several impromptu speech topics, there is one simple rule to follow: Choose the topic on which you are best qualified to speak. When you are making your choice, consider your audience and the occasion.

Preparing

There is little to fear from impromptu speaking if you follow a preconceived plan of attack. The way to do this is to refuse to allow yourself to become panicky, to recognize that some nervousness is a good sign, and to realize that your audience will expect nothing extraordinary because they know you are speaking impromptu. You may even discover that they're rooting for you!

Naturally you can't prepare for an unknown topic, but you can have a plan of attack for situations that offer surprise topics from an audience. One of the best methods is to have in mind organizational processes you can use to develop your ideas.

Organizing

Select from the following organizational methods for impromptu speaking: chronological, spatial, cause-effect, problem-solution or a creative combination of your choice. For a review of these methods, see Organizing Your Materials on pages 25–26.

Bear in mind that no matter what organizational method you choose, for impromptu speaking you will need to keep your wits about you and utilize only those portions of the device that are appropriate to the particular speech, occasion, and audience.

Presenting

In presenting an impromptu speech, your attitude is the deciding factor in determining your effectiveness. First of all, you must maintain poise. It does not matter how surprised you are in the moment of being asked to speak or how difficult your topic is. It does not make any difference what happens when you receive your subject or while you are speaking or after you conclude your speech—you still must maintain poise. How do you do that? Here are some suggestions.

1. Do not fidget around at your seat before you speak. It might be hard to sit still when you know you will soon be on the spot. But fidgeting won't help, and it might hurt you in terms of what the audience thinks of your speech.

2. When you are called on to speak, rise calmly and take your place before your audience.

3. If you know your topic when you take the platform, begin your remarks calmly, without hurrying. Maintain some vigor and force, and be sure that you have an organizational plan in mind by which you will develop your thoughts. Do not apologize to your audience in any way, by word or action.

4. If you do not know your topic when you rise to speak but are offered several choices after you take the floor, simply stand calmly before the group and listen carefully to the suggestions.

If you do not understand a topic, you should ask to have it repeated. After you have received all of the proposed subjects, either stand quietly or walk calmly back and forth for a few seconds while you decide which topic you will select. Ten seconds should be the maximum time you take to decide.

Once you make your selection, decide immediately on what organizational method or plan you will use to develop it. This plan should have been committed to memory before you ever attended class or placed yourself in a position where you might be asked to give an impromptu speech. After you have chosen your method of development, make your introductory remarks by telling why the subject is important to your listeners.

In actually delivering an impromptu talk, it is wise to begin slowly and pick up speed and power as you go along. Aside from this, you should make bodily actions and gestures that are in keeping with the speech situation. Your voice should be vigorous and easy for all audience members to hear. Naturally, your articulation, pronunciation, and grammar must be of a high standard.

Remember that whenever you are called upon to speak in class or in a meeting, you are responsible for staying in control of the situation. Many impromptu speakers say essentially the first thing that comes into their heads, but that is not always the most appropriate way to respond to the situation. In fact, it can be disastrous, especially if *nothing* comes to mind! Use the tips in this lesson to help you make the most of an on-the-spot situation.

Evaluating

Evaluate a classmate's impromptu speaking. Be prepared to give oral feedback to the speaker on the following questions.

- Did the speaker seem poised?
- Did the speaker use an effective organizational method?
- Did the speaker use eye contact to connect with the audience?
- Did the speaker deliver the speech with authority?
- Were the speaker's gestures and facial expressions appropriate to the material?

Remember that impromptu speaking can be a bit nerve-wracking for the speaker. Try to keep in mind your own efforts in this area as you consider what the speaker did or did not do well.

UNIT 6

Speeches for Special Occasions

As has been said throughout the text so far, public speaking is about building and maintaining relationships between speakers and audiences. Nowhere is this more directly illustrated than in speeches for special occasions. As you can tell from the list of speech experiences in this unit, there are many special occasions for which spoken remarks are essential elements. This unit is designed to introduce you to a wide variety of those occasions in order to provide experiences you can draw upon when you encounter these contexts.

Speech Experiences in This Unit

The Eulogy or Tribute Speech

Ron Reagan delivers a eulogy at his father's funeral.

Specs for the Eulogy or Tribute Speech

Time limits
5–6 minutes.

Speaker's notes
10-word maximum.

Sources of information
Two are required, preferably three. For each source give the specific magazine, book, or Internet site it was taken from, the title of the article, author's full name, date of publication, and the chapter or pages telling where the material was found. If the source is a person, identify the source completely by title, position, and occupation. List these on the outline form. For Internet sites include the address (URL).

Outlining
Prepare a 75- to 150-word complete sentence outline.

Speak Up!

Choose an inanimate object that is no longer serviceable such as a fallen tree, a worn-out backpack, a missing running shoe, a sweater with moth holes, a chewed-up pencil, and so forth. Outline a eulogy commemorating this item telling its good qualities, how it helped you, how owning it made you a better person, and how much you miss it. Be ready to present your eulogy to the class.

Purpose and Expectations of this Assignment

Sooner or later we all experience the loss of someone important in our lives. When these occasions happen, people often gather to hear speeches in praise of that person's life and the contributions he/she made to the community. This assignment offers you an opportunity to study the elements of such a speech in order to be better prepared if such an occasion rises.

In completing this assignment you will

- select appropriate information to include in the speech,
- understand the importance and role of sincerity in a speech of praise, and
- organize and present a speech praising another person.

Defining the Eulogy or Tribute Speech

The **eulogy** is a speech of praise that is usually delivered in honor or commemoration of someone who has died. However, one of the synonyms for *eulogy* is *tribute*. A **tribute** is usually given for a person as an honor for achievement.

The purpose of a eulogy is to praise and evaluate favorably that which is eulogized; it commends and lifts up the finer qualities and characteristics of the subject eulogized. It stresses the personality of the person that it concerns; it tells of their greatness and achievements, their benefits to society, and their influence upon people. It is not merely a simple biographical sketch. Eulogies are given at memorials and funerals.

Occasions for tributes are many. For persons who are living, the speech may be given on a birthday, a retirement, at a dinner in honor of an individual, or at the dedication of a project someone has created and/or donated. Tributes often appear at the formal announcement of a political candidate or at an inauguration.

Choosing a Person to Eulogize or Tribute

First, it is essential that you give a tribute to someone whom you greatly admire and who, in your opinion, is living or has lived a commendable life. This is necessary for your tribute to be completely sincere. Second, select someone about whom you can secure adequate information. Here are some possibilities.

- A well-known person in your community
- A former president
- A leader for minority or women's rights
- A grandparent or other relative
- A classmate
- A religious leader
- A teacher

Preparing and Organizing

The purpose of a eulogy is a set objective, regardless of the time, place, or occasion. The eulogy is intended to stimulate audience members to think favorably about the subject and to inspire them to nobler heights by virtue of the examples set by the person being praised. The speaker is not required to determine a purpose in preparing a eulogy.

Having selected the person to be eulogized, you should decide on the method that you will use in developing the eulogy.

must state how the person reacted to the events and what happened as a result of them.

For example, if you were eulogizing former President Franklin D. Roosevelt, you could recount, as one event, how he was stricken with infantile paralysis. You would not merely make a statement regarding the tragedy that befell him and then move on. Rather, you would show how his illness became a challenge to him, how he resolved to live a great life despite a pair of useless legs, and how he overcame his handicap. You would show that, as a result of his illness, he became more resolute and more determined. Other important incidents in his life should be given similar treatment.

Once you have a chronology, look back over it and remove any unimportant events. Second, in developing your speech, point out the struggles that the person met in order to achieve his or her goals. Avoid overemphasis and exaggeration when you are doing this. Third, show the development of ideas and ideals. Fourth, describe relations and services to others and indicate their significance.

In constructing your speech, be sure you pay careful attention to your introduction and conclusion, but do not neglect the logical organization and arrangement of the remainder of your talk. Actually, a eulogy is a difficult speech to prepare. However, if you go about it knowing what you wish to put into it, you should have no particular trouble. When you have the eulogizing speech ready for rehearsal, practice it aloud until you have thoroughly mastered the sequence of ideas. Do not memorize the speech word for word.

Materials for eulogies may be found in *Who's Who*, histories, biographies, autobiographies, encyclopedias, newspapers, magazines, the Internet, and similar sources.

Most eulogies follow a **chronological order**; that is, you will present events in the order in which they occurred. As you touch upon these broad and influential events in the subject's life, you will point to them as evidence of (1) what the person has accomplished, (2) what the person stood for, (3) the nature of his or her influence upon society, and (4) the subject's probable place in history. In building your speech chronologically, do not end by composing a simple biographical sketch. If you do, you will have an informative speech but not a eulogy. It is not enough to list the significant happenings in a person's life chronologically and consider that you have built a eulogy. You

Presenting

Your overall attitude must be one of undoubted sincerity. Be a true believer in the person about whom you speak. Aside from your attitude, you will, of course, observe all the requirements of good speech. There should be no showiness or gaudiness in your presentation that will call attention to you instead of your ideas about the subject of your speech.

You will need to be fully aware of the occasion and atmosphere into which you will step when you deliver the eulogy. Make sure you are dressed appropriately, especially if the occasion is a solemn one. It is your responsibility to know what will be required of you in the way of carrying out rituals or ceremonies if they are a part of the program. Since you will be in the limelight, you should fit easily into the situation without awkwardness. Naturally you must adjust your bodily actions and gestures to your environment—and your audience. Your voice should reach the ears of all present. In giving a eulogy at a funeral or memorial service, it is often appropriate to recognize family and friends and offer words of comfort. This is best accomplished by letting them know how the person touched other lives and will live on through the influence he or she had on others. If you are sincere, well prepared, and mean what you say, the eulogy you present should be inspirational to all who hear it.

Evaluating

Evaluate a classmate's eulogy or tribute. Rate the following criteria on a scale from 1 to 5 with 1 being "needs much improvement" and 5 being "outstanding."

- Did the speaker provide appropriate information about the person being eulogized?

- Was the material organized in a logical fashion?

- Did the speaker maintain eye contact with the audience?

- Did the speaker seem sincere?

- Did the speech include what the subject accomplished, what he or she stood for, how he or she influenced society, and the person's probable place in history?

Give an overall score to the speech. Then choose one area of the speaker's performance that may have given you new ideas about your own speaking skills. Write a short paragraph to explain.

Example Speech

Tribute to Thurgood Marshall

by Senator Carol Moseley Braun

Delivered to the United States Senate, Washington, D.C., January 26, 1993

Thurgood Marshall died last Sunday of heart failure. I still have great difficulty believing it. I know he was born over 84 years ago, and I know that he himself said he was "old and falling apart," but it is nonetheless hard to conceive that a heart as mighty and as courageous as his is no longer beating.

Thurgood Marshall epitomized the best in America; he was, in fact, what this country is all about. That may seem to be an odd thing to say about him. After all, he himself was very aware of the fact that the United States did not, and in too many instances still does not, live up entirely to its founding principles. He knew that the phrases of the Declaration of Independence, "that all men are created equal" and are endowed "with certain inalienable rights," including those to "life, liberty and the pursuit of happiness…," were not, all too much of the time, the principles that govern everyday life in America.

Thurgood Marshall was born in Baltimore in 1908. He lived and felt the humiliation of racism, of not being able even to use the bathroom in downtown Baltimore simply because of the color of his skin.

But Thurgood Marshall was not defeated by racism. He knew that racial inequality was incompatible with American ideals, and he made it his life's unending fight to see that

this country's ideals became true for all of its citizens.

And what a fight it has been. It took Thurgood Marshall from Baltimore's segregated public schools to Lincoln University, where he graduated with honors, to Howard University Law School, to the NAACP, to the circuit bench, to the U.S. Solicitor General's office, to become the first African-American member of the U.S. Supreme Court.

That quick biography does not begin to measure the battles Thurgood Marshall fought and won, and the strength, conviction and power he put into that fight.

Thomas Jefferson said that "a little rebellion, now and then, is a good thing, and as necessary in the political world as storms in the physical." Thurgood Marshall took Jefferson at his word, and played a key role in creating a rebellion in America, a

continued

rebellion not of violence, but of law. What Marshall did was to use the U.S. legal system to bludgeon and destroy state-supported segregation.

What Marshall did was to use the courts and the law to force the United States to apply the promises made to every American in our Declaration of Independence and our Bill of Rights to African-Americans who had little or no protection under the law up until the Marshall legal rebellion. What Marshall did was to make the 13th, 14th, and 15th amendments to our Constitution the law of the land in reality, instead of just an empty promise.

The history of the civil rights movement in this country is, in no small part, the history of Marshall's battles before the Supreme Court. As lead counsel of the National Association for the Advancement of Colored People, Marshall appeared before the Supreme Court 32 times, and won 29 times. His legal skills, grounded in sound preparation and sensitivity to the evidence helped him win such landmark decisions as *Smith versus Allwright, Shelley versus Kramer, Sweatt versus Painter*, and the biggest case of them all, *Brown versus Board of Education.*

I am somewhat reluctant to dwell on Thurgood Marshall's many successes, because I know he would not like that. He would not like it because he knew only too well that there are many more battles that must be fought and won if America's

founding principles and American reality are to become one and the same for every American of every color. In his dissent in the Bakke case, Marshall said:

"The position of the Negro today in America is the tragic but inevitable consequence of centuries of unequal treatment. Measured by any benchmark of comfort or achievement, meaningful equality remains a distant dream for the Negro."

However, the fact that the battle is not yet won does not lessen Marshall's many accomplishments. He was a man who worked and fought to make a difference, he was a man who did make a difference.

He certainly made a difference in my life, opening doors of opportunity measured only by merit. He helped ensure that I was able to attend public schools and the University of

Chicago Law School, and not schools for blacks only. His work helped make my election to the U.S. Senate possible. He opened closed doors and created new opportunities for me and for many, many others. His life was the most convincing evidence that a change is possible.

I want to close, Mr. President, by quoting Thurgood Marshall one more time. In the Bakke case, he said:

"In the light of the sorry history of discrimination and its devastating impact on the lives of Negroes, bringing the Negro into the mainstream of American life should be a state interest of the highest order."

I share his view. Elimination of racism is not just an interest of African-Americans, but of all Americans. Only then will we be able to tap the full potential of our people. Only then will we live the greatness of the American promise.

I hope we will all remember Thurgood Marshall by continuing his lifetime of struggle. I hope we will all remember Marshall by dedicating ourselves to the principles and goals he dedicated himself to: making American opportunity available to every American. And as we work toward those goals, I hope we can all live our lives as completely as he did, enjoy ourselves as much as he did, and poke as much fun at ourselves as Thurgood Marshall did all of his life.

I will miss Thurgood Marshall. America will miss Thurgood Marshall. I am proud to have the opportunity, in some small way, to continue his work, and to try to build on his legacy.

The
Dedication Speech

Christopher Reeve speaks at the dedication of the Lois Pope LIFE Center in Miami, 2000.

Specs for the Dedication Speech

Time limits
3–4 minutes.

Speaker's notes
This is a short speech. No notes are necessary.

Sources of information
Two are required, preferably three. For each source, give the specific magazine, book, or Internet site it was taken from, title of the article, author's full name, date of publication, and the chapter or pages telling where the material was found. If a source is a person, identify the source completely by title, position, and occupation. List these on the outline form. For Internet sites give the address (URL).

Outlining
Prepare a 75- to 150-word complete sentence outline.

Speak Up!

How many things can you think of that could be dedicated? Choose one, such as a building, a statue, a book, or a song, and outline a few things you might say if you were called on to give this object a dedication speech.

Purpose and Expectations of This Assignment

You may not give a speech at dedication ceremonies for a long time, then again the occasion for a speech of this kind may arise sooner than you had thought possible. But regardless of when you are called on, one thing is sure—you must know the requirements for this kind of speech. The dedication speech occurs on an occasion and in an atmosphere that requires very strict observance of certain aspects of speech presentations. This speech assignment is designed to give an experience like the "real thing," so that you give a creditable performance when the opportunity presents itself.

In completing this assignment, you will

- identify the required elements of a dedication speech,
- identify ideals to be celebrated, and
- present a speech with dignity appropriate to the occasion.

Defining the Dedication Speech

The **dedication speech** is one presented on commemorative occasions. It is generally brief and carries a serious tone. It employs excellent language and demands careful construction, fine wording, and polished delivery. Its purpose should be to commemorate, to honor, and to praise the spirit of endeavor and progress that the dedication symbolizes.

The speech should thrill the audience with pride regarding their community, ideals, and progress. Occasions for the dedication speech usually involve a group enterprise. Common among these

are occasions such as erecting monuments; completing buildings, stadiums, and baseball parks; or laying cornerstones and opening institutions. Similar events considered as marks of progress are also occasions for dedication speeches. Lincoln's Gettysburg Address is one of the finest dedication speeches ever made.

Choosing a Topic

This will involve a bit of imagination on your part; however, choose an occasion that you wish were actually true. For instance, think about dedicating a statue to someone you consider a hero or heroine. Would you like to have a new community center in your neighborhood where you could relax with your friends? Then, create a ceremony to break ground, lay a cornerstone, or dedicate a completed building. If you are having trouble developing a topic, consult your teacher for additional suggestions.

Preparing

First, know your purpose. It must dominate this speech just as the purpose dominates every speech. This means that you are to compliment the ideals and achievements that the dedicated structure symbolizes, thus setting it apart for a certain purpose.

These are the points to cover in the speech. Give a brief history of events leading up to the present time. Mention the sacrifice, the work, the ideals, and the service that lie behind the project. Next, explain the future use of the work, the influence or significance that will be associated with the structure being dedicated. Place the emphasis upon what the object dedicated stands for (ideals, progress, loyalty) rather than upon the object itself.

The items on the facing page will constitute your material. Now, organize your speech carefully. To accomplish the organization of the speech you will first outline it; then word it. Do this meticulously. Use understandable and simple language. The speech is serious, not frivolous. Leave your humor at home.

Next, you are ready to practice. Do this orally. Rehearse aloud until you have definitely fixed the order of the speech in your mind. Avoid complete word-for-word memorization. You may memorize certain words and phrases, but you should not memorize the entire speech. When you have mastered an effective presentation, you will be ready to speak. Remember to include appropriate body language, gestures, and tone as you practice.

Presenting

Your attitude should be one of self-confidence and dignity. Body language must be keyed to the tone of the speech. The environment surrounding the speaker may permit much action or limit it severely. If a public address system is used, you will not be able to move from the microphone; however, you can and should utilize gestures.

Whether speaking with the aid of a microphone or not, your voice should be full and resonant and easily heard. If the crowd is large, a slower speaking rate should be used. Articulation must be carefully attended, yet not so much so that it becomes ponderous and labored. Voice and action must be in tune, with neither one overbalancing the other. The speaker must be animated, alive to the purpose, desirous of communicating, and capable of presenting a polished speech.

Evaluating

Evaluate a classmate's dedication speech. Rate the following criteria on a scale from 1 to 5 with 1 being "needs much improvement" and 5 being "outstanding."

- Did the speaker provide information about the purpose of the object or building being dedicated?
- Was the material organized in a logical fashion?
- Did the speaker choose appropriate vocabulary and sentence construction?
- Was the speaker's presentation serious and dignified?
- Would the speech engender feelings of pride among audience members?

Give an overall score to the speech. Then write down one area of the speaker's performance that was excellent and one area that needs work.

Example Speech

Dedication of the Holocaust Museum

by Elie Wiesel

Washington, D.C. April 22, 1993

Mr. President, Mrs. Clinton, President Herzog, Mrs. Herzog, Mr. Vice President, Mrs. Gore, Excellencies, distinguished members of Congress, Mr. Speaker, fellow survivors and friends, as one who was privileged to have been present at the inception of this noble and singular enterprise, may I say how deeply grateful I am to the American people, to its leadership in Congress and the White House, and to its many benefactors, and to the survivors—especially to the survivors— for helping us further the cause of remembrance. This impressive museum could not have been built without your understanding and generosity, for with the exception of Israel, our country is the only one who has seen fit to preserve the memory of the Holocaust and made it a national imperative to do so.

Mr. President, you have brought change to this city and to this country. Some of the changes you have brought to Washington have been instant. One such notable change is that the average age has dropped by some 30 years. It is to that new, young generation that you symbolize, Mr. President, that we now turn this awesome legacy to so that you, Mr. President, can implement our vision.

What has been my vision? When President Carter entrusted me with this project in 1978, I was asked about that vision, and I wrote then one sentence. And now my words are here engraved in stone at the entrance to this edifice. And those words are "For the dead and the living, we must bear witness." For not only are we responsible for the memories of the dead, we are also responsible for what we are doing with those memories.

Now, a museum is a place, I believe, that should bring people together, a place that should not set people apart. People who come from different horizons, who belong to different spheres, who speak different languages—they should feel united in memory. And, if possible at all, with some measure of grace, we should, in a way, be capable of reconciling ourselves with the dead. To bring the living and the dead together in a spirit of reconciliation is part of that vision.

Now, may I tell you a story? Fifty years ago, somewhere in the Carpathian Mountains, a young Jewish woman read in a Hungarian newspaper a brief account about the Warsaw ghetto uprising. Astonished, dismayed, she wondered aloud, "Why," she said, "are our Jewish brothers doing that? Why are they fighting? Couldn't they wait quietly"—the word was *quietly*—"until the end of the war?" Treblinka, Ponar, Belzec, Chelmno, Birkenau. She had never heard of these places. One year later, together with her entire family, she was already in a cattle car traveling to the black hole in time, the black hole in history, named Auschwitz.

But Mr. President and distinguished guests, these names and others were known to officials in Washington, and London, and Moscow, and Stockholm, and Geneva, and the Vatican. After all, by April 1943, nearly 4 million Jews from surrounding countries had already vanished, had already perished. The Pentagon knew, the State Department knew, the White House knew, most governments knew. Only the victims did not know. Thus the painful, disturbing question—why weren't Hungarian Jews in 1944—they were then the last remnant of Eastern European Jewry, why were they not even warned of the impending doom? For one year later, in 1944, three weeks before D-Day, that young woman and husband, all of them were already turned into ashes. Jews from everywhere, old and young, beggars and industrialists, sages and madmen, military men, diplomats, professors, students, children—children!—they were all entering the shadow of flames.

An Italian philosopher/theologian, Giordano Bruno said, "Light is the shadow of God." No, it is not. It is fire that is the shadow of God, that fire that consumed a third of my people. Inside the kingdom of night we who were there tried to understand, and we could not. We found ourselves in an unfamiliar world, a creation parallel to God's, with its

continued

own hierarchy, with its own hangmen, its own laws and customs. There were only two categories—those who were there to kill and those who were there to be killed.

In Poland, SS officers used Jewish infants for target practice. The only emotion they ever showed was anger when they missed. In Kiev, an SS officer beheaded two Jewish children in front of their mother, who in her anguish, in prey of some mystical madness, held them to—close to her bosom and began to dance. In Rumania, the Aryan guards hanged Jews on meat hooks and displayed them in butcher shops with signs, "Kosher Meat."

So as you walk through the museum, so magnificently conceived and built by James Freed, and illustrated, in a way, artistically by Raye Farr and her colleagues—as you walk through those exhibits, looking into the eyes of the killers and their victims, ask yourselves how could murderers do what they did and go on living? Why was Berlin encouraged in its belief that it could decree with impunity the humiliation, persecution, extermination of an entire people? Why weren't the railways leading to Birkenau bombed by Allied bombers? As long as I live I will not understand that. And why was there no public outcry of indignation and outrage?

More questions—there were fighters in every ghetto—Jewish fighters, there were resistance members in every city and every camp. Why weren't they helped? Help came to every resistance movement from every single occupied country. The only ones who never received any help, not even an encouragement, were the Jewish fighters in the Warsaw ghetto, the Bialice ghetto, the Vilna ghetto. And for me, a man who grew up in a religion, the Jewish religion, a man who his entire life thought that God is everywhere, how is it that man's silence was matched by God's?

Oh, I don't believe there are answers. There are no answers. And this museum is not an answer; it is a question mark. If there is a response, it is a response in responsibility.

In one of my tales, an SS officer says to a young yeshiva student, "You want to live," he said. "Some will laugh at you. Others will try to redeem themselves through you. People will refuse to believe you. You will possess the truth, but it will be the truth of a mad man."

In 1942, a Jew called Yakov Grabovsky escaped from Chelmno. He came to the Rabbi in Grabov and in Yiddish he said to him, 'Rabbi,' he said—(in Yiddish)—

"They are killing our people." And when the Rabbi looked at him, the Jew said, "Rabbi—(in Yiddish)—you think I am crazy. I am not crazy."

We are not crazy. We are not crazy because we still believe in human beings. We still believe and we still have faith. And, President Herzog, you who came from Israel—and we are so grateful to you for coming—you know that you are part of that belief. It is because of the passion that we have for Israel, we are Jews, and decent people in America, that we have faith in humanity and in America.

We also believe in the absolute necessity to communicate a tale. We know we cannot, we never will explain. My good friends, it is not because I cannot explain that you won't understand, it is because you won't understand that I cannot explain. How can one understand that human beings could choose such inhumanity? How can one understand that in spite of everything there was goodness in those times, in individuals? There were good people even in occupied countries, and there was kindness and tenderness and love inside the camps among the victims.

What have we learned? We have learned some lessons, minor lessons, perhaps, that we are all responsible, and indifference is a sin and a punishment. And we have learned that when people suffer we cannot remain indifferent.

And, Mr. President, I cannot not tell you something. I have been in the former Yugoslavia last fall. I cannot sleep since for what I have seen. As a Jew I am saying that we must do something to stop the bloodshed in that country! People fight each other and children die. Why? Something, anything must be done.

This is a lesson. There are many other lessons. You will come, you will learn. We shall learn together.

And in closing, Mr. President and distinguished guests, just one more remark. The woman in the Carpathian Mountain of whom I spoke to you, that woman disappeared. She was my mother.

The
Anniversary Speech

Coretta Scott King celebrates the
40th anniversary of her husband's
"I Have a Dream" speech.

Specs for the Anniversary Speech

Time limits

5–6 minutes.

Speaker's notes

It is advisable to use none. Try it.

Sources of information

Two are required, preferably three. For each source, give the specific magazine, book, or Internet site it was taken from, title of the article, author's full name, date of publication, and the chapter or pages telling where the material was found. If a source is a person, identify the source completely by title, position, and occupation. List these on the outline form. For Internet sites give the address (URL).

Outline your speech

Prepare a 75- to 100-word complete sentence outline.

Speak Up!

Before a more serious presentation, have some fun with a humorous anniversary speech. Write out a silly speech topic consisting of a subject and a time span. For example, The Six-Month Anniversary of the Sewer System Back-Up, or The 15th Year of Brady Bunch Reruns. Go around the class with each student standing and reading his or her topic aloud.

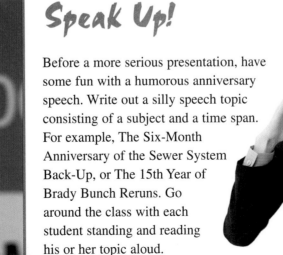

Purpose and Expectations of This Assignment

The experience of presenting an anniversary speech may well prove helpful to you at some later time. If in the future you are called upon to give such a speech, knowledge of the structure and style of such a presentation will serve you well. A person can be nervous and ill-at-ease when speaking on an occasion they have never previously experienced.

In completing this assignment, you will

- identify the necessary elements of an anniversary commemoration and
- create and present a speech that celebrates an historical event.

Defining the Anniversary Speech

The **anniversary speech** is presented in commemoration of an event, a person, or occasion. Its purpose is to recall and remember the past, so that we may more adequately serve the present and prepare for the future. It will weigh the past, observe the blessings of the present, and look to the future optimistically. Elements of loyalty and patriotism usually are contained in the remarks.

This talk is similar to the dedication speech. The selection of the speaker should be a person who represents the community both in character and ability. The speaker should be fully acquainted with the history of the event, the present status of the anniversary, and any future plans that are pertinent. You might think of the anniversary as a birthday celebration and incorporate all the ideals and ideas associated with such a day in order to create an innovative presentation.

Occasions for anniversary speeches arise whenever the passing of time is marked by a pause in which people lay aside their work long enough to note what has been accomplished. The remembrance of Independence Day, landing of the Pilgrims; Armistice; Thanksgiving; Labor Day; Christmas; and birthday of a national, state, or local figure are all examples of such occasions. Observance of the progress during a certain number of years of a business firm, school, church, city, state, nation, or any organization may form the basis of an anniversary speech.

Choosing a Topic

If you have a special loyalty or devotion to a particular holiday, construct your speech around it. National holidays are natural subjects for anniversary speeches. They commemorate historical events or individuals. However, you

can also use this assignment as a way of learning about the history of your school or community by choosing a more local subject as the topic of your presentation.

Preparing

Remember that your purpose is to commemorate the event and leave a lasting impression with your audience. Keep this purpose in mind constantly. Your thoughts must be constructed to achieve this end. The research and organization of your speech is important. You should include the following points: Explain why you are especially interested in this anniversary and show how the ideals of the past have led to the current celebration.

Anecdotes, stories, incidents, and humor are appropriate if used properly. The past should vividly live again for your audience. Turn next to the present; compare it with the past. Avoid references to or implications of partisan or class views. Speak broadly for all the people by utilizing a spirit of friendliness and goodwill. Bend your energies toward unity and interest for the common good. Speak next of the future. By virtue of a splendid past and a significant present, the future holds promises of greater things to come.

After constructing the speech, be sure to rehearse it aloud until you have fixed the order of points in your mind. Do not memorize it. Practice body language and gestures while rehearsing, but be sure to avoid mechanical movements.

Presenting

Speak sincerely. If you cannot and do not mean what you say, you should not speak. Your body language and your voice must evoke sincerity and knowledge about the event. Maintain good eye contact with your audience. You should be easily heard by all and be completely in their view. Your dress should be appropriate to the occasion.

Evaluating

Evaluate a classmate's anniversary speech. Rate the following criteria on a scale from 1 to 5 with 1 being "needs much improvement" and 5 being "outstanding."

- Did the speaker provide background information about the purpose of the anniversary celebration?
- Did the speaker connect the past with the present?
- Did the speaker choose appropriate vocabulary and sentence construction?
- Was the speaker's presentation serious and dignified?
- Would the speech engender positive feelings among audience members?
- Was the speech fluent and well rehearsed?

Give an overall score to the speech. Then write down one area of the speaker's performance that was excellent and one area that needs work.

Example Speech

The President's Remarks One Year After 9/11

by President George W. Bush

Ellis Island, New York
September 11, 2002

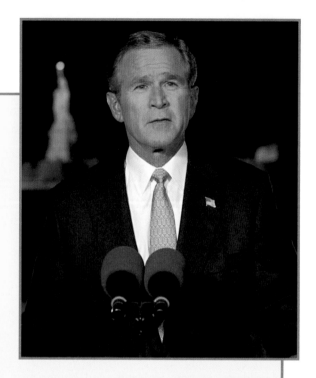

Good evening. A long year has passed since enemies attacked our country. We've seen the images so many times they are seared on our souls, and remembering the horror, reliving the anguish, re-imagining the terror, is hard—and painful.

For those who lost loved ones, it's been a year of sorrow, of empty places, of newborn children who will never know their fathers here on earth. For members of our military, it's been a year of sacrifice and service far from home. For all Americans, it has been a year of adjustment, of coming to terms with the difficult knowledge that our nation has determined enemies, and that we are not invulnerable to their attacks.

Yet, in the events that have challenged us, we have also seen the character that will deliver us. We have seen the greatness of America in airline passengers who defied their hijackers and ran a plane into the ground to spare the lives of others. We've seen the greatness of America in rescuers who rushed up flights of stairs toward peril. And we continue to see the greatness of America in the care and compassion our citizens show to each other.

September 11, 2001, will always be a fixed point in the life of America. The loss of so many lives left us to examine our own. Each of us was reminded that we are here only for a time, and these counted days should be filled with things that last and matter: love for our families, love for our neighbors and for our country; gratitude for life and to the Giver of life.

We resolved a year ago to honor every last person lost. We owe them remembrance and we owe them more. We owe them, and their children, and our own, the most enduring monument we can build: a world of liberty and security made possible by the way America leads, and by the way Americans lead their lives.

The attack on our nation was also an attack on the ideals that make us a nation. Our deepest national conviction is that every life is precious, because every life is the gift of a Creator who intended us to live in liberty and equality. More than anything else, this separates us from the enemy we fight. We value every life; our enemies value none—not even the innocent, not even their own. And we seek the freedom and opportunity that give meaning and value to life.

There is a line in our time, and in every time, between those who believe all men are created equal, and those who believe that some men and women and children are expendable in the pursuit of power. There is a line in our time, and in every time, between the defenders of human liberty and those who seek to master the minds and souls of others. Our generation has now heard history's call, and we will answer it.

America has entered a great struggle that tests our strength, and even more our resolve. Our nation is patient and steadfast. We continue to pursue the terrorists in cities and camps and caves across the earth. We are joined by a great coalition of nations to rid the world of terror. And we will not allow any terrorist or tyrant to threaten civilization with weapons of mass murder. Now and in the future, Americans will live as free people, not in fear, and never at the mercy of any foreign plot or power.

This nation has defeated tyrants and liberated death camps, raised this lamp of liberty to every captive land. We have no intention of ignoring or appeasing history's latest gang of fanatics trying to murder their way to power. They are discovering, as others before them, the resolve of a great country and a great democracy. In the ruins of two towers, under a flag unfurled at the Pentagon, at the funerals of the lost, we have made a sacred promise to ourselves and to the world: we will not relent until justice is done and our nation is secure. What our enemies have begun, we will finish.

I believe there is a reason that history has matched this nation with this time. America strives to be tolerant and just. We respect the faith of Islam, even as we fight those whose actions defile that faith. We fight, not to impose our will, but to defend ourselves and extend the blessings of freedom.

We cannot know all that lies ahead. Yet, we do know that God had placed us together in this moment, to grieve together, to stand together, to serve each other and our country. And the duty we have been given—defending America and our freedom—is also a privilege we share.

We're prepared for this journey. And our prayer tonight is that God will see us through, and keep us worthy.

Tomorrow is September the 12th. A milestone is passed, and a mission goes on. Be confident. Our country is strong. And our cause is even larger than our country. Ours is the cause of human dignity, freedom guided by conscience and guarded by peace. This ideal of America is the hope of all mankind. That hope drew millions to this harbor. That hope still lights our way. And the light shines in the darkness. And the darkness will not overcome it.

May God bless America.

The Commencement Address

Specs for the Commencement Address

Time limit

5–7 minutes.

Speaker's notes

10-word maximum limit.

Sources of information

Two are required, preferably three. For each source give the specific magazine, book, or Internet site it was taken from, title of the article, author's full name, date of publication, and the chapter or pages telling where the material was found. If a source is a person, identify the source completely by title, position, and occupation. List these on the outline form. For Internet sites give the address (URL).

Outlining

Prepare a 75- to 100-word complete sentence outline.

Speak Up!

Interview a parent, relative, or other adult about a graduation in which he or she participated or recall one that you attended. Who were the speakers? How were they received? Were the speeches relevant and interesting or cliche-ridden and boring? What elements made them appealing or dull? As a class, brainstorm a list of *dos* and *don'ts* that commencement speakers should follow.

Purpose and Expectations of This Assignment

How many times have you been to a graduation of a friend or relative hoping that the speeches will be short so you can get on with the ceremony? Unfortunately, this is the way many people feel about the speeches presented at graduation ceremonies. However, the commencement speech need not be boring. A well-executed commencement address will cause the audience to reflect on the past and inspire them to action in the future. This speech has its own unique difficulties. The speaker must be able to relate to an audience of parents and relatives along with the graduates. The ability to communicate to both of these audiences and present an interesting, stimulating speech is the focus of this address.

In completing this assignment, you will

- determine the objectives of a commencement address and

- create and deliver a commencement speech.

Defining the Commencement Address

Occasions for **commencement speeches** are not as numerous as are those for other types of speeches. Commencement ceremonies usually limit their speakers to (1) a special guest, (2) the senior class president, and (3) the valedictorian and/or salutatorian. There are several objectives for the commencement speech. The speech should congratulate the students and family members on their accomplishments that led to graduation. It is important not to neglect parents and relatives in the audience who had a part in

the student's education. A similar objective is to pay tribute to the teachers and administrators who helped the students through the education system.

Another element of the commencement address is reflecting on past memories and traditions. This part of the speech is the one most appreciated by the students in the audience. The speaker relates stories about the things that have happened over the years and shares special memories. The speech should have a serious overtone, but humorous anecdotes and stories can add life to the presentation. Another objective is to issue a challenge for the future. The speaker should inspire the graduates to do great things as they embark on a new chapter in their lives.

Choosing a Topic

One of the most important things to remember about choosing a topic is that it needs to be interesting to a wide variety of audience members. The speaker will be dealing with the students who are anxious to graduate, along with parents, grandparents, siblings, and friends. Many of these people have attended graduation ceremonies before and have certain expectations of what should be included in commencement speeches. The student speakers should remember that "inside" stories of past experiences might not be of interest, or make much sense, to anyone other than their classmates.

Preparing and Organizing

As with any speech presentation, careful attention should be paid to organization and supporting material. The speaker should prepare examples and stories that support the themes of the presentation. The examples should be vivid, and interesting, making the principles of the speech come alive. Quotations from philosophers or other respected individuals may be utilized. Use of contrast may be helpful as the speaker issues challenges for the students' new endeavors. Commencement is a beginning along with an ending and may be contrasted with other beginnings. The speech must leave the audience with a sense of accomplishment and an eagerness to move into the future. Therefore, organization of the presentation must build to these points.

A guest speaker should attempt to impart some personal wisdom, which comes with age, to the audience. The speaker becomes the expert, leading the younger generation into their new world. A senior class president, valedictorian, or salutatorian becomes the representative of the student body at the commencement ceremony. Their presentations should reflect the themes that are important to their classmates. They should include memories of happy times, sad times, and important times in their school experience.

Presenting

Since the commencement speaker is not the real highlight of the ceremony, the speaker needs to grab and hold on to the attention of the audience. The speaker must be dynamic and enthusiastic. The speaker must be sincere and earnest and as brief as possible.

Since this may be an emotional time for the student speakers, practice is essential. Practice in front of people should be a requirement. The parts of the speech that need to be inspiring should be delivered in an enthusiastic, dynamic tone. Other parts of the speech, which call for earnest reflection and sincere gratitude, also need to be delivered in the appropriate tone. The speech should be long enough to get the message across but not so long that the audience feels trapped or bored. The speaker must remember that there are other parts to the ceremony. A long commencement speech is generally not well received by the audience.

All other presentational skills for speaking to large audiences should be observed. Speakers may wish to review the Talking Points: Working with a Microphone on page 339 prior to presenting this speech. Also prior to presenting, a review of the chapters that cover speeches to persuade and convince might be helpful.

Evaluating

Evaluate a classmate's commencement speech. Rate the following criteria on a scale from 1 to 5 with 1 being "needs much improvement" and 5 being "outstanding."

- Did the speaker choose a topic appropriate to the situation?
- Would the presentation be of interest to all members of the audience?
- Was the material organized in a logical fashion?
- Did the speaker maintain eye contact with the audience?
- Did the speaker challenge the graduates about their future?

Give an overall score to the speech. Then choose one area of the speaker's performance that was especially good and write him or her a note about it.

Example Speech

Commencement Speech to Mount Holyoke College

by Suzan-Lori Parks

Thank you, graduating class of 2001, fellow honorary degree recipients, distinguished administration and faculty, alumnae, parents, family and friends; thank you all so much for inviting me to speak with you today. I graduated from Mount Holyoke in 1985. Here I am 16 years later. The learned faculty is seated there behind me, and so, before I get into the swing of things, I want to state that any grammatical errors, historical fabrications, and inappropriate flights of fancy contained within the following speech are the sole responsibility of the commencement speaker and, if found objectionable, should in no way be viewed as an example of the caliber of education one would receive at Mount Holyoke College.

It is commencement and you all are commencing—you are beginning. Today is your birthday. It's a sort of birthday for me too: this is my first honorary degree. You're sitting there looking forward into me and I'm standing here looking forward into you. I'll be your mirror for a few minutes, if you'll be mine. All of us together, we are commencing. It is the beginning of things, it's also the end of things and I've brought along 16 suggestions which may be of use—as you walk through the rest of your lives.

Suggestions and advice are funny things. In 1982 I took a creative writing class with James Baldwin. He suggested to me that I try playwriting, and I tried playwriting and here I am today. That was some good advice.

But it wasn't the best advice I ever got.

The best advice I ever got was also the worst advice anyone ever gave me. In high school I had a very stern English teacher, and one gloomy day she summoned me into her gloomy office. She knew I loved English and that I wanted to study literature and perhaps someday become a writer—"Don't study English," she said, "you haven't got the talent for it." What a horrible thing to say. What an excellent suggestion. It was an excellent suggestion because it forced me to think for myself. And that's my first suggestion for you.

SUGGESTION #1: CULTIVATE THE ABILITY TO THINK FOR YOURSELF. When someone gives you advice, you lay their advice alongside your own thoughts and feelings, and if what they suggest jives with what you've got going on inside, then you follow their suggestion. On the other hand—there are lots of people out there who will suggest all kinds of stupid stuff for you to incorporate into your life. There are lots of people who will encourage you to stray from your heart's desire. Go ahead and let them speak their piece, and you may even want to give them a little smile depending on your mood, but if what they suggest does not jive with the thoughts and feelings that are already alive and growing beautifully inside you, then don't follow their suggestion. THINK for yourself, LISTEN to your heart,

TUNE IN to your gut. These are just the things for which Mount Holyoke has educated you. You've all received an excellent education here, and education, excellent education, is just a kind of ear training. That's all it really is—inner ear training.

SUGGESTION #2: EMBRACE DISCIPLINE. Give yourself the opportunity to discover that discipline is just an extension of the love you have for yourself—discipline is not, as a lot of people think, some horrid exacting torturous self-flagellating activity—discipline is just an expression of love—like the Disciples—they didn't follow Christ because they HAD TO.

SUGGESTION #3: PRACTICE PATIENCE, whether you sit around like I do, working for that perfect word, or you're working toward a dream job, or wishing for a dreamy sweetheart. Things will come to you when you're ready to handle them—not before. Just keep walking your road.

SUGGESTION #4: And as you walk your road, as you live your life, RELISH THE ROAD. And relish the fact that the road of your life will probably be a windy road. Something like—the yellow brick road in *The Wizard of Oz*. You see the glory of Oz up ahead—but there are lots of twists and turns along the way—lots of tin men, lots of green women.

SUGGESTION #5: DEVELOP THE ART OF MAKING A SILK PURSE FROM A SOW'S EAR.

'Cause, you know, it ain't whatcha got, it's how you work it.

SUGGESTION #6: FOR EVERY 30 MINUTES OF TV YOU WATCH, READ ONE POEM OUT LOUD. For every work of literature you read, spend at least 30 minutes in the mall, or in a mall equivalent such as Wal-Mart. This is cross-fertilization—a new-age form of crop rotation—a way to cross train your spirit and keep interested in everything and not get too stuck in your ways.

Speaking of your ways and your way:

SUGGESTION #7: GET OUT OF YOUR WAY. You can spend your life tripping on yourself; you can also spend your life tripping yourself up. Get out of your own way.

You're young, brilliant, and today is your birthday. You've got your whole lives ahead of you, and each of you will spend your life doing something, or maybe a host of things. Don't just spend your life.

SPLURGE.

SUGGESTION #8: SPLURGE YOUR LIFE BY DOING SOMETHING YOU LOVE. My husband Paul is a musician. He says that the concept of talent is overrated because "talent" is really the gift of love. "Talent" happens when you're in love with something and you devote your life to it, and it's your love of it that makes you want to keep doing it, it's your love of it which helps you overcome the obstacles along the way, and it's your love of it that begets a talent for it.

continued

Example Speech cont.

SUGGESTIONS #9, 10, 11, 12, and 13: Eat Your Vegetables, Floss Your Teeth, Try Meditation, Get Some Exercise, and SHARPEN YOUR SEVEN SENSES: the basic Five Senses plus the Sixth Sense: ESP, and the Seventh Sense, which is your sense of HUMOR.

Sixteen years ago I sat where one of you is sitting now. The class of 1985 was graduating. And we were lucky as we had a great poet speaking to us. She was a great writer and an MHC alum. She was pretty and poised and she had such grace—so much grace that I sat there looking at her thinking that she looked more as if she had gone to Smith. Anyway it was sunny and we were all in black, probably sweating a little, and she spoke brilliantly and eloquently, and to this day I have absolutely no memory of what she said. I don't remember one word of her brilliant commencement address, the address that launched the class of 1985. Not one word. I want you to catch my drift. I'm not saying our speaker was boring. I'm saying that I don't remember what she said. But I do remember some words that went through my head at the very moment our speaker's words were passing by. It was a voice, coming from my gut, a voice coming from my heart and the voice said: "Ah, Suzan-Lori Parks, the next degree you're going to receive is an honorary degree from MHC."

Yep, I really said that to myself. And here I am today.

SUGGESTION #14: SAY "THANK YOU" at least once a week.

SUGGESTION #15: LOVE YOURSELF. Why not.

Sixteen years from now who will remember these words? Maybe no one. But maybe someone will. Maybe, from back in 1985, there is a classmate of mine who, to this day, remembers every word of our commencement address and this classmate repeats those words, and they lighthouse her stormy days, maybe. Or if not a classmate remembering, then maybe an alum, if not an alum maybe a family member, maybe a parent, up there, gathered in the background having given so much, helping you get to this special day. Whether my words today will be remembered is not the issue because, you see, what I'm saying to you right now isn't as important as what you are saying, right now, to yourselves.

SUGGESTION #16: BE BOLD. ENVISION YOURSELF LIVING A LIFE THAT YOU LOVE. Believe, even if you can only muster your faith for just this moment, believe that the sort of life you wish to live is, at this very moment, just waiting for you to summon it up. And when you wish for it, you begin moving toward it, and it, in turn, begins moving toward you.

As the great writer James Baldwin said: "Your crown has been bought and paid for. All you have to do is put it on your head."

Thank you.

Example Speech

Choices and Change: Your Success as a Family

by Barbara Bush, Former First Lady of the United States

Delivered at Severance Green, Wellesley College, Wellesley, Massachusetts, June 1, 1990

Thank you, President Keohane, Mrs. Gorbachev,[1] trustees, faculty, parents, Julie Porer, Christine Bicknell, and the Class of 1990. I am thrilled to be with you today, and very excited, as I know you must all be, that Mrs. Gorbachev could join us.

More than ten years ago when I was invited here to talk about our experiences in the People's Republic of China, I was struck by both the natural beauty of your campus and the spirit of this place.

Wellesley, you see, is not just a place, but an idea, an experiment in excellence in which diversity is not just tolerated, but is embraced.

The essence of this spirit was captured in a moving speech about tolerance given last year by the student body president of one of your sister colleges. She related the story by Robert Fulghum about a young pastor who, finding himself in charge of some very energetic children, hit upon a game called "Giants, Wizards, and Dwarfs." "You have to decide now," the pastor instructed the children, "Which are you . . . a giant, a wizard, or a dwarf?" At that, a small girl tugging on his pants leg asked, "But where do the mermaids stand?"

The pastor told her there are *no* mermaids. "Oh yes there are," she said. "I am a mermaid."

This little girl knew what she was and she was not about to give up on either her identity *or* the game. She intended to take her place wherever mermaids fit into the scheme of things. Where *do* the mermaids stand . . . all those who are different, those who do not fit the boxes and the pigeonholes? "Answer that question," wrote Fulghum, "And you can build a school, a nation, or a whole world on it."

As that very wise young woman said . . . "Diversity, like anything worth having, requires *effort*." Effort to learn about and respect difference, to be compassionate with one another, and to cherish our own identity, and to accept unconditionally the same in all others.

You should all be very proud that this is the Wellesley spirit. Now I know your first choice for today was Alice Walker, known for *The Color Purple*. Instead you got me—known for the color of my hair! Of course, Alice Walker's book has a special color, and for four years the class of '90 has worn the color purple. Today you meet on Severance Green to say good-bye to all that, to begin a new and very personal journey, a search for your own true colors.

In the world that awaits you beyond the shores of Lake Waban, no one can say what your true colors will be. But this I know: You have a first-class education from a first-class school. And so you need not, probably cannot, live a "paint-by-numbers" life. Decisions are not irrevocable. Choices

[1] Raisa Gorbachev, wife of Mikhail Gorbachev, former president of the U.S.S.R.

continued

do come back. As you set off from Wellesley, I hope that many of you will consider making three very special choices.

The first is to believe in something larger than yourself, to get involved in some of the big ideas of your time. I chose literacy because I honestly believe that if more people could read, write, and comprehend, we would be that much closer to solving so many of the problems plaguing our society.

Early on I made another choice which I hope you will make as well. Whether you are talking about education, career, or service, you are talking about life, and life must have joy. It's supposed to be fun!

One of the reasons I made the most important decision of my life, to marry George Bush, is because he made me laugh. It's true, sometimes we've laughed through our tears, but that shared laughter has been one of our strongest bonds. Find the joy in life, because as Ferris Bueller said on his day off: "Life moves pretty fast. Ya don't stop and look around once in a while, ya gonna miss it!"

The third choice that must not be missed is to cherish your human connections: your relationships with friends and family. For several years, you've had impressed upon you the importance to your career of dedication and hard work. This is true, but as important as your obligations as a doctor, lawyer, or business leader will be, you are a human being first, and those human connections, with spouses, with children, with friends, are the most important investments you will ever make.

At the end of your life, you will never regret not having passed one more test, not winning one more verdict, or not closing one more deal. You will regret time not spent with a husband, a friend, a child, or a parent.

We are in a transitional period right now, fascinating and exhilarating times, learning to adjust to the changes and the choices we, men and women, are facing. I remember what a friend said, on hearing her husband lament to his buddies that he had to baby-sit. Quickly setting him straight, my friend told her husband that when it's your own kids, it's not called baby-sitting!

Maybe we should adjust faster, maybe slower. But whatever the era, whatever the times, one thing will never change: fathers and mothers, if you have children, they must come first. Your success as a family, our success as a society, depends not on what happens at the White House, but on what happens inside your house.

For over 50 years, it was said that the winner of Wellesley's annual hoop race would be the first to get married. Now they say the winner will be the first to become a C.E.O. Both of these stereotypes show too little tolerance for those who want to know where the mermaids stand. So I offer you today a new legend: the winner of the hoop race will be the first to realize her dream, not society's dream, her own personal dream. And who knows: Somewhere out in this audience may even be someone who will one day follow in my footsteps, and preside over the White House as the president's spouse. I wish him well!

The controversy ends here. But our conversation is only beginning. And a worthwhile conversation it is. So as you leave Wellesley today, take with you deep thanks for the courtesy and honor you have shared with Mrs. Gorbachev and me. Thank you. God bless you. And may your future be worthy of your dreams.

UNIT 7 Contest Speaking

Competitive public speaking can build and hone valuable communication skills. In this unit we present experiences to guide you in some of the most common speaking contest events. Your school may be a member of the State High School Activities Association (SHSAA), which sponsors individual events in competitive public speaking and/or dramatic presentation. If regional events are not available in your area, you might consider setting up a small contest within your class or school.

Competition has a way of getting the adrenaline flowing, which may allow you to hone your communication skills in a whole new way. In so doing, it will provide you with a fresh way to rehearse and develop important skills that will benefit your public speaking for years to come.

Speech Experiences in This Unit

Oral Interpretation

Specs for Oral Interpretation

Time limits

4–5 minutes.

Speaker's notes

Do not use notes for oral interpretation.

Sources of information

If you have difficulty finding materials
for an oral interpretation project, consult with your instructor
or coach. The school librarian may also be able to help.

Outline

Do not use an outline for this assignment.

Speak Up!

Borrow some picture books for young children.
With a partner, take turns reading one of the
books aloud. Use expressions, vocal variety,
and movement to make the story entertaining
for your "young" listener. When you have
finished, switch roles and have your partner
read a different book to you. Discuss any
difficulties you had and how you each could
improve your oral interpretation skills.

Purpose and Expectations of This Assignment

Many people have a hard time measuring up to the demands of oral reading. Too many readers have no idea how to get the material across with expression. As a result, excellent literary materials go unread or are read so poorly that much of their beauty and thought are lost. No one expects you to master the field of oral interpretation after concluding one appearance before your classmates, but after this assignment you will have a much clearer understanding of and facility for reading aloud. This speech experience will help you improve your oral reading from the standpoint of personal enjoyment and the ability to read for others.

In completing this assignment, you will

- research an author's background,
- discover the meaning and thoughts intended by the author of a selected text,
- understand the process of a formal oral interpretation presentation, and
- rehearse and present an oral interpretation to an audience.

Defining Oral Interpretation

Oral Interpretation is a formal public speaking event that features oral expression to bring out the emotions and deeper meanings implanted in a text and to express those meanings to an audience. The purpose may be to inform, to entertain, to arouse, to persuade, or to incite action. Successful oral interpretation demands that the speaker know the material well enough to interpret fully and accurately the ideas, meanings, and subtleties of the composition. This form of expression requires meticulous preparation on the part of the reader/performer.

As an oral interpreter, you must have a thorough understanding of what the author is saying. Through your performance you assume the responsibility of discovering and interpreting the author's meaning by using your voice and body language.

There are many occasions for this type of public speaking. Any gathering at which it is appropriate to read aloud is an opportunity for oral interpretation. School, church, and civic gatherings are perhaps the most common venues. Clubs, societies, private groups, private parties, and even commercial organizations utilize oral reading for education and for entertainment. Perhaps you remember a parent or older sibling reading to you when you were young. This is one of the most common examples of oral interpretation.

Choosing a Selection

Choosing what to read for an oral interpretive presentation is not easy. So be sure to make your choice early and give yourself plenty of time to prepare. The selection should be suited to your strengths as a reader. In other words, choose something that you are capable of preparing and later interpreting. For this reading experience—particularly the first time—stick with an interpretation that does not require you to create multiple characters. Of course, if you

have had some prior experience and you are sure you have what it takes to portray different characters and make the necessary transitions between them, go ahead.

Your selection must be applicable to you and your audience. This means that you should analyze both your audience and the occasion carefully. You must ascertain the kind of environment in which you will be reading. The size of the building, the seating arrangement, outside noises, building distractions, and other factors should definitely influence your selection. If you observe all of these elements before you settle on a selection, you have a good chance of presenting a credible oral reading.

Preparing

Sources for oral interpretive material are available in your school library. Check the card catalog for poetry, prose readings, and dramatic scenes or monologues. Your instructor and the librarian can help you.

Once you have found your selection, study it in depth. Know the meaning of every word, and pay special attention to the punctuation. The author wrote it a certain way for a reason. Learn all you can about the author so that you may understand what underlies the specific words, phrases, and punctuation. Try to understand the philosophy and point of view. Learn about the circumstances surrounding the writing of your particular selection. Practice telling why you chose this piece. Tell something about the author so that the listeners may better understand his or her circumstances and background; provide information concerning the setting of the prose or poetry; and include anything else that will contribute to the audience's appreciation and enjoyment of your reading.

To better understand your selection's meaning, it is often helpful to paraphrase and pantomime it. By doing this, you may discover deeper layers of meaning within the selection.

The quality and tone of your voice must tell and imply a great deal. You must provide vocal variety as to rhythm, rate, pitch, melody, and intensity—everything should be in keeping with the material you are interpreting. All of these qualities should be determined during rehearsal. Mark your manuscript to indicate where you need to slow down or read more rapidly. You can also use different colored highlighters to identify vocal changes. If you emphasize the emotion and meaning of the story, the audience will be better able to visualize and relate to the overall presentation.

Use body language to further enhance the words you read. Include any activity and gesture that will add to the interpretation of your reading. Whatever will assist in imparting the mood, emotion, and meaning should be a part of your presentation. Your goal is to make the reading an *interpretation* and not an impersonation of the author's characters. That means you must strive to put something of yourself into the presentation.

For ease in handling your material, you may want to type or photocopy the section of the book you are reading and place it in a folder. That way you won't have to deal with handling a larger text in a clumsy manner.

Practice reading aloud until you know the entire selection well enough that you can give most of your attention and eye contact (80 to 90 percent) to your audience. This will necessitate a form of memorization that will permit you to use the printed copy as merely a guide.

You may wish to videotape your rehearsals to give you insight about how to improve your interpretation. (See Talking Points: Using Video to Improve Your Speech Performance on page 247.)

Presenting

Keep in mind that your audience is watching you at all times. This includes before and after you read. As you approach the front of the room or the stage, the audience will be observing you and forming opinions. Thus it is imperative that you constantly maintain an alert, poised, and friendly appearance. When you rise to read, your confidence and poise should be evident. Do not hurry to your position. Take your place politely and without hesitation. Pause a few seconds to glance over your audience before you begin.

After you have introduced your selection with a short discussion of the author or the material itself, begin your reading.

Hold your script in such a way that it does not hide your face or block the flow of your voice. One hand placed palm down on the page will permit you to mark your place with your forefinger. With your other hand, hold the script palm up; this will act as a support. You need not hold your book in only one position, especially while you are looking at your audience. The main point to remember is to raise your book when you read. If you do this, you will avoid bowing your head, which makes it hard for the audience to hear you. Give them the best chance to see your face to catch your emotions and meanings.

If you are reading several selections, treat each one separately. Allow sufficient time in between that the audience may applaud and relax slightly and otherwise express their enjoyment of your performance. When concluding a reading, pause a second or two before politely returning to your chair. Avoid quickly closing your book or manuscript and leaving the stage before you're completely finished with your performance.

Evaluating

Evaluate a classmate's oral interpretation using the criteria below.

- Did the speaker provide interesting information about the author or background of the selection?

- Was the speaker able to maintain eye contact with the audience?

- Did the speaker seem to know the material well?

- Did the speaker use vocal variety, including changing the speed, rhythm, and volume of the presentation?

- Did the speaker end the presentation with a moment or two of silence?

Give an overall score to the speech. Then choose one area of the speaker's performance that may have given you new ideas about your own oral interpretation skills. Write a short paragraph to explain.

Talking Points

Using Video to Improve Your Speech Performance

Many people cringe the first time they see themselves on videotape. But a critical look at your oral interpretation skills by means of a videotaped rehearsal can do wonders for your eventual performance. Here are a few tips to help make videotaping your rehearsal as positive and effective as possible.

1. If you are using a stationary camera, set it up so that your entire body is in the picture. This allows you to observe your posture, stance, body movements, and gestures.

2. If you have a friend videotape you, make sure he or she gets some close-ups of your upper body and face to allow you to observe your gestures and facial expressions.

3. Tape the entire performance, including walking to where you will present your oral interpretation and leaving the area when you have finished.

4. Replay and watch the tape, reviewing the strengths and weaknesses of just your verbal delivery.

5. Play the tape again without the audio and evaluate your nonverbal communication.

6. Practice the speech once more without taping it. Work on the areas you noted as needing improvement.

7. Tape the speech again. Be sure to keep the first practice session on the tape. Watch the first practice and the second in sequence. Did you improve your performance? If not, work more without the tape.

8. Tape a final practice when you feel you have the speech ready for presentation. As you view it, concentrate on the improvements you made.

Extemporaneous Speaking

Specs for Extemporaneous Speaking

Time limit

6–7 minutes.

Speaker's notes

Key words only.

Sources of information

For this type of public speaking the references are called **cites**. Two are required, preferably three. For each cite, state the specific magazine or book from which it was taken, the title of the article, the author's full name, and the date of publication, if available. If a source is a person, identify him or her as completely as possible, including full name, title or position, occupation, and date of interview.

Outline

You will not need an outline for this assignment.

Speak Up!

Share some details about a news story or current event that has been on your mind lately. As you tell the class about it, assume that they have no prior knowledge on this subject. Give them what you consider to be the facts—and also your opinion.

Purpose and Expectations of This Assignment

Many forensics tournaments include extemporaneous speaking. The skills you can discover and develop by participating in this event include the ability to organize your thoughts quickly, critically analyze current events, frame your opinions and ideas about national and international issues, and express these opinions concisely and effectively to others.

Keeping up with current events helps demonstrate that you are aware of the larger world, a trait that can be very attractive to colleges and employers you wish to impress. Extemporaneous speaking is a valuable skill to have in today's job market. While experience in this type of speaking is definitely recommended for anyone interested in pursuing a career as an on-air personality in radio or television, strong communication skills are important no matter what field you enter. With sincere effort, you can master these skills in a relatively short time—and reap the benefits for years to come.

In completing this assignment, you will

- understand the procedures of tournament extemporaneous speaking,

- analyze a current event or issue,

- determine an opinion on a current event or issue, and

- organize speech materials in a limited amount of time.

Defining Extemporaneous Speaking

When speaking extemporaneously in formal speech situations such as tournaments or contests, you may be given the option to choose either national or international issues. International issues would include topics dealing with other countries, or with U.S. foreign relations.

The typical system allows you to draw three topics, then select one of those on which to prepare your speech. Typically, you will have 30 minutes for your preparation.

During the preparation time, you are allowed to consult source materials such as newspapers and magazines, or notes you may have made in advance from broadcast sources. You are not allowed to consult another person. At the end of the designated preparation time, you are expected to present your speech to a panel of judges and, sometimes, an audience. The judges will be aware that you have had a limited amount of time to prepare. Still they will expect from you a smooth delivery of well-organized ideas and a concise thesis statement.

Choosing a Topic

For this assignment your instructor will ask you to supply a topic from time to time as needed. Phrase each topic as a question. Examples of suitable topics for extemporaneous speaking are

- Will the recent crime bills passed by Congress reduce violent crimes by juveniles?

- Is the U.S. economy stable, or is it ready for a major "course correction"?

- How should the U.S. respond to the human rights abuses committed by military personnel at prisoner-of-war camps?

- Are college costs excessive?

- Should children under the age of 18 who commit murder be tried as adults?

Write one suggestion for each of the following general categories.

- National issues
- Economic issues
- International issues

Your topic suggestions should not be so narrow that they are unsuitable for your classmates. Aim for a topic that your fellow classmates are likely to know something about.

When you have a choice of topics, keep one simple rule in mind: Choose the topic on which you are best equipped to speak. Also take into consideration your audience and the occasion.

Preparing

As is true of impromptu speaking, you cannot use standard speech preparation practices here. That's because it's impossible to prepare fully for an unknown topic. However, unlike impromptu speaking, extemporaneous speaking does allow you a small amount of preparation time before you speak. Therefore, several suggestions are in order to help you make the most of that time.

1. To be a competent extemporaneous speaker, you must keep up with current events. A minimum effort in this regard is to listen to at least one radio or TV newscast per day, or read a daily newspaper. More than one source per day will add to your ability to see the issues from various points of view.

2. Review the material in the Preparing section of Speech Experience 19, "Impromptu Speaking," as many of the same organizational principles apply to extemporaneous speaking as well.

3. Have someone help you prepare by suggesting a topic in one of the three areas named above. He or she can time your preparation. Part of developing these speaking skills to their maximum effectiveness is simply practicing the process over and over again. The more opportunity you have to rehearse, the stronger your skills will become.

Once you have selected your topic, review your knowledge of the particular issue. Make notes about key ideas you recall. If you have brought clippings from current news publications with you, you may review and cite them as sources in your speech. Take a moment now to think clearly about what position you want to take on the topic. Write out a clear thesis statement that tells the audience both what you think is important about the topic and how your talk will reveal that.

Next, decide what organizational method will both fit your topic and make it easiest for the audience to follow what you are saying. You don't necessarily need three main points. Some topics require only two, and trying to create three can cause you to misuse your speaking time unnecessarily. Organize your key ideas on the issue and then check to be sure they make sense and fit together logically.

Take the last few minutes of your preparation time to plan an attention-getting introduction and a solid conclusion. Do not neglect this part of your preparation, as the conclusion and introduction are likely to be the parts of your speech that your audience will notice most. Search through your information on the issue to find a startling statistic or poignant story that could capture your listeners' imaginations. Use such an example to begin your speech, followed by your thesis statement and a preview of your main ideas. Your conclusion should restate your thesis, summarize your main points, and, if possible, refer back to that opening attention-getter.

Presenting

As with impromptu speaking, your attitude toward your audience and your subject has a tremendous impact on your effectiveness when speaking extemporaneously. Maintaining your poise is crucial. You may wish to review the suggestions for this in the Presenting section of Speech Experience 19.

When you are ready to speak, begin by making eye contact with members of the audience and the judges. (Some events do not have an audience. In this case you will make eye contact with the judge(s).) Begin your introduction with confidence; be careful not to speak too fast. Use gestures when appropriate, but avoid movements that only serve to communicate nervousness. You may wish to cross the room as you progress to a new main point. However, do not make these moves if they do not feel natural to you. Stagy movements are almost always obvious. They serve to reduce your credibility rather than enhance it.

Evaluating

Evaluate a classmate's extemporaneous speech. Be prepared to give oral feedback to the speaker on the following questions.

- Did the speaker make eye contact with the audience before beginning to speak?
- Did the presenter organize the information in a clear progression of ideas?
- Were the speaker's gestures and facial expressions appropriate to the occasion?

- Did the speaker have an interesting or attention-getting introduction?
- Did the speaker have a point of view about the issues?
- Were the speaker's movements appropriate and spontaneous?

When you share your thoughts with the speaker, try to avoid undue negativity. Open your comments by citing something the speaker did well. Try to be specific and cite examples whenever you can.

Parliamentary Procedure and Student Congress

A joint session of the U.S. Congress

Specs for Parliamentary Procedure and Student Congress

Time limit

Unless otherwise stated in the organization's constitution, 5 minutes is the generally recognized maximum time limit for a speaker's proposal.

Speaker's notes

Do not use notes for this assignment.

Sources of information

Robert's Rules of Order.

Outline

No outline is required for this assignment.

Speak Up!

Discuss courtroom dramas you have witnessed or films that take place partly on the floor of the Senate or the House of Representatives. What, for example, do you know about the following terms:

- out of order
- pass the motion
- passed by a narrow margin
- table the motion
- objection
- adjourned

Participate in a class discussion of these and other terms that might come to mind when you think about legally functioning entities.

Purpose and Expectations of This Assignment

For students who wish to learn how to conduct fair and orderly business meetings, many speaking tournaments offer an event called *Parliamentary Law* or *Student Congress*. This format requires knowledge of parliamentary procedure. It offers students a chance to apply their knowledge within the context of a lively debate. This assignment explains parliamentary procedure and related events in detail so that you may begin your participation in such events should you desire to do so.

By mastering the rules of parliamentary procedure, you will be able to take your place in any gathering whether you chair it or merely participate. Furthermore, you will be qualified to assist in carrying on all matters of business pertaining to the group's needs.

In completing this assignment, you will

- be able to identify and explain basic rules of parliamentary procedure,
- identify the basic duties of parliamentary officers and participants,
- understand the parliamentary process of conducting business, and
- compose and deliver a formal motion and arguments in its support.

Defining Parliamentary Law

To master parliamentary procedure, you must study *Robert's Rules of Order* and be prepared to follow the rules that govern participation in any organization that has a constitution and bylaws. Many people attempt to dominate an assembly in which group discussion is paramount, or they try to participate in a group discussion when they are totally uninformed regarding orderly and proper procedure. The results of haphazard procedure are notorious; ill will, upset feelings, confusion, stalled progress, and circuitous thinking are only a few of its byproducts.

Parliamentary procedure is a recognized procedure for conducting the business of a group. Its purpose is to expedite the transaction of business in an orderly manner by observing definite procedures, which may vary according to the constitutions and bylaws adopted by a group. In the many state legislatures and the national congress, parliamentary procedures are basically the same, but differ in terms of some of their interpretations. The rules of each assembly determine the procedures that prevail. There is no one set of rules that applies to all assemblies, despite the fact that they may all adopt the same text on parliamentary procedure. Each group follows its own laws, which they adopt, interpret, and enforce. The Kansas and Indiana legislatures might each adopt *Robert's Rules of Order* as their rulebook for conducting business, yet in carrying out the rules, they may differ widely. In fact, the house and senate in the same state legislature normally operate under different regulations. This is also true of the two houses in the national Congress. One of the obvious divergences here is the Unlimited Debate Ruling in the Senate (which allows senators to hold the floor for hours in filibusters) and the Limited Debate allowed in the House. There are other differences, which need not be discussed here. The fundamental point is that assemblies do operate under definite laws and regulations.

Situations for using parliamentary procedure arise any time a group meets to transact business—whether the occasion is a meeting in a church, a school, or one of 10,000 other places. The formality is dependent upon the group's knowledge and interpretation of the rules. Generally, the larger organized groups are more formal and observe their regulations more strictly than do smaller informal gatherings.

In all parliamentary meetings, however, members proceed through the business at hand by making motions. A **motion** is a call for action made by a member. No business takes place without a motion. Once a motion is made the members must act upon it.

For this assignment, you need to know three types of motions: **privileged**, **subsidiary**, and **incidental**. Following is a listing of the various kinds of motions and their purposes and rules within parliamentary procedure.

Using the Precedence of Motions and Their Rules

The best, if not the only, way to prepare for participation in parliamentary procedure is to be familiar with the precedence of motions and their applications. You can gain this familiarity with a reasonable amount of study using any standard parliamentary law book. Without this knowledge, you are likely to flounder during an assembly and slow down the proceedings. If you wish to master many of the technicalities, you should definitely make a detailed study of a parliamentary text. For now, you will find some fundamentals discussed in the following paragraphs.

Precedence of motions Motions are debated in a certain order. In the chart of Precedence of Motions and Their Rules on page 258, you will notice that number 13 is a **main motion**. There might be a main motion, for example, "That the Parliamentary Law Club have a party." This main motion is what the assembly must discuss. It is the *only* main motion that can be under discussion until it is disposed of. Once the motion has been disposed of, the assembly can legally entertain another main motion. If after discussion the group votes to have a party, the main motion is disposed of. If it votes not to have a party, the motion is disposed of. But let's suppose that the club does not want to adopt the motion as it stands. This raises another question—that of an **amendment**.

Amendments You see, as the motion stands, it simply suggests that the "Parliamentary Law Club have a party." It does not say *when* that party should take place. It is obvious that a change will have to be made. Now look at number 11 in the chart of Precedence of Motions. It is "to amend." It is in a position *above* the main motion of the chart. Hence, someone moves "to amend the main motion by adding the words *Saturday night, June 16.*" This is in order. It is discussed and voted on. If it carries, the group has decided to add the words "Saturday night, June 16" to the motion. If it fails, the main motion stands as it was originally made and is open to discussion or is ready to be voted on. Assuming for a moment that the amendment carried, the business before the house becomes that of disposing of the *main motion as amended*. It is debated and voted on.

Precedence of Motions and Their Rules

Key to the abbreviations of the rules:
2/3—Requires a 2/3 vote for adoption
Int.—May interrupt a speaker
Lim.—Limited debate
No-S.—No second required
Und.—Undebatable

Privileged Motions

These motions regulate the actual running of the meeting. They fulfill such functions as ending or pausing a meeting. Privileged motions may also concern basic physical functions, such as controlling the temperature of the meeting room, adjusting the lighting, or eliminating disturbances outside the room. Because the effects are immediate, these motions take precedence over all other types.

1.	To fix the time to adjourn	Lim.
2.	To adjourn (unqualified)	Und.
3.	To take a recess	Lim.
4.	To raise to a question of privilege	Int., Und., No-S.
5.	To call for orders of the day	Int., Und., No-S.

Subsidiary Motions

6.	To lay on the table	Und.
7.	To move the previous question (this stops debate)	Und., 2/3
8.	To limit or extend the limits of debate	Lim., 2/3
9.	To postpone definitely	Lim.
10.	To refer to committee	Lim.
11.	To amend	1/3 S
12.	To postpone indefinitely	Lim.
13.	A Main Motion –	
	a. "To reconsider" is a specific main motion	Int.

Incidental Motions

These have no precedence of order.

To suspend the rules	Und., 2/3
To withdraw a motion	No-S., Und.
To object to a consideration	Int., No-S., Und., 2/3
To rise to a point of order	Int., No-S., Und.
To rise to a point of information	Int., No-S., Und.
To appeal from the decision of the chair	Int., Lim.
To call for a division of the house	Int., No-S., Und.
To call for a division of a question	Und.

If an assembly wishes to, it can amend an amendment in the same manner it amends the main motion. It then discusses and votes on the amendment to the amendment. If this does not carry, the amendment remains untouched. If it does carry, the amendment *as amended* is next discussed and voted on. If it, in turn, does not carry, then the main motion remains unchanged and the amendment plus the amendment to the amendment is lost. If it does carry, the main motion as amended is debated and voted on. It is illegal to change an amendment beyond adding one amendment to it.

Other motions Let's suppose that the group decided to amend the main motion by adding the words "Saturday night, June 16," but still is not ready to decide definitely about having a party. You will note that number 10 in the chart of Precedence of Motions is "to refer to committee." When a motion is referred to a committee, all amendments automatically go with it. The motion to refer will be debated and voted on. If it carries, the main motion is *disposed of* and the assembly is ready for another main motion. If the motion to refer fails, then the main motion remains before the house as though the motion to refer to a committee had never been offered.

Now look at the chart of Precedence of Motions again. Notice that many more motions are listed above number 10. The higher you move up this list, the smaller the number of the motion is, but the more important it becomes, until you arrive at the very top. This is the most powerful motion of all. The motion on the chart may be placed before the assembly at any time during debate on a main motion, provided the new motion has precedence. In other words, John moves a main motion; Susan immediately moves number 9, to postpone the main motion definitely; Adam moves number 6, to lay the main motion on the table; Mary follows by moving number 3, to take a recess. This is all in order. However, when Adam moved number 6, Mary could not move number 8, since Adam's motion had precedence.

Actually, the precedence of motions in its simplest form means that a person may place any of the motions on the floor as long as he or she follows the rules of precedence. When you participate in parliamentary procedures, you have to understand that the numbers appearing before each motion are not put there for counting purposes. Instead they tell you exactly what motion has precedence over other motions. The most important motion, as far as having power over other motions is concerned, is number 1, to fix the time at which to adjourn. The second most important motion in order of precedence is number 2, to adjourn—unqualified; next is number 3; then number 4; and so on, clear down to number 13, the main motion itself.

Now let's look at the chart of Precedence of Motions once more. You see the 13 motions divided into three specific groups: namely, Privileged Motions (number 1 through number 5), Subsidiary Motions (number 6 through number 12), and the Main Motion, number 13, which can be a motion about anything from abolishing taxes to having a party.

Here is the main point you should take away from studying these 13 motions. After you have a main motion on the floor, there are seven actions you can take on it. These are the motions numbered 6, 7, 8, 9, 10, 11, and 12. They are called *subsidiary* because they pertain to things you can do to a main motion. At a glance you can see that an assembly can do anything from postponing a motion indefinitely to laying it on the table and taking it off again.

These motions do not conflict with the ruling that you can have only one main motion at a time. They are not main motions. They are the ways you change (amend) or dispose of a motion (postpone indefinitely, refer to a committee, or lay on the table). Of course, you can dispose of a motion by adopting or rejecting it. It is obvious that once you have a main motion before the assembly, you have to do something with it, and rules concerning precedence of motions tell you how to do it.

If you examine the privileged motions, 1 through 5, you will see that they do not do anything to a main motion. They are the actions a group can take while it is disposing of a main motion. For example, if the club were discussing a main motion to have a party, someone could move number 3, to take a recess. If the group wanted to take a recess, they would vote to do so and then recess for five minutes (or whatever time the motion to recess specified). When the recess was over, they would convene again and resume discussing the main motion where they left off when they voted to recess.

The section entitled Incidental Motions is largely self-explanatory. You will note that it concerns those things a person would normally do during debate on a motion. For example, if the assembly were debating the motion to have a party, you might want to find out whether it was in order to offer an amendment to the main motion at that time. In this case you would *rise to a point of information*, sometimes called a *point of parliamentary inquiry*. If you observed an infraction of the rules that the chair had overlooked, you would immediately rise to a point of order. You will notice that most incidental motions require no second and also permit interruption of a speaker. This is true because certain matters must be clarified while debate is in progress. Otherwise too many corrections would have to be made after a motion was adopted or defeated.

Preparing

For this assignment, each student will be required to place at least three motions before the assembly and seek their adoption. Motions that are adopted should be reported to your instructor. To prepare for this assignment, you will have to become familiar with a number of duties and protocols. Here is a list to get you started.

Duties

The chairperson This is the person who must call the meeting to order, conduct the business of the assembly, enforce rules, appoint committees and their chairpersons, and appoint a secretary for each meeting if one has not been elected. The chairperson refrains from discussing any motion before the house. If the chairperson wants to speak on a proposal, he or she appoints a member to substitute, then assumes the position of a participant in the assembly. The chairperson must gain recognition from the newly appointed chairperson, make remarks on an equal basis with other members of the group, and then resume the chair at any time desired.

The secretary This is the officer who must keep an accurate record of all business transacted by the house. This includes all motions, whether carried or defeated, who seconded the motions, and the votes upon them. The secretary also keeps a record of all committees appointed and any other actions of the assembly.

Protocols

To gain recognition from the chairperson
Rise and address the chairperson by saying "Mr. (or Madam) Chair." The chair will then address you by name, nod to you, point toward you, or give some other sign of recognition. You are not allowed to speak until you get the chair's permission to do so.

To place a motion on the floor Gain recognition from the chair; then state your motion, beginning with the phrase, "I move that _____."

To dispose of a motion The assembly must adopt, reject, or apply subsidiary motions to it.

To second a motion Simply call out the word *second*. You need not rise or have recognition from the chairperson.

To change (amend) a motion Gain recognition, and then say, "I move to amend the motion (or amendment) by adding the words _____," or "by striking out the words _____," or "by striking out the words _____ and inserting the words _____."

To ask for information Rise without gaining recognition, interrupt a speaker if necessary, and say, "Mr. (or Madam) Chair, point of information" or "I rise to a point of parliamentary inquiry." When the chair says, "State your point," ask your question.

To ask a member of the assembly a question First gain recognition; then say, "Will the speaker yield to a question?" The chair then asks the person if he or she will yield. If the member says yes, you may ask one question. If not, you may not proceed with your question.

To exercise personal privilege Rise without recognition, interrupt a speaker if necessary, and say, "Mr. (or Madam) Chair, personal privilege!" The chair will say, "State your privilege." You may then ask whatever happens to be your privilege—even if it is something off the point, such as whether you might have a window closed because a draft is blowing on you.

To call for "division of the house" Without rising to gain recognition, simply call out, "Division of the house." This means that you want the voting on a measure to be taken by a show of hands or by asking members to stand to indicate their vote. "Division of the house" is called for when there has been a voice vote that was so close it was hard to determine what the vote actually was.

To call out "question" If you are ready to vote, call out "question." It is not compulsory that the chair put the motion to a vote at this time. However, he or she will generally do so if enough persons call out "question."

To reverse a ruling made by the chair As soon as the chair makes the ruling, the person who disagrees with it calls out without recognition, "Mr. (or Madam) Chair, I appeal from the decision of the chair." A second is necessary to make the appeal valid. If there is a second, the chair asks the person who made the appeal to state the reasons for doing so. This done, discussion follows after which the chair asks for a vote from the assembly by saying, "All those in favor of sustaining the chair raise their hands." Then after counting the votes the chairperson says, "Those opposed the same sign." The chairperson announces the vote by saying, "The chair is sustained by a vote of seven to three" or "The chair stands corrected by a vote of six to four."

To adjourn a meeting Adjournment may be made by a declaration from the chair, or it may be made after the motion to adjourn is placed on the floor, voted on, and carried.

To ascertain the order of business The assembly agrees upon an order of business. It is the chair's duty to see that this order is carried out unless rules are suspended by a two-thirds vote by the group, which will permit a temporary change.

To suspend the rules A motion is put before the assembly that the rules be temporarily suspended to consider certain urgent business. The motion requires a two-thirds vote to carry. If the motion receives a two-thirds vote, the rules are suspended.

To vote on a motion The chair asks for a vote. It may be by voice ("yes" and "no"), roll call, show of hands, standing, or ballot.

To object to the consideration of a motion Rise without recognition, interrupt a speaker if necessary, and say, "Mr. (or Madam) Chair, I object to the consideration of the motion (or question)." No second is required. The chair immediately asks the assembly to vote as to whether they want to consider the question. If two-thirds vote against consideration of the question, it cannot be considered. The objection must be made immediately after the motion to which the member objects is placed before the assembly.

To conduct nominations for office The chair opens the floor to nominations for a certain office. A member rises and says, "Mr. (or Madam) Chair, I nominate _____." The secretary records nominations. After a reasonable time, the chair rules that nominations are closed, or someone moves that nominations be closed. This is a main motion. It is seconded, debated, and voted on. If it carries, nominations are closed. If not, they remain open. The chair may rule a quick motion to close nominations out of order if such a motion is obviously an attempt to railroad a certain party into office before other nominations can be made.

To put a motion before the assembly If the motion requires a second, the chair waits a short time to hear the second. If it does not come, the motion is ruled dead for want of a second. If a second is made, the motion is repeated as follows: "It has been moved and seconded that the Parliamentary Law Club will have a party Friday night. Is there any discussion?" This officially places the motion in the hands of the assembly.

Presenting

Your instructor will advise you in this matter. However, every class member should take at least one turn acting as chair and one turn as secretary. The instructor will appoint the chair until you and your classmates learn how to nominate and elect a chair. Then you will carry out the following steps.

1. The chair should appoint a committee to draw up a proposed constitution and bylaws. (The committee may be elected if the group wishes to do it this way.) If time is limited, the instructor may dispense with drawing up a constitution and bylaws.

2. An order of business should be set up. Normally, it will be something similar to the following:

   A. Call the meeting to order.

   B. Have the minutes from the preceding meeting read. Ask if there are any additions or corrections, and make any changes required. A formal vote is not required to approve the minutes. The chairman should state the minutes are approved as amended or as read, whichever is appropriate.

   C. Ask for old business. This may be any unfinished business.

   D. Ask for committee reports.

   E. Ask for new business.

   F. Adjourn.

3. In carrying out practice parliamentary law sessions, motions will have to be placed before the assembly. Each student is required to put at least three main motions on the floor and seek their adoption. Here are some examples.

   • A motion to petition teachers that all written examinations be limited to one hour

   • A motion that tardy students should pay a 25-cent fine for each incidence of tardiness, with revenues to be contributed to a school building fund

Your instructor will give you a form on which to write your motions.

The Student Congress

A **student congress** may be composed of a house and senate, with different speech classes acting in each capacity, or one group may form a unicameral (single-chamber) legislature. In either instance the group's purpose is to formulate bills, discuss them, and adopt or reject them by vote. To accomplish these activities the group must know parliamentary procedure and conduct its business in an orderly manner. This involves

1. determining the scope of legislation to come before the assembly,

2. organizing the legislature by electing officers, forming committees, and assigning seats,

3. holding committee meetings to consider and/or draft bills, and

4. debating and disposing of bills brought before the assembly.

The First Meeting of the General Assembly

At the first meeting of the general assembly a temporary chair and a temporary secretary should be appointed or elected. Both will take office immediately. The instructor will act as parliamentarian unless one is elected or appointed. The temporary chair will then open the meeting to nominations for a permanent chair (speaker of the house or president of the senate) who will take office as soon as elected. The chair will call for nominations for a permanent secretary who will be elected and take office at once. As next business the presiding officer will appoint standing committees and a chair for each. The assembly may then discuss matters relative to its general objectives and procedures. When the discussion is finished, the meeting is adjourned.

Committee Meetings

Committee meetings are next in order, and, though these are informal, you should follow parliamentary procedure by having an elected or appointed secretary keep minutes for the group. A committee may originate its own bills and consider bills submitted by members of the assembly, which the speaker of the house or president of the senate has referred to them. The committee can amend bills. It will report bills out or "kill them" in committee, according to votes taken after discussion in the committee.

Sample Resolutions and Bills

A resolution is a recommendation of action and does not carry the weight of law as it has no enforcement and penalty clause. A resolution must have a title and a body. A preamble is optional. The body is composed of sections and each line is numbered. Resolutions should be brief—keep them under 175 words.

A Resolution Limiting Student Drivers at Central High School

WHEREAS, Space is limited around Central High School, and

WHEREAS, Parking on the street is limited to one hour, and

WHEREAS, Student enrollment is increasing each year, and

WHEREAS, Many students are within walking distance of Central High School, therefore,

BE IT RESOLVED BY CENTRAL HIGH SCHOOL SPEECH CLASS THAT:

1 SECTION I. The governing officials
2 of Central High School should
3 prohibit all students living within
4 one mile of this school from
5 operating a vehicle to and from
6 school as a means of transportation.

This resolution introduced by

_____

A Bill Providing for Limiting Student Drivers at Central High School

BE IT ENACTED BY THE CENTRAL HIGH SCHOOL SPEECH CLASS, THAT:

1 SECTION I. All students living
2 within one mile of the school shall
3 not operate a vehicle to and from
4 school as a means of transportation.

5 SECTION II. Any exceptions to
6 Section I must be approved by the
7 school board upon petition.

8 SECTION III. The policy will take
9 effect at the beginning of the next
10 school year after passage.

11 SECTION IV. Any student in
12 violation of the policy will serve a
13 three-day in-school suspension.

This bill introduced by

_____

The General Assembly in Deliberation

Some student congresses follow the procedures and rules of their state legislatures. Others follow established rules of parliamentary procedure by designating a certain text as their guide. In either case, an agreed-upon procedure must be used. To have a successful general assembly, members should know parliamentary procedure and how to use it. It's especially important that they know the precedence of motions, and how to apply the privileged and subsidiary motions. Incidental motions, which have no order of precedence, are of vital importance in the general conduct of the assembly's deliberations. As such they should be thoroughly familiar to all participants.

Under a bicameral (two-chamber) student congress the requirement is that each bill must pass the house in which it originates. It is then filed with the secretary of the other house after which the presiding officer of the house refers it to the proper committee. If reported out of this committee and passed by the second house, it may be considered passed unless there is a governor who must act on it before it can be so considered. When a governor is used, a lieutenant governor is ordinarily elected and serves as presiding officer in the senate. It thus becomes doubly important that all plans be laid before a student assembly convenes for the first time in order to know what officials to elect, what their duties are, what committees to set up, and which procedures will be relative to activities of the congress.

A Suggested Order of Business

The following order of business meets most student congress needs.

1. The meeting is called to order.

2. Minutes of the last meeting are read and adopted as read or corrected.

3. The presiding officer announces the order in which committees will report and the group decides on (a) time limits for individual speakers and (b) the total time allowed for each bill.

4. The spokesperson for the first committee reads the bill, moves its adoption, and gives a copy to the secretary. Another member seconds. If the bill belongs to an individual, he or she presents it in a similar manner when granted permission by the chairperson. Another member seconds. Whoever presents a bill then speaks for it. The bill is debated and disposed of according to the rules of the assembly.

5. Each succeeding committee reports and the process of discussing and disposing of each bill continues until all bills have been acted upon.

6. The secretary announces the bills that were passed and those that were defeated.

7. The assembly conducts any business that is appropriate.

8. Adjournment is in order.

Evaluating

As you will be participating in this assignment right alongside your classmates, pay attention to your own performance. Check your progress on the following.

*   Have you made a study of parliamentary procedure?

*   Have you acted in accordance with the new protocols you have learned?

*   Do you know the precedence of motions?

*   Have you worked cooperatively with your classmates in making and passing motions?

Debate

Specs for Debate

Time limits

The time limits shown here are standard for competitive debate. They may be shortened proportionately for class debates.

First Affirmative Constructive—8 minutes
Cross-Examination of First Affirmative by Negative—3 minutes
First Negative Constructive—8 minutes
Cross-Examination of First Negative by Affirmative—3 minutes
Second Affirmative Constructive—8 minutes
Cross-Examination of Second Affirmative by Negative—3 minutes
Second Negative Constructive—8 minutes
Cross-Examination of Second Negative by Affirmative—3 minutes
First Negative Rebuttal—4 minutes
First Affirmative Rebuttal—4 minutes
Second Negative Rebuttal—4 minutes
Second Affirmative Rebuttal—4 minutes

Speaker's notes

Use notes sparingly but efficiently. They are necessary in good debating.

Sources of information

You will need many. In your debate you will be required to state your sources of information to prove the validity of your statements.

Outline

Prepare a 75- to 150-word complete sentence outline to be handed to your instructor before the debate starts.

Speak Up!

Have you ever participated in a debate? You probably have at least argued your case a few times in your life! Share a recent example of a time when you used examples, anecdotes, hard facts, and other methods to win an argument. If you have had some experience with formal debating, share that experience.

Purpose and Expectations of This Assignment

Many opportunities in life invite us to formally debate particular topics within decision-making bodies to which we belong. The contest version of formal debate is particularly ordered to present two strong sides of an issue.

Debate provides excellent experience in communicating, as it pits two or more speakers with opposing ideas against each other. It tests your ability to express your ideas and to defend them under direct challenge. This teaches tact and resourcefulness, and strengthens your ability to think on your feet. It also demands that you back your ideas with solid evidence, not mere conjecture or opinion. This assignment will familiarize you with the rules for debate and prepare you to participate in a competitive event. But it will also give you skills you can carry with you throughout your life.

In completing this assignment, you will

- express ideas and defend them under direct challenge,

- understand how to support arguments with evidence,

- understand how formal debates are organized and conducted,

- prepare and deliver a case on one side of a proposition, and

- analyze and cross-examine an opponent's case.

Defining a Debate

A **debate** is a speaking situation in which two opposing speakers or teams present and argue their ideas on a specified topic. The ideas represent solutions to a problem. The proponents of each solution attempt to convince the audience that their idea should be adopted in preference to all others. In fact, a debate, in the sense used here, consists of two opposing persuasive speeches.

A debate team may be composed of one or two people depending on the debate format. Two-person teams are the most common for topics that deal with a policy change. This assignment is structured for that format.

Debates are divided into **constructive speeches** and **rebuttals**. Constructive speeches introduce the arguments and position of each speaker while the rebuttals review and extend the constructive issues. Refer to the time limits at the beginning of this assignment for the order of speeches. You will note that the affirmative team leads off and closes the debate. While this may seem like an unbeatable advantage, both teams have the same amount of time, and the second negative constructive followed by the first negative rebuttal can be a powerful advantage for the negative.

After each of the constructive speeches, a member of the opposite team will be given three minutes to **cross-examine** or question the speaker. Each team member will take turns asking questions. One negative team member will cross-examine the first affirmative speaker and the other negative team member will cross-examine the second affirmative after the constructive speech. The same is true when the affirmative cross-examines the negative. The purpose of cross-examination is to gain additional information from the speaker or to clarify what the speaker said. Cross-examination is not a time to argue; it is a time for questions to be asked and answered.

Occasions for debates occur in practically every academic class, although regularly organized debate groups and speech classes participate in them most frequently. There are nationwide inter-school debates among high schools, as well as inter-college contests. Debates provide excellent programming in schools; over TV and radio; and within civic organizations, churches, business groups, and clubs. Many different kinds of people enjoy listening to or taking part in a good debate. The format need not be completely humorless. Some debates are very entertaining. But even for a lighthearted debate, the purpose of which is to entertain, you will have to do the same skillful preparation you would do for a regular debate.

Choosing a Topic

Topics for debates are worded in a statement of resolve that asks for a change to be made in the way we currently do something. The affirmative team supports the topic. The negative team defends the present way of doing things. The topic is also called a **resolution**.

Each year one topic is chosen for national interscholastic high school competitions and another is chosen for national college competitions. Ask your instructor what the current national high school or college debate topic is. You may want to debate one of those topics or some element of them.

As your team and the opposing team will be concerned with the choice of topic, you'll have to consult your opponents to reach agreement. Remember that one team will uphold the proposition under debate, while the other will argue against it. So, in choosing a topic, the two teams should also decide which of them will debate **affirmative** (*for* the topic) and which will debate **negative** (*against* it).

Before you arrive at an agreement, be sure that all of you have an interest in the subject and that you can find information about it. If you are in doubt about the availability of source materials, check with your school and city libraries before making a final decision. One way to solve the problem of what to debate is to ask your instructor to assign the topic and the side each team will argue. The following are sample topics. Notice that they all use the word *should* and they all suggest a policy change.

- Resolved: That the federal government should significantly increase social services to homeless individuals in the United States.

- Resolved: That the federal government should initiate and enforce safety guarantees on consumer goods.

- Resolved: That the federal government should guarantee comprehensive medical care for all citizens in the United States.

- Resolved: That smoking should be prohibited by law.

- Resolved: That students caught cheating should be expelled from school.

- Resolved: That capital punishment should be abolished.

Preparing

As stated earlier in this chapter, a debate is really two or more opposing speeches to persuade. Your purpose then is to convince your audience that your point of view is the correct one. To refresh your memory about the speech to persuade, reread Speech Experience 9.

Because a debate is an activity in which two colleagues team up against two other colleagues, you must prepare for the contest in cooperation with your teammate. You will find this easy to accomplish if you carry out the following suggestions.

1. Decide who will be the first speaker.

2. Make a mutual agreement that both of you will search for materials to prove your side of the question. Later these materials can be exchanged to help each of you strengthen your individual arguments.

3. Begin your hunt for information on your subject. Whenever you find something pertinent, take notes. Be sure you are able to give the exact reference for the information. Record the author's name and qualifications; the title of the article; the magazine, newspaper, or book in which you found the item; and the exact date of publication. Take your notes on 4-inch by 6-inch cards; then at the top of each card write a heading that tells you in brief what the notes on that card concern. For instance, on a health-care topic, labels might be: "cost of care," "uninsured," and "Canadian system."

4. Use only complete and exact quotes. It is very important in a debate to have accurate information. Therefore, when quoting sources, copy the information exactly as it appears in the publication. Don't leave anything out or add anything. You could set yourself up for an attack by the opposition if you do try to paraphrase a quotation.

5. Plan and rehearse your case with your partner. You should each have your material so well in mind that you will have to make little reference to your notes during the debate, except when bringing up objections raised by the opposition. Practice until you and your teammate are in complete mastery of the material. However, you should not memorize a debate speech word for word. Know the sequence of points and the evidence to prove the point. Remember to create a well-planned introduction and conclusion.

The following briefly states what each speaker should do in each speech.

First Affirmative Constructive

1. State the resolution.
2. Define terms of resolution.
3. Present affirmative reasons for change.
4. Present proof for reasons for change.
5. Present affirmative plan.

First Negative Constructive

1. Explain basic negative approach.
2. Present negative position.
3. Argue affirmative definition of terms (optional).
4. Prove affirmative reasons for change are not significant.
5. Prove status quo can achieve affirmative reason for change without affirmative plan (inherency).

Second Affirmative Constructive

1. Attack negative position.
2. Rebuild affirmative reasons for change.
3. Answer all first negative attacks.
4. Present added advantages.

Second Negative Constructive

1. Extend (develop in light of opponent's attacks) negative position.

2. Attack affirmative plan as unworkable and undesirable.

First Negative Rebuttal

1. Extend first negative constructive arguments in light of second affirmative responses.
2. Review reasons for change and why they are insufficient.

First Affirmative Rebuttal

1. Answer second negative attacks on plan.
2. Return to affirmative case to rebuild affirmative reason for change.

Second Negative Rebuttal

1. Review first negative attacks on reasons for change.
2. Return to plan attacks—show how plan is still unworkable and undesirable in light of first affirmative rebuttal.

Second Affirmative Rebuttal

1. Answer attacks on affirmative plan by proving it workable and desirable.
2. Return to case and emphasize reason for change.

Organizing

Use the following outline to create an overview of your team's argument.

I. Divide your entire case into four parts. These parts are called **stock issues**. An affirmative must prove all issues; a negative can win by disproving any one of the issues.

   A. **Harm** This shows a need for the specific proposal you are offering by showing some harm is currently happening that needs to be solved.

   B. **Inherency** This shows that there is something that currently exists in our present system that prevents us from solving the harm. You must show that the harm is inherent. For example, in a topic that would ask for the right of doctors to prescribe marijuana for medical purposes, we have a law in the present system that states that marijuana use is a federal offense. Therefore, the law prevents the present system from solving the problem.

   C. **Plan** You have to come up with a plan of action to solve the harm you identify. In other words, you need a solution to the problem, and you need to show that your solution works.

   D. **Disadvantages** You need to show that there will not be problems that occur (disadvantages) if your solution is accepted.

II. Your finished affirmative case should be set up as follows.

   A. Introduce the topic's importance and state your resolution.

   B. Define your terms. If you are arguing that compulsory military training should be established in the United States, you must tell what you mean by *compulsory*. Will there be any exceptions? What does *military training* mean? Does it refer to the infantry, the air force, or a technical school for nuclear specialists? In other words, state *exactly* what you are talking about.

   C. Show that your proposal is needed (stock issue of harm).

      1. Give examples, illustrations, opinions of authorities, facts, and analogies that point to the need for your proposition. Give enough of these proofs to establish your point.

   D. Show that we cannot solve the problem in the present system.

   E. Show that your proposition is practical (it will work).

      1. Give proofs as you did to establish need in point C, above.

   F. Show that your proposal is desirable (its results will be beneficial). Prove that there will be no disadvantages to it.

      1. Give proofs as you did in point C.

G. Summarize your speech; then close it by stating your belief in your proposal.

III. Negative colleagues should set up their case as follows.

A. Prepare material that denies that there is a problem.

B. Prepare to defend the fact that the present system can take care of any problem on its own, assuming one exists.

C. Find reasons the affirmative solution will not work.

D. Prepare material that shows problems or disadvantages that would occur if the affirmative plan were adopted.

Note: All of your arguments should be presented in constructive speeches. The rebuttal speeches are used to provide further support for your arguments, to deny the opposition's arguments, and to summarize why you are winning.

IV. Rebuttal is easy if you keep certain factors in mind.

A. In refuting points, try to run the debate. Take the offensive. This is easy but you must follow a plan. The plan is to take your main speech point by point. Reiterate the first point you made, tell what the opposition did to disprove it. Then give more evidence to re-establish it. Now take your second point and do exactly the same thing over again. Continue this strategy throughout your rebuttal and close with a summary, followed by a statement of your belief in the soundness of your proposal.

Do not talk about points brought up by your opponents, except as you refer to them while you re-emphasize your own points. You must carry out this plan of advancing your own case or you will be likely to confuse yourself and your audience. Refuse to be budged from the consideration of your plan for advancing your own case.

B. The final speech by each side in the debate should be the strongest. Each side needs to prove why it should win the debate. Concentrate on those points you know you are winning. Remember, the affirmative must win all the stock issues, but the negative side only needs to win one.

V. When each team tries to run the debate, that is, take the offensive, there is a real argument. Because each team plays upon its own case, the two proposals and their arguments are easy to follow.

Presenting

A debater's attitude should be one of confidence, not cockiness. Debaters should be friendly, firm, polite, and eager to be understood. A sense of humor is helpful if well applied.

Use movement, gestures, and notes without awkwardness. Your posture should be relaxed and alert. Your voice should be conversational in quality, earnest, and sincere. Speak loudly enough to be heard by everyone in the room.

When you rise to speak, address the audience and your opponents. Simply make a few introductory remarks about the occasion, the audience, and the pleasure of debating a timely question. No more is needed. Some debaters utter trite, stereotyped sentiments that would be better left unsaid.

Next, move into the debate by defining the terms. This should all be done informally and sincerely in a communicative manner. There is no reason why a debate should be a formal, cold, stilted, unfriendly affair.

After the debate is over, it is customary for the teams to rise, walk to the center of the room, and shake hands. If your team won the debate, don't gloat. If you lost, don't be peevish. Do the best you can and accept the outcome.

Following is the standard protocol you will use when you take part in a debate.

1. The two teams sit at tables on opposite sides of the room facing the audience.

2. A timekeeper sits in the front row of the audience. The timekeeper signals the debaters by raising time cards. If the 2-card is up, this means that the speaker has two minutes left. When time is up, the timekeeper raises the stop card. The speaker should stop speaking within ten seconds after the final signal.

3. There may be one, three, or five judges. Each is provided with a ballot. When the debate is over, the judges, without consultation, immediately fill out their ballots.

4. Debaters may refer to their teammates by name, or as "my colleague." Opponents may be referred to by name or as "my opponent" or "the first affirmative (or negative) speaker" or "the second negative (or affirmative) speaker." Debaters may refer to their team as "we," or "my colleague and I."

Evaluating

Evaluate a classmate's constructive argument. Rate the following criteria on a scale from 1 to 5 with 1 being "needs much improvement" and 5 being "outstanding."

- Was the speech clearly and effectively organized?
- Did the introduction catch your attention?
- Did the speaker give you a reason why the speech was important to you personally?
- Was the speech delivered well with good posture, appropriate gestures, eye contact, and adequate rate and volume of speech?

- Did the speech contain sufficient and appropriate supporting materials?
- Was the conclusion effective?
- Did the speech achieve its intended result? Did you find the argument persuasive?

Give an overall score to the speech. As always, when evaluating a speech, be positive and take time to comment on good points as well as areas for improvement. Choose one area of the speaker's performance that may have given you new ideas about your own debate skills. Write a short paragraph to explain.

UNIT 8

Business and Career Speaking

A quick survey of help-wanted advertisements will reveal that one of the most sought-after qualities in the job market is the ability to communicate well. This unit is designed to highlight some of the speaking and listening skills needed in the workplace. Regardless of what path you pursue, these skills will be the ones you will draw upon most frequently.

Speech Experiences in This Unit

The
Sales Talk

Michael Levey, TV Infomercial king

Specs for the Sales Talk

Time limit

5–6 minutes.

Speaker's notes

Do not use notes when trying to sell something to an audience; however, you can use overheads or handouts.

Sources of information

Two and preferably three sources are required for this speech. You will need to acquire and become familiar with the data about the product you will sell, manufacturer's specifications, uses for the product, and reasons people buy the product. Sources of information will come from brochures or publications. The Internet is also a good source. For each source, cite where the information was found—the specific magazine, brochure, Web site, or book it was taken from; title of the article; author's full name; date of publication; and the chapter or page telling where the material was found. If a source is a person, identify the source completely by title, position, and occupation. List these on the outline form.

Outline

Prepare a 75- to 100-word complete sentence outline.

Speak Up!

Share a particularly good or bad sales experience you have had as either a salesperson or a customer. How did you feel? Describe the salesperson. Was he or she pushy, knowledgable? Was a demonstration or a visual aid used? What traits would describe a good salesperson? a bad one?

Purpose and Expectations of This Assignment

The sales talk is something you may be called upon to present much sooner than you now expect. It involves a situation in which you usually try to trade or sell a group of persons an article in exchange for their money. Sometimes this is a difficult task. Many persons have had little or no experience in this particular type of speaking and selling. This one experience is not intended to make a sales expert out of anyone, but certainly it will help the person who later finds it necessary to sell something.

In completing this assignment, you will

- identify speaking strategies used to sell products to others,
- understand the competitive nature of sales talks,
- adapt arguments for the sale of a product to a particular audience,
- identify the motivation for buyers of the product, and
- prepare responses to anticipated questions.

Defining the Sales Talk

A **sales talk** is a speech in which you attempt to persuade others to buy a product from you now or at a later date. In some instances, you will actually take orders at the conclusion of your remarks; in other cases, you will merely develop an interest in your goods so prospective customers will buy from you later. But in either case, your purpose is to sell by stimulating the customer to want what you have and to be willing to part with money to acquire the goods you have for sale.

The sales talk makes special demands on the speaker. You must be pleasing in appearance, pleasant to meet, congenial, and friendly. You must be thoroughly familiar with the product and with most matters pertaining to it. You must be honest and truthful with your answers, and if a question is asked that you cannot answer at the time, you should say, "I do not have an answer to that question right now, but I will get the answer for you."

You should, by all means, be able and willing to answer questions regarding the production, the manufacturer (or the company sponsoring it, such as an insurance company), the cost, terms of selling, guarantees, repairs, cost of upkeep, and other such matters. You should know how to answer objections, questions, or comparisons made to a competitive product.

Occasions for the sales talk are many. We might say that any time a speaker appears before one or more persons with the purpose of selling, it is a sales talk. Think about occasions where you have heard the sales pitch—someone at your door selling Girl Scout cookies, college recruiting fairs, soliciting for school funds, someone at your school telling you about class rings, infomercials on television. The main idea is that prospective customers can be any kind of people and be met anywhere and at any time.

Choosing a Topic

Choose a product for sale that you believe in; then build your talk around it. Be sure to select something your audience needs and can use. Some natural topics are athletic equipment, computers, food, schoolbooks, a movie or play, or an article of clothing. For additional suggestions, ask your instructor.

Preparing

First of all, follow the regular steps of preparation used for any speech. Pay particular attention to analyzing your audience. It would be fatal to misjudge your prospective buyers. You should know as much as possible about their personal situations: probable incomes, credit ratings, occupations, religions, education, local issues, and anything else that concerns them.

A wise salesperson will find out what other salespeople have sold or tried to sell in the way of competitive products. Salespeople will also be familiar enough with these products to make comparisons favorable to their own.

Whenever possible, demonstrate what you are selling. This means that you must know how to show it to the best advantage. Be sure, very sure, that it looks good and is in working order. Let your customers try it out. If it is candy, pass samples around. If it is a computer, let people work on it.

It is essential that you be ready to sign order contracts. This will necessitate your having pen and ink, order forms, credit information, checkbooks, and receipts on hand. Do not make buyers wait when they are ready to buy.

Be prepared to greet your audience promptly. Go to the designated meeting place early. Have everything arranged before your audience arrives. After you think you have every display most advantageously placed, all sales forms in order, and everything in tip-top shape, go back for a final check. If you have omitted nothing, then you are ready.

As for your speech, have it well in mind. Do not use notes. It would be foolish to attempt to sell something while referring to notes in order to discover the good points of your product.

Organizing

The organization of your speech should be well thought out. One plan that can be recommended is the one that follows.

1. **Start with a friendly introduction,** stating your pleasure in meeting the audience. Be sincere.

2. **Present information about your product and yourself.** Talk about your credibility or experience with the product. What position do you hold? How long have you been with this company? Why did you choose to work for your particular company? What is the name of the company? How old is it? Is it a nationwide organization? Is it financially sound? Is it reliable? Does it stand behind its products? Does it guarantee its products? Does it quibble over an adjustment if a customer asks for one? Does it have a larger dealer organization? Can you get parts and repairs quickly if these are needed? Does the company plan to stay in business? Does it test all of its products before placing them on the market? How large is its business? What special recommendations does the company have? Of course, it may not be necessary to answer all of these questions; however, many of them will have to be answered by giving information that establishes you as a reputable salesperson and your company as a reputable firm.

3. **Explain and demonstrate how the product operates.** In doing this, be sure to play up its advantages, its special features, new improvements, economy of operation, dependability, beauty, ease of

handling, and the like. Give enough details to be clear but not so much that you confuse your listeners.

4. **Show the advantages and benefits of ownership.** Let the audience see vividly how your product will benefit them. If the article is a box of chocolates, the buyer will delight family and friends by serving them. If the salesperson is offering a correspondence school course, the buyer will make more money, gain prestige, and secure advancements by buying the course. Sometimes it is helpful to mention the names of other persons who have bought the product from you and are now benefiting from ownership of it.

5. **Close the sale.** How may they buy it? Where? When? Who sells it, if you carry only samples? How much does it cost? Do you sell on the installment plan? What are the interest charges? How much do you require as a down payment? How many months are allowed in paying for it? What is the amount of the monthly payment? Or is it cash? Is any discount allowed for cash? What special inducement is offered to those who buy now? How much can they save? Will future prices be higher? Do you take trade-ins? How much allowance is made on a trade-in?

Presenting

Look good; be good. In other words have a neat and pleasing appearance, plus a friendly and polite attitude. These points are extremely important. Your own good judgment will tell you what is appropriate dress. Your common sense will provide the background for the right attitude. And by all means, avoid looking like the salesman below! Generally, you should begin your speech directly, if this procedure is appropriate to the mood of your listeners. Avoid being smart or using questionable stories to impress your listeners. Put the group at ease and get on with the speech.

Your manner should be conversational; your voice should be easily heard by all but not strained. Your bodily action should be suitable for holding attention, making transitions, and demonstrating what you are selling. Your language, of course, should be simple, descriptive, vivid, and devoid of technical terms.

Allow your audience time to ask questions after concluding your talk. It may be that some of them will wish to ask questions during your speech. It is your choice as to when you answer the questions. You can delay the answer until you finish with the main part of your presentation or you can pause briefly to answer the question. Do not allow the questions to sidetrack your presentation. You must maintain control and keep the audience focused on your agenda. You can delay the answer to any question by stating, "You have asked a good question, and I will answer it in just a moment." Be sure you make a note of the question and when you are ready to answer questions you should always repeat the question that was asked before you answer it. Try to take the questions in the order in which they were asked. Be sure to answer them clearly; however, do not turn the meeting into a question and answer occasion before you have presented your product. Do not allow your audience to dictate the direction or details of your presentation.

In order to present the above information effectively, to demonstrate the product, to show the prospective customers how they will benefit from owning your goods, and how they may have the purchase, you will rehearse the demonstration and accompanying speech aloud many times. Do this until you have attained complete mastery.

Evaluating

Evaluate a classmate's sales talk. Rate the following criteria on a scale from 1 to 5 with 1 being "needs much improvement" and 5 being "outstanding."

- Was the talk well organized and easy to understand?
- Did the speaker seem confident and knowledgable?
- Did the speaker make effective use of visual aids?
- Were the product's attributes and benefits explained clearly?
- Would you be inclined to purchase the speaker's product?

Finally, give an overall score to the speech and be ready to explain it.

Talking Points

Handling Visual Aids

Visual aids are always a bonus when making a presentation because so many audience members may be "visual learners," meaning they remember material best when it is put into a visual format.

When you use charts, pictures, diagrams, or the objects, your familiarity with these articles should be so great that you can point out any information or refer to any part of the product while retaining a posture that permits focusing your attention on the audience. In answering questions, you should be as clear as possible and sure that your questioner is satisfied with the information you give. Avoid embarrassing anyone. An alert and enthusiastic yet friendly attitude should be your goal.

Using Visual Aids Effectively

1. Choose visuals that are clear and easy to see across the entire room.

2. Place them in view of all audience members.

3. Keep them out of sight until they are ready to be used. Place them out of sight after they are used.

4. Try using different media such as posters, overhead transparencies, objects, videotapes, slides, or computer-generated graphics.

5. Practice with the visual aids so they can be used smoothly during the speech.

6. Face the audience and not the visual aid when presenting.

Tips for Visual Aid Use

Chalkboard/Whiteboard

Write or print large enough so those in the back can see.

Don't write too far down on the board. Your writing won't be visible to people at the back of the room.

Don't face the board while speaking.

Posters

Do use an easel with a large tablet, or have your information on large pieces of paper that you can put on the wall or chalkboard. Check beforehand to make sure that your posters will stick to the surface where you intend to put them.

Take down the poster or turn to a clean sheet on the easel after you have finished with it.

Use dark-colored markers. Red, black, and blue are best.

Computer-Generated Visuals

Be at the presentation room *early* to make sure you have any electrical cords or outlets needed and that there is a good spot for your computer so you can operate it and connect with the audience at the same time.

See Experience 30 for more information about computer-assisted presentations.

Handouts

Don't pass out handouts until they are needed. You want the audience to focus on you, not on a piece of paper. Some speakers wait until the end of their presentation to pass them out.

Make sure you have enough handouts for the maximum number of people you expect to attend.

Slides, Movies, Videotapes, DVDs, CDs

Arrive early to make sure any necessary equipment is in place and that you know how to operate it.

If you have a colleague to help you, make sure you two coordinate when to dim the room lights and how the equipment will be used.

continued

Talking Points cont.

Objects

Keep your item out of sight until you are ready to use it. When you are done, put it back in a space that is concealed from the audience.

Plan and rehearse how you will work with the object. Don't hide behind the podium. You want your audience to clearly see what you are showing. Also, since you will probably be using both hands, make sure you can run through this part of your presentation without note cards.

Do not hand out the object to the audience for passing around. Again, you want attention focused on *you*. Let audience members know that the object will be available to them after your presentation is finished.

Overhead Projector

Using transparencies with an overhead projector is one of the most common visual aids.

Prepare your transparencies by using special markers or by using your computer to create the copy and printing it out on transparency film. In either case, make sure the type size is large enough to be seen easily from the back of the room. (Transparency film and markers can be found at office supply stores.)

If you have several main points on one transparency, use a piece of heavy paper or cardboard to cover them up until you are ready to address them.

Come early to practice operating the equipment. Make sure that the lens is in focus and that the projector is at the right distance from the screen. Practice placing and removing your transparencies so you can work with them fluently when you give your talk.

As soon as you are done with a transparency, remove it from the projector. When you are through with the last one, turn the machine off.

Example Speech

The Jayhawk Mug

by Margie Hapke

Good morning . . . Excuse me . . . Just a minute [Spills water on herself] . . . Oh man, I hate it when that happens . . . You know what the problem is. It's these Styrofoam cups. They are so flimsy and unreliable. I'm sure it's happened to you too. It happens to everyone at one time or another. These Styrofoam cups are just worthless. But today I've got a product to show you that will solve the problem of these flimsy and unreliable cups forever.

It's the Jayhawk Mug. Now the Jayhawk Mug has numerous features that give it a definite advantage over Styrofoam and paper cups, and produces benefits not only to you the user, but to the environment as well. Now the Jayhawk Mug is made from hard plastics that are guaranteed not to split or crack, eliminating the problem that you all just witnessed. The mug also features double-wall construction that provides it with thermal insulation, keeping your hot drinks hot and your cold drinks cold without changing the outside temperature of the mug. How many times have you filled a styrofoam cup with hot coffee only to find out it's so hot you can't hold on to it? And what about in the summertime when you have the Styrofoam cup full of ice and Coke and the thing sweats and gets your hand all wet and drips all over your shoes? It's really a nuisance. The Jayhawk Mug's double-wall construction eliminates that problem—a definite advantage.

Another benefit of the mug is a reduced charge for refills offered at all the Kansas Union concession outlets. This mug holds 32 ounces of any beverage, like Coke, coffee, iced tea, and can be refilled with any beverage for just 60 cents. That same amount of product in a one-time-use Styrofoam cup would cost you at least a dollar.

And speaking of one-time-use-only, that's probably the biggest benefit of using the Jayhawk Mug—the benefit to the environment. Styrofoam is a hazard in our landfills because it just doesn't biodegrade. By reusing the Jayhawk Mug you can help significantly reduce the amount of non-degradable Styrofoam that the KU campus sends to landfills each week.

Now, how can you get your very own Jayhawk Mug? It's easy. You just stop in at any one of KU's concession outlets. The Mug sells for two dollars and fifty cents. It's a great price. It's affordable. And the savings from just six refills will pay for it. So run across the street to the Wescoe Beach and pick yourself up a Jayhawk Mug today. You'll never walk around with a wet T-shirt again.

The
Lecture Forum

Specs for the Lecture Forum

Time limits

Speech: 7–8 minutes.

Question-and-answer period: 5 minutes.

Speaker's notes

15-word maximum.

Sources of information

Three are required, preferably four. For each source, give the specific magazine, book, or Internet site from which it was taken; the title of the article; the author's full name; the date of publication; and the chapter or page numbers. If a source is a person, identify him or her completely by title, position, occupation, etc. For Internet sites, include the address (URL).

Outline

Prepare a 75- to 150-word complete sentence outline.

Speak Up!

Share an experience you have had as a member of an audience during a question-and-answer period. How did the speaker handle the audience? Was he or she comfortable and relaxed? Were the answers complete? In your opinion, was there anything the speaker could have done to be more effective?

Purpose and Expectations of This Assignment

Many people who give speeches on a regular basis never know how many unanswered questions they leave in the minds of their audience. As a speaker, you can be more helpful to your listeners if you remain on stage after your talk to field their questions.

Most students do not receive training in answering questions about the material they present in speeches; thus, when they are later confronted with a **forum** (question period) following a speech they may handle the situation awkwardly. This assignment will provide experience in speaking as well as answering questions.

In completing this assignment, you will

- experience the need to be better informed on a topic than the audience,

- demonstrate the ability to answer questions from the audience, and

- understand the procedures to follow in conducting a lecture forum with an audience.

Defining the Lecture Forum

The **lecture forum** is a speech followed by a period in which members of the audience are permitted to direct questions to the speaker. The lecturer's general purpose is to inform the listeners on a worthwhile subject. The speaker could present a speech intended to motivate or one to persuade; however, the persuasive speech would probably not suit the lecture forum atmosphere as well as the speech to inform would. We cannot preclude speeches to motivate and to persuade—they can often be followed by a question period—but we suggest that for most lecture forums the speaker should use the time to present an informative subject.

The lecture forum demands that the speaker be better informed than any member of the audience. It demands further that he or she be capable of receiving and answering questions from an audience. In short, the lecture forum demands an excellent speaker who is also something of an expert on the subject at hand.

Occasions for the lecture forum occur whenever an informative speech is in order. These speeches may be given before committees, business groups, church organizations, civic audiences, educational meetings, fraternal orders, and so on.

Choosing a Topic

You will be expected to know your subject unusually well, as you will inform your audience about it and then take their questions. So choose a topic that will be of interest to you and your listeners, and one about which you can find plenty of information. Do not select a subject that has only limited sources. Making an apology to an audience for ignorance on your subject is not a good way to gain their confidence in you as a speaker. Base your choice then, on interest, appropriateness, and the availability of source materials. Here are some suggestions to get you started.

- How may our government be improved?
- Drug abuse today
- TV and movie violence
- Teen pregnancy
- Population control
- AIDS education
- Multilingual education
- Saving the family farm
- The right to die
- Best vacation spots in the united states

Preparing

As this will be an informative speech, you should review Speech Experience 7, "The Speech to Inform." There you will find complete information relative to preparing this type of speech.

Presenting

Immediately after the conclusion of your lecture you or your host will advise the audience that they may question you. (While the following points pertain to live questions from the audience, sometimes the speaker will specify that the questions be written.) In making this announcement, explain the following points politely but thoroughly.

1. Ask that the audience confine their questions to the material presented in the lecture because you are not prepared to answer questions outside this scope.

2. Request that your audience ask questions only, unless you wish to permit short speeches on the subject. Whatever policy you intend to follow—that is, strictly a questioning period or a question and short speech period—announce it specifically; otherwise you may run into trouble with audience members who want to make long comments. If you allow comments or short speeches, announce a definite time limit for each. For the classroom, one minute is enough. In large public gatherings, two minutes is generally adequate.

3. If the audience is small and informal, permit the questioners to remain seated during the forum period; that is, do not ask them to stand while participating. If the gathering is large, require them to stand so that the rest of the audience will have a better chance of hearing them.

4. Announce the exact amount of time that you will allow for questioning. Do not make this period too long. You can always extend the time if the questions are coming briskly at the moment you are scheduled to close. On the other hand, do not continue to hold an audience for the announced time if

it becomes obvious that they no longer care to ask questions. It is better to have them go away wanting more than having had too much.

5. Once you have made your announcements, open the question-and-answer period by telling the audience to direct their questions to you. Also explain that you will answer the questions in the order in which they are asked. Thus, if two persons speak at once you will designate which one may ask a question first. Speakers should be urged to raise their hands and wait to be called on.

Having made these explanations to your audience, tell them you will be glad to answer their questions as best you can. Do not promise to answer all questions, since it is likely that no one could do that. If someone raises a question that you do not feel qualified to answer, tell the questioner you do not have the information necessary to give a reliable answer. Promise to find the answer and ask the questioner to see you after the speech to give you a phone number, mailing address, or e-mail address so you can forward the answer when you have it. If, on the other hand, you do not know the answer because you are poorly prepared, you will quickly—and deservedly—lose the confidence and respect of your audience.

If an audience member asks a question that does not pertain to the subject under discussion, politely tell him or her that the question is beyond the scope of your talk and you are not prepared to answer it. Should you by chance possess information that will enable you to answer it, mention briefly that the question is somewhat off the topic and then give whatever information you have. Make this a very brief reply. Do not let it take you off your subject for more than a moment. Should hecklers trouble

you, handle them politely but firmly. Do nothing drastic. Always repeat the question so the audience can hear it.

If some questions are obscure and/or drawn out, it may be necessary for you to rephrase them. If you do this, inquire of the person who asked the question as to whether or not your rephrasing asks what they want to know. At other times it may be necessary for you to ask for a restatement of the question. Do this any time that you do not hear or understand the question clearly. Never try to answer a question you do not fully understand.

Observe acceptable speaking practices throughout your lecture and the period following. Retain an alert and friendly attitude. Do not become ruffled when you meet obvious disagreement or criticism. Simply explain your position firmly but politely. Do not engage in a debate or an exchange of unfriendly remarks or accusations. Dismiss the matter and move on to the next question. If some of the questions are pointed, sarcastic, or overly confrontational, keep your head and perhaps add a touch of humor; then reply as capably as you can. If any person asks a question that cannot be heard by the entire audience, repeat it for the audience. Then give your answer. When you are ready to turn the meeting back to the chair, conclude with appropriate remarks in which you sincerely express your pleasure about the time you've spent with the audience. Also compliment them for their interest in the subject.

Evaluating

Evaluate a classmate's lecture forum. Take notes and be prepared to ask questions during the question-and-answer period. Then rate the presentation on the following criteria.

- Did the speaker seem confident of the material?
- Did the presenter organize the information in a clear progression of ideas?
- Were the speaker's gestures and facial expressions appropriate to the occasion?
- Did the speaker have an interesting or attention-getting introduction?
- Did the speaker have a point of view about the issues?
- Did the speaker rephrase or repeat the questions for the audience?
- Did the speaker have all the answers to the questions asked?
- Did the speaker allow a reasonable amount of time for the questions?
- Did the speaker end the presentation politely but firmly?

When you share your thoughts with the speaker, try to avoid undue negativity. Open your comments by citing something the speaker did well. Try to be specific and cite examples whenever you can.

Example Speech

Everybody recently has said, "You have so much courage to do this." This is so funny to me because you cannot imagine the courage of the Afghan women I have met in the course of pursuing this. My perception of myself is that I was born in paradise and upgraded to heaven. So the least I can do is pay some attention to people who didn't win the lottery, and these women sure as hell didn't win the lottery.

Back in college when I was taking art appreciation, I remember learning that during the Middle Ages there was a repellent religious theme that was often depicted in paintings of those times. Hieronymus Bosch was particularly fond of this theme. People would be going down a thoroughfare, where there would be rich people, poor people, tradesmen selling their goods, wealthy people off to a party in their finery, poor people in the streets begging—everybody going about their business on an ordinary day in their lives. That would be a first panel. Second panel, the ground would suddenly open with no warning, gape open, and all of these people would be swallowed into the fires of hell, and particularly in the Bosch paintings, you'd see little tiny people plummeting into the mouths of grotesque beasts and limbs being severed, etc. Violence didn't originate with American films. The worst part of these paintings, and the theme

that they depicted, was not actually shown. After these people fell into the gaping jaws of hell with no warning, in the middle of their lives, the earth would close and they would be forgotten. No one would know what happened to them, and they would be lost.

This is what happened to the women of Afghanistan. When I first heard what was going on there, fairly early in the situation—it was about three months old—I found myself, in my mind, in the same position as a person who happens to be walking by a lake when someone's going down for the third time, and you know that you can swim. I couldn't know this and not do something about it.

Let me give you a little history about the situation in Afghanistan. This country has been decimated by a 20-year-old civil war. I believe it is either the first or second most land-mined country in the world. It is mainly an agrarian society, and this is particularly hard because it's difficult for people to farm countryside that is thickly sown over with land mines. Most of the infrastructure of the country has been destroyed. There is great poverty, great hardship, and all of these things were true before the Taliban took over.

Nevertheless, women were contributing members of that society at every level—as is true in almost every country in the world—

in the urban areas women were living modernized lives. Some of them wore Western dress, some more traditional dress, but it was entirely their choice, and they had had equal rights under the law since the '60s. They held down an enormous quantity of all the important positions in the government, and in the professions. In the countryside, women did live more conservative lives, but they had a rich support system among the other women of their community, and although some of them did wear the burqa, the garment that all women have to wear if they leave their houses, according to the Taliban edict—they wore the burqa mainly for visits to the town.

The burqa is a very expensive garment. One of the great hardships that has been visited upon women in Afghanistan since the Taliban took over falls heavily on the rural areas where women cannot afford a burqa, and therefore as many as 12 or 14 women share in the use of one garment. And should you have an emergency, should your child fall ill, break a leg—you need to take this kid to the hospital or any available medical care right now—if it's not your turn for the burqa, too bad.

One of the many Afghan women that I have come to know told me that it is ridiculous to suggest that the women in rural areas wore the burqa as a common thing. Not only is it too expensive for most of them to have owned, but in most farming areas, most women worked in the fields alongside their husbands, which you cannot do in a burqa.

Mavis Leno, center, describes the head-to-toe shroud, called a *burqa*.

continued

In fact, there is almost nothing you can do in a burqa. One of the singular qualities of this garment is that it renders you incapable of almost any independent action. It is the case under the Taliban edicts that you must go out of your house not only wearing the burqa, but accompanied by a close male relative. But in truth, it would be very difficult for somebody to navigate and manage their tasks while wearing the burqa if they did not go out accompanied by someone.

You have no peripheral vision in this garment. In fact, the only vision provided to you is through an approximately two and a half by two inch square of mesh which sits over your eyes.

The Feminist Majority has started wearing these, and we are sending them to people who are interested in taking action as a token of remembrance for the women in Afghanistan. This little 2.5 x 2 inch square of dense mesh, which is hard to see through, provides no peripheral vision and also does not allow for breathing. You breathe through the solid cloth of the burqa itself. It's the only view of the outside world that is left to these women anymore, since their windows have to be painted an opaque color; they cannot look out of them. If a woman rides in a car, all the windows except for the front window must also be either curtained or painted opaque.

These are the kinds of egregious, excessive restrictions which have prompted us to call this "gender apartheid." In reality, the people who suffered under apartheid in South Africa had fewer restrictions, by far, than these women do. They can no longer work in any capacity, even if their families have no other means of support, which is a serious issue in a country where so many men have been killed in war, and where women far outnumber men. There are many widows. Many women are the sole support of their families. Now that they can no longer work, they are sometimes allowed to beg, but there is almost no other form of self-support left open to them, even though these women were once lawyers, doctors, professors, midwives, nurses, teachers.

When we made the film, we had to go to the Afghan American community to get enough pictures of how the women lived before the Taliban took over. We asked people to give us home movies, family photographs, anything that showed the good times that they had enjoyed prior to the takeover. We had to do this because the Taliban insists that many of these situations never occurred.

This desire to erase history has plagued people for a long time. It was a feature of the Nazis in the concentration camps that they would often tell the Jews that when the war was over and they had won, they would destroy the concentration camps, they would hide all the evidence of what had happened there, and they would tell the populace at large that the Jewish population had gone to live in other non-fascist countries so that no one would ever know what had happened to them.

Many people that were interned in those camps have said that one of their main motives for surviving in such a terrible environment was that they were determined to live to tell their story and call the Nazis liars. These films and photographs that we got from the Afghan American community do the same thing on a smaller scale. The Taliban would like to say that their country was always a conservative, Islam culture, that women never enjoyed the freedoms that in fact they enjoyed. But that is not the case, and we are here to put the lie to it.

The Taliban is essentially a tribal group; they are predominantly Pashtun. There are three major ethnic groups that live in Afghanistan: Pashtun, Tajik, and Hazara. The Hazara have always been subjected to a certain amount of prejudice. They have some Mongolian ancestry. The Pashtun occupy not only Afghanistan but a great deal of Pakistan. When the lines of demarcation were drawn to create the state of Pakistan, the Pashtun population was essentially divided in half between the two countries. So it is not so odd that Pakistan has helped promulgate the Taliban and recognized them as the legal government of Afghanistan. Pakistan is one of only three countries that makes that recognition, and they give them fiscal support.

One of the things that the Feminist Majority would like the United States to do is to address this issue with Pakistan. Pakistan has a long, strong relationship with America. We give them money; we help them out and have a lot of interaction with them. We need to say to them, "You have to speak to these people."

The fact is that there is no fabulous alternative government for Afghanistan at the moment. I can't say, "If only the Taliban weren't there, the such-and-such could take over." There is no really rich, wonderful, democratic alternative. And even if there were, that's none of my business. That's not America's business. I am strictly concerned with the human rights of the women and girls there. I do not want to displace the Taliban. I want them to understand how enormously wrong their treatment of women is to the rest of the world, and to moderate it. Give these women back the lives and the freedoms that they enjoyed before.

Recently, some people have been suggesting that the Taliban has in fact moderated. They have yet to rescind their edicts, and it is from these edicts that we get the information that I have just given you about how the women are treated. In other words, this is not word of mouth from people who witnessed it. This is from the Taliban themselves. If they wish to be seen as moderating their position, they must rescind these edicts. They must allow observers into the country to confirm that they are, in fact, treating the women in a fair, humane, and equal way. That's all we ask. We don't want any sort of revolution there. We simply want these people to listen to reason.

There are a lot of things that everybody can do to help this cause along. The Taliban does not have a lot of money. The country is destroyed. It will take a lot of money and effort to rebuild it. One of the things that gives me hope about moderation of the Taliban stance is that I see no possible way that it or any other government can rebuild this country while it keeps better than half of its population under what essentially amounts to house arrest.

One of the things that I believe has made the West so strong and powerful and successful is that we use all our human resources. Who knows how many ideas, how many

continued

Example Speech cont.

inventions and innovations are lost to countries that will not give equal rights to women, certain racial groups, and whatever these particular people decide is a group that should be singled out to have no opportunity in their society? Afghanistan needs every single citizen to rebuild the country. The people that I speak to from the Afghan community say, "Do not imagine that this is a monolithic group. They have lots of factions, some of whom are much more moderate. It happens that the extremists are in power now."

It is my hope that the more moderate, more reasonable people will realize that not only will they never gain acceptance in the world community while they treat women like this, but they'll never fix their country unless they want to spend the rest of their natural lives walking up and down the streets of the country with shotguns and chains hitting people because they're not conforming with some tiny minutiae come up with by the Taliban developers. They're not going to be able to reconstruct the society that will live on its own.

We need to increase immigration to this country from Afghanistan so that people who have fled or are able at some point in the future to leave can come to this country. You would imagine that we would be inundated by Afghan immigrants, but when the Feminist Majority checked the statistics, we found that thousands of Afghans were led into this country and welcomed during the war with the Soviets. But since the Taliban takeover two and a half years ago, guess how many Afghan people have been admitted to this country? Zero.

No one is a political refugee if these people aren't political refugees. And if you don't think that this is a human rights violation, then I don't know what you mean by human, or I don't know what you mean by rights.

So that is the first step that we can take: pressuring the government to take this action. Then we can ask America to speak to three nations in the Middle East who are alone in recognizing the legal government of Afghanistan, and alone in giving them money: Saudi Arabia, Pakistan, and the United Arab Emirates. We have strong influence with Saudi Arabia and Pakistan; we should use it. We should speak to them in the name of decency and reason and say, "This is your family. There's one in every family. You go talk to them. Tell them it won't fly."

Another thing that we need to do is to be concerned about United States companies setting up in Afghanistan and financing—not perhaps as a direct result of their business being set up there, but as an indirect result— the Taliban. If the Taliban had a lot of financial support, it would have no need to listen to the world community. They could take the ball and go home. We don't want that to happen. The problem is that Afghanistan is, by far, the most viable country through which to run a gas pipeline from Turkmenistan, which has no coast, to Pakistan. Some people have suggested that the gas deposit there is so large it might last as long as 500 years. It is this pipeline which brought me into direct contact with Unocal. I spoke at a stockholders' meeting that they had, and I participated in a number of actions to try to persuade them not to build a pipeline and fund this terrible regime.

Let me be very clear about this. Somebody's going to get this gas. I would like it to be the United States. We're a decent and humane country; we stand for human rights as much as anybody in the world. The business of business is to make money; there's nothing wrong with wanting to put the pipeline through there. But you don't have to become a fiscal giant at the expense of being a moral dwarf. Go to the Taliban and say, "You can have hundreds of millions of dollars right now. Let the women out of their houses. Knock it off." Is that so hard? Is that such a big deal? I think a company could say that.

Furthermore, the Feminist Majority has made it their business to look into which other countries might want to put the gas pipeline through there. Some of you may be aware that there are feminist organizations even in some very unlikely places, including almost all the Middle Eastern countries. We intend to speak to our sisters in Japan, which are trying to involve themselves with the Taliban on the basis of this pipeline, and we intend to speak to our sisters in Great Britain, which also have an interest in putting a pipeline through there. In both of these countries, the gender gap in voting is similar to what it is in the United States. In other words, it behooves the government of both these countries, as it behooves the government of this country, to listen up when women say, "We're really bothered by this. You could find yourself out of office if you don't listen up."

We are going to speak to these women and make sure that no one can do business in Afghanistan comfortably and with the sanction of their population. Eventually, we will make it clear to the Taliban, which is a very young, inexperienced group of people, that women are significant in the cultures of all other countries in the world, that they are a force to be reckoned with, and they do not want—and nor do men who have mothers whom they love, and daughters whom they have great hopes for—the next 1000 years to be like the last 1000 years for women. The work that the Feminist Majority has done to try to help the women of Afghanistan is beginning to yield some results. We have some profoundly conservative people on board with us, as well as some renowned liberals. This is human rights, human decency; it has nothing to do with political attitudes whatsoever, except the political attitude that the world, if it cannot get better, should at least not get worse.

I was privileged to make a tape for Voice of America, which they promised me they would take into Afghanistan, so that the women there would know that women in the rest of the world know what has happened to them and were not going to rest until something was done. These women were like people buried in a mine cave who had no idea if somebody was searching for them. They had no idea if anybody even knew what happened to them. That's how fast and overwhelming the takeover was.

While making the short tape, they taught me how to say "Maba shuma hasteem," which in Pashtun means, "We are with you." I got a lot of response. What I wanted to tell those women, and what I want to make a reality, is that they're not going to be like those pathetic people in those medieval paintings.

continued

Example Speech cont.

That the ground will not close over them, that they will not be forgotten; that it will not be as if they never lived.

Answers to written questions from the floor:

Q. How did you first get involved with both the Feminist Majority and this particular subject?

A. I first got involved with the Feminist Majority two and a half years ago, because I was looking for a feminist organization to join. I wanted a small group of people, and I had certain things I wanted to happen in feminism. I wanted the gains that women have made here in America over the last 25 years not to be rolled back, and I wanted to do something for women in other countries who were right at the beginning of the struggle. Every major group that has suffered bigotry and oppression in the world eventually learns that they have to take care of their own, and I felt that American women—and women generally in the West—were strong enough to take care of their own abroad, to not be so parochial, to not imagine that sisterhood stops at the border. So when I heard about Afghanistan, I realized that this is exactly where my heart is, this is exactly what I want to do, and this is the most extreme situation that I have encountered. It seemed like an urgent issue to draw a line in the sand and say, "No more. Enough."

Q. How much influence can President Clinton have in bringing about change in Taliban policies? Has Secretary of State Albright taken a position on this, and why hasn't the United Nations taken a stand against the Taliban? Will the recent consideration of President Clinton and nonprofits like Amnesty International expedite global change?

A. President Clinton, Hillary Clinton, and Madeleine Albright have all taken extremely firm and public stances against Taliban abuses towards women and their abuses of human rights in general. They also bury homosexuals alive; they punish thieves by cutting their hands off. These are not human rights activists. Kofi Annan has spoken out vehemenly against the Taliban, and the U.N. has continually drafted stronger legislation against them, and coined a very fitting term: gender apartheid. As far as organizations like Amnesty International go, what can I say? I revere these people. Their work is superlative, and we stand beside them. We're all trying to contribute, each in our own way, and I believe that the current government is extremely disposed to look favorably upon this—not least because President Clinton has publicly acknowledged that he is aware of it. He was elected because of the gender gap. A lot of conservatives feel strongly about this, because people like Cal Thomas have come over firmly to our side. I have optimism, regardless of what administration comes in in the next couple of years;

this is not something that people will overlook.

Q. Do you think that the benefits of celebrity, namely the media attention that it brings, is outweighed by the fact that Hollywood political causes aren't taken all that seriously?

A. I'm married to a celebrity. I live in Hollywood. I refuse to be disenfranchised on either of those grounds. I don't see why anybody else who is a celebrity or lives in Hollywood should be disenfranchised on those grounds. I'm a little bit puzzled why people make such a production out of this.

Most media companies in this country belong to extremely wealthy men. They did not acquire their papers, magazines, and networks because they were so knowledgeable about politics and foreign affairs. They got them because they were rich. What is the difference between using your fiscal resources to influence world affairs and using other resources you can bring to the table such as renown? Many rich people inherited their money. Most famous people earned their fame themselves. There must be something about them that makes what they have to say worth listening to.

The Computer-Assisted Presentation

Specs for the Computer-Assisted Presentation

Time limit
4–5 minutes.

Speaker's notes
None needed besides slides/transparencies from the software preparations.

Sources of information
Two are required, preferably three. For each source, give the specific magazine, book, or Internet site from which it was taken; the title of the article; the author's full name; the date of publication; and the chapter or pages numbers where the material was found. If a source is a person, identify him or her by title, position, and occupation. List these on the outline form. For Internet sites give the address (URL).

Outline
Follow the computer software instructions.

Speak Up!

Share a recent experience you had working with computers. It may be something you learned through a computer program or a Web site, a new game or research information that was enhanced by sound and video, or even a presentation for another class.

Purpose and Expectations of This Assignment

Software programs for creating effective presentations have become increasingly popular in many business settings over the past two decades. These technologies allow you to create visual aids that will lead your audience through the points of your speech just the way you planned it. Because these programs are now so common, we encourage you to familiarize yourself with how and when to use them. This assignment will help you gain some skills in this area. When you can use technology to enhance an already effective speech, you reveal your competence in several areas all at once.

In completing this assignment, you will

- apply a computer presentation program to speech preparation,
- create and present appropriate visual aids to illustrate the speech, and
- practice proofreading created materials.

Defining Computer-Assisted Presentations

Computer-assisted presentations begin with the same purposes, topics, and research as many of the other speeches you have given so far. The software simply provides guidance for organizing speech materials into standardized formats. It offers the opportunity to create transparencies of an outline, as well charts, graphs, or illustrations.

Software programs are valuable tools for creating clear, visual presentations quickly and relatively easily. However, the formats are limited and should not be considered appropriate for all speaking occasions and topics.

Choosing a Topic

In selecting a topic for a presentation, your first consideration should be the audience, just as it has been in the other assignments. The types of speech you can effectively develop using, for example, the PowerPoint software program include recommending a strategy; selling a product, service, or idea; training; reporting on progress; and communicating bad news. Once you have determined the purpose of your presentation, you can select an appropriate topic.

For additional topic ideas, consult some related chapters in this text, such as Experience 7, "The Speech to Inform"; Experience 9, "The Speech to Persuade"; and Experience 28, "The Sales Talk."

Preparing

For this assignment, we will use the PowerPoint program as an example.

Begin to craft your presentation by identifying key ideas and subpoints from the research you've done on your topic.

Choose a title. Identify any other information you wish to include on the opening slide of your presentation.

Select the Auto Content Wizard from the PowerPoint menu to begin the presentation-development process. Then select the type of presentation you wish to create. Clicking on the Finish button will take you to the Outline View of your format. Follow the software's prompts to edit the outline in the format provided, organizing your ideas by key words, phrases, or simple sentences.

After you have completed your outline, check out the software's options for adding backgrounds, charts, graphs, or other artwork to your slides. Follow the prompts and graphics menus to enhance your basic format.

Before you print out your slides, you must proofread the material. Be sure your spelling, punctuation, and grammar are absolutely perfect, as your audience will no doubt spot any glitches. One small typographical error unchecked can severely reduce your credibility as a presenter.

Once you are satisfied with your presentation, print out your slides to create transparencies to use with an overhead projector. The software will also allow you to print out your outline in the form of speaking notes. If you have a correctly configured computer, you may be able to connect directly to a projector.

Presenting

Before you present your speech, be sure you have all the equipment you need. Ideally, you should rehearse with this equipment in the room where you will be presenting. Pay close attention to when you will change slides. Check and refocus to ascertain optimal visibility for the audience.

Delivery skills for this speech are no less important than for other speeches you have given. Volume, rate, and clarity are vitally important, as are gestures and posture. Until you are completely comfortable with changing the slides, rehearsal is a must. Your goal should be a fluid vocal delivery and efficient, appropriate gestures.

The following is a thumbnail layout of a PowerPoint presentation.

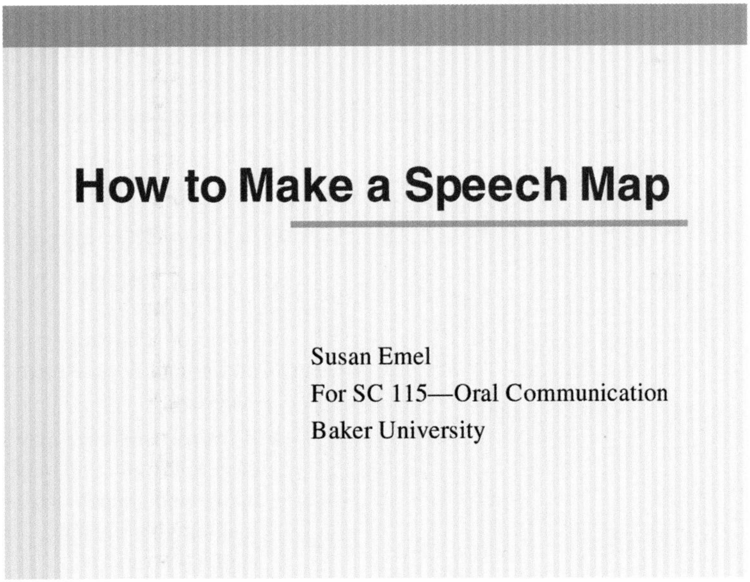

How to Make a Speech Map

Susan Emel
For SC 115—Oral Communication
Baker University

(1)

Why Map a Speech?

To clarify the flow of ideas

(2)

Communicating Competently

- Speeches must be audience-friendly.
- Ideas must flow logically.
- Speech mapping helps a speaker visualize:
  - placement of main ideas
  - relationship of the main ideas

(3)

How to Begin

- Identify the main points you wish to make.
- Create an outline of main ideas and sub-points.

(4)

Making the Map

- How do ideas fit together?
  - Do ideas represent a time progression?
  - Do ideas build like a pyramid?
  - Are ideas like recipe ingredients?
  - Is there a problem and a solution, as in a mystery?

(5)

Making the Map, cont'd

- Select a visual image that best fits your ideas.
- Draw the image; label each part to identify main ideas.
- Do the ideas fit the image?
  - If no, rearrange the order; try another image
  - If yes, you correctly identified a relationship
  - Ideas should be easy for your audience to follow

(6)

Making the Most of Your Map

- Now you are ready to test your flow of ideas on a friend or classmate to check your success.
- If the test audience agrees that your ideas are easy to follow, you may want to consider using your speech map as a visual aid, making your presentation even more audience-friendly.

Evaluating

Evaluate a classmate's computer-assisted presentation. Be prepared to give feedback to the speaker on the following questions.

- Did the presenter handle the equipment efficiently?
- Did the presenter integrate the computer portion of the speech with the spoken thoughts and concepts?
- Did the presenter speak clearly and follow a clear progression of ideas?
- Was the computer portion of the speech effective?
- Did the speaker use appropriate gestures and body language?
- Did the recipient speak clearly?

When you share your thoughts with the speaker avoid being overly negative. Begin your comment by citing something the speaker did well. Try to be specific and cite examples whenever you can.

Talking Points
Getting the Technology to Work for You

In today's world of high technology, hand-drawn posters are no longer appropriate visual aids. It is now so easy to prepare and display professional-looking visuals with computer graphics and fonts that it makes little sense not to take advantage of this technology. With adequate preparation, a computer-assisted presentation can be very impressive.

Using technology such as PowerPoint can be fun, challenging, and exciting. But keep in mind that computer presentations are meant to *enhance* your speech, not *replace* it. When you have decided on an interesting topic and finished your research, use the tips on the following page to help you run your chosen technology—and to keep it from running *you*!

Tips for Effective PowerPoint Presentations

1. Simplify and limit the number of words on each transparency. Use key phrases and include only essential information. Link the ideas for your audience throughout your speech.

2. Avoid writing words in all capital letters. Make sure the letters are spaced evenly and not too close together. Empty space on the slide will enhance readability.

3. Use contrasting colors for text and background. Dark text on a light background works best.

4. Avoid patterned backgrounds. They reduce readability.

5. Avoid special effects such as animation and sound. While you may think these will add interest to your presentation, they can turn out to be distracting and/or annoying to the audience.

6. Limit the number of transparencies you use. There should be no more than one per minute. Constantly changing transparencies is likely to confuse the audience.

7. Audiences often ask to have another look at the previous screen, so get familiar with moving forward and backward through your presentation.

8. Be sure you have an alternate plan in case you experience technical difficulties. You might be able to give the speech without visual aids, or you might provide a handout.

9. Rehearse in front of someone who has never seen your presentation. Ask for honest feedback about all aspects of the speech, with an emphasis on the visual.

10. Avoid reading from your slides. What's on the slides is for the audience, not for the speaker.

11. Face the audience. There is nothing more annoying than a presenter who spends his or her whole time talking to the visual aids rather than the audience.

12. Never apologize for anything in your presentation. If you believe something in the presentation is a little off, embarrassing, or wrong, *don't include it!*

The Interview

Specs for the Interview

Time limits

4–6 minutes for report of an interview.

$1/2$–2 minutes for role-played telephone appointment.

5–10 minutes for role-played interview.

Speaker's notes

25–50 words for interview report.

Sources of information

List the person interviewed.

Outline

Prepare a 75- to 100-word complete sentence outline.

Speak Up!

If you had a chance to interview anyone in the world living or dead, who would it be? List four questions you would ask and be prepared to share your responses with the class. Next, as a group, brainstorm on what makes a good interview question. Keep these criteria in mind as you work through the following assignment.

Purpose and Expectations of This Assignment

If you're like most people you will take part in a number of interviews over the course of your life. Perhaps you have already interviewed for a job or are planning to do so. Whether or not you get the job, or any other favorable response, will depend on how well you present yourself during the interview. And if you are interviewing for other reasons—for example, to gain information for a report, to prepare a newscast, to prepare a legal brief for a case in court, or to write an article to sell to a magazine—the maturity, skill, and judgment you exercise will be the keys to your success or failure.

In completing this assignment, you will

- prepare appropriate interview questions,
- conduct an interview to acquire information,
- understand the role of research in preparation of the interview,
- identify types of questions to ask employers when being interviewed for a job, and
- understand the communication effects of interviewing by phone or in person.

Defining the Interview Situation

When you go to an interview, you talk with another person or group for a specific purpose. The **interview format** is a series of questions and answers. Most are planned. Impromptu interviews, however, occur among business-people and others. You can often see this type of interview going on at a restaurant, on the street, in a store, or at someone's home. Unplanned interviews tend to sound like normal conversation while formal interviews proceed in a more structured manner. It is the latter we will focus on here.

The formal interview requires certain protocols from the parties involved, such as (1) making an appointment, (2) operating within a limited time period, and sometimes (3) having several different meetings.

One element that is common to all interviews is talk. If you can express yourself well, things should go smoothly. If you cannot, you may have trouble. Another important element is your physical behavior—your grooming and appearance, your walk, your posture, subtle movements of your hands and feet, eye contact, and facial expressions. Everything you say and do tells something about you. Your thoughts and moods, attitudes and feelings, are all symbolized by your total behavior, and you can't hide them. You are only fooling yourself if you think you have mastered the art of deception. Personnel officers, business executives, and sales personnel are quick to spot a phony.

As the interview situation tends to place the involved parties in close physical proximity, often in a small office, it permits many personal judgments and subconscious reactions on both sides. This can be stressful, but so far a better way to formulate final evaluations of another person—whether it's a prospective employee or prospective boss—has yet to be invented.

A group may conduct an interview. One example you will recognize is when news reporters interview a governor or other public official. Or a single reporter might interview an executive or administrative group. Companies often have more than one person present during an interview. Applicants for key positions usually go through more than one interview.

Choosing an Interview Situation

Select an interview situation that interests you and one you can complete within the designated time frame. Avoid a person or group that is too distant to reach or that cannot grant the interview within a short time or at a time when you are available to meet. Make your choice and arrangements within 24 hours of receiving your assignment. Why so soon? You may find out that the person you want to interview is not available; if you do, you will have time to contact someone else.

Because many people you might want to interview could have last-minute conflicts, it's a good idea to schedule the interview as far as possible in advance of your due date. Thus, if the person must cancel, you still have time to reschedule or find another person to interview before your presentation is due.

For this assignment, think about a person who holds a job you might want to have someday. Use the interview to learn more about the job. You can also interview someone who makes policies that affect your life—school administrators or local and state officials. If you are interested in learning more about a historic or current events topic, interview an expert.

Preparing (as Interviewer)

As you are the interviewer, call and make an appointment. When you make the appointment, be prepared to conduct it on the spot should the interviewee suggest that you do so. If your appointment is by telephone, be pleasant and efficient by using a carefully prepared and rehearsed request. Structure this request as follows:

1. Make sure you are talking with the right person.

2. Introduce yourself.

3. Explain why you want the interview, and suggest the amount of time you will need, the date, hour, and place.

4. Do not apologize.

5. Once you have made the appointment, leave the person your name and telephone number, and ask to be called should it be necessary for him or her to change the appointment. Sometimes a secretary will take down your appointment. It is appropriate to confirm the appointment with a letter or fax in advance or a telephone call on the day of the appointment.

Regardless of whether you are interviewing for a job or to acquire information, you should acquaint yourself with background data about your interviewee. Ask an assistant to send you information about the interviewee and the business.

Now comes the crux of your interview preparation. What is your purpose, and what do you want to know? Determine the purpose first. Then prepare a list of ten broad-based lead questions and 20 specific, detail-oriented questions that will bring out the information you want. Do not read your list of questions verbatim during the interview. Memorize selected questions from it to be used as needed. Refer to your list occasionally and originate other questions as the interview proceeds.

Dress neatly and appropriately. Casual school

clothes are not suitable. You can fail an interview before opening your mouth to speak if your appearance suggests carelessness or disregard for the situation.

Get the correct address and exact time for the interview. Be sure of this. Allow yourself more time than you need to get there. Plan to be ten minutes early for the interview because this will demonstrate your enthusiasm. Do not take any chances on being late; you might have car trouble or traffic problems. If you are going somewhere unfamiliar, do a test run before the interview date or use a Web site such as mapquest.com to get printed and graphic directions.

Study the background information and your list of questions. Be sure you have your questions laid out with adequate space for writing responses to them or bring an additional notebook for recording the interviewee's answers. Make sure you have a pencil or pen that works. Tape recording is a good idea, but be sure to ask permission for this at the time when you make the appointment.

Above all, approach the interview as an enjoyable experience. Most people are fairly accommodating when it comes to talking about themselves or their business.

Presenting

Arrive ten minutes early for the interview. Inquire where to locate the interviewee, or tell the person in charge of the front office who you are and that you have an appointment. When you are invited to do so, go into your interviewee's office, introduce yourself, and shake hands. Use a firm grip. Thank the interviewee for making the time for you.

Take a seat when your interviewee invites you to do so, or seat yourself when your judgment tells you it is appropriate. The host may be busy and request that you wait a moment longer. You may stand or sit politely, or look over the office furnishings and arrangements casually, but don't fidget or pace nervously. Glance over your list of questions to refresh your memory. When your host is ready, be prepared to make a sincere remark about the office, the view, or something of general interest.

Start your interview by explaining why you are there. Then ask your questions courteously, tactfully, and directly. Initial questions may concern (1) the history of the business; (2) the nature of the business, such as products sold or services performed; (3) the number of employees, labor practices, qualifications of employees, vacations, employee benefits; and (4) advantages of being in this business. Do not press questions on any subject the interviewee obviously doesn't want to discuss. It's your obligation to direct the interview into the desired areas and bring the discussion back if it gets off track. Remember this is *your* interview.

Bring the interview to a pleasant conclusion (perhaps by saying you have one more question). Do not overstay your time. Should the interviewee offer to show you the place of business, have a cup of coffee, or tour the grounds, accept graciously but don't forget that his or her time may be limited—in other words, don't overstay your welcome. Thank the interviewee when it seems appropriate and extend an invitation for him or her to visit your school.

While the interview is under way, take notes quickly and accurately. Write clearly so you can read your notes later. Listen attentively so you won't have to ask to have information repeated. If your time runs out, you can request a later appointment to finish the interview. Accept the interviewee's response gracefully either way. Thank the interviewee before leaving.

Be courteous at all times. Avoid random, nervous movements, any over-familiar gestures or comments, excessive throat clearing, and mumbling.

✳ The Job Interview

You will take a turn as both the interviewee and the interviewer. As the interviewee, you will answer questions about yourself and ask questions about the work. Reread the preceding section on conducting an interview to refresh your thinking.

You should have a copy of your resume, which includes personal information such as honors you've received, offices you've held, activities you've participated in, clubs and organizations of which you are a member, and a record of your work experience. There are several good books available on resume preparation. Check your school or public library.

You should have a list of at least three personal references with complete contact information including addresses and telephone numbers. Each reference should be a businessperson, teacher, or other professional. You may also use letters of recommendation. You should contact each reference in advance and request permission to use his or her name.

Before you are interviewed, you may be required to fill out an application form. If so, fill it out completely and make sure you answer every question fully. Be neat and accurate. Omit nothing, and don't assume that a stranger studying the form will be able to read your mind and fill in blank spaces.

When you go into the job interview, conduct yourself as you would with any business or professional person. Greet the interviewer cordially, shake hands if appropriate, and state your purpose.

It's likely that you will be asked questions about your experience, background, training, and education. Answer these questions honestly and directly, but don't belittle yourself. Suggest that the interviewer might like to examine the summaries of your personal history, training, experience, and recommendations you have with you. Sit politely while the interviewer reads these materials. Besides the job you are applying for, he or she may be looking for someone to fill a different position—one that is not advertised. If you conduct a superior

interview showing alertness and intelligence, it's possible the job would be yours. Ask about the qualifications, responsibilities, duties, benefits, and requirements of the job position.

As the interview progresses you should be ready to talk and give answers or to wait with poise if anything unusual occurs. Sometimes interruptions are planned to test your reactions: the telephone might ring, a secretary might bring a message, or an employee might come in. The interviewer might even ask you a startling or unexpected question. Don't be surprised at anything—just respond intelligently and respectfully.

Before the interview ends, ask when you will be notified about the job. If you receive a vague or indefinite answer, ask if you may contact the interviewer or write him or her at a future date. It is only fair before you leave that you have some word about when you will be notified.

When the interviewer indicates that the interview is ending, bring your remarks to a close, extend thanks again, and leave. Sometimes it may be necessary for you to close the interview. Do not stay too long.

Hint: If you weren't asked to fill out an application and you want the interviewer to remember you over the dozen other applicants, hand him or her a three-by-five card as the interview ends. On it, neatly typed, should be your name, address, telephone number, fax number, education, work experience, and the type of work you are most interested or qualified to do.

Your instructor may develop the interview assignment in three role-playing activities.

1. **Role-play Making the Appointment** Two people at a time sit back-to-back eight to ten feet apart and carry out an imagined telephone conversation. One is a businessperson; the other is a student seeking an interview appointment. Don't overdo the role-playing. Keep it realistic. As the prospective job interviewee, be sure to have a specific job description in mind when you ask for the interview.

2. **Role-play the Job Interview** Two people role-play the job interview for five to ten minutes. The interviewee should enter the classroom door after the instructor has set up any special circumstances the interviewer will confront. The businessperson, a secretary, or someone else will admit the student who will take it from there. The participants

should not rehearse because a real interview is not rehearsed; however, the participants should be well prepared to conduct their individual parts and try to make the entire experience as true to life as possible.

3. **The Actual Interview** You should have successfully role-played the appointment and interview aspects of this assignment before attempting an interview with an actual businessperson. However, once you have fulfilled parts 1 and 2, you may proceed to this step, and to number 4 below.

   a. By telephone, make an appointment with a business or professional person whom you do not know personally.

   b. Complete an interview to learn about the business, its general operations, policies (labor, products, organization), and future plans. Take notes. Prepare a five- to six-minute oral presentation on the interview and what you learned from it.

      Your instructor will keep a list of all businesspersons interviewed so that future classes will not interview the same ones too often. However, a letter of appreciation from the interviewer and the instructor to the businessperson for the cooperation is a good practice.

4. Students who want to work should conduct actual job interviews and then prepare a five- to six-minute oral report of their experiences for the class.

Evaluating

Evaluate a classmate's interview presentation. Rate the following criteria on a scale from 1 to 5 with 1 being "needs much improvement" and 5 being "outstanding."

Interviewer:

- Did the interviewer ask questions that elicited needed information?
- Did the interviewer put the interviewee at ease?
- Did the interviewer describe the job opening and the necessary qualifications?

Interviewee:

- Did the interviewee seem relaxed and confident?
- Did the interviewee answer all questions in a straightforward manner?
- Did the interviewee have a resume and references or letters of recommendation?
- Did the interviewee ask pertinent questions about the workplace?

Choose one element of your classmate's performance that you think might be improved. Encourage him or her to role-play that portion of the interview with you. Stop and start at the point in the interview where you feel your classmate might improve.

The
Panel Discussion

Specs for the Panel Discussion

Participants

Three to six panelists and a moderator.

Time limits

30 minutes for most classroom performances. Others vary according to the amount of time available.

Speaker's notes

Participants usually find it necessary and convenient to have notes to provide them with figures, facts, and sources for the information and points of view they present.

Sources of information

At least three, preferably more.

Outline

See the Preparing section on pages 323–324.

Speak Up!

You have no doubt participated in brainstorming sessions with friends, fellow club members, and even your family members. As you know, when brainstorming, you listen to every group member's ideas, no matter how far-fetched. Discuss with your classmates what this type of discussion accomplishes. Do you think group discussions are generally worthwhile? Why or why not?

Purpose and Expectations of This Assignment

There is no better method for resolving problems than by talking them over. A panel discussion, when operating successfully, uses this method to great advantage. In a panel discussion, students work together in small groups to focus on the communication skills necessary to solve a problem. Each panel member prepares his or her own thoughts and ideas on the problem in advance, then comes to the panel with a clearly outlined problem-solving process to try to work out a single solution through discussion with the group. This process makes the most of each member's best thinking. Every student should have the experience of deliberately sitting down in the company of others to find the answers to problems of mutual concern. This assignment will provide this vital experience. Studying it carefully now will bring big benefits later on. Being able to function successfully in a group setting and address problem-solving in cooperation with others are qualities that every employer wants in his or her employees.

In completing this assignment, you will

- work as a group member to solve a problem,

- use the steps of a problem-solving process, and

- understand the importance of open-mindedness in problem-solving.

Defining the Panel Discussion

A **panel discussion** is a speaking event in which people sit down together to try to solve one or more problems by pooling their knowledge and thus arriving at decisions that are satisfactory to the majority. If they reach these decisions, their purpose is fulfilled. This requires each panelist to enter the panel with an open mind and a desire to hear other viewpoints, opinions, and evidence. Thus by gathering all possible information (facts) and combining it, the group can examine a problem point by point to arrive at a logical solution.

No one should consent to join a panel unless he or she is capable of participating without holding on to preconceived ideas, prejudices, and opinions. An attitude of open-mindedness is the most valuable asset a panel speaker can possess. This does not mean he or she is wishy-washy. Instead it implies that the participant is willing to change his or her mind when confronted with new information.

A panel may vary greatly in terms of the number of members; however, if there are too many participants, progress tends to be slow and laborious. It is therefore advisable to limit the panel to five or six people in addition to the moderator.

There are a wide variety of occasions for panel discussions. Clubs, societies, and other organizations use this common method of problem solving. Naturally, if an organization has a large membership, its problems will be submitted to committees that will in turn attack them through a panel.

Today radio and television often feature the panel as a public service, and even a form of entertainment. Don't believe that every panel must have a huge audience or that TV programs dominated by sarcasm, acrimony, and quibbling represent true discussion. Such examples are not good panel discussions because they often lack both the quality of open-mindedness and a sincere desire to solve a problem.

Choosing a Topic

If the problem is not assigned, the panel should meet under the leadership of the moderator or chair. At the meeting, the participants should suggest several topics. Then they can vote. Whichever topic gets the majority of votes is the one the participants will use as the basis of their panel. Think of school or community problems that affect you directly. Your selection should be based on the interests of the panelists and the availability of materials for research and study. If the discussion will be conducted before an audience, the panel should take the audience into consideration when selecting the topic. In either case the group should select a question that the members are capable of discussing in some depth. Here are some sample discussion problems/questions.

1. How may more people be encouraged to vote?

2. How may teacher's salaries be raised?

3. What should be done to improve high school and college curricula?

4. What should be done about cheating at school?

5. What should be the policy relative to paying athletes or granting them special privileges?

6. Should required courses in marriage and parenting be taught in high schools?

7. Should all physically and mentally capable students be required to attend school until they reach 18 years of age, or until they graduate?

Preparing

As participants, you and your fellow panel members should give careful thought to the purpose of a panel discussion, which is to problem-solve. You should prepare your material with this in mind. Your attitude should be similar to that of a farmer who sees a strange plant growing in a field. What should be done about it? Is it harmful? Is it valuable? Should it be dug out by the roots or cut off? Who can tell what kind of a plant it is? In other words, try not to jump to conclusions immediately after selecting a problem. Like the farmer, the student should find out everything possible about the question under discussion and then determine which solutions are most sound.

Let's assume for a moment that you have selected your problem and that the panelists are ready to begin searching for possible solutions. Imagine that the question you and your fellow panelists have chosen is "What should be done to decrease the number of divorces?" Following are the procedures each individual participant should follow to arrive at possible solutions.

1. Find out all the effects of divorce, both good and bad. Ask your teacher and librarian to help you locate sources of information. Keep detailed notes on this and all data you uncover.

2. Find out what caused these good and bad effects.

3. Now that you know the results of divorce and what causes it, you should establish a set of standards by which you can analyze each solution that you come up with. In this case, the standards might be:

   • Any solution must be fair to both men and women.

- Any solution must be fair to the children of divorced parents.

- Any solution must be legal and constitutional.

4. State several tentative solutions to the problem. Be sure these answers meet each of the standards you set up. Under each suggested solution, list both its advantages and its disadvantages. Remember that you are not to be biased toward your solutions. You must be willing to say to the other panelists, "Here are my ideas with their good and bad points. This is what I believe on the basis of the information I could find. However, I'm willing to change my views if your information indicates I should."

5. Now select the one solution that you think is the best from all those you have constructed.

6. Suggest ways and means to put your best solution into action.

Note: Outline all your points, one through six, using complete sentences. State your sources of information, including dates, authors, titles of books or magazines, and volume and page numbers. Be sure to identify your authorities. Hand this outline to your instructor as evidence of your preparation.

Now that you have gathered all of the information on your problem, outlined it, and learned its contents sufficiently well, you are ready to meet with the other members of the panel to see what they have discovered. Each of them should have done the same thing you did in aiming for a solution to the problem of the high divorce rate. You will all get together and pool your knowledge. Obviously you will not all have the same information, because you won't have read the same magazines and books and talked to the same people. This means you will not agree with each other because your information is different. Your possible solutions will be different too. Nevertheless, you will pool your knowledge, and after thoroughly talking it over and examining all the data carefully, you will decide on a possible solution that is agreed upon by a majority of the panel. These solutions will represent the cooperative effort of the entire group.

Presenting

In presenting a panel you merely meet as a group and discuss the information and ideas each member has brought. To do this effectively, each participant should approach the panel with an open mind. You must have a desire to find the answer to the problem, not a desire to press your own agenda or get the others to adopt your ideas and solutions. Again, an attitude of open-mindedness is the most important aspect of the discussion.

Let's assume that the members of the panel have assembled. The moderator should have arrived early and placed the chairs in a semicircle so that each participant can easily see everyone else during the discussion. The moderator will sit near the middle of the group. If there is an audience, the moderator should make sure that all the panelists are seated in such a way that they are both visible and audible. The speakers should remember to direct their voices toward the audience as well as the panel.

As the panel gets under way, try not to dominate the occasion. Nor should you withdraw and say little or nothing. All participants should remember that they are not to be angry, impolite, sarcastic, or acrimonious. They should be earnest and sincere—and persistent if necessary.

The moderator should insist on a policy of fairness, and promote harmony and goodwill among the group. He or she should encourage the most timid to speak their minds. A good moderator permits some digression from the main question but will direct the discussion in such a way as to bring it back on point. The moderator also keeps track of the time and makes certain that the discussion ends within the allotted period.

The moderator will make brief introductory remarks in which he or she will mention the occasion and reasons for discussing the topic at hand, and introduce the members of the panel (if there is an audience). He or she should tell where each panelist is from, their occupations, and any other appropriate information. If there is no audience, the moderator should be certain that all members of the panel are acquainted with one another.

The procedure for the actual discussion should be informal throughout. It should be a spontaneous give-and-take with questions, answers, and contributions from everyone without prompting from the moderator. This does not mean the chair may not call on a member if he or she finds it necessary to bring out that person's thoughts.

The points to discuss should develop in the following order through informal talk.

1. **Define the terms.** Be sure you all agree on what you are talking about.

2. **Limit your subject** if it is too broad. Perhaps you should talk about decreasing divorce rates only in the United States or in a single state or city. (Note: The statement of your question does not limit the discussion in this respect.)

3. **Talk about the effects** of the high divorce rate.

4. **Discuss the causes.**

5. **Set up standards** on which you will base any solutions to your problem.

6. **Arrive at several tentative solutions** or conclusions to your question. Be sure you discuss advantages and disadvantages of each one.

7. **Select one tentative solution** as the best one to put into action.

8. **Decide on ways and means** to go about putting your solution into action.

At that point, the moderator summarizes briefly what the panel has accomplished. He or she may permit the audience (if there is one) to direct questions to the panel members. It is their job to rule on questions that obviously have no bearing on the discussion or other questions that are out of order. The moderator concludes the meeting with a brief summary at the end of the allotted or appropriate time.

Note: To follow through all of these steps will necessitate a constant alertness on the part of all panelists and the moderator. Of course, if a number of meetings are scheduled, you may move gradually through the various stages on your way to a solution. It is not wise, however, to have sessions so long that the members become tired.

Evaluating

Evaluate the panel discussion of a group of your classmates. Rate the following criteria on a scale from 1 to 5.

- Did the moderator introduce all the panel members?

- Did the panel members listen well to one another?

- Did members refrain from shutting down anyone's ideas?

- Did every member take part in the discussion?

- Did the panelists come up with sound solutions?

- Did all the panelists and the moderator speak clearly and loudly enough?

- Did the solution they reached seem like the best one that was discussed?

Using this list as a basis for your notes, give oral feedback to the group.

Talking Points
Listening to and Reading the News

By regularly viewing television news, listening to radio news, and reading newspapers and magazines, you will become familiar with a wide array of potential speech topics. As a bonus, you will observe good writing and speaking practices. Here are some techniques to help you remember and use new information about current events.

1. Keep a place in your notebook or journal to list ideas for potential speech topics you heard or read about in the news. Record the date you heard or read the news item. This will allow you to locate additional material in a variety of sources on similar dates.

2. Read a wide range of magazines. Don't overlook specialized "news" publications such as sports magazines or arts journals.

3. Go to the library and read a magazine you have never read before. If you live in a rural area or a small town, read a newspaper from a major city. Most major newspapers have an online edition you can read free of charge via the Internet.

4. As you watch the news on television, observe the way the visuals complement the voiceovers. Think about ways you can incorporate visuals to add life to your speech.

5. Listen to the news on the radio. Pay attention to the way reporters use changes in inflection, volume, and tone to add interest to their reports.

6. Read editorials and op-ed pieces (these are the articles appearing on the page opposite the editorial page). Analyze the way writers build their arguments. Locate articles from two columnists or editorial writers on the same topic with different viewpoints. Analyze how they consider the other side in preparing their columns.

The
Symposium

John Payne (left) and Dr. Henry Samueli take part in an Internet symposium.

Specs for the Symposium

Participants

Three to four speakers and a moderator.

Time limit

5–6 minutes per speech.

Speaker's notes

None for the speakers. The moderator may use notes in order to make sure that the order of speakers, topics for discussion, and other information do not become confused.

Sources of information

Three or more.

Outline

Prepare your own to ensure proper organization. You need not hand it in to the instructor.

Speak Up!

Share an experience in which you were in the audience when a group of speakers presented various sides of a single problem or question. What was this experience like for you? Do you think you gained more from multiple points of view than you would have from a single well-informed speaker? Tell the class why or why not.

Purpose and Expectations of This Assignment

Another form of group discussion, the symposium, is becoming more and more common as a means of informing and enlightening the public on current issues. In a symposium members of a small group prepare public statements on differing aspects of a single topic and present their speeches in turn before opening the discussion up to the audience for questions. Like many people, you may be unaware of the different types of discussions and the advantages or disadvantages inherent in each. Because it will be to your advantage to understand the structure and techniques of the symposium, this assignment is designed to take you through the basics.

In completing this assignment, you will

- organize one speech topic among several speakers,

- participate in presenting a speech with several others,

- coordinate presenting a speech topic from several different points of view, and

- coordinate answering audience-generated questions with several panel members.

Defining the Symposium

The **symposium** is a method of presenting representative aspects of a problem. Usually three or four speakers talk about one general question, with each speaker presenting views on a particular aspect. A moderator acts as the discussion leader. It is up to the moderator to synchronize the different speeches so that unification of ideas begins to emerge rather than a series of unrelated lectures. Speakers are charged with the responsibility of fitting their remarks into the main question by making sure that they contribute to the proposition being explored.

The time allotted to each speaker is the same, except that the length of the speeches may vary from symposium to symposium—some allow speeches of only a few minutes, while others allow 15 or 20 minutes each if time permits. Following the speeches, the participants may form a panel, after which the audience is invited to ask them questions. Either the panel or the questions from the audience may be omitted.

The whole program may continue as long as an hour and a half if time permits or more if the audience is actively engaged and the panelists are able to continue.

The purpose of a symposium is to inform and stimulate the listeners. Each speaker may support a very different point of view from the others. There are many appropriate occasions for symposiums. A symposium may take place in any situation in which a group of people gather. It may be at the meeting of a club; a society; a religious, fraternal, or business organization; an educational group; or any civic gathering. Today radio and television shows frequently use the symposium format.

Choosing a Topic

The participants in your symposium should meet with the moderator and, by general agreement, decide on a **proposition**. If possible, you should choose one that is interesting to everyone. However, if all of the members of the group do not agree, go with the topic most suitable to the majority. You are unlikely to find a topic on which everyone is equally well informed. Be sure that the topic you and your fellow participants select is one about which you can secure information via interviews and/or reading. Consider some of the following topics:

1. What should be done to conserve energy?

2. Should the United States have a program of compulsory military service?

3. What should be done about the nation's homeless population?

4. Should scholarships be given to all high school graduates who have outstanding academic records?

5. What should be done to decrease gang violence?

Preparing

First of all, keep in mind that each individual speaker should prepare his or her speeches according to the suggestions laid down for any speech to inform or stimulate. Include all the steps of preparation—from audience analysis to rehearsal.

You and your fellow members should meet with the moderator. Then work together to figure out how the selected topic is to be divided among you so that you can each present a different aspect of it. Let's imagine that the topic is "What should be done to improve the streets of our city?" If there are three speakers, you could divide the question so that each of you addressed one of the following aspects:

1. What should the city administration do to improve the streets?

2. What should the citizens do to improve the streets?

3. What should be done to improve the current level of efficiency and use of equipment?

Having agreed on the above divisions of the question, you and your fellow speakers must next prepare the discussion, making sure to observe the time limits closely.

The moderator should be well prepared on the entire subject so that he or she can direct the discussion effectively. A routine responsibility of the moderator is to set up the order of speakers.

The moderator should prepare brief introductory remarks, including the following facts.

- History and statement of the proposition
- Reasons for its discussion
- Relationship and importance of the topic to the audience
- Definitions of terms of the proposition
- Names, qualifications, topics, and order of the speakers
- Manner in which the symposium will be conducted

The moderator should be familiar with the point of view each speaker will take. He or she should also make a brief summary of the overall presentation at the conclusion of the event.

Let's assume that everyone is now ready for the symposium. Each participant should briefly go through the following list of reminders.

- Does each speaker have sufficient authorities and accurate data to back up his or her information, ideas, and conclusions?
- Are these proofs in a form that the speaker can use while participating as a member of the symposium or during the audience's question period?

- Does each member know how to answer questions from the audience, to meet objections, to restate arguments, and to summarize his or her point of view?
- Will the speakers keep their sense of humor and remain calm and polite when under fire?
- Does the moderator know how to lead the audience and direct questions to the speakers?
- Does the speaker know which types of questions to permit as legitimate and which to rule out of order?

If the participants do not know the answers to these questions, they are obligated to do more work.

Presenting

Throughout the entire symposium, follow the usual good speech habits. Present the symposium as follows.

1. The symposium members take their seats side by side with the moderator at one end.

2. The moderator makes introductory remarks, introduces the members of the symposium to the audience, and presents the topic and the first speaker.

3. The first speaker delivers his or her comments after which the moderator presents the other speakers in a similar manner.

4. At the conclusion of the speeches, the moderator briefly summarizes the speakers' ideas.

5. Following the moderator's summary, the symposium continues according to one of the alternatives listed below:

   a. The speakers form a panel for a limited time and further discuss the ideas they presented. Then the chair summarizes briefly and adjourns the meeting.

   b. The speakers form a panel as indicated in (a) above, after which the audience is permitted to question the speakers for a limited or unlimited time by directing questions via the moderator. The moderator concludes the symposium with a brief summary followed by adjournment.

   c. Following the speeches and the moderator's brief summary, the audience is permitted to question the speakers for a definite or indefinite period of time by directing questions through the chair. At the conclusion of audience participation, the chair will summarize the matter of the individual speakers and then adjourn the meeting. In this case there is no speaker panel.

Evaluating

Evaluate a group of your classmates' symposium. Rate the following criteria on a scale from 1 to 5 with 1 being "needs much improvement" and 5 being "outstanding."

- Did each speaker stick to his or her assigned aspect of the main question?

- Did each speaker appear to be attentive while the others were speaking?

- Did the moderator give strong introductions and summarize the proceedings following the speeches?

- Did the moderator and the speakers handle the questions from the audience effectively?

Now think about what you might suggest to each individual participant in the symposium and to the group as a whole. Write down your comments and share them with the group.

The Keynote Address

Specs for the Keynote Address

Time Limit

5 minutes.

Speaker's notes

Write out a full manuscript with notes for emphasis and other delivery cues as suggested in this chapter.

Sources of information

You should use at least two, preferably more. List them at the end of your written speech.

Outline

Prepare a 75- to 100-word complete sentence outline to hand in to your instructor.

Speak Up!

Share with the class something in which you have great confidence or faith. It might be a team, a current movement or trend, a club, a friend, a talent, a religious belief, or an event. If you were asked to give a speech about this very special issue, what would you say? How would you get people to feel and understand the things you believe about it?

Purpose and Expectations of This Assignment

This assignment introduces you to a type of speech that is common in a variety of business, professional, and political settings. The **keynote address** is a formal speech usually delivered to a large gathering. It sets the stage for an entire conference or meeting. Often this speech inspires and motivates the audience for the future. It provides a unifying theme and, often, a challenge to listeners. Most keynote addresses are carefully worded; thus, an important element of this assignment is the preparation of a full manuscript for the speech. The speaker typically stands behind a lectern or podium on a stage or platform and uses a microphone. While you will most likely not have a large audience for your speech, you should deliver it in an auditorium or other large room/venue to provide the experience of being elevated and distant from the audience. This assignment offers you the chance to practice your speaking skills while coordinating your remarks with a conference theme or focus.

In completing this assignment, you will

- organize one speech topic coordinated with an overall theme,

- present a nearly memorized speech in a large venue, and

- use a microphone when presenting the speech.

Defining the Keynote Address

The two short words that are joined together to name this type of speech explain much about its purpose. Something that is *key* is important or fundamental. The word *note* has many meanings, but one is a "call" or a "sound." Therefore, a keynote address calls attention to something important. If you are a musician you know that the word **keynote** refers to the first tone of a scale that is harmonically fundamental to the scale. A keynote address is usually the first address given at a conference, convention, or meeting. It is designed to identify the key issues participants will address in their sessions and meetings. The address generates enthusiasm and motivation for the work the group must face. In some instances, especially at political conventions, it is intended to promote unity among subgroups of a party that supported different candidates. At a political convention the keynote reminds everyone that the primary elections are over, the winner has emerged, and it is now time for everyone to stand firm behind the party's nominee.

A good keynote address makes use of a conference theme or builds on the goals that the group's officers have chosen for the meeting. The speaker should be aware of all of the events that are to take place during the conference because workshop titles or other activities might provide examples or starting points for developing challenges to the audience. The address also sets the tone for the meeting. If it is a meeting with an agenda that requires the group to solve a problem, then the speaker should challenge the audience to work together to meet that goal. If it is a conference that is intended to share information through workshops, then the keynote should encourage participants to take advantage of the learning opportunities. In other words, the speaker's goals are influenced by the goals of the audience and the overall conference.

Keynote addresses can be persuasive or informative. Often they include humor to build goodwill with the audience. The speaker is usually someone the audience knows—either personally or by reputation—as an expert on topics they will address during their meetings. Occasionally keynotes are controversial; in this case, the speaker should be aware that some members of the audience disagree. A good keynote, regardless of its persuasive or informative intent, prepares everyone in the audience for what is to come and motivates them to take full advantage of the speeches and workshops that follow.

Choosing a Topic

Most keynote speakers are assigned a topic on a general theme. In most cases, they are expected to incorporate not only a general theme, but also the specific theme of the conference. For example, a computer conference may have a title such as "Beyond the Three Rs: Computer Literacy in a Technological Age." Given a general topic assignment, you the speaker must still narrow the focus of the address. The theme of computer literacy is broad, and the speaker could approach it many ways. For instance, you might develop the speech to call for a state-mandated computer-literacy requirement for graduation from high school. Or you might discuss novel ways that computer literacy is being incorporated throughout the K–12 curriculum. The composition of the audience, as with any other type of speech, should guide you in the specific development of your topic.

Another source for a topic is the mission statement of the organization. As a keynote speaker, you should be very familiar with such goals in order for the speech to address in some way the overall mission of the organization.

Preparing

For this assignment, you should make a list of all of the organizations within your school. These can be local, state, or national organizations.

Develop conference themes suitable to the missions of each organization. Select a theme for a hypothetical conference composed of students from schools throughout the city or state. For example, prospective audiences might be participants in the student government or drama club. The possibilities are nearly limitless, but you should choose an organization that interests you on several levels.

Decide the general purpose of your speech as informative, persuasive, or a combination of the two. Review information in earlier chapters on both types of speech (for example, Experience 7, "The Speech to Inform" and Experience 9, "The Speech to Persuade"). Narrow your topic and develop it using the same methods you would for any other speech.

Your research should be appropriate for the organization and for the theme. This will involve talking to the sponsor and members of the organization to learn more about its history and mission. You will also need to do library or Internet research that is appropriate to your specific purpose.

Outline your speech. Then prepare a manuscript. When preparing a manuscript, it is best to talk through your speech as you would if you were giving it from an outline. Tape-record the speech. Before you write the manuscript for your speech, play back the recording and listen to the way you spoke it when you delivered it from an outline. Then as you write, review the manuscript for sentences that ramble or ideas that are not clearly stated. Revise where needed.

As you prepare the manuscript, make sure that you are using vivid language. Your style here can include contractions, sentence fragments, or single-word statements for emphasis. For example, the phrase "Well, don't," could be a complete thought in a speech if it follows a rhetorical question such as "Have you ever put off studying until the hour before an exam?" After a pause, a reminder of the problems that such behavior could create for a student could follow. Use words that sound natural to your ear. We tend to use smaller vocabularies when we speak than we do when we write. While you might use a thesaurus to write an essay, you should use common language for the speech. Read the manuscript aloud to others. Ask them if it sounds natural. In other words, does it sound like the way you talk, or does it sound as if you're reading? If you find out that you sound robotic, go back to your outline and revise the speech again.

Prepare your final manuscript using triple spacing and a font size of 18 points or larger. You want to be able to read it easily and not lose your place. You will have multiple pages, so be sure to number them.

Presenting

Because you will be giving your keynote address from a stage with the audience at a distance, it is important to maintain good eye contact. This means that you need to practice the speech to the point where you have it almost memorized. It is important to remember that the audience doesn't have a manuscript to follow. If you say something differently from the way you wrote it, don't go back and try to pick up the lost phrasing. It's likely that the way you said it will be more natural than the way you wrote it.

Place the manuscript with the page you are reading from on the left and the remaining pages in a stack on the right. As you begin speaking from the page on the right, slide it to the left. Don't turn the pages over.

Your nonverbal presentation will be limited because you will be changing pages every minute or so. Use vocal emphasis to get your point across. Because you will have two pages visible at all times, you can still use gestures; however, your movement will be limited unless you have large segments of the speech memorized and you have a portable microphone. If you have a stationary microphone, you must stay behind the podium. Speak into it at a natural rate and in a normal volume, as the microphone will do the work of carrying your voice to all parts of the auditorium. For more tips on using a microphone, see the Talking Points featured on the facing page.

Evaluating

Evaluate a classmate's keynote address. Rate the following criteria on a scale from 1 to 5 with 1 being "needs much improvement" and 5 being "outstanding."

- Did the speaker's presentation conform to his or her stated conference goals?

- Did the speaker make eye contact with the audience?

- Did the speaker's words and presentation seem natural and unforced?

- Did the speaker handle the microphone efficiently and effectively?

Give an overall score to the presentation. Then tell your classmate the highlight of his or her speech, as well as one or two areas where you believe he or she could have done better.

Talking Points
Working with a Microphone

There may be many occasions during your life when you will speak in front of an audience. If the audience is large, you may be asked to use a microphone. It may be a standing microphone, a tiny microphone clipped to your collar, or a handheld device. No matter what type of microphone you end up using, it pays to keep these tips in mind.

1. Always make sure the microphone is plugged in and turned on. This may sound obvious, but when you are nervous, you may start speaking and assume that you are all hooked up when in fact the audience can't hear a word.

2. If you are wearing a lapel mic, be sure it is pinned to a place where your clothes won't cause a rustling sound.

3. Speak clearly and distinctly. Avoid slurring your words.

4. The most common mistake when it comes to using a microphone is holding it too close or too far from your mouth. To avoid distortion, hold the microphone at least two to three inches from your mouth.

5. Certain consonants create sounds that can become abrasive when amplified. Words with the letters *B* and *P* can cause a popping sound. The *C, S*, and *Z* sounds can produce a hiss that is very unpleasant to the ear. Be aware of the danger and remember that the best way to combat it is to hold the microphone far enough away from your mouth.

6. Speak in a normal tone of voice. The purpose of a microphone is to amplify your voice; there is no need to be exceptionally loud.

7. Avoid speaking too rapidly. This may cause words and sounds to run together.

8. If possible, practice your speech using a microphone before you give your performance.

Example Speech

Star Trek's Lessons for the Disability Community: Adapting to Change, While Holding On to Values

by Sue Suter, Former U.S. Commissioner Of Rehabilitation/President of World Institute On Disabilities Services

Keynote Address for the Annual Conference of The Association for the Severely Handicapped, September 22, 1999, Springfield, Illinois

Thank you for this honor, and for making this day one of the highlights of my life.

In a new book called *Quotable Star Trek*, Jill Sherwin uses thousands of quotations to encourage people to think about their lives and the lessons they can learn from this popular series. Today, I want to share some of those lessons with you, as we open this conference on systems change.

The first lesson from *Star Trek* comes from one of televisions' first leading characters to be portrayed as having a disability—the blind chief engineer, Geordi LaForge.

In a scene where LaForge is confronted by a culture that euthanizes its members with disabilities, he answers:

> Who gave them the right to decide whether or not I should be here? Whether or not I might have something to contribute?

Who has the right to judge whether people with disabilities belong? People have been raising their hands for centuries. From Greek philosophers who endorsed the humane disposal of disabled infants over cliffs, to 1940s German purification policies, to declarations by today's elites.

One example can be found in a September 7th *Newsweek* column by George Will about Princeton's new professor of Bioethics. The teacher's name is Peter Singer, and he is noted for advocating a utilitarian approach to children with disabilities. This includes applying utilitarian calculations to determine whether a disabled child's life should be spared, based on the painful life they might face and costs to society for keeping them alive.

He also advocates letting parents consider the option of infanticide of a severely disabled newborn. This to relieve them of the burden of caring for a disabled child, and to allow them to replace the child with a normal baby that would certainly enjoy a happier life. Part of our battle is to fight the mentality that says the greatest goal is the perfection of the human race. And we see that message in the most common of places. Billions are spent on cosmetic surgery, diets, beer commercials and beauty contests—all with the same message. You're not having fun, you're not normal, until you can fit into this ideal mold—and buy our products. It's a condition that psychologists call the Lake Wobegon Effect. It's related to an American radio program about a fictional town called Lake Wobegon. A place where "all the women are strong, all the men are handsome, and all the children are above average." There's no such place. There never will be. More than anything else, the world needs to rediscover what's normal. Disability is a normal part of being human. People with disabilities are ordinary people. This is not a form of denial. It is a fundamental recognition of our undeniable worth and our inseparable membership in the human race. Yet women with disabilities, especially, are often devalued by the institutions they should be able to count on most—their families and the women's movement. One feminist activist said, "Why study women with disabilities? They reinforce traditional stereotypes of women being dependent, passive, and needy." To that I ask, who is an accomplice to that image? Who is abandoning the universal ideals of freedom and dignity in exchange for the easy path of appeasement? Appeasement has been defined as feeding your friends to the alligator in hopes that he'll eat you last. Everyone loses with that strategy. We must be flexible in our strategies, but we must stay honest to our cause.

The next lesson comes from Captain Picard, who said that one of the most important things in a person's life is to feel useful. This kind of usefulness implies more than identity. It's the source of pleasure for so much of life. As the character Alexis in *Deep Space Nine* once said, "We all work for our supper." You'll be surprised how much sweeter it tastes when you do.

Unfortunately, a majority of people with disabilities don't have the chance to taste the sweet rewards of work. Unfortunately, it's usually stereotypes, not physical barriers, that stand in the way. And these prejudices can come from the most troubling of sources.

I contracted polio when I was two years old. I don't remember it. But I do remember my parents telling me about the advice the doctor gave when it was time for me to leave the hospital. He told them, "Just put her in bed, she's going to be staying there the rest of her life." I had a college counselor who advised me that going after more education might hurt me. He warned that it was hard enough for a woman with a disability to get married; a master's degree would only intimidate a man more.

And I remember when I went after my first job as a secretary. The boss nearly didn't hire me because he worried that I couldn't carry

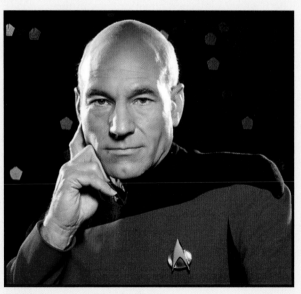

Patrick Stewart as Captain Picard

continued

Example Speech cont.

coffee to him every morning. Talk about a double barrel insult—being doubted whether you could do something that you really shouldn't have to do in the first place! I should have been more assertive. But I was newly married and getting that first job was important to me. I did get the job. I'm embarrassed to admit that I actually practiced carrying the coffee. And I never spilled coffee on the boss's lap, although the temptation was real. These were all well-meaning professionals who believed that they knew what was best for me. But my life would be much different, and I probably wouldn't be with you today, if I had stayed within the boundaries of their expectations.

We are all unique. Each one of us has special gifts to add to the tapestry we call community. But I have been among those rehabilitation counselors and administrators who have shortchanged client dreams in the name of risk management.

If a person with a severe disability says they want to become a doctor, should I dismiss their dreams as fantasy? Dreams are important. They reflect deeply held values. Even if the dreams seem far beyond reach, they deserve to be explored. And with a little work, they can show the path to a person's giftedness, and how they can make a difference in the world. But too often, people in our business are afraid to risk client failures. We want to shelter them from defeat. And we're afraid that their failure at a job or an educational goal will be seen as a black mark against the system that tried to help. Yet as Rabbi Harold Kushner once said, pain is an unavoidable part of a normal life. Risk-

taking and failures are normal for both individuals and organizations.

The next lesson comes from the powerful Klingon, Lt. Commander Worf, who after tasting prune juice for the first time, declared it a warrior's drink. Sometimes we need a new perspective to see familiar things as they really are. That's why this conference is so important. It brings together people with disabilities and families and professionals and advocates under one roof.

TASH may be the only professional association dedicated to people with severe disabilities, but its organization of nearly 9,000 members reaches beyond the professional ranks. And that's so important! Years ago, there was a bill in our state legislature to increase wages for personal attendants, so that high turnover rates could be reduced. Many prominent rehabilitation professionals came to the legislative hearings in support of the bill. But it was one consumer, named Terry Gutterman, who made the issue understandable to legislators by simply asking them to "Imagine giving the keys to your house to 14 different people in a single year." That message got through—I believe—in large part because of one small action by one person. The bill passed. In a September 8th speech, President Clinton relied on a similar story to bring home the urgent message that the pending work incentive improvement act must be passed before many people with disabilities can afford to work. Clinton described meeting a man in New Hampshire who, if he had to pay his own health bills, would have had bills of $40,000 a year, and he desperately wanted to take a $28,000 job. President Clinton called the old system foolish, and then asked, "Wouldn't you rather have the man making $28,000 and giving some of it back in taxes as a productive citizen?" Groups and individuals have made a difference. And I believe with all my heart that it can happen again.

There's another reason why this conference is so important. And it can be summed up in Captain Picard's admonition that "Things are only impossible until they're not."

I remember what my father said to me when I was in the second grade. He loved me very much. He wanted me to be prepared for the future. So he warned me that I would probably never get married. He told me that I should become a clinical psychologist. I eventually did. Then he said that I should work to be the best, so that I could be independent, because some day there might not be anybody around to take care of me. Hard words for a seven-year-old girl to hear. But my father loved me. And he wanted me to be prepared. What a difference it would have made, for myself and my parents, if there was a family next door where the mother also wore braces. A role model. A person with a disability who was married, who raised children, who was nurturing and independent in her own right. Maybe even a corporate leader.

Professionals aren't the only ones who need to know that those labels can also belong to a person with a disability. People with disabilities need that affirmation, as well. The truth is, most boundary-breaking work has been done by people with disabilities who had the courage to challenge the status quo. Now we are facing the greatest challenges in the past 25 years. Last spring's Olmstead decision bought us a temporary victory in the courts to protect the Americans with Disabilities Act, but the Florida Assistant Attorney General is now challenging the constitutionality of the ADA. The same backlash is being felt on the Individuals with Disabilities Education Act front.

Meanwhile, the waiting lists for services people with disabilities are entitled to are effectively creating their own blockades. Bureaucratic Quality Assurance systems are bogging down our service deliveries. We need to find ways to get monies to self advocates. We need to support vouchers for people with disabilities, so that they have choices about where to go for services. We need to have a Medicaid buy-in, so people can afford to go to work. And we need to provide more leadership opportunities for people with disabilities and self advocates.

At a time when college football stars are pleading guilty to illegally using handicapped parking permits and at a time when schools are refusing to pay for assistive technology, but buy elaborate lab equipment that only a few students will ever use and at a time when our most basic rights are being systematically attacked as too costly in an era of national prosperity—then it's time for us to say enough with the abuse, the preferential treatment of the elite, and the pleading of poverty at a time of budget surpluses. It's time for us to say that Social Security Insurance is not the next and final step after high school graduation.

If detractors say we can't afford to do the right thing now, how long will it be before they say the time is right?

continued

Example Speech cont.

That brings us to the final lesson from *Star Trek*. I'd like to leave you with two quotations from Captain Picard that define what it means to be human.

In *The Next Generation*, Picard confronts discrimination by agreeing that, yes, we may be different in appearance. Then he adds, "But we are both living beings. We are born, we grow, we live, and we die. In all the ways that matter, we are alike."

Then, later in the movie *Generations*, Picard confesses that "Recently, I've become very much aware that there are fewer days ahead than there are behind. But I took some comfort from the fact that the family would go on."

Much of what we do in the next two days will center on these fundamental beliefs: that we are alike, and that no matter who we are, we only have only a short time to accomplish what we desire to do.

Will our action steps create the world we want? No.

But they will bring that world closer. And the swifter we act, the more days of opportunities will be given to people with disabilities, and the fuller our own accomplishments will be. And for as long as it takes to reach our goal, there will be people like you and me, who will share that same vision.

I'm proud that you, and I, belong to that family.

The Mass Media

Speaking for broadcast by the mass media increases the usual concerns about the speaker's relationship to the audience in two important ways. The actual audience receiving the message is potentially much larger than the audience that will hear a single speech. Tailoring a message to such an audience can be significantly more challenging because the parameters, or limits, of their needs or concerns are more difficult to define. This unit contains assignments that will allow you to apply many of the speaking skills introduced in previous units to the entirely different contexts of mass media.

Speech Experiences in This Unit

The
Radio Commercial

Specs for the Radio Commercial

Time limit

   1 minute.

Speaker's notes

   A full script of the commercial, complete
   with all voices, pauses, and sound effects
   indicated, and notation of each 5-second
   interval of the material.

Sources of information

   At least two, preferably more. List them at the end of your script.

Outline

   None is required for instructor.

Speak Up!

Have each person in the class record himself or
herself reading three or four sentences. Listen to
the recordings. After hearing the recordings,
each student should answer the following
questions: Did you like the way your voice
sounded? Did it take you a moment to recognize it?
What word would you use to describe your voice?
Many people are surprised the first time they hear
themselves recorded. Discuss why this might be.

Purpose and Expectations of This Assignment

This assignment introduces you to the demands of persuading a mass audience to buy a product.

Producing a radio commercial can provide you with valuable communication skills, including the ability to analyze a message for its maximum auditory impact and to coordinate several voices and sound effects. In this assignment, you will create a dramatic story line that sells a product and develops a concise message within a very limited time frame. Such skills provide a unique opportunity for developing self-expression, enhancing your understanding of the listening process, and giving you the chance to practice making precise but complete language choices. You will also build your audience-analysis skills and your ability to write and edit messages for maximum precision.

In completing this assignment, you will

- create a media presentation to fit within a given time limit,
- assess effectiveness of various auditory message designs,
- coordinate a multifaceted project, and
- identify and develop a dramatic story line.

Defining the Radio Commercial

Radio commercials take a variety of forms, but this assignment is designed to focus on presenting a brief drama, or enactment, that illustrates why an audience should buy a certain selected product.

The economic interests of the broadcast station and its advertisers will directly influence any mass media creation. In order to maintain the opportunities to use the mass media, financial support for the programming must be obtained and sustained. Therefore, as a speaker, you must focus even more on your audience to persuade listeners that they want and need what you are selling.

Voice, musical background, detailed sound effects, and a lack of nonverbal action characterize the **radio commercial**. The various parts are read rather than memorized. An announcer may be used to narrate or describe the scene. He or she usually delivers the closing call for action.

Choosing a Topic

Select a product you would like to sell through a radio commercial. To lend credibility to your product you will need some background information such as scientific studies of its effectiveness or testimony from credible sources that your audience will easily recognize. Keep in mind that your audience is very diverse and your choice of product should appeal to a wide range of people.

Preparing

Once you have selected the product you wish to advertise, choose an appropriate format for your commercial. There are four general formats:

1. A **univocal** ad is one that depends solely on one voice delivering the message. This format is the closest to other assignments you have had in this text.

2. In a **multivoiced** commercial, two or more voices deliver the message; both speak directly to the listeners, not to each other.

3. A **dialogue** commercial features multiple voices carrying on a conversation in which the selected product is the topic being discussed among them.

4. A **dramatized** commercial includes appropriate sound effects added to the dialogue conversation in order to give the impression of physical action or environment to the scene.

After selecting the format, gather all the appropriate resource materials and identify the key message, or thesis statement, you wish to convey by the end of the ad. When you have selected the essential information required (what the product is, how it works, when to use it, where it is available, advantages of this product over others), prepare the script keeping in mind the principles of good speech organization. Above all, remember that this is a *persuasive* message and you have only one minute to get your message across.

The next step in preparing your radio commercial is to carefully time the script, noting the point at which each five-second increment passes. You will likely need to adjust your script to fit the assigned time limit. Once you have done this, show the completed script to your instructor for approval.

When your script has been approved, you can begin rehearsing. Practice by performing your commercial into a tape recorder and reviewing it for possible improvements. If you use other performers, make sure that they have scored their scripts in such a way as to emphasize the key words and concepts. Run through the material with them several times until their delivery is flawless.

Presenting

Even though a radio audience is usually very large and diverse, remember that people listen to the radio when they are alone or in small groups. Therefore, you should imagine that you are presenting your commercial to a small group of people or to an individual consumer.

Avoid rustling papers or making any other extraneous background noise. Be sure you do not cough, sneeze, or clear your throat. Speak into the microphone from a uniform distance; do not shout. Six inches from the microphone is an adequate distance in most cases. You may use gestures if you like. Of course no one would see them, but they may add vitality to your expression.

Evaluating

Listen closely to a classmate's radio commercial. Answer the following questions.

- Did the speaker adhere to the one-minute time limit?

- Did the speaker use strong persuasive techniques?

- Would you buy this product based on the commercial? Tell your classmate why or why not.

The In-Depth News Report Interview

College basketball coach Bobby Knight is interviewed by CNN's Larry King.

Specs for the In-Depth News Report Interview

Time limit
5 minutes.

Speaker's notes
Interview questions and background data on interviewee.

Sources of information
Two or more, including the person being interviewed. List them at the end of your outline.

Outline
Prepare a 75- to 100-word complete sentence outline.

Speak Up!

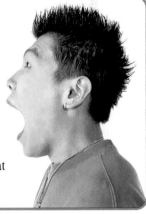

What is your usual reaction when you watch news programming? What parts of the broadcast do you find most interesting? Why? Is there a particular broadcaster you enjoy listening to? If so, describe what he or she does that you find so appealing.

Purpose and Expectations of This Assignment

Interviewing someone for your own information, as you did for the assignment in Experience 31, is different from interviewing someone for a group of listeners. A public or broadcast interview is more complex because you need to know about the topic in order to intelligently ask questions of the person you are interviewing. Also, you must ask questions to which you believe your listeners will want to have answers. You will have to structure the questioning so that the interviewee discusses the information and his or her opinions in a manner that is easy for the audience to follow. Interviewing for a news report can help you sharpen your timing and audience-analysis skills as well as provide practice in sharing a public speaking platform with others.

In completing this assignment, you will

- analyze audience interest in a speaker or topic,
- research a topic and prepare interview questions tailored to audience interests,
- facilitate the flow of dialogue, and
- monitor an ongoing interview to fit within a given time limit.

Defining the In-Depth News Interview

A **radio or television news interview** is not a discussion. Therefore, the interviewer must avoid offering an opinion on the subject at hand. The interviewer's opinion is irrelevant in this situation. The objective of the interview is to allow the interviewee to present his or her ideas to the listeners as coherently as possible. The interviewer serves solely as a *facilitator* and should not openly agree, disagree, or comment in any substantive way upon the information offered by the one being interviewed.

Questions should be carefully prepared in advance of the interview; however, the interview should not be rehearsed. Rehearsing the interview can take away the conversational tone of the delivery. It can also give the listener the impression that the interview has been edited or censored, thus damaging the credibility of either or both participants.

Choosing a Topic

For this assignment, you will need to select a topic that is of interest to your audience and an interviewee who is an authority on that topic. Look for topics of interest around your school and invite a teacher, coach, or administrator to be interviewed about it. Community policies that affect your audience may also be of interest. People to interview may come from state or local government agencies. Avoid a person or group that is too distant to reach and interview effectively within a short time frame.

Preparing

It is very important that you know what you wish to accomplish in the interview before you begin. As you determine the questions to be asked, place yourself in the role of the listener. From your research on the topic you have chosen, determine the main points you want to cover. Prepare a list of questions and rank them from most important to least important so that if you should run short on time you will not have missed the most vital ones. You will also want to remain open to new information coming from the interviewee that might lead you to a new, better question. You don't want to get so stuck on the order of your questions that you leave no room to respond and build on your subject's answers. Frame the questions in a manner that allows the interviewee to expound on the subject. Refrain from questions with yes or no answers. Develop questions that are open-ended.

Who, what, when, where, why and *how* questions are acceptable. You must keep in mind why you are interviewing the person and what pertinent information he or she can reveal. Be sure you narrow the scope of your question enough to help the interviewee get to the points you are interested in hearing about. "Tell us what you do as principal," is too broad for a five-minute interview. A better question might be, "Tell us what is the best thing about being principal of this school."

Once you have prepared the questions you wish to ask, get the specific information from your instructor on when and where the talk show interview is to be conducted. With this in mind, refer to the Preparing section of Experience 31, and follow the suggestions there.

You will be responsible for monitoring the time throughout the interview. You won't be able to go over the time limit and edit out parts of the interview later. Plan to stick to your schedule. You may wish to rehearse by interviewing a friend or parent who can help you role-play so that you can get a feel for controlling the time.

Presenting

Start the interview by introducing yourself and your guest. Indicate to the audience what topic the two of you will discuss. State your questions courteously, tactfully, and directly. As you go through your list of questions, remember that you must listen carefully to the answers and follow up with relevant questions and responses.

Pay attention to the time. However, it is very important that you do not become so absorbed with the timing that you fail to listen to your interviewee. Something he or she says may be left unclear and it will be up to you to ask a follow-up or clarifying question.

When you are ready to wrap up the interview, be sure you signal the end only once. If you indicate to the audience that you have come to your final question, don't ask another one after you get your answer! Conclude by thanking your interviewee, repeating his or her name and title, and restating your name and affiliation as well.

Evaluating

Pay careful attention to a classmate's in-depth news interview. Answer these questions.

- Did the interviewer attempt to put the interviewee at ease?

- Did the interviewer remain unbiased?

- Did the interview stay within the time limit?

- Were the interviewer's questions strong? Did they lead to informative answers?

- What was the best element of this presentation?

- What element needed the most improvement?

Share your thoughts with your classmate.

Example Speech

An In-Depth News Report Interview

by Mark S. Redding

MSR: Today we welcome Dr. Susan Emel to Radioactive KNBY. Dr. Emel is the sponsor of the OWL group here on campus. Dr. Emel, you're the sponsor of the OWLs. Now that stands for...

Dr. E: It stands for Organization for Women Leaders.

MSR: And what do OWLs do?

Dr. E: The primary purpose of the organization is to provide opportunities for women students to network with women in all types of leadership positions...to learn how they got into those positions and how they view women in leadership.

MSR: Wow, that's cool. So how did the organization get started?

Dr. E: Four students—Holly Davis, Heather Cessna, Stephanie Cauble, and Mary Tolman—and I attended a workshop held in St. Louis last summer, conducted by Center for American Women in Politics from Rutgers University. The goal of the workshop was to introduce college women from schools in the Midwest to several women in leadership roles and to encourage them to go back to their campuses and initiate some kind of ongoing service project that promotes leadership development in women. Our group, together with two students selected as alternates for the workshop, Cassie Haas and Stefanie Balzer, chose to start a networking organization for women on campus to connect with women leaders and discuss related issues.

MSR: How often do you have those discussions? What happens?

Dr. E: We have had two to three meetings each semester in which we have invited prominent women leaders to speak. This year we hosted Kansas' First Lady Linda Graves, Kansas' Attorney General Carla Stovall, and several women from the Kansas legislature, in addition to an outstanding woman professor here at Baker, Martha Harris. We also held two open business meetings for anyone interested in helping us plan.

MSR: You mentioned earlier that other schools attended the workshop last summer. Do you know if there are groups like this in other universities?

Dr. E: Yes. Although many schools came to the workshop and designed service projects of different kinds, one of the groups we became friends with was the group from Iowa State University. After returning home and laying the groundwork for our organization, we learned that they had started a similar group AND had come up with a similar name! In April, some of our group went to their campus to hear featured speaker Anita Hill.

MSR: What has been the response from the members?

Dr. E: Well, Mark, we don't actually have formal membership, but we have had excellent responses from students on campus and women in the Baldwin community as well. Several students have joined our leadership team in making plans for the future.

MSR: And what about men?

Dr. E: Well, as a matter of fact, we have had men attend some of these presentations. But other times we have had only women attend.

MSR: Finally—we only have a minute left—is there anything else your group hopes to accomplish?

Dr. E: Yes, Mark, one of the most exciting things the OWL group has begun is a service project in which our students mentor young girls from the inner city. Through an association with the YWCA of Kansas City, Kansas, this spring several elementary and junior high girls from the Y came to Baker and followed our members around to classes, to lunch and to their jobs on campus to see what it was like to be in college. It was a very successful experience, and we hope to continue it next year.

MSR: Okay. Well, thanks for being on the show today. We've been talking with Dr. Susan Emel, assistant professor of speech communication and sponsor of the OWL group here on campus. I'm your host, Mark Redding.

The Film or TV Program Review

Richard Roeper (left) and Roger Ebert

Specs for the Film or TV Program Review

Time limit
> 5 minutes.

Speaker's notes
> Write out a full manuscript with 30-second time intervals indicated throughout the speech.

Sources of information
> Radio and television broadcasts of film and television reviews.

Outline
> None is required for instructor. For your own convenience, you may wish to outline your major points.

Speak Up!

Share with the class your favorite type of television show or film. Is the plot easy to follow? Are subplots necessary to develop the major plot? Are the characters believable? What elements or action keeps your attention?

Purpose and Expectations of This Assignment

Most people share opinions about films or television programs they have seen. A formal review, however, gives the listener a more complete picture of the reviewer's response. Delivering a review of a TV program or film will help you understand the complexities of broadcasting media production. Building upon analytical skills introduced in Experience 8, "The Book Review," you can use this assignment to tailor your reviews to the needs and interests of the mass media audience.

In completing this assignment, you will

- identify elements of program composition,
- draw conclusions about the effectiveness of those elements,
- determine levels of sensitivity in a captive audience to material being reviewed, and
- present a complete assessment of a program within a given time limit.

Defining the Film or TV Program Review

Though a **review of a film or television program** may begin with ideas about the plot, style, and author similar to those of a book review, the film or television review must include assessment of many other production factors such as the acting, directing, and editing. Like the book review, the purposes of the film or TV review may be to inform, to entertain, or to persuade. The reviewer is expected to know the program very well and to be able to present the review in an organized and interesting manner.

Like the in-depth news report interview, the film or TV reviewer must anticipate the general interests of the audience and answer the questions they would be most likely to ask about the production.

Many audience members depend on film or TV program reviews for recommendations as to whether or not a given vehicle is worth seeing. A reviewer must be prepared to offer such an assessment and to back it up with a well-reasoned argument.

Choosing a Topic

The best choices for films or TV programs to review are those with which you are already familiar. If you wish to review a show with which you are not familiar, choose one you will be able to see more than once.

In the classroom setting your primary audience (your classmates and instructor) will be what is known as a *captive audience*. In other words, they are obligated to listen to your speech for educational purposes. Such audiences might not otherwise choose to hear a review of a program they might find offensive. Because of this unique circumstance, you will be ethically obligated in this assignment to select a vehicle that minimizes the chances of offending the captive audience.

Be sure to get your instructor's approval of your selection before proceeding with your review.

Preparing

As with the book review, begin your preparation by determining the purpose of your speech. Once you have decided whether you wish to inform, persuade, or entertain, begin the review with some information that will give the audience the context of the show's origin and development.

Within the body of the review, discuss the **elements of composition** in the piece. Judge and report on the quality of such things as the lighting, sound, editing, set, acting, plot or purpose of the program, camera movements, and special effects. Decide whether these attributes add to the meaning of the program or detract from it.

Additionally, provide your audience with answers to questions you feel they would need answered. Such questions may include

- For whom is the program intended?

- What is the point of view of the program?

- Do you believe the program portrays life realistically? Why or why not?

- What is the overall message of the program?

- What effect, if any, did it have on your opinions or actions?

In the broadcast review, it can be important to use a short video clip of the program you are discussing to illustrate one of your strongest points. However, if you choose to do this, you must carefully select the clip to be sure it illustrates your point very clearly and efficiently. You must also time the clip precisely so that it fits well within your time limit and does not intrude on the other important ideas you wish to convey.

One of the best ways to master your preparation is to view the program once for your own enjoyment. Then view it a second and third time looking for the information you wish to include in your review. You may wish to make a list of elements to look for as you watch in order to be sure you have been a careful enough observer.

When reviewing for either a radio station or a TV studio, you will need to become familiar with signals you'll receive from the production manager. A visit to a radio or television station will reveal many methods used to make speeches more effective for broadcasting. Plan to become acquainted with these methods *before* you make your presentation.

Presenting

In presenting your review, speak clearly and use a deliberate pace so that your listeners will be able to follow you easily. Pay careful attention to your enunciation and pronunciation. Due to the lack of visuals, your radio voice will need more than usual animation, clarity, force, and emphasis to keep the audience interested in listening. For television, you will need to give attention to posture, gestures, movement, and appearance.

Be sure you are close enough—but not too close—to the microphone. For television, look directly into the camera as if to make eye contact with your audience.

Evaluating

Listen closely to a classmate's radio or television review. Answer the following questions.

- Were the reviewer's points easy to follow and well reasoned?

- Was the speaker's voice animated?

- Did you feel the reviewer presented an unbiased assessment?

- Would you base your decision to watch the show based on this reviewer's response?

Share your thoughts with your classmate.

Example Speech

The Lord of the Rings: The Return of the King

By Roger Ebert, December 17, 2003

At last the full arc is visible, and the *Lord of the Rings* trilogy comes into final focus. I admire it more as a whole than in its parts. The second film was inconclusive, and lost its way in the midst of spectacle. But *Return of the King* dispatches its characters to their destinies with a grand and eloquent confidence. This is the best of the three, redeems the earlier meandering, and certifies the "Ring" trilogy as a work of bold ambition at a time of cinematic timidity.

That it falls a little shy of greatness is perhaps inevitable. The story is just a little too silly to carry the emotional weight of a masterpiece. It is a melancholy fact that while the visionaries of a generation ago, like Coppola with *Apocalypse Now*, tried frankly to make films of great consequence, an equally ambitious director like Peter Jackson is aiming more for popular success. The epic fantasy has displaced real contemporary concerns, and audiences are much more interested in Middle Earth than in the world they inhabit.

Still, Jackson's achievement cannot be denied. *Return of the King* is such a crowning achievement, such a visionary use of all the tools of special effects, such a pure spectacle, that it can be enjoyed even by those who have not seen the first two films. Yes, they will be adrift during the early passages of the film's 200 minutes, but to be adrift occasionally during this nine-hour saga comes with the territory; Tolkien's story is so sweeping and Jackson includes so much of it that only devoted students of the Ring can be sure they understand every character, relationship and plot point.

The third film gathers all of the plot strands and guides them toward the great battle at Minas Tirith; it is "before these walls, that the doom of our time will be decided." The city is a spectacular achievement by the special-effects artisans, who show it as part fortress, part Emerald City, topping a mountain, with a buttress reaching out over the plain below where the battle will be joined. In a scene where Gandalf rides his horse across the drawbridge and up the ramped streets of the city, it's remarkable how seamlessly Jackson is able to integrate computer-generated shots with actual full-scale shots, so they all seem of a piece.

I complained that the second film, *The Two Towers*, seemed to shuffle the hobbits to the sidelines—as humans, wizards, elves and Orcs saw most of the action. The hobbits are back in a big way this time, as the heroic little Frodo (Elijah Wood) and his loyal friend Sam (Sean Astin) undertake a harrowing journey to return the Ring to Mount Doom—where, if he can cast it into the volcano's lava, Middle Earth will be saved and the power of the enemy extinguished. They are joined on their journey by the magnificently eerie, fish-fleshed, bug-eyed creature Gollum, who started in life as a hobbit named Smeagol, and is voiced and modeled by Andy Serkis in collaboration with CGI artists, and introduced this time around with a brilliant device to illustrate his dual nature: He talks to his reflection in a pool, and the reflection talks back. Gollum loves Frodo but loves the Ring more, and indeed it is the Ring's strange power to enthrall its possessors (first seen through its effect on Bilbo Baggins in *The*

Fellowship of the Ring) that makes it so tricky to dispose of.

Although the movie contains epic action sequences of awe-inspiring scope (including the massing of troops for the final battle), the two most inimitable special-effects creations are Gollum, who seems as real as anyone else on the screen, and a monstrous spider named Shelob. This spider traps Frodo as he traverses a labyrinthine passage on his journey, defeats him, and wraps him in webbing to keep him fresh for supper. Sam is very nearly not there to save the day (Gollum has been treacherous), but as he battles the spider we're reminded of all the other movie battles between men and giant insects, and we concede that, yes, this time they got it right.

The final battle is kind of magnificent. I found myself thinking of the visionary films of the silent era, like Lang (*Metropolis*) and Murnau (*Faust*), with their desire to depict fantastic events of unimaginable size and power, and with their own cheerful reliance on visual trickery. Had they been able to see this scene, they would have been exhilarated. We see men and even an army of the dead join battle against Orcs, flying dragons, and vast lumbering elephantine creatures that serve as moving platforms for machines of war. As a flaming battering-ram challenges the gates of the city, we feel the size and weight and convincing shudder of impacts that exist only in the imagination. Enormous bestial Trolls pull back the springs for catapults to hurl boulders against the walls and towers of Minas Tirith, which fall in cascades of rubble (only to seem miraculously restored in time for a final celebration).

And there is even time for a smaller-scale personal tragedy; Denethor (John Noble), steward of the city, mourns the death of his older and favored son, and a younger son named Faramir (David Wenham), determined to gain his father's respect, rides out to certain death. The outcome is a tragic sequence in which the deranged Denethor attempts to cremate Faramir on a funeral pyre, even though he is not quite dead.

The series has never known what to do with its female characters. J.R.R. Tolkien was not much interested in them, certainly not at a psychological level, and although the half-elf Arwen (Liv Tyler) here makes a crucial decision—to renounce her elfin immortality in order to marry Aragorn (Viggo Mortensen)—there is none of the weight or significance in her decision that we feel, for example, when an angel decides to become human in *Wings of Desire*.

There is little enough psychological depth anywhere in the films, actually, and they exist mostly as surface, gesture, archetype and spectacle. They do that magnificently well, but one feels at the end that nothing actual and human has been at stake; cartoon characters in a fantasy world have been brought along about as far as it is possible for them to come, and while we applaud the achievement, the trilogy is more a work for adolescents (of all ages) than for those hungering for truthful emotion thoughtfully paid for. Of all the heroes and villains in the trilogy, and all the thousands or hundreds of thousands of deaths, I felt such emotion only twice, with the ends of Faramir and Gollum. They did what they did because of their natures and their free will, which were explained to us and known to them. Well, yes, and I felt something for Frodo, who has matured and grown on his long journey, although as we last see him it is hard to be sure he will remember what he has learned. Life is so pleasant in Middle Earth, in peacetime.

Radio/Television Commentary

Former President Jimmy Carter

Specs for Radio/Television Commentary

Time limit
See your instructor for the exact time.

Speaker's notes
Unless your instructor directs otherwise, you will write out your speech word for word.

You should hand in a copy of your speech to your instructor at least one day before you are scheduled to speak.

Sources of information
Two or more. List them at the end of your written speech.

Outline
None is required for your instructor.

Speak Up!

Have you ever listened to talk radio or seen and heard commentary from a controversial figure from the political or entertainment world? Share your experience. How would you describe what you heard? What stuck with you? Did you agree with the commentator?

Purpose and Expectations of This Assignment

In general, listening or viewing audiences can only hear or see the subject one time—in other words, in broadcast media they cannot reread the information as they might do with a newspaper. Therefore the key to good broadcast journalism is to communicate to the audience what they need to know about a subject and then tell them one more time in an interesting way what you have already told them. As you begin to understand the preparation and presentation of media commentaries through firsthand knowledge and experience, you will be much more equipped to identify, evaluate, and appreciate these factors as a media consumer. This assignment is designed to pose real-world problems. As you go through the assignment, you will take part in audience analysis and adaptation, and carefully select and apply various persuasive elements to the mass audience situation.

In completing this assignment, you will

- identify opposing viewpoints on a selected topic,

- gather information on a topic of importance to a community of listeners/viewers,

- use divergent thinking and originality to analyze and suggest solutions to a controversial topic, and

- prepare a concise persuasive appeal to fit a given time limit.

Defining Radio/Television Commentary

A **commentary** is a statement of a subjective point of view by a broadcast professional or by selected listeners/viewers. Not all radio or television stations use them because they can be controversial. Some stations attempt to avoid offending any listeners in any way. However, sometimes commentaries are broadcast as a public service to promote community discussion on particular topics of concern. (Subjective views presented by station owners or managers are called *editorials*.)

Good commentaries have impact, are personal (making reference to the speaker), are timely, and involve controversy, meaning that the topic has at least two clearly defined and advocated points of view. In other words, commentaries are similar to persuasive speeches.

Choosing a Topic

There are three levels for topics of public concern: national, statewide, and local. To maintain timeliness in your commentary, a good place to look for topics is the media sources around you. Medical discoveries, governmental policies, and social needs are examples of potential topics for commentary.

Some public issues are viable concerns over long periods of time and across all three levels. These might include such elements as stereotypes in programming, violence in the media, TV ratings systems proposals, censorship/First Amendment issues, and trying accused persons in the media rather than the courts.

Follow the principles discussed in earlier chapters (Experience 7, "The Speech to Inform"; Experience 9, "The Speech to Persuade") for topic selection.

Preparing

As you prepare your commentary, use the methods you learned in Experience 9. Give special attention to facts and details. You can make no excuses when you have a printed copy lying before you. It should be double-spaced for easy reading.

When you have written, edited, and proofread your commentary, submit it to your instructor for approval. Once it's been approved, rehearse a number of times until you feel ready to step before the microphone or camera. If possible you should practice with such equipment while a friend listens critically and offers you suggestions for improvement. Using a tape recorder or a video camera for practice will greatly add to the quality of your speech. If you like, after several rehearsals you can write time signals in the margin of your paper to tell you where you should be at the end of two, three, and four minutes.

Presenting

Ordinarily, these speeches are presented with the idea that the audience will be scattered throughout the nation, possibly the world. Listeners may be alone or congregated in groups of two, three, or four. Your presentation should be tempered to meet all occasions. If you ask yourself how you would speak if you were to step before these small groups of people in person, your style of presentation will become quite clear. Remember that for radio, only your voice will be heard. This calls particular attention to your vocal qualities. If you opt for television, then of course you are in full view for all to see and hear. This calls attention to not only your vocal qualities, but also your posture, gestures, movements, and appearance.

As mentioned in other media assignments, avoid rustling your manuscript in any way. Do not cough, clear your throat, or shout into the microphone. Stay a uniform distance from the microphone at all times to prevent sudden fades or increases in volume.

Evaluating

Evaluate a classmate's radio or television commentary. Rate the following criteria on a scale from 1 to 5 with 1 being "needs much improvement" and 5 being "outstanding."

- Did the commentator use vocal variety?
- Were the commentator's points persuasive?
- Did the commentator handle the microphone effectively?
- Did the television commentator look into the camera when speaking?
- Did the commentator look and/or sound at ease?

Give an overall score to the presentation. Then tell your classmate the highlight of his or her commentary, as well as one or two areas where you believe he or she might improve.

Example Speech

The President's Radio Address to the Nation

by President Bill Clinton
Saturday, March 2, 1996

THE PRESIDENT: Good morning. Something remarkable happened this week; something that can forever help parents, children, and anybody who cares about what our children watch on television. We took an enormous step toward controlling the images of violence and bias that can enter our homes and disturb our children. Television is one of the most influential voices that can enter a home. It can be entertaining, enlightening, and educating. But when it transmits pictures or words we wouldn't want our children to see and hear in real life, television can become an unwelcome intruder, one that parents have too often found too difficult to control.

In study after study, the evidence has steadily mounted that television violence is numbing and corrosive. It can have a destructive impact on young children. In my State of the Union speech, I challenged the members of Congress to give control back to parents. I asked them to require TVs to include the V-chip, a device that lets parents filter out programs they don't want to let into their homes and their children's lives.

Congress answered that challenge and, three weeks ago when I signed the Telecommunications Bill into law, the V-chip also became law. Now it will be standard in new television sets sold in our country. We need this.

To make the V-chip work, I invited leaders of the media and entertainment industry to come to the White House to work with us to help our families. And this past Thursday I met with the leaders of the television networks, the production studios, the cable companies, actors, directors, and writers. Their response was overwhelming, and our meeting was a great success.

For the first time ever, leaders of the television and entertainment industry have come together as one force and agreed to develop a rating system for their programming that will help parents to protect their children from violence and other objectionable content on television. They said this system will be in place by next January.

Like the movie ratings have done for 27 years, the ratings for television will help parents to guide their children's entertainment choices. The system will provide families with a standard they can rely on from show to show, from channel to channel. Parents are the best judges of what their children should and shouldn't see, and this new rating system will help them to make those critical judgments. The best programming director for our children is a parent.

At my meeting with the entertainment industry, we also discussed the need for more programming that is suitable for children, and that is educational and attractive to them. I want to preserve public broadcasting and the innovation it has brought in educational shows for children.

These days, a typical child will watch 25,000 hours of television before his or her eighteenth birthday. It's up to us whether these shows stimulate their minds or numb them. Let's build on the good shows that we have as models for educating and informing our children. I applaud the entertainment leaders for what they have done voluntarily. Through their action, they are being responsible for the product they produce, and they are showing greater concern for our American community and our children's future.

With the V-chip and the rating system, we mark a sea change. We are harnessing technology, creativity, and responsibility, bringing together parents, business, and government to meet a major challenge to our society. After all, it doesn't do a family any good to have a nice television if the images it brings to our children erode their values and diminish their future.

We should look at this breakthrough as part of the bigger picture and as a lesson for even greater achievement. As I have said many times, this is an age of great possibility when more Americans will have more opportunities to live out their dreams than ever before. But we also know that this is a time of stiff challenges as well. If we are to meet those challenges, all of us must take our proper responsibility. Government must play a part, but only a part. Only if each of us measures what we do by basic standards of right and wrong, taking responsibility for our actions, moving us together, will we be able to move forward as a nation.

Let me say again—only if we work together in our businesses, our schools, our places of worship, our civic groups—will we transform our lives and our country. That is what I mean when I talk about corporate responsibility.

The actions of the television industry show us what can happen when visionary business leaders make a commitment to values and the common good as well as to the bottom line, and when they live up to their responsibilities as corporate citizens of our great country. I hope their example will be matched by the executives in other industries to address other problems and other challenges we face as a people. That means corporations helping to improve our schools, helping to connect them to the information superhighway, helping to demand high standards. That means corporations finding new ways to protect our environment even as they grow the bottom line and improve our economy.

That means businesses recognizing that workers are an asset, not a liability, and that a well-trained work force is any business's most important competitive edge. All these things demand a renewed commitment from business. And I am confident that the leaders of other industries will also rise to the challenge just the way the leaders of the entertainment industry did this week.

We can celebrate a giant step toward realizing the possibility of a great instrument of communication in the homes of our families. I believe we can meet our other challenges to the nation in the same way. We'll all want to stay tuned for that.

Thanks for listening.

Collected Speeches

I Claim a Right to Live on My Land

by Chief Joseph of the Nez Percés

The earth was created by the assistance of the sun, and it should be left as it was . . . the country was made without lines of demarcation, and it is no man's business to divide it . . . I see the whites all over the country gaining wealth, and see their desire to give us lands which are worthless. . . . The earth and myself are of one mind. The measure of the land and the measure of our bodies are the same. Say to us if you can say it, that you were sent by the Creative Power to talk to us. Perhaps you think the Creator sent you here to dispose of us as you see fit. If I thought you were sent by the Creator I might be induced to think you had a right to dispose of me. Do not misunderstand me, but understand me fully with reference to my affection for the land. I never said the land was mine to do with as I chose. The one who has the right to dispose of it is the one who has created it. I claim a right to live on my land, and accord you the privilege to live on yours.

Speech in the Virginia Convention

by Patrick Henry

This speech was delivered on March 23, 1775, before the Second Revolutionary Convention of Virginia, in the old church in Richmond.

No man thinks more highly than I do of the patriotism, as well as abilities, of the very worthy gentlemen who have just addressed the House. But different men often see the same subject in different lights; and, therefore, I hope it will not be thought disrespectful to those gentlemen, if, entertaining as I do opinions of a character very opposite to theirs, I shall speak forth my sentiments freely and without reserve. This is not time for ceremony.

The question before the House is one of awful moment to this country. For my own part, I consider it as nothing less than a question of freedom or slavery; and in proportion to the magnitude of the subject ought to be the freedom of the debate. It is only in this way that we can hope to arrive at truth, and fulfill the great responsibility, which we hold to God and our Country. Should I keep back my opinions at such a time, through fear of giving offense, I should consider myself as guilty of treason toward my country, and of act of disloyalty toward the Majesty of Heaven, which I revere above all earthly kings.

Mr. President, it is natural to man to indulge in the illusions of hope. We are apt to shut our eyes against a painful truth, and listen to the song of that siren, till she transforms us into beasts. Is this the part of wise men, engaged in a great and arduous struggle for liberty? Are we disposed to be of the number of those, who having eyes, see not, and having ears, hear not, the things which so nearly concern their temporal salvation? For my part, whatever anguish of spirit it may cost, I am willing to know the whole truth; to know the worst, and to provide for it.

I have but one lamp by which my feet are guided, and that is the lamp of experience. I know of no way of judging of the future but by the past. And judging by the past, I wish to know what there has been in the conduct of the British ministry for the last ten years to justify those hopes with which gentlemen have been pleased to solace themselves and the House. Is it that insidious smile with which our petition has been lately received? Trust it not, sir; it will prove a snare to your feet. Suffer not yourselves to be betrayed with a kiss. Ask yourselves how this gracious reception of our petition comports with those warlike preparations which cover our water and darken our land. Are fleets and armies necessary to a work of love and reconciliation? Have we shown ourselves so unwilling to be reconciled that force must be called in to win back our love? Let us not deceive ourselves, sir. These are the implements of war and subjugation; the last arguments to which kings resort.

I ask gentlemen, sir, what means this martial array, if its purpose be not to force us to submission? Can gentlemen assign any other possible motive for it? Has Great Britain any enemy in this quarter of the world to call for all this accumulation of navies and armies? No, sir, she has none. They are meant for us: they can be meant for no other. They are sent over to bind and rivet upon us those chains which the British ministry have been so long forging. And what have we to oppose to them? Shall we try argument? Sir, we have been trying that for the last ten years. Have we anything new to offer upon the subject? Nothing. We have held the subject up in every light of which it is capable; but it has been all in vain.

Shall we resort to entreaty and humble supplication? What terms shall we find which have not been already exhausted? Let us not, I beseech you, sir, deceive ourselves longer. Sir, we have done everything that could be done, to avert the storm which is now coming on. We have petitioned; we have remonstrated; we have supplicated; we have prostrated ourselves before the throne, and have implored its interposition to arrest the tyrannical hands of the ministry and Parliament. Our petitions have been slighted; our remonstrations have produced additional violence and insult; our supplications have been disregarded, and we have been spurned, with contempt, from the foot of the throne!

In vain, after these things, may we indulge the fond hope of peace and reconciliation. There is no longer any room for hope. If we wish to be free—if we mean to preserve inviolate those inestimable privileges for which we have been so long contending—if we mean not basely to abandon the noble struggle in which we have been so long engaged, and which we have pledged ourselves never to abandon, until the glorious object of our contest shall be obtained—we must fight! I repeat it, sir, we must fight! An appeal to arms to the God of Hosts is all that is left us!

They tell us, sir, that we are weak—unable to cope with so formidable an adversary. But when shall we be stronger? Will it be the next week, or the next year? Will it be when we are totally disarmed, and when a British guard shall be stationed in every house? Shall we gather strength by irresolution and inaction? Shall we acquire the means of effectual resistance by lying supinely on our backs and hugging the delusive phantom of hope, until our enemies shall have bound us hand and foot?

Sir, we are not weak if we make a proper use of those means which the God of nature has placed in our power. Three millions of people armed in the holy cause of liberty, and in such a country as that which we possess, are invincible by any force which our enemy can send against us. Besides, sir, we shall not fight our battles alone. There is a just God who presides over the vigilant, the active, the brave. Besides, sir, we have no election. If we were base enough to desire it, it is now too late to retire from the contest. There is no retreat but in submission and slavery! Our chains are forged! Their clanking may be heard on the plains of Boston! The war is inevitable—and let it come! I repeat it, sir, let it come!

It is in vain, sir, to extenuate the matter. Gentlemen may cry, Peace, Peace—but there is no peace. The war is actually begun! The next gale that sweeps from the north will bring to our ears the clash of resounding arms! Is life so dear, or peace so sweet, as to be purchased at the price of chains and slavery? Forbid it, Almighty God! I know not what course others may take, but as for me, give me liberty or give me death!

On the Federal Constitution

by Benjamin Franklin

From a speech in Philadelphia before the Constitutional Convention of 1787. The Constitution was adopted only after much debate. In the following speech one well-known individual expressed his feelings about signing the document.

I confess that I do not entirely approve of this Constitution at present; but, sir, I am not sure I shall never approve of it, for, having lived long, I have experienced many instances of being obliged, by better information or fuller consideration, to change opinions even on important subjects, which I once thought right, but found to be otherwise. It is therefore that, the older I grow, the more apt I am to doubt my own judgment of others. Most men, indeed, as well as most sects in religion, think themselves in possession of all truth, and that wherever others differ from them, it is so far error. Steele, a Protestant, in a dedication, tells the pope that the only difference between our two churches in their opinion of the certainty of their doctrine is, the Romish Church is infallible, and the Church of England is never in the wrong. But, though many private persons think almost as highly of their own infallibility as of that of their sect, few express it so naturally as a certain French lady, who, in a little dispute with her sister, said: "But I meet nobody but myself that is always in the right."

In these sentiments, sir, I agree to this Constitution with all its faults—if they are such—because I think a general government necessary for us, and there is no form of government but what may be a blessing to the people if well administered; and I believe, further, that this is likely to be well administered for a course of years, and can only end in despotism, as other forms have done before it, when the people shall become so corrupted as to need despotic government, being incapable of any other. I doubt, too, whether any other convention we can obtain may be able to make a better Constitution; for, when you assemble a number of men, to have the advantage of their joint wisdom, you inevitably assemble with those men all their prejudices, their passions, their errors of opinion, their local interests, and their selfish views. From such an assembly can a perfect production be expected?

It therefore astonishes me, sir, to find this system approaching so near to perfection as it does; and I think it will astonish our enemies, who are waiting with confidence to hear that our counsels are confounded like those of the builders of Babel, and that our States are on the point of separation, only to meet hereafter for the purpose of cutting one another's throats. Thus I consent, sir, to this Constitution, because I expect no better, and because I am not sure that it is not the best. The opinions I have had of its errors I sacrifice to the public good. I have never whispered a syllable of them abroad. Within these walls they were born, and here they shall die. If every one of us, in returning to our constituents, were to report the objections he has had to it, and endeavor to gain partisans in support of them, we might prevent its being generally received, and thereby lose all the salutary effects and great advantages resulting naturally in our favor among foreign nations, as well as among ourselves, from our real or apparent unanimity. Much of the strength and efficiency of any government, in procuring and securing happiness to the people, depends on opinion, on the general opinion of the goodness of that government, as well as of the wisdom and integrity of its governors. I hope, therefore, for our own sakes, as a part of the people, and for the sake of our posterity, that we shall act heartily and unanimously in recommending this Constitution wherever our influence may extend, and turn our future thoughts and endeavors to the means of having it well administered.

On the whole, sir, I can not help expressing a wish that every member of the convention who may still have objections to it, would, with me, on this occasion, doubt a little of his own infallibility, and, to make manifest our unanimity, put his name to this instrument.

Ain't I a Woman?

by Sojourner Truth

At the Ohio Women's Rights Convention in 1851, former slave Sojourner Truth quieted a crowd of indignant men with this impromptu speech.

Well, children, where there is so much racket there must be something out of kilter. I think that 'twixt the Negroes of the South and the women at the North, all talking about rights, the white men will be in a fix pretty soon. But what's all this here talking about?

That man over there says that women need to be helped into carriages, and lifted over ditches, and to have the best place everywhere. Nobody ever helps me into carriages, or over mud puddles, or gives me any best place! And ain't I a woman? Look at me! Look at my arm. I have plowed and planted, and gathered into barns, and no man could head me! And ain't I a woman? I could work as much and eat as much as a man—when I could get it—and bear the lash as well! And ain't I a woman? I have borne thirteen children, and seen them most all sold off to slavery, and when I cried out with my mother's grief, none but Jesus heard me! And ain't I a woman?

Then they talk about this thing in the head; what's this they call it? [Intellect, someone whispers.] That's it, honey. What's that got to do with women's rights or Negro's rights? If my cup won't hold but a pint, and yours holds a quart, wouldn't you be mean not to let me have my little half-measure full?

Then that little man in black there, he says women can't have as much rights as men, 'cause Christ wasn't a woman! Where did your Christ come from? Where did your Christ come from? From God and a woman! Man had nothing to do with Him.

If the first woman God ever made was strong enough to turn the world upside down all alone, these women together ought to be able to turn it back, and get it right side up again! And now they is asking to do it, the men better let them.

Obliged to you for hearing me, and now old Sojourner ain't got nothing more to say.

The Gettysburg Address

by President Abraham Lincoln

In this brief, eloquent speech, President Lincoln dedicates a cemetery on the spot where thousands lost their lives during the Battle of Gettysburg in July of 1863.

Four score and seven years ago our fathers brought forth upon this continent a new nation, conceived in liberty, and dedicated to the proposition that all men are created equal.

Now we are engaged in a great civil war, testing whether that nation so conceived, and so dedicated, can long endure. We are met on a great battlefield of that war. We have come to dedicate a portion of that field as a final resting-place for those who here gave their lives that that nation might live. It is altogether fitting and proper that we should do this.

But in a larger sense, we cannot dedicate—we cannot consecrate—we cannot hallow this ground. The brave men, living and dead, who struggled here, have consecrated it far above our poor power to add or detract. The world will little note, nor long remember, what we say here, but it can never forget what they did here. It is for us, the living, rather, to be dedicated here to the unfinished work which they who fought here have thus far so nobly advanced. It is rather for us to be here dedicated to the great task remaining before us—that from these honored dead we take increased devotion to that cause for which they gave the last full measure of devotion—that we here highly resolve that these dead shall not have died in vain—that this nation, under God, shall have a new birth of freedom and that government of the people, by the people, and for the people, shall not perish from the earth.

On Women's Right to Vote

by Susan B. Anthony

Susan B. Anthony delivered this speech in 1873 after she had been arrested, put on trial, and fined one hundred dollars for voting at the presidential election in 1872. She refused and never did pay the fine.

Friends and Fellow Citizens:

I stand before you tonight under indictment for the alleged crime of having voted at the last presidential election, without having a lawful right to vote. It shall be my work this evening to prove to you that in thus voting, I not only committed no crime, but, instead, simply exercised my citizen's rights, guaranteed to me and all United States citizens by the National Constitution, beyond the power of any State to deny. The Preamble of the Federal Constitution says:

"We, the people of the United States, in order to form a more perfect union, establish justice, insure domestic tranquility, provide for the common defense, promote the general welfare, and secure the blessings of liberty to ourselves and our posterity, do ordain and establish this Constitution for the United States of America."

It was we, the people, not we, the white male citizens; nor yet we, the male citizens; but we, the whole people, who formed the Union. And we formed it, not to give the blessings of liberty, but to secure them; not to the half of ourselves and the half of our posterity, but to the whole people—women as well as men. And it is downright mockery to talk to women of their enjoyment of the blessings of liberty while they are denied the use of the only means of securing them provided by this democratic-republican government—the ballot.

For any State to make sex a qualification that must ever result in the disfranchisement of one entire half of the people is to pass a bill of attainder, or an ex post facto law, and is therefore a violation of the supreme law of the land. By it the blessings of liberty are forever withheld from women and their female posterity. To them this government has no just powers derived from the consent of the governed. To them this government is not a democracy. It is not a republic. It is an odious aristocracy; a hateful oligarchy of sex; the most hateful aristocracy ever established on the face of the globe; an oligarchy of wealth, where the rich govern the poor. An oligarchy of learning, where the educated govern the ignorant, or even an oligarchy of race, where the Saxon rules the African might be endured; but this oligarchy of sex, which makes father, brothers, husband, sons, the oligarchies over the mother and sisters, the wife and daughters of every household—which ordains all men sovereigns, all women subjects, carries dissension, discord and rebellion into every home of the nation.

Webster, Worcester, and Bouvier all define a citizen to be a person in the United States, entitled to vote and hold office.

The only question left to be settled now is: Are women persons? And I hardly believe any of our opponents will have the hardihood to say they are not. Being persons, then, women are citizens; and no State has a right to make any law, or to enforce an old law, that shall abridge their privileges or immunities. Hence, every discrimination against women in the constitutions and laws of the several States is today null and void, precisely as in every one against Negroes.

First Inaugural Address

by President Franklin Delano Roosevelt

Washington D.C., March 4, 1933

Roosevelt was elected during the Great Depression. His inaugural address helped to ease the despair of the nation and provide hope for the future.

I am certain that my fellow Americans expect that on my induction into the Presidency I will address them with a candor and a decision which the present situation of our nation impels. This is preeminently the time to speak the truth, frankly and boldly. Nor need we shrink from honesty facing conditions in our country today. This great nation will endure, will revive, and will prosper. So, first of all, let me assert my firm belief that the only thing we have to fear is fear itself—nameless, unreasoning, unjustified terror which paralyzes needed efforts to convert retreat into advance. In every dark hour of our national life a leadership of frankness and vigor has met with that understanding and support of the people themselves which is essential to victory. I am convinced that you will again give that support to leadership in these critical days.

In such a spirit on my part and on yours, we face our common difficulties. They concern, thank God, only material things. Values have shrunken to fantastic levels; taxes have risen; our ability to pay has fallen; government of all kinds is faced by serious curtailment of income; the means of exchange are frozen in the current of trade; the withered leaves of industrial enterprise lie on every side; farmers find no market for their produce; the savings of many years in thousands of families are gone.

More important, a host of unemployed citizens face the grim problems of existence and an equally great number toil with little return. Only a foolish optimist can deny the dark realities of the moment.

Yet our distress comes from no failure of substance. We are stricken by no plague of locusts. Compared with the perils which our forefathers conquered because they believed and were not afraid, we still have much to be thankful for.

Their Finest Hour

By British Prime Minister Winston Churchill

The excerpt contains the conclusion only. The speech was delivered to the House of Commons, London, England, then broadcast June 18, 1940, in the early stages of World War II.

The Battle of France is over. I expect that the Battle of Britain is about to begin. Upon this battle depends the survival of Christian civilization. Upon it depends our own British life, and the long continuity of our institutions and our Empire. The whole fury and might of the enemy must very soon be turned on us. Hitler knows that he will have to break us in this Island or lose the war. If we can stand up to him, all Europe may be free and the life of the world may move forward into broad, sunlit uplands. But if we fall, then the whole world, including the United States, including all that we have known and cared for, will sink into the abyss of a new Dark Age made more sinister, and perhaps more protracted, by the lights of perverted science. Let us therefore brace ourselves to our duties, and so bear ourselves that, if the British Empire and its Commonwealth last for a thousand years, men will still say, "This was their finest hour."

Inaugural Address

by President John F. Kennedy

January 20, 1961

Vice President Johnson, Mr. Speaker, Mr. Chief Justice, President Eisenhower, Vice President Nixon, President Truman, Reverend Clergy, Fellow Citizens: We observe today not a victory of party but a celebration of freedom—symbolizing an end as well as a beginning—signifying renewal as well as change. For I have sworn before you and Almighty God the same solemn oath our forebears prescribed nearly a century and three quarters ago.

The world is very different now. For man holds in his mortal hands the power to abolish all forms of human poverty and all forms of human life. And yet the same revolutionary beliefs for which our forebears fought are still at issue around the globe—the belief that the rights of man come not from the generosity of the state but from the hand of God.

We dare not forget today that we are the heirs of that first revolution. Let the word go forth from this time and place, to friend and foe alike, that the torch has been passed to a new generation of Americans—born in this century, tempered by war, disciplined by a hard and bitter peace, proud of our ancient heritage—and unwilling to witness or permit the slow undoing of those human rights to which this nation has always been committed, and to which we are committed today, at home and around the world.

Let every nation know, whether it wishes us well or ill, that we shall pay any price, bear any burden, meet any hardship, support any friend or oppose any foe to assure the survival and the success of liberty. This much we pledge—and more.

To those old allies whose cultural and spiritual origins we share, we pledge the loyalty of faithful friends. United, there is little we cannot do in a host of cooperative ventures. Divided, there is little we can do—for we dare not meet a powerful challenge at odds and split asunder. To those new states whom we welcome to the ranks of the free, we pledge our word that one form of colonial control shall not have passed away merely to be replaced by a far more iron tyranny. We shall not always expect to find them supporting our view. But we shall always hope to find them strongly supporting their own freedom—and to remember that, in the past, those who foolishly sought power by riding the back of the tiger ended up inside.

To those people in the huts and villages of half the globe struggling to break the bonds of mass misery, we pledge our best efforts to help them help themselves, for whatever period is required—not because the Communists may be doing it, not because we seek their votes, but because it is right. If a free society cannot help the many who are poor, it cannot save the few who are rich.

To our sister republics south of our border, we offer a special pledge—to convert our good words into good deeds—in a new alliance for progress—to assist free men and free governments in casting off the chains of poverty. But this peaceful revolution of hope cannot become the prey of hostile powers. Let all our neighbors know that we shall join with them to oppose aggression or subversion anywhere in the Americas. And let every other power know that this hemisphere intends to remain the master of its own house.

To that world assembly of sovereign states, the United Nations, our last best hope in an age where the instruments of war have far outpaced the instruments of peace, we renew our pledge of support—to prevent it from becoming merely a forum for invective—to strengthen its shield of the new and the weak—and to enlarge the area in which its writ may run.

Finally, to those nations who would make themselves our adversary, we offer not a pledge but a request: That both sides begin anew the quest for peace, before the dark powers of destruction unleashed by science engulf all humanity in planned or accidental self-destruction.

We dare not tempt them with weakness. For only when our arms are sufficient beyond doubt can we be certain beyond doubt that they will never be employed. But neither can two great and powerful groups of nations take comfort from our present course—both sides overburdened by the cost of modern weapons, both rightly alarmed by the steady spread of the deadly atom, yet both racing to alter that uncertain balance of terror that stays the hand of mankind's final war.

So let us begin anew—remembering on both sides that civility is not a sign of weakness, and sincerity is always subject to proof. Let us never negotiate out of fear. But let us never fear to negotiate. Let both sides explore what problems unite us instead of belaboring those problems which divide us. Let both sides, for the first time, formulate serious and precise proposals for the inspection and control of arms—and bring the absolute power to destroy other nations under the absolute control of all nations. Let both sides seek to invoke the wonders of science instead of its terrors.

Together let us explore the stars, conquer the deserts, eradicate disease, tap the ocean depths and encourage the arts and commerce. Let both sides unite to heed in all corners of the earth the command of Isaiah—to "undo the heavy burdens. . . [and] let the oppressed go free." And if a beachhead of cooperation may push back the jungle of suspicion, let both sides join in creating a new endeavor: not a new balance of power, but a new world of law, where the strong are just and the weak secure and the peace preserved.

All this will not be finished in the first one hundred days. Nor will it be finished in the first one thousand days, not in the life of this administration, nor even perhaps in our lifetime on the planet. But let us begin.

In your hands, my fellow citizens, more than mine, will rest the final success or failure of our course. Since this country was founded, each generation of Americans has been summoned to give testimony to its national loyalty. The graves of young Americans who answered the call to service surround the globe.

Now the trumpet summons us again—not as a call to bear arms, though arms we need—not as a call to battle, though embattled we are—but a call to bear the burden of a long twilight struggle, year in and year out, "rejoicing in hope, patient in tribulation"—a struggle against the common enemies of man: tyranny, poverty, disease and war itself.

Can we forge against these enemies a grand and global alliance, north and south, east and west, that can assure a more fruitful life for all mankind? Will you join in that historic effort?

In the long history of the world, only a few generations have been granted the role of defending freedom in its hour of maximum danger.

I do not shrink from this responsibility—I welcome it. I do not believe that any of us would exchange places with any other people or any other generation. The energy, the faith, the devotion which we bring to this endeavor will light our country and all who serve it—and the glow from that fire can truly light the world.

And so, my fellow Americans: Ask not what your country can do for you—ask what you can do for your country.

My fellow citizens of the world: Ask not what America will do for you, but what together we can do for the freedom of man.

Finally, whether you are citizens of America or citizens of the world, ask of us here the same high standards of strength and sacrifice which we ask of you. With a good conscience our only sure reward, with history the final judge of our deeds, let us go forth to lead the land we love, asking His blessing and His help, but knowing that here on earth God's work must truly be our own.

I Have a Dream

by Reverend Martin Luther King, Jr.

Dr. King delivered this speech on August 28, 1963, at the Lincoln Memorial, Washington D.C.

I am happy to join with you today in what will go down in history as the greatest demonstration for freedom in the history of our nation.

Five score years ago, a great American, in whose symbolic shadow we stand today, signed the Emancipation Proclamation. This momentous decree came as a great beacon light of hope to millions of Negro slaves, who had been seared in the flames of withering injustice. It came as a joyous daybreak to end the long night of their captivity.

But one hundred years later, the Negro still is not free. One hundred years later, the life of the Negro is still sadly crippled by the manacles of segregation and the chains of discrimination. One hundred years later, the Negro lives on a lonely island of poverty in the midst of a vast ocean of material prosperity. One hundred years later, the Negro is still languished in the corners of American society and finds himself an exile in his own land. And so we've come here today to dramatize a shameful condition.

In a sense we have come to our nation's capital to cash a check. When the architects of our republic wrote the magnificent words of the Constitution and the Declaration of Independence, they were signing a promissory note to which every American was to fall heir. This note was a promise that all men, yes, black men as well as white men, would be guaranteed the unalienable rights of life, liberty, and the pursuit of happiness. It is obvious today that America has defaulted on this promissory note, insofar as her citizens of color are concerned. Instead of honoring this sacred obligation, America has given the Negro people a bad check, a check which has come back marked "insufficient funds."

But we refuse to believe that the bank of justice is bankrupt. We refuse to believe that there are insufficient funds in the great vaults of opportunity of this nation. And so we have come to cash this check, a check that will give us upon demand the riches of freedom and the security of justice.

We have also come to this hallowed spot to remind America of the fierce urgency of Now. This is no time to engage in the luxury of cooling off or to take the tranquilizing drug of gradualism. Now is the time to make real the promises of democracy. Now is the time to rise from the dark and desolate valley of segregation to the sunlit path of racial justice. Now is the time to lift our nation from the quicksands of racial injustice to the solid rock of brotherhood. Now is the time to make justice a reality for all of God's children.

It would be fatal for the nation to overlook the urgency of the moment. This sweltering summer of the Negro's legitimate discontent will not pass until there is an invigorating autumn of freedom and equality. Nineteen sixty-three is not an end but a beginning. Those who hope that the Negro needed to blow off steam and will now be content will have a rude awakening if the nation returns to business as usual. There will be neither rest nor tranquility in America until the Negro is granted his citizenship rights. The whirlwinds of revolt will continue to shake the foundations of our nation until the bright day of justice emerges.

But there is something that I must say to my people who stand on the warm threshold which leads into the palace of justice. In the process of gaining our rightful place we must not be guilty of wrongful deeds. Let us not seek to satisfy our thirst for freedom by drinking from the cup of bitterness and hatred. We must ever conduct our struggle on the high plane of dignity and discipline. We must not allow our creative protest to degenerate into physical violence. Again and again we must rise to the majestic heights of meeting physical force with soul force.

The marvelous new militancy which has engulfed the Negro community must not lead us to a distrust of all white people, for many of our white brothers, as evidenced by their presence here today, have come to realize that their destiny is tied up with our destiny. And they have come to realize that their freedom is inextricably bound to our freedom. We cannot walk alone.

And as we walk, we must make the pledge that we shall always march ahead. We cannot turn back. There are those who are asking the devotees of civil rights, "When will you be satisfied?" We can never be satisfied as long as the Negro is the victim of the unspeakable horrors of police brutality. We can never be satisfied as long as our bodies, heavy with the fatigue of travel, cannot gain lodging in the motels of the highways and the hotels of the cities. We cannot be satisfied as long as a Negro in Mississippi cannot vote and a Negro in New York believes he has nothing for which to vote. No, no, we are not satisfied and we will not be satisfied until justice rolls down like waters and righteousness like a mighty stream.

I am not unmindful that some of you have come here out of great trials and tribulations. Some of you have come fresh from narrow jail cells. Some of you have come from areas where your quest for freedom left you battered by the storms of persecutions and staggered by the winds of police brutality. You have been the veterans of creative suffering. Continue to work with the faith that unearned suffering is redemptive. Go back to Mississippi, go back to Alabama, go back to South Carolina, go back to Georgia, go back to Louisiana, go back to the slums and ghettos of our northern cities, knowing that somehow this situation can and will be changed. Let us not wallow in the valley of despair, I say to you today, my friends. And so even though we face the difficulties of today and tomorrow, I still have a dream. It is a dream deeply rooted in the American dream.

I have a dream that one day this nation will rise up and live out the true meaning of its creed: We hold these truths to be self-evident that all men are created equal.

I have a dream that one day on the red hills of Georgia the sons of former slaves and the sons of former slave owners will be able to sit down together at the table of brotherhood.

I have a dream that one day even the state of Mississippi, a state sweltering with the heat of injustice, sweltering with the heat of oppression, will be transformed into an oasis of freedom and justice.

I have a dream that my four little children will one day live in a nation where they will not be judged by the color of their skin but by the content of their character. I have a dream today!

I have a dream that one day, down in Alabama, with its vicious racists, with its governor having his lips dripping with the words of interposition and nullification; one day right down in Alabama little black boys and black girls will be able to join hands with little white

boys and white girls as sisters and brothers. I have a dream today!

I have a dream that one day every valley shall be exalted, and every hill and mountain shall be made low, the rough places will be made plain, and the crooked places will be made straight, and the glory of the Lord shall be revealed and all flesh shall see it together.

This is our hope. This is the faith that I will go back to the South with. With this faith we will be able to hew out of the mountain of despair a stone of hope. With this faith we will be able to transform the jangling discords of our nation into a beautiful symphony of brotherhood. With this faith we will be able to work together, to pray together, to struggle together, to go to jail together, to stand up for freedom together, knowing that we will be free one day. And this will be the day, this will be the day when all of God's children will be able to sing with new meaning, "My country 'tis of thee, sweet land of liberty, of thee I sing. Land where my fathers died, land of the Pilgrim's pride, from every mountainside, let freedom ring!" And if America is to be a great nation, this must become true.

And so let freedom ring—from the prodigious hilltops of New Hampshire.

Let freedom ring—from the mighty mountains of New York.

Let freedom ring—from the heightening Alleghenies of Pennsylvania.

Let freedom ring—from the snow-capped Rockies of Colorado.

Let freedom ring—from the curvaceous slopes of California.

But not only that.

Let freedom ring—from Stone Mountain of Georgia.

Let freedom ring—from Lookout Mountain of Tennessee.

Let freedom ring—from every hill and molehill of Mississippi; from every mountainside, let freedom ring!

And when this happens, when we allow freedom to ring, when we let it ring from every village and every hamlet, from every state and every city, we will be able to speed up that day when all of God's children, black men and white men, Jews and Gentiles, Protestants and Catholics, will be able to join hands and sing in the words of the old Negro spiritual,

"Free at last, free at last.

Thank God Almighty, we are free at last."

Democratic Convention Keynote Address

by Representative Barbara Jordan

This speech was delivered July 12, 1976, in New York City.

One hundred and forty-four years ago, members of the Democratic Party first met in convention to select a Presidential candidate. Since that time, Democrats have continued to convene once every four years and draft a party platform and nominate a Presidential candidate. And our meeting this week is a continuation of that tradition.

But there is something different about tonight. There is something special about tonight. What is different? What is special? I, Barbara Jordan, am a keynote speaker.

A lot of years passed since 1832, and during that time it would have been most unusual for any national political party to ask that a Barbara Jordan deliver a keynote address . . . but tonight here I am. And I feel that notwithstanding the past that my presence here is one additional bit of evidence that the American Dream need not forever be deferred.

Now that I have this grand distinction what in the world am I supposed to say? I could easily spend this time praising the accomplishments of this party and attacking the Republicans, but I don't choose to do that. I could list the many problems which Americans have.

I could list the problems which cause people to feel cynical, angry, frustrated: problems which include lack of integrity in government; the feeling that the individual no longer counts; the reality of material and spiritual poverty; the feeling that the grand American experiment is failing or has failed. I could recite these problems, and then I could sit down and offer no solutions. But I don't choose to do that either.

The citizens of America expect more. They deserve and they want more than a recital of problems.

We are a people in a quandary about the present. We are a people in search of our future. We are a people in search of a national community. We are a people trying not only to solve the problems of the present—unemployment, inflation—but we are attempting on a larger scale to fulfill the promise of America. We are attempting to fulfill our national purpose; to create and sustain a society in which all of us are equal.

Throughout our history, when people have looked for new ways to solve their problems, and to uphold the principles of this nation, many times they have turned to political parties. They have often turned to the Democratic Party.

What is it, what is it about the Democratic Party that makes it the instrument that people use when they search for ways to shape their future? Well I believe the answer to that question lies in our concept of governing. Our concept of governing is derived from our view of people. It is a concept deeply rooted in a set of beliefs firmly etched in the national conscience of all of us. Now what are these beliefs?

First, we believe in equality for all and privileges for none. This is a belief that each American regardless of background has equal standing in the public forum, all of us. Because we believe this idea so firmly, we are an inclusive rather than an exclusive party. Let everybody come.

I think it no accident that most of those emigrating to American in the 19th century identified with the Democratic Party. We are a heterogeneous party made up of Americans of diverse backgrounds.

We believe that the people are the source of all governmental power; that the authority of the people is to be extended, not restricted. This can be accomplished only by providing each citizen with every opportunity to participate in the management of the government. They must have that.

We believe that the government which represents the authority of all the people, not just one interest group, but all the people, has an obligation to actively, underscore actively, seek to remove those obstacles which would block individual achievement . . . obstacles emanating from race, sex, economic condition. The government must seek to remove them.

We are a party of innovation. We do not reject our traditions, but we are willing to adapt to changing circumstances, when change we must. We are willing to suffer the discomfort of change in order to achieve a better future. We have a positive vision of the future founded on the belief that the gap between the promise and reality of America can one day be finally closed. We believe that.

This my friends, is the bedrock of our concept of governing. This is a part of the reason why Americans have turned to the Democratic Party. These are the foundations upon which a national community can be built.

Let's all understand that these guiding principles cannot be discarded for short-term political gains. They represent what this country is all about. They are indigenous to the

American idea. And these are principles which are not negotiable.

In other times, I could stand here and give this kind of exposition on the beliefs of the Democratic Party and that would be enough. But today that is not enough. People want more. That is not sufficient reason for the majority of the people of this country to vote Democratic. We have made mistakes. In our haste to do all things for all people, we did not foresee the full consequences of our actions. And when the people raised their voices, we didn't hear. But our deafness was only a temporary condition, and not an irreversible condition.

Even as I stand here and admit that we have made mistakes I still believe that as the people of America sit in judgment on each party, they will recognize that our mistakes were mistakes of the heart. They'll recognize that.

And now we must look to the future. Let us heed the voice of the people and recognize their common sense. If we do not, we not only blaspheme our political heritage, we ignore the common ties that bind all Americans.

Many fear the future. Many are distrustful of their leaders, and believe that their voices are never heard. Many seek only to satisfy their private work wants. To satisfy private interests.

But this is the great danger America faces. That we will cease to be one nation and become instead a collection of interest groups: city against suburb, region against region, individual against individual. Each seeking to satisfy private wants.

If that happens, who then will speak for America? Who then will speak for the common good? This is the question which must be answered in 1976. Are we to be one people bound together by common spirit sharing in a common endeavor or will we become a divided nation?

For all of its uncertainty, we cannot flee the future. We must not become the new puritans and reject our society. We must address and master the future together. It can be done if we restore the belief that we share a sense of national community, that we share a common national endeavor. It can be done.

There is no executive order; there is no law that can require the American people to form a national community. This we must do as individuals and if we do it as individuals, there is no President of the United States who can veto that decision.

As a first step, we must restore our belief in ourselves. We are a generous people so why can't we be generous with each other? We need to take to heart the words spoken by Thomas Jefferson: "Let us restore to social intercourse that harmony and that affection without which liberty and even life are but dreary things."

A nation is formed by the willingness of each of us to share in the responsibility for upholding the common good. A government is invigorated when each of us is willing to participate in shaping the future of this nation.

In this election year we must define the common good and begin again to shape a common future. Let each person do his or her part. If one citizen is unwilling to participate, all of us are going to suffer. For the American idea, though it is shared by all of us, is realized in each one of us.

And now, what are those of us who are elected public officials supposed to do? We call ourselves public servants but I'll tell you this: we as public servants must set an example for the rest of the nation. It is hypocritical for the public official to admonish and exhort the people to uphold the common good if we are derelict in upholding the common good. More is required of public officials than slogans and handshakes and press releases. More is required. We must hold ourselves strictly accountable. We must provide the people with a vision of the future.

If we promise as public officials, we must deliver. If we as public officials propose, we must produce. If we say to the American people it is time for you to be sacrificial; sacrifice. If the public official says that we (public officials) must be the first to give. We must be. And again, if we make mistakes, we must be willing to admit them. We have to do that. What we have to do is strike a balance between the idea that government should do everything and the idea, the belief, that government ought to do nothing. Strike a balance.

Let there be no illusions about the difficulty of forming this kind of a national community. It's tough, difficult, not easy. But a spirit of harmony will survive in America only if each of us remembers that we share a common destiny. If each of us remembers, when self-interest and bitterness seem to prevail, that we share a common destiny.

I have confidence that we can form this kind of national community. I have confidence that the Democratic Party can lead the way. I have that confidence. We cannot improve on the system of government handed down to us by the founders of the Republic, there is no way to improve upon that. But what we can do is to find new ways to implement that system and realize our destiny.

Now, I began this speech by commenting to you on the uniqueness of a Barbara Jordan making the keynote address. Well I am going to close my speech by quoting a Republican President and I ask you that as you listen to these words of Abraham Lincoln, relate them to the concept of a national community in which every last one of us participates: "As I would not be a slave, so I would not be a master. This expresses my idea of Democracy. Whatever differs from this, to the extent of the difference is no Democracy."

Eulogy for the Challenger Astronauts

by President Ronald Reagan

On January 28, 1986, only seconds after liftoff, the space shuttle Challenger exploded, and all seven astronauts were lost. Because one of the crew, Christa McAuliffe, was a teacher, live coverage of the flight was being watched in thousands of classrooms across the country.

Ladies and gentlemen, I'd planned to speak to you tonight on the state of the Union, but the events of earlier today have led me to change those plans. Today is a day for mourning and remembering.

Nancy and I are pained to the core by the tragedy of the shuttle Challenger. We know we share this pain with all of the people of our country. This is truly a national loss.

Nineteen years ago, almost to the day, we lost three astronauts in a terrible accident on the ground. But we've never lost an astronaut in flight; we've never had a tragedy like this. And perhaps we've forgotten the courage it took for the crew of the shuttle; but they, the Challenger Seven, were aware of the dangers, but overcame them and did their jobs brilliantly. We mourn seven heroes: Michael Smith, Dick Scobee, Judith Resnik, Ronald McNair, Ellison Onizuka, Gregory Jarvis, and Christa McAuliffe. We mourn their loss as a nation together.

For the families of the seven, we cannot bear, as you do, the full impact of this tragedy. Bur we feel the loss, and we're thinking about you so very much. Your loved ones were daring and brave, and they had that special grace, that special spirit that says, "Give me a challenge and I'll meet it with joy." They had a hunger to explore the universe and discover its truths. They wished to serve, and they did. They served all of us.

We've grown used to wonders in this century. It's hard to dazzle us. But for 25 years the United States space program has been doing just that. We've grown used to the idea of space, and perhaps we forget that we've only just begun. We're still pioneers. They, the members of the Challenger crew, were pioneers.

And I want to say something to the schoolchildren of America who were watching the live coverage of the shuttle's takeoff. I know it is hard to understand, but sometimes painful things like this happen. It's all part of the process of exploration and discovery. It's all part of taking a chance and expanding man's horizons. The future doesn't belong to the fainthearted; it belongs to the brave. The Challenger crew was pulling us into the future, and we'll continue to follow them.

I've always had great faith in and respect for our space program, and what happened today does nothing to diminish it. We don't hide our space program. We don't keep secrets and cover things up. We do it all up front and in public. That's the way freedom is, and we wouldn't change it for a minute.

We'll continue our quest in space. There will be more shuttle flights and more shuttle crews and, yes, more volunteers, more civilians, more teachers in space. Nothing ends here; our hopes and our journeys continue.

I want to add that I wish I could talk to every man and woman who works for NASA or who worked on this mission and tell them: "Your dedication and professionalism have moved and impressed us for decades. And we know of your anguish. We share it."

There's a coincidence today. On this day 390 years ago, the great explorer Sir Francis Drake died aboard ship off the coast of Panama. In his lifetime the great frontiers were the oceans, and an historian later said, "He lived by the sea, died on it, and was buried in it." Well, today we can say of the Challenger crew: Their dedication was, like Drake's, complete.

The crew of the space shuttle Challenger honored us by the manner in which they lived their lives. We will never forget them, nor the last time we saw them, this morning, as they prepared for their journey and waved goodbye and "slipped the surly bonds of earth" to "touch the face of God."

Opportunities for Hispanic Women: It's Up to Us

by Janice Payan

Thank you. I felt as if you were introducing someone else because my mind was racing back ten years, when I was sitting out there in the audience at the Adelante Mujer Conference. Anonymous. Comfortable. Trying to relate to our "successful" speaker, but mostly feeling like Janice Payan, working mother, glad for a chance to sit down.

I'll let you in on a little secret. I still am Janice Payan, working mother. The only difference is that I have a longer job title, and that I've made a few discoveries these past ten years that I'm eager to share with you.

The first is that keynote speakers at conferences like this are not some sort of alien creatures. Nor were they born under a lucky star. They are ordinary Hispanic women who have stumbled onto an extraordinary discovery.

And that is: Society has lied to us. We do have something up here! We can have not only a happy family but also a fulfilling career. We can succeed in school and work and community life, because the key is not supernatural powers, it is perseverance. Also known as hard work!

And God knows Hispanic women can do hard work! We've been working hard for centuries, from sun-up 'til daughter-down!

One of the biggest secrets around is that successful Anglos were not born under lucky stars, either. The chairman of my company, Jack MacAllister, grew up in a small town in eastern Iowa. His dad was a teacher; his mom was a mom. Jack worked, after school, sorting potatoes in the basement of a grocery store. Of course I realize, he could have been hoeing them, like our migrant workers.

Nevertheless, Jack came from humble beginnings. And so did virtually every other corporate officer I work with. The major advantage they had was living in a culture that allowed them to believe they would get ahead. So more of them did.

It's time for Hispanic women to believe we can get ahead, because we can. And because we must. Our families and workplaces and communities and nation need to reach our full potential. There are jobs to be done, children to be raised, opportunities to be seized. We must look at those opportunities, choose the ones we will respond to, and do something about them.

We must do so, for others. And we must do so, for ourselves. Yes, there are barriers. You're up against racism, sexism, and too much month at the end of the money. But so was any role model you choose. Look at Patricia Diaz-Denis. Patricia was one of nine or ten children in a Mexican-American family that had low means, but high hopes. Her parents said Patricia should go to college. But they had no money. So, little by little, Patricia scraped up the money to send herself.

Her boyfriend was going to be a lawyer. And he told Patricia, "You should be a lawyer too, because nobody can argue like you do!" Well, Patricia didn't even know what a lawyer was, but she became one—so successful that she eventually was appointed to the Federal Communication Commission in Washington, D.C.

Or look at Toni Panteha, a Puerto Rican who grew up in a shack with dirt floors, no father, and often no food. . . But through looking and listening, she realized the power of community—the fact that people with very little, when working together, can create much.

Dr. Panteha has created several successful institutions in Puerto Rico, and to me, she is an institution. I can see the wisdom in her eyes, hear it in her voice, wisdom far beyond herself, like Mother Teresa.

Or look at Ada Kirby, a Cuban girl whose parents put her on a boat for Miami. Mom and Dad were to follow on the next boat, but they never arrived. So Ada grew up in an orphanage in Pueblo, and set some goals, and today is an executive director at U.S. West's research laboratories.

Each of these women was Hispanic, physically deprived, but mentally awakened to the possibilities of building a better world, both for others and for themselves.

Virtually every Hispanic woman in America started with a similar slate. In fact, let's do a quick survey. If you were born into a home whose economic status was something less than rich...please raise your hand.

It's a good thing I didn't ask the rich to raise their hands. I wouldn't have known if anyone was listening.

All right. So you were not born rich. As Patricia, Toni and Ada have shown us, it doesn't matter. It's the choices we make from there on, that make the difference.

If you're thinking, "that's easy for you to say, Payan," then I'm thinking: "little do you know. . ."

If you think I got where I am because I'm smarter than you, or have more energy than you, you're wrong.

If I'm so smart, why can't I parallel park?

If I'm so energetic, why do I still need eight hours of sleep a night?

And I mean need. If I hadn't had my eight hours last night, you wouldn't even want to hear what I'd be saying this morning!

I am more like you and you are more like me than you would guess.

I'm a third generation Mexican-American. . . born into a lower middle class family right here in Denver. My parents married young; she was pregnant. My father worked only about half the time during my growing-up years. He was short on education, skills, and confidence. There were drug and alcohol problems in the family. My parents finally sent my older brother to a Catholic high school, in hopes that would help him. They sent me to the same school to watch him. That was okay.

In public school I never could choose between the "Greasers" and the "Soshes." I wanted desperately to feel that I "belonged." But I did not like feeling that I had to deny my past to have a future.

Anybody here ever feel that way?

Anyway, the more troubles my brother had, the more I vowed to avoid them. So, in a way, he was my inspiration. As Viktor Frankl says, there is meaning in every life.

By the way, that brother died after returning from Vietnam.

I was raised with typical Hispanic female expectations. In other words: if you want to do well in life, you'd better . . . Can anybody finish that sentence?

Right!

Marry well.

I liked the idea of loving and marrying someone, but I felt like he should be more than a "meal ticket." And I felt like I should be more than a leech. I didn't want to feel so dependent.

So I set my goals on having a marriage, a family and a career. I didn't talk too much about those goals, so nobody told me they bordered on insanity for a Hispanic woman in the 1960s.

At one point, I even planned to become a doctor. But Mom and Dad said, "wait a minute. That takes something like 12 years of college."

I had no idea how I was going to pay for four years of college, let alone 12. But what scared me more than the cost was the time: In 12 years I'd be an old woman.

Time certainly changes your perspective on that.

My advice to you is, if you want to be a doctor, go for it!

You may be several years older when you finish, but by that time you'd be several years older if you don't finish college, too.

For all my suffering in high school, I finished near the top of my graduating class. I dreamed of attending the University of Colorado, at Boulder. You want to know what my counselor said? You already know. That I should go to business college for secretaries, at most.

But I went to the University of Colorado, anyway. I arranged my own financial aid: a small grant, a low-paying job, and a big loan.

I just thank God that this was the era when

jeans and sweatshirts were getting popular. That was all I had!

I'm going to spare you any description of my class work, except to say that it was difficult—and worth every painful minute. What I want to share with you is three of my strongest memories—and strongest learning experiences—which have nothing to do with books.

One concerns a philosophy professor who, I was sure, was a genius. What I liked best about this man was not the answers he had—but the questions. He asked questions about the Bible, about classic literature, about our place in the universe. He would even jot questions in the margins of our papers. And I give him a lot of credit for helping me examine my own life.

I'm telling you about him because I think each of us encounters people who make us think—sometimes painfully. And I feel, strongly, that we should listen to their questions and suffer through that thinking. We may decide everything in our lives is just like we want it. But we may also decide to change something.

My second big "non-book" experience was in UMAS—the United Mexican American Students. Lost in what seemed like a rich Anglo campus, UMAS was an island of familiarity: people who looked like me, talked like me, and felt like me.

We shared our fears and hopes and hurts—and did something about them. We worked hard to deal with racism on campus, persuading the university to offer Chicano studies classes. But the more racism we experienced, the angrier we became.

Some members made bombs. Two of those members died. And I remember asking myself: "Am I willing to go up in smoke over my anger? Or is there another way to make a difference?"

We talked a lot about this, and concluded that two wrongs don't make a right. Most of us agreed that working within the system was the thing to do. We also agreed not to deny our Hispanic heritage: not to become "coconuts"—brown on the outside and white on the inside—but to look for every opportunity to bring our culture to a table of many cultures.

That outlook has helped me a great deal as a manager, because it opened me to listening to all points of view. And when a group is open to all points of view, it usually chooses the right course.

The third experience I wanted to share from my college days was the time they came nearest to ending prematurely. During my freshmen year, I received a call that my mother had been seriously injured in a traffic accident. Both of her legs were broken. So was her pelvis.

My younger brother and sister were still at home. My father was unemployed at the time, and I was off at college. So who do you think was elected to take on the housework? Raise your hand if you think it was my father.

No???

Does anybody think it was me?

I am truly amazed at your guessing ability.

Or is there something in our Hispanic culture that says the women do the housework?

Of course there is.

So I drove home from Boulder every weekend; shopped, cleaned, cooked, froze meals for the next week, did the laundry, you know the list.

And the truth is it did not occur to me until some time later that my father could have done some of that. I had a problem; I was part of the problem.

I did resist when my parents suggested I should quit school. It seemed better to try doing everything than to give up my dream. And it was the better choice. But it was also very difficult.

Which reminds me of another experience. Would it be too much like a soap opera if I told you about a personal crisis? Anybody want to hear a story about myself that I've never before told in public?

While still in college, I married my high school sweetheart. We were both completing our college degrees. My husband's family could not figure out why I was pursuing college instead of kids, but I was. However, it seemed like my schoolwork always came last.

One Saturday night I had come home from helping my mom, dragged into our tiny married-student apartment, cooked a big dinner for my husband, and as I stood there washing the dishes, I felt a teardrop trickle down my face.

Followed by a flood.

Followed by sobbing.

Heaving.

If you ranked crying on a scale of 1 to 10, this was an 11.

My husband came rushing in with that . . . you know . . . that "puzzled-husband" look. He asked me what was wrong.

Well, it took me a while to figure it out, to be able to put it into words. When I did they were 12 words:

"I just realized I'll be doing dishes the rest of my life."

Now, If I thought you'd believe me, I'd tell you my husband finished the dishes. He did not. But we both did some thinking and talking about roles and expectations, and, over the years, have learned to share the domestic responsibilities. We realized that we were both carrying a lot of old, cultural "baggage" through life.

And so are you.

I'm not going to tell you what to do about it. But I am going to urge you to realize it, think about it, and even to cry over the dishes, if you need to. You may be glad you did. As for me, what have I learned from all this?

I've learned, as I suggested earlier, that Hispanic women have bought into a lot of myths through the years. Or at least I did. And I want to tell you now, especially you younger women, the "five things I wish I had known" when I was 20, 25, even 30. In fact, some of these things I'm still learning at 37.

Now for that list of "five things I wish I had known."

First: I wish I had known that I—like most Hispanic women—was underestimating my capabilities.

When I first went to work for Mountain Bell, which has since become U.S. West Communications, I thought the "ultimate" job I could aspire to would be district manager. So I signed up for the courses I knew would help me achieve and handle that kind of responsibility. I watched various district managers, forming my own ideas of who was most effective—and why. I accepted whatever responsibilities and opportunities were thrown my way, generally preparing myself to be district manager.

My dream came true.

But then it almost became a nightmare. After only eighteen months on the job, the president of the company called me and asked me to go interview with his boss—the president of our parent company. And the next thing I knew, I had been promoted to a job above that of district manager.

Suddenly, I was stranded in unfamiliar territory. They gave me a big office at U.S. West headquarters down in Englewood, where I pulled all the furniture in one corner. In fact, I sort of made a little "fort." From this direction, I could hide behind the computer. From that direction, the plants. From over here, the file cabinet. Safe at last.

Until a friend from downtown came to visit me She walked in, looked around, and demanded to know: "What is going on here? Why was your door closed? Why are you all scrunched up in the corner?"

I had all kinds of excuses.

But she said, "You know what I think? I think you're afraid you don't deserve this office!"

As she spoke, she started dragging the plants away from my desk. For a moment, I was angry. Then afraid. Then we started laughing, and I helped her stretch my furnishings—and my confidence.

And it occurred to me that had I pictured, from the beginning, that I could become an executive director, I would have been better prepared. I would have pictured myself in that big office. I would have spent more time learning executive public speaking. I would have done a lot of things. And I began to do them with my new, expanded vision of becoming an officer—which subsequently happened.

I just wish that I had known, in those early years, how I was underestimating my capabilities.

I suspect that you are, too.

And I wonder: What are you going to do about it?

Second: I wish I had known that power is not something others give you.

It is something that comes from within yourself . . . and which you can then share with others.

In 1984, a group of minority women at U.S. West got together and did some arithmetic to confirm what we already knew. Minority women were woefully under-represented in the ranks of middle and upper management. We had a better chance of winning the lottery. We gathered our courage and took our case to the top. Fortunately, we found a sympathetic ear. The top man told us to take our case to all the officers.

We did. But we were scared. And it showed. We sort of "begged" for time on their calendars. We apologized for interrupting their work. Asked for a little more recognition of our plight. And the first few interviews went terribly.

Then we realized: we deserve to be on their calendars as much as anyone else does. We realized that under-utilizing a group of employees is not an interruption of the officers' work—it is the officers' work. We realized that we should not be asking for help—we should be telling how we could help.

So we did.

And it worked. The company implemented a special program to help minority women achieve their full potential. Since then, several of us have moved into middle and upper management, and more are on the way.

I just wish we had realized, in the beginning, where power really comes from. It comes from within yourself. . . and you can then share with others.

I suspect you need to be reminded of that, too.

And I wonder: What are you going to do about it?

Third: I wish I had known that when I feel envious of others, I'm really just showing my lack of confidence in myself.

A few years ago, I worked closely with one of my co-workers in an employee organization. She is Hispanic. Confident. Outgoing. In fact, she's so likable I could hardly stand her!

But as we worked together, I finally realized: She has those attributes; I have others. And I had to ask myself: do I want to spend the time it would take to develop her attributes, or enjoy what we can accomplish by teaming up our different skills? I realized that is the better way.

I suspect that you may encounter envy from time to time.

And I wonder: What are you going to do about it?

Fourth: I wish I had realized that true success is never something you earn single-handed.

We hear people talk about "networking" and "community" and "team-building." What they mean is an extension of my previous idea: We can be a lot more effective working in a group than working alone.

This was brought home to me when I was president of my Hispanic employees' organization at U.S. West Communications. I wanted my administration to be the best. So I tried to do everything myself, to be sure it was done right. I wrote the newsletter, planned the fund-raiser, scheduled the meetings, booked the speakers, everything.

For our big annual meeting, I got the chairman of the company to speak. By then the other officers of the group were feeling left out. Come to think of it, they were left out.

Anyway, we were haggling over who got to introduce our big speaker. I was determined it should be me, since I so "obviously" had done all the work.

As it turned out, I missed the big meeting altogether. My older brother died. And I did a lot of painful thinking. For one thing: I was glad my team was there to keep things going while I dealt with my family crisis. But more important: I thought about life and death and what people would be saying if I had died.

Would I prefer they remember that "good ol' Janice sure did a terrific job of arranging every last detail of the meeting"? Or that "we really enjoyed working with her. Together, we did a lot."

All of us need to ask ourselves that question from time to time.

And I wonder: What are you going to do about it?

Hispanic women in America have been victims of racism, sexism, and poverty for a long, long time.

I know, because I was one of them. I also know that when you stop being a victim is largely up to you.

I don't mean you should run out of here, quit your job, divorce your husband, farm out your kids or run for President of the United States.

But I do mean that whatever you can dream, you can become.

A couple of years ago, I came across a poem by an Augsburg College student, Devoney K. Looser, which I want to share with you now.

I wish someone had taught me long ago

How to touch mountains

Instead of watching them from breathtakingly safe distances.

I wish someone had told me sooner

That cliffs are neither so sharp nor so distant nor so solid as they seemed.

I wish someone had told me years ago

That only through touching mountains can we reach peaks called beginnings, endings, or exhilarating points of no return.

I wish I had learned earlier that ten fingers and the world shout more brightly from the tops of mountains

While life below only sighs with echoing cries.

I wish I had realized before today

That I can touch mountains

But now that I know, my fingers will never cease to climb.

Please, my sisters, never, ever, cease to climb.

Adelante Mujer.

Women's Rights Are Human Rights

by Senator Hillary Rodham Clinton

These are Senator Clinton's remarks to the United Nations Fourth World Conference on Women.

Plenary Session in Beijing, China, September 5, 1995

Mrs. Mongella, Under Secretary Kittani, distinguished delegates and guests:

I would like to thank the Secretary General of the United Nations for inviting me to be part of the United Nations Fourth World Conference on Women. This is truly a celebration—a celebration of the contributions women make in every aspect of life: in the home, on the job, in their communities, as mothers, wives, sisters, daughters, learners, workers, citizens and leaders.

It is also a coming together, much the way women come together every day in every country.

We come together in fields and in factories. In village markets and supermarkets. In living rooms and boardrooms.

Whether it is while playing with our children in the park, or washing clothes in a river, or taking a break at the office water cooler, we come together and talk about our aspirations and concerns. And time and again, our talk turns to our children and our families. However different we may be, there is far more that unites us than divides us. We share a common future. And we are here to find common ground so that we may help bring new dignity and respect to women and girls all over the world—and in so doing, bring new strength and stability to families as well.

By gathering in Beijing, we are focusing world attention on issues that matter most in the lives of women and their families: access to education, health care, jobs and credit, the chance to enjoy basic legal and human rights and participate fully in the political life of their countries.

There are some who question the reason for this conference.

Let them listen to the voices of women in their homes, neighborhoods, and workplaces.

There are some who wonder whether the lives of women and girls matter to economic and political progress around the globe.

Let them look at the women gathered here and at Huairou—the homemakers, nurses, teachers, lawyers, policymakers, and women who run their own businesses.

It is conferences like this that compel governments and people everywhere to listen, look and face the world's most pressing problems.

Wasn't it after the women's conference in Nairobi ten years ago that the world focused for the first time on the crisis of domestic violence?

Earlier today, I participated in a World Health Organization forum, where government officials, NGOs [non-governmental organizations], and individual citizens are working on ways to address the health problems of women and girls.

Tomorrow, I will attend a gathering of the United Nations Development Fund for Women. There, the discussion will focus on local—and highly successful—programs that give hard-working women access to credit so they can improve their own lives and the lives of their families.

What we are learning around the world is that if women are healthy and educated, their families will flourish. If women are free from violence, their families will flourish. If women have a chance to work and earn as full and equal partners in society, their families will flourish.

And when families flourish, communities and nations will flourish.

That is why every woman, every man, every child, every family, and every nation on our planet has a stake in the discussion that takes place here.

Over the past 25 years, I have worked persistently on issues relating to women, children, and families. Over the past two-and-a-half years, I have had the opportunity to learn more about the challenges facing women in my own country and around the world.

I have met new mothers in Jojakarta, Indonesia, who come together regularly in their village to discuss nutrition, family planning, and baby care.

I have met working parents in Denmark who talk about the comfort they feel in knowing that their children can be cared for in creative, safe, and nurturing after-school centers.

I have met women in South Africa who helped lead the struggle to end apartheid and are now helping build a new democracy.

I have met with the leading women of the Western Hemisphere who are working every day to promote literacy and better health care for the children of their countries.

I have met women in India and Bangladesh who are taking out small loans to buy milk cows, rickshaws, thread, and other materials to create a livelihood for themselves and their families.

I have met doctors and nurses in Belarus and Ukraine who are trying to keep children alive in the aftermath of Chernobyl.

The great challenge of this Conference is to give voice to women everywhere whose experiences go unnoticed, whose words go unheard.

Women comprise more than half the world's population. Women are 70 percent of the world's poor, and two-thirds of those who are not taught to read and write.

Women are the primary caretakers for most of the world's children and elderly. Yet much of the work we do is not valued—not by economists, not by historians, not by popular culture, not by government leaders.

At this very moment, as we sit here, women around the world are giving birth, raising children, cooking meals, washing clothes, cleaning houses, planting crops, working on assembly lines, running companies, and running countries.

Women also are dying from diseases that should have been prevented or treated; they are watching their children succumb to malnutrition caused by poverty and economic deprivation; they are being denied the right to go to school by their own fathers and brothers; they are being forced into prostitution; and they are being barred from the bank lending office and banned from the ballot box.

Those of us who have the opportunity to be here have the responsibility to speak for those who could not.

As an American, I want to speak up for women in my own country—women who are raising children on the minimum wage, women who can't afford health care or child care, women whose lives are threatened by violence, including violence in their own homes.

I want to speak up for mothers who are fighting for good schools, safe neighborhoods, clean air, and clean airwaves; for older women, some of them widows, who have raised their families and now find that their skills and life experiences are not valued in the workplace; for women who are working all night as nurses, hotel clerks, and fast food cooks so that they can be at home during the day with their kids; and for women everywhere who simply don't have time to do everything they are called upon to do each day.

Speaking to you today, I speak for them, just as each of us speaks for women around the world who are denied the chance to go to school, or see a doctor, or own property, or have a say about the direction of their lives, simply because they are women. The truth is that most women around the world work both inside and outside the home, usually by necessity.

We need to understand that there is no formula for how women should lead their lives. That is why we must respect the choices that each woman makes for herself and her family. Every woman deserves the chance to realize her God-given potential.

We also must recognize that women will never gain full dignity until their human rights are respected and protected.

Our goals for this Conference, to strengthen families and societies by empowering women to take greater control over their own destinies, cannot be fully achieved unless all govern-ments—here and around the world—accept their responsibility to protect and promote internationally recognized human rights.

The international community has long acknowledged—and recently affirmed at Vienna—that both women and men are entitled to a range of protections and personal freedoms, from the right of personal security to the right to determine freely the number and spacing of the children they bear.

No one should be forced to remain silent for fear of religious or political persecution, arrest, abuse, or torture.

Tragically, women are most often the ones whose human rights are violated.

Even in the late 20th century, the rape of women continues to be used as an instrument of armed conflict. Women and children make up a large majority of the world's refugees. When women are excluded from the political process, they become even more vulnerable to abuse.

I believe that, on the eve of a new millennium, it is time to break our silence. It is time for us to say here in Beijing, and the world to hear, that it is no longer acceptable to discuss women's rights as separate from human rights.

These abuses have continued because, for too long, the history of women has been a history of silence. Even today, there are those who are trying to silence our words.

The voices of this conference and of the women at Huairou must be heard loud and clear: It is a violation of human rights when babies are denied food, or drowned, or suffocated, or their spines broken, simply because they are born girls.

It is a violation of human rights when women and girls are sold into the slavery of prostitution.

It is a violation of human rights when women are doused with gasoline, set on fire and burned to death because their marriage dowries are deemed too small.

It is a violation of human rights when individual women are raped in their own communities and when thousands of women are subjected to rape as a tactic or prize of war.

It is a violation of human rights when a leading cause of death worldwide among women ages 14 to 44 is the violence they are subjected to in their own homes.

It is a violation of human rights when young girls are brutalized by the painful and degrading practice of genital mutilation.

It is a violation of human rights when women are denied the right to plan their own families, and that includes being forced to have abortions or being sterilized against their will.

If there is one message that echoes forth from this conference, it is that human rights are women's rights—and women's rights are human rights. Let us not forget that among those rights are the right to speak freely—and the right to be heard.

Women must enjoy the right to participate fully in the social and political lives of their countries if we want freedom and democracy to thrive and endure.

It is indefensible that many women in nongovernmental organizations who wished to participate in this conference have not been able to attend—or have been prohibited from fully taking part.

Let me be clear. Freedom means the right of people to assemble, organize, and debate openly. It means respecting the views of those who may disagree with the views of their governments. It means not taking citizens away from their loved ones and jailing them, mistreating them, or denying them their freedom or dignity because of the peaceful expression of their ideas and opinions.

In my country, we recently celebrated the 75th anniversary of women's suffrage. It took 150 years after the signing of our Declaration of Independence for women to win the right to vote.

It took 72 years of organized struggle on the part of many courageous women and men. It was one of America's most divisive philosophical wars. But it was also a bloodless war. Suffrage was achieved without a shot being fired.

We have also been reminded, in V-1 Day observances last weekend, of the good that comes when men and women join together to combat the forces of tyranny and build a better world.

We have seen peace prevail in most places for a half century. We have avoided another world war.

But we have not solved older, deeply rooted problems that continue to diminish the potential of half the world's population.

Now it is time to act on behalf of women everywhere. If we take bold steps to better the lives of women, we will be taking bold steps to better the lives of children and families too.

Families rely on mothers and wives for emotional support and care; families rely on women for labor in the home; and increasingly, families rely on women for income needed to raise healthy children and care for other relatives.

As long as discrimination and inequities remain so commonplace around the world—as long as girls and women are valued less, fed less, fed last, overworked, underpaid, not schooled, and subjected to violence in and out of their homes—the potential of the human family to create a peaceful, prosperous world will not be realized.

Let this Conference be our—and the world's—call to action.

And let us heed the call so that we can create a world in which every woman is treated with respect and dignity, every boy and girl is loved and cared for equally, and every family has the hope of a strong and stable future.

Thank you very much.

God's blessings on you, your work, and all who will benefit from it.

Our First Amendment Rights in Cyberspace

by Senator Patrick Leahy

This speech was delivered at the Media Institute Friends and Benefactors Banquet, October 22, 1996.

I am deeply honored to be the recipient of the Freedom of Speech Award. Long before I got the nickname "CyberSenator," and long before I ever began using the Internet, I was a confirmed Dead Head. Following John Perry Barlow to this podium is the closest I'll come to a Dead Head experience this year, so I'm doubly pleased to be here tonight.

Let me tell you another reason why this award has special meaning to me. My parents published a weekly newspaper and owned a printing business while I was growing up in Vermont. They instilled in me an enduring respect for the First Amendment and our rights to free speech, to practice the religion of our choice—or no religion at all—and to associate with whom we want. These rights are the surest footing for a sound democracy.

When a dynamic new technology like the Internet explodes onto the scene, some cultural indigestion is inevitable. The exhilarating freedom to speak that is part and parcel of the Internet invites more speech and more participation, and wherever there is such freedom, there will be some who abuse it. Computer technology and the Internet make it easier to gossip, search, collect, and dispense personal information without knowledge or consent and to do it on an unprecedented scale.

What we need in the on-line world is to cultivate an ethic of self-restraint to check these temptations to invade privacy or to venture into other excesses. What the on-line world patently does not need are government restraints to limit speech freedom on the Internet.

Unfortunately, our free speech rights on the Internet have been under siege. The same Congress that promised to get government off our backs passed the Communications Decency Act to regulate on-line speech.

The CDA imposes far-reaching new federal criminal penalties on Americans for exercising their free speech rights on-line, including on the Internet. This law was recognized to be seriously flawed and unconstitutional every place but where it counted—in the Congress of the United States. And, it passed overwhelmingly.

Specifically, the Communications Decency Act penalizes with two-year jail terms and large fines anyone who transmits indecent material to a minor, or displays or posts indecent material in areas where a minor can see it.

An e-mail message to a teenager with a four-letter swear word would violate this law. So, too, would posting in a Usenet discussion group, on electronic bulletin boards, or in a chat room accessible to children, any quote from the racier parts of some of the great works of literature. Information on AIDS, birth control, or prison rape could all be out of bounds on the Internet. Advertisements that would be perfectly legal in print could subject the advertiser to criminal liability if circulated online.

Of course, in the borderless world of the Internet, enforcement of the Communications Decency Act, or other speech restrictions, also presents stark practical problems. And then there is the definitional issue. The CDA targets speech that is either, quote, "indecent," or,

quoting again, "patently offensive." What strikes some as "indecent" or "patently offensive" may look very different to others in another part of the country, let alone the world. Now, I might find some of the speeches that Phil Gramm gives on the Senate Floor to be patently offensive, quote, unquote, but some others would disagree with me about that. Given these cultural, social, and regional differences, the end result is to leave in the hands of the most aggressive prosecutor in the least tolerant community the power to set standards for what every other Internet user may say on-line. This will have a significant chilling effect on all the speech that is put on-line, including the speech between consenting adults.

The myth is that Members of Congress passed the CDA because most do not use and do not understand the Internet. That was certainly part of it. There still are some policy makers here and there who think a computer monitor is simply a TV on the fritz!

Unfortunately, ignorance about the Internet is only a partial excuse. The First Amendment has always provided fertile ground for demagoguery and political posturing. Just look at the number of times Congress has voted on flag burning bans and on legislation to control the content of TV and cable programming.

The United States is certainly not alone in its efforts to censor the Internet. As the *Washington Post* opined yesterday, the governments of China, Singapore, Iran, and Burma have all taken steps to maintain control of their citizens by controlling what their citizens may access on the Internet.

As these issues are raised and debated around the globe, the United States—with the oldest and most effective constitutional protections of free speech anywhere—is uniquely situated to provide cultural leadership in answering these questions.

The Internet is a home-grown American technology that has swept the world. Americans should take the high ground to protect the future of the Internet and fight censorship efforts springing up here at home and around the globe. Instead of championing the First Amendment, however, responses such as the Communications Decency Act trample the principles of free speech and free flow of information that have fueled the growth of democracy around the world.

Make no mistake, there is a global battle being waged over what the Internet will look like in the near and distant future. Many of the heroes of this battle have formed a coalition to make it easy for us to identify them. Organized by the Center for Democracy and Technology, America On Line, the American Library Association, Microsoft, the Recording Industry Association of America, and others, the Citizens Internet Empowerment Coalition won a stunning victory when the CDA was declared unconstitutional in Philadelphia in June. I was proud to support their effort with a declaration. We are all counting on them to win the case before the Supreme Court this term.

Even if we win this case—and my legislation to wipe the books clean of the CDA is then able to pass—the battle over First Amendment rights in Cyberspace will simply shift to other areas. For example, the debate over the extent to which we can engage in anonymous communications over the Internet looms as one of the future First Amendment battles in cyberspace.

The Supreme Court has made crystal clear that speaking anonymously is protected by the First Amendment and that "anonymity is a shield from the tyranny of the majority." Indeed, our freedom to speak anonymously on the Internet is one way to protect our privacy, and is particularly important for those Internet users who access sensitive information anonymously to avoid stigma or embarrassment.

Yet, a Justice Department official has testified that our ability to have anonymous communications in cyberspace poses problems for law enforcement that may generate proposals to restrict our ability to communicate anonymously over the Internet.

Vigilant defense of freedom of thought, opinion, and speech will be crucially important as the Internet graduates from infancy and on to adolescence and maturity. Members of Congress each are sworn custodians of the Constitution during our brief terms in office. We were given a Bill of Rights that has served to protect our rights and speech for more than two centuries. We should provide no less to our children and grandchildren, who are growing up with computers and the Internet. For the Internet to fulfill its promise as a communications medium, we need to give it the full breadth of protection under the First Amendment.

Funeral Oration for Princess Diana

by Ninth Earl Spencer, September 6, 1997

I stand before you today the representative of a family in grief, in a country in mourning before a world in shock.

We are all united not only in our desire to pay our respects to Diana but rather in our need to do so.

For such was her extraordinary appeal that the tens of millions of people taking part in this service all over the world via television and radio who never actually met her, feel that they, too, lost someone close to them in the early hours of Sunday morning. It is a more remarkable tribute to Diana than I can ever hope to offer her today.

Diana was the very essence of compassion, of duty, of style, of beauty. All over the world she was a symbol of selfless humanity, a standard-bearer for the rights of the truly downtrodden, a truly British girl who transcended nationality, someone with a natural nobility who was classless, who proved in the last year that she needed no royal title to continue to generate her particular brand of magic.

Today is our chance to say "thank you" for the way you brightened our lives, even though God granted you but half a life. We will all feel cheated that you were taken from us so young, and yet we must learn to be grateful that you came along at all.

Only now you are gone do we truly appreciate what we are now without and we want you to know that life without you is very, very difficult.

We have all despaired at our loss over the past week and only the strength of the message you gave us through your years of giving has afforded us the strength to move forward.

There is a temptation to rush to canonize your memory. There is no need to do so. You stand tall enough as a human being of unique qualities not to need to be seen as a saint. Indeed to sanctify your memory would be to miss out on the very core of your being, your wonderfully mischievous sense of humor with the laugh that bent you double, your joy for life transmitted wherever you took your smile, and the sparkle in those unforgettable eyes, your boundless energy which you could barely contain.

But your greatest gift was your intuition, and it was a gift you used wisely. This is what underpinned all your wonderful attributes. And if we look to analyze what it was about you that had such a wide appeal, we find it in your instinctive feel for what was really important in all our lives.

Without your God-given sensitivity, we would be immersed in greater ignorance at the anguish of AIDS and HIV sufferers, the plight of the homeless, the isolation of lepers, the random destruction of land mines. Diana explained to me once that it was her innermost feelings of suffering that made it possible for her to connect with her constituency of the rejected.

And here we come to another truth about her. For all the status, the glamour, the applause, Diana remained throughout a very insecure person at heart, almost childlike in her desire to do good for others so she could release herself from deep feelings of unworthiness of which her eating disorders were merely a symptom.

The world sensed this part of her character and cherished her for her vulnerability, whilst admiring her for her honesty. The last time I saw Diana was on July the first, her birthday, in London, when typically she was not taking time to celebrate her special day with friends but was guest of honor at a charity fund-raising evening.

She sparkled of course, but I would rather cherish the days I spent with her in March when she came to visit me and my children in our home in South Africa. I am proud of the fact that apart from when she was on public display meeting President Mandela, we managed to contrive to stop the ever-present paparazzi from getting a single picture of her.

That meant a lot to her.

These are days I will always treasure. It was as if we'd been transported back to our childhood, when we spent such an enormous amount of time together, the two youngest in the family.

Fundamentally she hadn't changed at all from the big sister who mothered me as a baby, fought with me at school and endured those long train journeys between our parents' homes with me at weekends. It is a tribute to her level-headedness and strength that despite the most bizarre life imaginable after her childhood, she remained intact, true to herself.

There is no doubt that she was looking for a new direction in her life at this time. She talked endlessly of getting away from England, mainly because of the treatment she received at the hands of the newspapers.

I don't think she ever understood why her genuinely good intentions were sneered at by the media, why there appeared to be a permanent quest on their behalf to bring her down. It is baffling. My own, and only, explanation is that genuine goodness is threatening to those at the opposite end of the moral spectrum.

It is a point to remember that of all the ironies about Diana, perhaps the greatest is this; that a girl given the name of the ancient goddess of hunting was, in the end, the most hunted person of the modern age.

She would want us today to pledge ourselves to protecting her beloved boys William and Harry from a similar fate. And I do this here, Diana, on your behalf. We will not allow them to suffer the anguish that used regularly to drive you to tearful despair.

Beyond that, on behalf of your mother and sisters, I pledge that we, your blood family, will do all we can to continue the imaginative and loving way in which you were steering these two exceptional young men, so that their souls are not simply immersed by duty and tradition but can sing openly as you planned.

We fully respect the heritage into which they have both been born, and will always respect and encourage them in their royal role. But we, like you, recognize the need for them to experience as many different aspects of life as possible, to arm them spiritually and emotionally for the years ahead. I know you would have expected nothing less from us.

William and Harry, we all care desperately for you today. We are all chewed up with sadness at the loss of a woman who wasn't even our mother. How great your suffering is we cannot even imagine.

I would like to end by thanking God for the small mercies he has shown us at this dreadful time; for taking Diana at her most beautiful and radiant and when she had so much joy in her private life.

Above all, we give thanks for the life of a woman I am so proud to be able to call my sister: the unique, the complex, the extraordinary and irreplaceable Diana, whose beauty, both internal and external, will never be extinguished from our minds.

Terrorism: Theirs and Ours

by Eqbal Ahmad

This presentation was made at the University of Colorado, Boulder, October 12, 1998.

Ahmad, a Pakistani, was a noted teacher, intellectual, historian, and journalist.

In the 1930s and 1940s, the Jewish underground in Palestine was described as "terrorist." Then new things happened.

By 1942, the Holocaust was occurring, and a certain liberal sympathy with the Jewish people had built up in the Western world. At that point, the terrorists of Palestine, who were Zionists, suddenly started to be described, by 1944–45, as "freedom fighters." At least two Israeli Prime Ministers, including Menachem Begin, have actually, you can find in the books and posters with their pictures, saying "Terrorists, Reward This Much." The highest reward I have noted so far was 100,000 British pounds on the head of Menachem Begin, the terrorist.

Then from 1969 to 1990 the PLO, the Palestine Liberation Organization, occupied the center stage as the terrorist organization. Yasir Arafat has been described repeatedly by the great sage of American journalism, William Safire of the *New York Times*, as the "Chief of Terrorism." That's Yasir Arafat.

Now, on September 29, 1998, I was rather amused to notice a picture of Yasir Arafat to the right of President Bill Clinton. To his left is Israeli Prime Minister Benjamin Netanyahu. Clinton is looking towards Arafat and Arafat is looking literally like a meek mouse. Just a few years earlier he used to appear with this very menacing look around him, with a gun appearing menacing from his belt. You remember those pictures, and you remember the next one.

In 1985, President Ronald Reagan received a group of bearded men. These bearded men I was writing about in those days in *The New Yorker*, actually did. They were very ferocious-looking bearded men with turbans looking like they came from another century. President Reagan received them in the White House. After receiving them he spoke to the press. He pointed towards them, I'm sure some of you will recall that moment, and said, "These are the moral equivalent of America's founding fathers." These were the Afghan Mujahiddin. They were at the time, guns in hand, battling the Evil Empire [*President Ronald Reagan's description of the Soviet Union*]. They were the moral equivalent of our founding fathers!

In August 1998, another American President ordered missile strikes from the American navy based in the Indian Ocean to kill Osama Bin Laden and his men in the camps in Afghanistan. I do not wish to embarrass you with the reminder that Mr. Bin Laden, whom fifteen American missiles were fired to hit in Afghanistan, was only a few years ago the moral equivalent of George Washington and Thomas Jefferson! He got angry over the fact that he has been demoted from "moral equivalent" of your "founding fathers." So he is taking out his anger in different ways. I'll come back to that subject more seriously in a moment.

You see, why I have recalled all these stories is to point out to you that the matter of terrorism is rather complicated. Terrorists change. The terrorist of yesterday is the hero of today, and the hero of yesterday becomes the terrorist of today. This is a serious matter of the constantly changing world of images in which we have

to keep our heads straight to know what is terrorism and what is not. But more importantly, to know what causes it, and how to stop it.

The next point about our terrorism is that posture of inconsistency necessarily evades definition. If you are not going to be consistent, you're not going to define. I have examined at least twenty official documents on terrorism. Not one defines the word. All of them explain it, express it emotively, polemically, to arouse our emotions rather than exercise our intelligence. I give you only one example, which is representative. October 25, 1984. George Shultz, then Secretary of State of the U.S., is speaking at the New York Park Avenue Synagogue. It's a long speech on terrorism. In the State Department Bulletin of seven single-spaced pages, there is not a single definition of terrorism. What we get is the following:

> Definition number one: "Terrorism is a modern barbarism that we call terrorism."

> Definition number two is even more brilliant: "Terrorism is a form of political violence." Aren't you surprised? It is a form of political violence, says George Shultz, Secretary of State of the U.S.

> Number three: "Terrorism is a threat to Western civilization."

> Number four: "Terrorism is a menace to Western moral values."

Did you notice, does it tell you anything other than arouse your emotions? This is typical. They don't define terrorism because definitions involve a commitment to analysis, comprehension, and adherence to some norms of consistency. That's the second characteristic of the official literature on terrorism.

The third characteristic is that the absence of definition does not prevent officials from being globalistic. We may not define terrorism, but it is a menace to the moral values of Western civilization. It is a menace also to mankind. It's a menace to good order. Therefore, you must stamp it out worldwide. Our reach has to be global. You need a global reach to kill it. Anti-terrorist policies therefore have to be global. Same speech of George Shultz: "There is no question about our ability to use force where and when it is needed to counter terrorism." There is no geographical limit. On a single day the missiles hit Afghanistan and Sudan. Those two countries are 2,300 miles apart, and they were hit by missiles belonging to a country roughly 8,000 miles away. Reach is global.

A fourth characteristic: claims of power are not only globalist they are also omniscient. We know where they are; therefore we know where to hit. We have the means to know. We have the instruments of knowledge. We are omniscient. Shultz: "We know the difference between terrorists and freedom fighters, and as we look around, we have no trouble telling one from the other." Only Osama Bin Laden doesn't know that he was an ally one day and an enemy another. That's very confusing for Osama Bin Laden. I'll come back to his story towards the end. It's a real story.

Five. The official approach eschews causation. You don't look at causes of anybody becoming terrorist. Cause? What cause? They ask us to be looking, to be sympathetic to these people.

Another example. *The New York Times* December 18, 1985, reported that the foreign minister of Yugoslavia, you remember the days when there was a Yugoslavia, requested the Secretary of State of the U.S. to consider the causes of Palestinian terrorism. The Secretary of State, George Shultz, and I am quoting from *The New York Times*, "went a bit red in the face. He pounded the table and told the visiting foreign minister, there is no connection with any cause. Period." Why look for causes?

Number six. The moral revulsion that we must feel against terrorism is selective. We are to feel the terror of those groups, which are officially disapproved. We are to applaud the terror of those groups of whom officials do approve. Hence, President Reagan, "I am a contra." He actually said that. We know the contras of Nicaragua were anything, by any definition, but terrorists. The media, to move away from the officials, heed the dominant view of terrorism. The dominant approach also excludes from consideration, more importantly to me, the terror of friendly governments. To that question I will return because it excused among others the terror of Pinochet (who killed one of my closest friends) and Orlando Letelier; and it excused the terror of Zia-ul-Haq, who killed many of my friends in Pakistan. All I want to tell you is that according to my ignorant calculations, the ratio of people killed by the state terror of Zia-ul-Haq, Pinochet, Argentinian, Brazilian, Indonesian type, versus the killing of the PLO and other terrorist types is literally, conservatively, one to one hundred thousand. That's the ratio.

History unfortunately recognizes and accords visibility to power and not to weakness. Therefore, visibility has been accorded historically to dominant groups. In our time, the time that began with this day, Columbus Day.

The time that begins with Columbus Day is a time of extraordinary unrecorded holocausts. Great civilizations have been wiped out. The Mayas, the Incas, the Aztecs, the American

Indians, the Canadian Indians were all wiped out. Their voices have not been heard, even to this day, fully. Now they are beginning to be heard, but not fully. They are heard, yes, but only when the dominant power suffers, only when resistance has a semblance of costing, of exacting a price. When a Custer is killed or when a Gordon is besieged. That's when you know that they were Indians fighting, Arabs fighting and dying.

My last point of this section: U.S. policy in the Cold War period has sponsored terrorist regimes one after another. Somoza, Batista, all kinds of tyrants have been America's friends. You know that. There was a reason for that. I or you are not guilty. Nicaragua, contra. Afghanistan, mujahiddin. El Salvador, etc.

Now the second side. You've suffered enough. So suffer more. There ain't much good on the other side either. You shouldn't imagine that I have come to praise the other side. But keep the balance in mind. Keep the imbalance in mind and first ask ourselves, What is terrorism? Our first job should be to define the damn thing, name it, give it a description of some kind, other than "moral equivalent of founding fathers" or "a moral outrage to Western civilization."

I will stay with you with Webster's Collegiate Dictionary: "Terror is an intense, overpowering fear." He uses terrorizing, terrorism, "the use of terrorizing methods of governing or resisting a government." This simple definition has one great virtue, that of fairness. It's fair. It focuses on the use of coercive violence, violence that is used illegally, extra-constitutionally, to coerce. And this definition is correct because it treats terror for what it is, whether the government or private people commit it. Have you noticed something? Motivation is left out of it. We're not talking about whether the cause is

just or unjust. We're talking about consensus, consent, absence of consent, legality, absence of legality, constitutionality, absence of constitutionality. Why do we keep motives out? Because motives differ. Motives differ and make no difference.

• • • • •

Why . . . this flurry of private political terrorism? Why now so much of it and so visible? The answer is modern technology. You have a cause. You can communicate it through radio and television. They will all come swarming if you have taken an aircraft and are holding 150 Americans hostage. They will all hear your cause. You have a modern weapon through which you can shoot a mile away. They can't reach you. And you have the modern means of communicating. When you put together the cause, the instrument of coercion, and the instrument of communication, politics is made. A new kind of politics becomes possible.

To this challenge rulers from one country after another have been responding with traditional methods. The traditional method of shooting it out, whether it's missiles or some other means. The Israelis are very proud of it. The Americans are very proud of it. The French became very proud of it. Now the Pakistanis are very proud of it. The Pakistanis say, "Our commandos are the best." Frankly, it won't work. A central problem of our time are the political minds, rooted in the past, and modern times, producing new realities.

Therefore in conclusion, what is my recommendation to America? Quickly. First, avoid extremes of double standards. If you're going to practice double standards, you will be paid with double standards. Don't use it. Don't condone Israeli terror, Pakistani terror, Nicaraguan terror, El Salvadoran terror, on the one hand,

and then complain about Afghan terror or Palestinian terror. It doesn't work. Try to be even-handed. A superpower cannot promote terror in one place and reasonably expect to discourage terrorism in another place. It won't work in this shrunken world. Do not condone the terror of your allies.

Condemn them. Fight them. Punish them. Please eschew, avoid covert operations and low-intensity warfare. These are breeding grounds of terror and drugs. Violence and drugs are bred there. The structure of covert operations, I've made a film about it, which has been very popular in Europe, called *Dealing with the Demon*. I have shown that wherever covert operations have been, there has been the central drug problem. That has been also the center of the drug trade. Because the structure of covert operations, Afghanistan, Vietnam, Nicaragua, Central America, is very hospitable to drug trade. Avoid it. Give it up. It doesn't help.

Please focus on causes and help ameliorate causes. Try to look at causes and solve problems. Do not concentrate on military solutions. Do not seek military solutions. Terrorism is a political problem. Seek political solutions. Diplomacy works. Take the example of the last attack on Bin Laden. You don't know what you're attacking. They say they know, but they don't know. They were trying to kill Qadaffi. They killed his four-year-old daughter. The poor baby hadn't done anything. Qadaffi is still alive. They tried to kill Saddam Hussein. They killed Laila Bin Attar, a prominent artist, an innocent woman. They tried to kill Bin Laden and his men. Not one but twenty-five other people died. They tried to destroy a chemical factory in Sudan. Now they are admitting that they destroyed an innocent factory, one-half of the production of medicine in Sudan has been

destroyed, not a chemical factory. You don't know. You think you know. Four of your missiles fell in Pakistan. One was slightly damaged. Two were totally damaged. One was totally intact. For ten years the American government has kept an embargo on Pakistan because Pakistan is trying, stupidly, to build nuclear weapons and missiles. So we have a technology embargo on my country. One of the missiles was intact. What do you think a Pakistani official told *The Washington Post*? He said it was a gift from Allah. We wanted U.S. technology. Now we have got the technology, and our scientists are examining this missile very carefully. It fell into the wrong hands. So don't do that. Look for political solutions. Do not look for military solutions. They cause more problems than they solve. Please help reinforce, strengthen the framework of international law. There was a criminal court in Rome. Why didn't they go to it first to get their warrant against Bin Laden, if they have some evidence? Get a warrant, then go after him.

Internationally. Enforce the U.N. Enforce the International Court of Justice, this unilateralism makes us look very stupid and them relatively smaller.

Q&A The question here is that I mentioned that I would go somewhat into the story of Bin Laden, the Saudi in Afghanistan and didn't do so, could I go into some detail? The point about Bin Laden would be roughly the same as the point between Sheikh Abdul Rahman, who was accused and convicted of encouraging the blowing up of the World Trade Center in New York City. *The New Yorker* did a long story on him. It's the same as that of Aimal Kansi, the Pakistani Baluch who was also convicted of the murder of two CIA agents.

Let me see if I can be very short on this. Jihad, which has been translated a thousand times as "holy war," is not quite just that. Jihad is an Arabic word that means, "to struggle." It could be struggle by violence or struggle by non-violent means. There are two forms, the small jihad and the big jihad. The small jihad involves violence. The big jihad involves the struggles with self. Those are the concepts.

The reason I mention it is that in Islamic history, jihad as an international violent phenomenon had disappeared in the last four hundred years, for all practical purposes. It was revived suddenly with American help in the 1980s. When the Soviet Union intervened in Afghanistan, Zia ul-Haq, the military dictator of Pakistan, which borders on Afghanistan, saw an opportunity and launched a jihad there against godless communism. The U.S. saw a God-sent opportunity to mobilize one billion Muslims against what Reagan called the Evil Empire. Money started pouring in. CIA agents starting going all over the Muslim world recruiting people to fight in the great jihad. Bin Laden was one of the early prize recruits. He was not only an Arab. He was also a Saudi. He was not only a Saudi. He was also a multimillionaire, willing to put his own money into the matter. Bin Laden went around recruiting people for the jihad against communism.

I first met him in 1986. He was recommended to me by an American official of whom I do not know whether he was or was not an agent. I was talking to him and said, "Who are the Arabs here who would be very interesting?" By here I meant in Afghanistan and Pakistan He said, "You must meet Osama." I went to see Osama. There he was, rich, bringing in recruits from Algeria, from Sudan, from Egypt, just like Sheikh Abdul Rahman. This fellow was an ally. He remained an ally. He turns at a particular moment.

In 1990 the U.S. goes into Saudi Arabia with forces. Saudi Arabia is the holy place of Muslims, Mecca, and Medina. There had never been foreign troops there. In 1990, during the Gulf War, they went in, in the name of helping Saudi Arabia defeat Saddam Hussein. Osama Bin Laden remained quiet. Saddam was defeated, but the American troops stayed on in the land of the kaba (the sacred site of Islam in Mecca), foreign troops. He wrote letter after letter saying, Why are you here? Get out! You came to help but you have stayed on. Finally he started a jihad against the other occupiers. His mission is to get American troops out of Saudi Arabia.

His earlier mission was to get Russian troops out of Afghanistan. See what I was saying earlier about covert operations? A second point to be made about him is these are tribal people, people who are really tribal. Being a millionaire doesn't matter. Their code of ethics is tribal. The tribal code of ethics consists of two words: loyalty and revenge. You are my friend. You keep your word. I am loyal to you. You break your word, I go on my path of revenge. For him, America has broken its word. The loyal friend has betrayed. The one to whom you swore blood loyalty has betrayed you. They're going to go for you. They're going to do a lot more. These are the chickens of the Afghanistan war coming home to roost. This is why I said to stop covert operations. There is a price attached to those that the American people cannot calculate.

Address on Animal Rights

by Ingrid Newkirk, Co-Founder and President of PETA

This talk was delivered in April, 2001, on Colorado's "Eleventh Hour," a series sponsored by the Public Broadcasting System.

In 1980, a small group of friends started People for the Ethical Treatment of Animals (PETA). Back then, no one had heard of "animal rights." Today, people remain confused as to what the term means, but they DO know that how we treat animals is important. Acknowledging animals' rights can be as simple as respecting their needs. Of course, animals don't need complex rights, like the right to drive or the right to vote—although considering the mess we sometimes make of our elections, perhaps that's not such a bad idea.

Animals enjoy the natural world without ruining it. All they need is to be able to take a drink of clean water, to be nourished, to have shelter from extreme weather, and to be left in peace. It isn't much to ask. Yet, today, few animals have those vital things. The reason they don't have them is because human beings dominate the world and, to put it bluntly, enslave animals. That may sound harsh, but think about it. If allowed to be themselves, animals are self-sufficient, whole, and vital. They raise their own young competently, make a home in the earth, on a riverbank, or in a tree, sharing that small space with at least 40 other species, from raccoons and frogs to birds and insects. Animals don't despoil the waterways or woods, as humans do with our pop top bottles and plastic bags, and, far worse, with the hog and chicken waste from our intensive farming systems. The Alaskan wilderness, which is often described as "uninhabited" and "unspoiled," has, in fact, always been heavily inhabited—by billions of animals who have kept it pristine.

Although animals have wants and needs and behaviors of their own, they are often treated as nothing more than hamburgers, handbags, living test tubes, cheap burglar alarms, or amusements for human beings. They are not allowed to live their lives, but instead are forced to serve us, giving us carriage rides, performing silly tricks, and having their skin used for clothing. We use their flesh as food, despite knowing that we can eat far healthier food, and they are the surrogate tasters of our poisons.

I was inspired to form People for the Ethical Treatment of Animals after reading a book called *Animal Liberation*, written by the philosopher Peter Singer. Dr. Singer suggests that instead of just being just kind to animals, which everyone knows one should be, we might try viewing animals as individuals like ourselves, as members of other cultures or, indeed, other nations—perhaps nations with languages we don't understand, but with rituals and behaviors similar to our own. After all, animals are not inanimate objects; they are feeling beings who experience love and joy, loneliness and fear, in much, if not exactly, the same way we do. Although we have set ourselves up as gods who can do anything we please simply because we please, biologically we are but one animal among many. Many anthropologists believe that we have miscategorized ourselves as a separate class of animal (hominids) out of pure conceit, for now that we have unraveled the human genome, we see that we share 99 percent of our DNA with other primates. When we think about it, perhaps all that keeps us from treating the other animals with respect— the ultimate respect being to leave them in peace to do what they wish to do—is simple prejudice.

Human beings have a sorry history of prejudice. Through the ages, our feelings of superiority have caused us to denigrate and abuse others we have felt were somehow less important or less intelligent than ourselves, instead of exercising magnanimity and protecting them. While we teach our children the Golden Rule of "do unto others as you would have others do unto you," insist that "might does not make right," and pronounce that it is wrong to discriminate on the basis of an arbitrary difference, like race or physical ability, somehow we continue to try to justify hurting, and even killing, other sentient beings, simply because we can get away with it. Our rationale is that they are not exactly like us.

Not that long ago, the philosopher Jeremy Bentham, noting that the French had abolished slavery, yet the British had not, said: "The day may come when the rest of the animal creation may acquire those rights which never could have been withholden from them but by the hand of tyranny. The question is not, Can they reason? Nor, Can they talk? but, Can they suffer?"

The questions for our generation, and for future generations, are: "Who are animals, what are we doing to them, and should we change, no matter how comfortable we may be in our old ways?"

Some members of our own species may have been to the moon, and some can split the atom, but there are many ways in which human talents pale in comparison to the animals'. This is not a competition, of course. We are all in this together. In the same way that establishing women's rights or rights for human minorities does not reduce men or white people, so facing up to our prejudices toward other species does not reduce humans; rather, it allows society to keep growing and expanding its ethical horizons, and individuals to become more compassionate, rather than just being bigger bullies.

There is a lot to respect and admire about animals. Our own military is still learning from dolphins, who use sonar not only to navigate, but also to stun their prey, and from bats who can find their way in total darkness. We cannot decipher animals' languages, but it is indisputable that they have them. Monkeys have separate warnings to alert the troupe to a threat from the sky, such as a hawk, and a threat from the ground, such as a poisonous snake. Prairie dogs use different calls to signal the approach of a single human being, a friend, and a foe. Whales sing their histories through the great oceans, adding new bits of information every year. The tree frog drums his messages to others far away, while other frogs "hear" with their skin. Elephants speak to each other across many miles by using infrasound—powerful, deep rumbles at frequencies too low for us to pick up—and mice also talk at frequencies inaudible to the human ear. Crows are now known not only to play (in St. Petersburg, they have worn the paint off the cathedral windows by sliding down them on their bottoms, just for fun), but to have dialects. Birds from the South of France, for example, can't understand birds of the same species from the North.

Animals use tools and have their own compasses. Ants fashion boats out of leaves with which to cross rivers. Wasps make a home out of a wood and sand mixture, as we make adobe huts. Orangutans in the rain forest, even very young ones, choose the right size leaf to use as an umbrella. Rabbits and beavers construct different rooms for sleeping, for food storage, and for waste. The humble newt can "read" the Earth's pulsating electromagnetic field. While we may whine if we miss a meal or two, the emperor penguin sits for up to 45 days on the ice without an iota of food, guarding the egg that contains his successor. The tiny desert mouse rolls a stone in front of her burrow to collect the dew so she can drink water in the morning before the heat sets in. The turtle navigates by the Earth's magnetic field, and starlings read the heavens for direction. It was an albatross, not a man, who first circumnavigated the globe and knew the Earth was round. As for family values, geese mate for life, and a male will risk hunters' guns to stick by his injured wife when she is shot.

When people say, "But all that is just instinct," I wonder how they think we human beings select our own mates, the people we love. Is it by cold logic? And how do we know to keep clean or to teach our children to walk? Our instincts are an integral part of us, yes, but all of us, from mice to cats, think: the dog who heads excitedly for the door when she sees you putting on your shoes and who relishes every moment of freedom; the bird who, seeing another bird in a bit of a personal dilemma, lends a hand; and the cat mother who enters a blazing home to rescue her kittens from a fire. From the extraordinary to the ordinary, all these acts demonstrate that all animals think, whether in the same exact ways or not.

We have all heard someone referring to criminal conduct say: "So and so behaved like an animal." The Spanish Child Welfare Society offers another perspective on human vs. animal behavior in its television commercial that shows a rhinoceros mother teaching her child how to avoid danger and other mothers instructing their infants on grooming, bathing, and how to choose safe foods. The narrator says, "For once, we're asking you to behave like animals!"

I was working for a humane society when I first started thinking about animals in a different way. I was already familiar with the often-terrible things that happen to dogs and cats and wildlife. People turn dogs and cats out into the countryside to fend for themselves; they also stab, beat, and shoot them and starve them to death on their chains at the far end of the yard. One afternoon, a cruelty call took me to a barn littered with broken glass. A family had moved away, leaving the animals behind. They were all dead except for one small pig. I lifted him up and held him in my arms, then gave him his first drink of water in perhaps a week. Then I bundled him off to the vet.

My job was to prosecute the people who had willfully caused this small animal's suffering, so I made sure that I dutifully collected all the evidence. But while driving home that night, I began to wonder what I could eat for dinner. Ah, I thought, conducting a mental inventory of the contents of my refrigerator, I have some pork chops. The penny dropped! I realized how inconsistent it was of me to be preparing to charge someone with a crime for abusing one little pig while paying someone else to hurt and kill the other little pig I was going to eat for dinner.

I had never been to a slaughterhouse then, but, like most people, I knew that such places must be appalling. Today, I can tell you firsthand about the look in the eyes of the animals. As they are prodded and kicked along to their death, they can smell and hear and see what is already happening to those in front of them in the slaughter line. I have stood on the "kill floors" in slaughterhouses for many different kinds of animals, including a slaughterhouse for dogs in China. In the West, we are appalled by dog-eating, but of course no animals wish to be killed, and all of them, dogs and chickens and pigs, struggle fiercely to avoid the man with the knife. All are equally filled with fear.

It is perhaps awful to say, but the moment of death in the slaughterhouse may be the best part of these animals' lives. I say that because to satisfy the tastes of so many people who crave chicken wings and burgers, animals raised for meat have a truly wretched existence. They are castrated and dehorned, have their tails amputated and their beaks seared off with a hot wire, all without benefit of anesthetics. Calves are separated from their loving mothers soon after birth so that the milk meant for these baby animals can become cheese and ice cream and the calf can be raised for veal. After weeks in darkness, the calves stumble down the same ramp their mothers will walk when their lives are considered insufficiently profitable. Animals on factory farms are crowded together in enormous numbers. Pigs must breathe in the ammonia from their own waste, collected in troughs beneath their pens. They suffer blackened lungs and have difficulty breathing, and their limbs become infected with open sores from lying on the hard cement. Undercover video footage shot by PETA shows pigs routinely clubbed with iron gateposts and beaten to death with claw hammers. The lame are thrown in and out of the trucks, and in bitter winter weather, the pigs' sensitive flesh freezes to the sides of the metal truck body.

"Broiler chickens" are bred to be so top-heavy that the bones in their legs splinter and they spend much of their lives in chronic pain. In the egg factories, chickens can never stretch a wing or find room to lie down. When their laying life is over, they are stuffed into crates so roughly that their wings often fracture. The dying are afforded no care. Sometimes you may pass a transport truck and see them looking out through the slats, their eyes filled with despair. What we do to them is neither "civilized" nor humane.

In 1981, People for the Ethical Treatment of Animals embarked on its first investigation. One of us took a job in a laboratory in Silver Spring, Maryland, where a group of macaque monkeys were kept. The monkeys had been taken as babies from their homes and families in the Philippines. The nerves in their spines had been cut, and this affected their ability to control their arms. The cages in which they were kept were rarely cleaned; in fact, they were so filthy that fecal matter rose to a height of a couple of inches in some places and fungus grew on it. The experimenter didn't bother to give the monkeys food bowls, so when their food was thrown into the cage, the pellets fell through the wire and landed in the waste collection trays below. The monkey would have to pick the food pellets out of these trays in order to eat. The animals' limbs were also injured from getting caught in the rusted and broken cage wires, and the monkeys had lost a great deal of their hair from malnutrition. The researcher had converted a small refrigerator into a shock box; inside it, the monkeys were punished if they failed to pick up objects with their damaged limbs.

We persuaded the police to do something unprecedented: to serve a search warrant on the laboratory and remove the monkeys. Seeing the faces of those monkeys turned up to the sunlight for the first time in many years as they came out of the lab encouraged people to seek alternatives to animal use. Scientists and lay people wondered aloud whether it was morally right to experiment on animals at all and whether, indeed, it was scientifically valid to do so. Some physicians, upset that modern research methods were being neglected in favor of old-fashioned animal-poisoning protocols, began clamoring for funding for human epidemiological studies, the cloning of human skin, and computer technology that can bring quick and directly applicable results.

When PETA started, most cosmetics, toiletries, and household products such as oven cleaner were still tested on animals. Today, more than 550 product companies have switched to using human skin patch tests, computer assays, and human corneas from eye banks, and from gathering guinea pig data to analyzing human data. The arguments that animals must be used faded into oblivion because consumers refused to buy the products until the companies changed.

The current challenge is to shift agencies, like the U.S. Environmental Protection Agency, away from animal use. The most common toxicity tests still in use take a substance, like weed killer or mustard gas, the effects of which we have long known from tragic human experience, and force-feed that substance to rabbits. Researchers poison kittens with it and finally feed it to other primates. No painkillers are given as substances like septic tank cleaner are smeared onto the animals' abraded skin to see how much flesh they corrode, the results being crudely recorded. Chemicals are also placed in animals' eyes and forced into animals' lungs. When enough people protest, this will stop.

Since PETA formed, the role of animals in education, too, has changed. Instead of cutting up frogs and piglets, many schools now use computer programs or human anatomy lessons or take children outdoors to observe animals in their natural setting, without intrusion. It can be inspiring to realize that an animal digs a den without tools, stocks her larder without a supermarket, and can tell what the weather will be by lifting her nose into the wind.

Today, medical students can use the Harvard Program, opting to learn the skills of their profession on a simulator or alongside a skilled practitioner in surgery. Because of lawsuits and protests, students are no longer compelled to violate their ethical beliefs by watching the death throes of a poisoned pig. Models now have lifelike "skin" that breathes, and software programs allow students to start over if they inadvertently "kill" the virtual patient. As PETA's message catches on, more people in all walks of life are beginning to embrace the idea that animals are not disposable tools, but individuals who need protection.

Most people, when shown how their actions contribute to cruelty and given options, will make compassionate choices. In the U.S. alone, while the demand for cheap flesh results in more than 9 billion animals suffering for the table each year—that's 1 million animals eaten every hour—the number of vegetarians is growing rapidly.

I hope that someday there will be no elephants in circuses, kept in shackles, beaten with bull hooks, and denied their family lives and their freedom, all for a human being's few moments of odd enjoyment; that the leg hold trap and the fur farm will be outlawed the world over, as they already have been in England and several other countries; that wonderful natural fibers and synthetics will be chosen over leather; that responsible parents will raise their children not to acquire the meat addictions of my generation, which have brought us heart attacks, cancer, and stroke, as well as causing immense suffering for animals. I hope that all the animal laboratories will have closed down and that it will be illegal to keep any dog on a chain, shivering through the cold weather while the families they long to interact with enjoy the warmth of their homes.

PETA's message is that each one of us is a vital player in life's great orchestra. Every day, our choices perpetuate or stop needless violence. I hope that People for the Ethical Treatment of Animals will continue to be a conduit for positive change, and I ask that you please join us in making the world a less violent place for all living beings. Thank you.

Ultimatum to Saddam Hussein

by President George W. Bush

President Bush delivered this speech on March 17, 2003, from the Cross Hall at the White House.

My fellow citizens, events in Iraq have now reached the final days of decision. For more than a decade, the United States and other nations have pursued patient and honorable efforts to disarm the Iraqi regime without war. That regime pledged to reveal and destroy all its weapons of mass destruction as a condition for ending the Persian Gulf War in 1991.

Since then, the world has engaged in 12 years of diplomacy. We have passed more than a dozen resolutions in the United Nations Security Council. We have sent hundreds of weapons inspectors to oversee the disarmament of Iraq. Our good faith has not been returned.

The Iraqi regime has used diplomacy as a ploy to gain time and advantage. It has uniformly defied Security Council resolutions demanding full disarmament. Over the years, U.N. weapon inspectors have been threatened by Iraqi officials, electronically bugged, and systematically deceived. Peaceful efforts to disarm the Iraqi regime have failed again and again—because we are not dealing with peaceful men.

Intelligence gathered by this and other governments leaves no doubt that the Iraq regime continues to possess and conceal some of the most lethal weapons ever devised. This regime has already used weapons of mass destruction against Iraq's neighbors and against Iraq's people.

The regime has a history of reckless aggression in the Middle East. It has a deep hatred of America and our friends. And it has aided, trained and harbored terrorists, including operatives of al Qaeda.

The danger is clear: using chemical, biological or, one day, nuclear weapons, obtained with the help of Iraq, the terrorists could fulfill their stated ambitions and kill thousands or hundreds of thousands of innocent people in our country, or any other.

The United States and other nations did nothing to deserve or invite this threat. But we will do everything to defeat it. Instead of drifting along toward tragedy, we will set a course toward safety. Before the day of horror can come, before it is too late to act, this danger will be removed.

The United States of America has the sovereign authority to use force in assuring its own national security. That duty falls to me, as Commander-in-Chief, by the oath I have sworn, by the oath I will keep.

Recognizing the threat to our country, the United States Congress voted overwhelmingly last year to support the use of force against Iraq. America tried to work with the United Nations to address this threat because we wanted to resolve the issue peacefully. We believe in the mission of the United Nations. One reason the U.N. was founded after the second world war was to confront aggressive dictators, actively and early, before they can attack the innocent and destroy the peace.

In the case of Iraq, the Security Council did act, in the early 1990s. Under Resolutions 678 and 687—both still in effect—the United States and our allies are authorized to use force in ridding Iraq of weapons of mass destruction.

This is not a question of authority, it is a question of will.

Last September, I went to the U.N. General Assembly and urged the nations of the world to unite and bring an end to this danger. On November 8th, the Security Council unanimously passed Resolution 1441, finding Iraq in material breach of its obligations, and vowing serious consequences if Iraq did not fully and immediately disarm.

Today, no nation can possibly claim that Iraq has disarmed. And it will not disarm so long as Saddam Hussein holds power. For the last four-and-a-half months, the United States and our allies have worked within the Security Council to enforce that Council's long-standing demands. Yet, some permanent members of the Security Council have publicly announced they will veto any resolution that compels the disarmament of Iraq. These governments share our assessment of the danger, but not our resolve to meet it. Many nations, however, do have the resolve and fortitude to act against this threat to peace, and a broad coalition is now gathering to enforce the just demands of the world. The United Nations Security Council has not lived up to its responsibilities, so we will rise to ours.

In recent days, some governments in the Middle East have been doing their part. They have delivered public and private messages urging the dictator to leave Iraq, so that disarmament can proceed peacefully. He has thus far refused. All the decades of deceit and cruelty have now reached an end. Saddam Hussein and his sons must leave Iraq within 48 hours. Their refusal to do so will result in military conflict, commenced at a time of our choosing. For their own safety, all foreign nationals—including journalists and inspectors—should leave Iraq immediately.

Many Iraqis can hear me tonight in a translated radio broadcast, and I have a message for them. If we must begin a military campaign, it will be directed against the lawless men who rule your country and not against you. As our coalition takes away their power, we will deliver the food and medicine you need. We will tear down the apparatus of terror and we will help you to build a new Iraq that is prosperous and free. In a free Iraq, there will be no more wars of aggression against your neighbors, no more poison factories, no more executions of dissidents, no more torture chambers and rape rooms. The tyrant will soon be gone. The day of your liberation is near.

It is too late for Saddam Hussein to remain in power. It is not too late for the Iraqi military to act with honor and protect your country by permitting the peaceful entry of coalition forces to eliminate weapons of mass destruction. Our forces will give Iraqi military units clear instructions on actions they can take to avoid being attacked and destroyed. I urge every member of the Iraqi military and intelligence services, if war comes, do not fight for a dying regime that is not worth your own life.

And all Iraqi military and civilian personnel should listen carefully to this warning. In any conflict, your fate will depend on your action. Do not destroy oil wells, a source of wealth that belongs to the Iraqi people. Do not obey any command to use weapons of mass destruction against anyone, including the Iraqi people. War crimes will be prosecuted. War criminals will be punished. And it will be no defense to say, "I was just following orders."

Should Saddam Hussein choose confrontation, the American people can know that every measure has been taken to avoid war, and every measure will be taken to win it. Americans understand the costs of conflict because we have paid them in the past. War has no certainty, except the certainty of sacrifice.

Yet, the only way to reduce the harm and duration of war is to apply the full force and might of our military, and we are prepared to do so. If Saddam Hussein attempts to cling to power, he will remain a deadly foe until the end. In desperation, he and terrorists groups might try to conduct terrorist operations against the American people and our friends. These attacks are not inevitable. They are, however, possible. And this very fact underscores the reason we cannot live under the threat of blackmail. The terrorist threat to America and the world will be diminished the moment that Saddam Hussein is disarmed.

Our government is on heightened watch against these dangers. Just as we are preparing to ensure victory in Iraq, we are taking further actions to protect our homeland. In recent days, American authorities have expelled from the country certain individuals with ties to Iraqi intelligence services. Among other measures, I have directed additional security of our airports, and increased Coast Guard patrols of major seaports. The Department of Homeland Security is working closely with the nation's governors to increase armed security at critical facilities across America.

Should enemies strike our country, they would be attempting to shift our attention with panic and weaken our morale with fear. In this, they would fail. No act of theirs can alter the course or shake the resolve of this country. We are a peaceful people—yet we're not a fragile people, and we will not be intimidated by thugs and killers. If our enemies dare to strike us, they and all who have aided them, will face fearful consequences.

We are now acting because the risks of inaction would be far greater. In one year, or five years, the power of Iraq to inflict harm on all free nations would be multiplied many times over. With these capabilities, Saddam Hussein and his terrorist allies could choose the moment of deadly conflict when they are strongest. We choose to meet that threat now, where it arises, before it can appear suddenly in our skies and cities.

The cause of peace requires all free nations to recognize new and undeniable realities. In the 20th century, some chose to appease murderous dictators, whose threats were allowed to grow into genocide and global war. In this century, when evil men plot chemical, biological and nuclear terror, a policy of appeasement could bring destruction of a kind never before seen on this earth.

Terrorists and terror states do not reveal these threats with fair notice, in formal declarations—and responding to such enemies only after they have struck first is not self-defense, it is suicide. The security of the world requires disarming Saddam Hussein now.

As we enforce the just demands of the world, we will also honor the deepest commitments of our country. Unlike Saddam Hussein, we believe the Iraqi people are deserving and capable of human liberty. And when the dictator has departed, they can set an example to all the Middle East of a vital and peaceful and self-governing nation.

The United States, with other countries, will work to advance liberty and peace in that region. Our goal will not be achieved overnight, but it can come over time. The power and appeal of human liberty is felt in every life and every land. And the greatest power of freedom is to overcome hatred and violence, and turn the creative gifts of men and women to the pursuits of peace.

That is the future we choose. Free nations have a duty to defend our people by uniting against the violent. And tonight, as we have done before, America and our allies accept that responsibility.

Good night, and may God continue to bless America.

Glossary

Acceptance speech A speech given in response to a formal nomination to office that is designed to establish the nominee as a competent leader in the minds of supporters and voters. May also refer to a speech given in response to the formal presentation of an award or gift that is designed to express sincere appreciation for the honor.

Action The last step of the Motivated Sequence method of organizing speeches in which the speaker clearly and directly states what response is desired from the audience.

Adaptable The ability of a speech to fit the needs of the occasion and the audience very closely with the intended message of the speaker.

Affirmative The team or speaker in a debate who supports the topic under discussion.

After-dinner speaking A speech presented at the end of a meal that may have a serious purpose or be designed primarily for entertainment.

Amendment A change in a bill or motion that adds to or deletes information.

Analogy A comparison between two things. A literal analogy compares similar things, such as two boats. A figurative analogy compares things that function similarly but are not actually the same, such as comparing a computer to the human brain.

Analysis of the audience This process involves learning as much as possible about your listeners either by inferring basic information about their demographics, interests, and attitudes, or by doing a formal survey of them. This information is used to tailor the message more specifically to their needs.

Anecdote A short story or recalling of an incident, usually humorous.

Anniversary speech The purpose of this speech is to recall events of the past and to relate their importance to the present while indicating how they might serve as guides for the future.

Attention The first step of the Motivated Sequence method of organizing speeches in which the speaker captures the focus and imagination of the listeners.

Audience The group of listeners in any public speaking situation who make the communication transaction with the speaker complete.

Auditory appeals Persuasive messages designed to be attractive to the human sense of hearing.

Background data General information about a company or person that gives the reader or interviewer a sense of the communication context for the interview. This could include information on the history of the company, what they produce and how they produce it, the management structure, career history of the interviewee, and so forth.

Bodily actions See "Body language."

Body language A type of nonverbal communication that involves use of the body such as gestures, posture, or movement.

Captive audience A group of listeners in a public speaking setting who are not in attendance first and foremost for the pleasure of hearing the speaker, but are rather in attendance due to other requirements.

Character studies The presentation of significant events in a person's life in terms of how the person responded to the events and how those events shaped who they became and what they valued; usually used in a speech of tribute.

Chronological Following an ordered pattern based on the flow of time; for example, from past to present to future.

Clarifying Active listening technique of asking questions that invite the speaker to offer more specific information about statements being made, examples to illustrate the intended meaning, or definitions of terms and ideas.

Codes Symbols, commonly agreed upon, used to express the thoughts, feelings, and meanings between people of a community; may be verbal or nonverbal.

Commemoration To honor, remember, or recognize with a formal observation.

Commemorative To have the nature of a commemoration.

Commencement address Speech presented in honor of graduates at a commencement ceremony.

Commentary A subjective analysis of one side or aspect of a controversial topic, presented in a mass media setting.

Common values Identification of particular values held in mutual regard by the speaker and the audience.

Communication Intentional or unintentional words, actions, or symbols that others interpret.

Communication apprehension The natural nervousness that occurs when communicating with others, usually in a public setting; commonly called "stage fright."

Conclusion The last part of a speech, which summarizes and emphasizes the speaker's main ideas.

Confidence In public speaking, this refers to the attitude of the speaker that springs from being well prepared and well rehearsed, and inspires the audience to assign credibility to the speaker in return.

Constructive speech The first speech given by a speaker in a debate, which presents or builds a case for acceptance or rejection of a topic.

Context The environment in which a communication transaction takes place, which has varying degrees of influence on the exchange of meanings.

Controversy See "Debatable proposition."

Conversationality The ability to make a well-planned public presentation flow at a rate and natural quality found in regular interpersonal conversation.

Convince To persuade.

Cooperative effort This is achieved when members of a group are successfully able to divide, combine, and present information together as a group.

Counterarguments Arguments made in response to original arguments, usually presenting an opposing viewpoint.

Credibility The quality or qualities of a speaker or of sources of information that an audience perceives as trustworthy, competent, and dynamic.

Criticisms Feedback designed to benefit the communicator by helping the speaker understand how his or her messages are being perceived by others.

Cross-examine In a debate, this is the process of asking the speaker questions to gain additional information and to clarify what the speaker said.

Debatable proposition A proposal that has at least two clearly distinguishable (and often opposing) points of view in which the speakers have an interest; a controversy.

Debate A contest in which the affirmative and negative sides of a proposition are advocated by opposing speakers.

Decoding The process of interpreting a message.

Dedication speech A speech of commemoration, usually part of a ceremony.

Demonstration This speech features the physical display and assembly of steps in a process while explaining each along the way.

Dialogue Conversation between two or more individuals.

Disadvantages In debate, these are problems showing that a team's position is unworkable and undesirable.

Dramatic story line The narrative or "plot" of a broadcast or film production.

Dynamic The quality of a speaker's presentation style that indicates enthusiasm for the message and a confident delivery.

Elements of composition The various aspects that combine to form the substance of a work of art; in film, for example, these would include acting, scriptwriting, costumes and makeup, set design, and so on.

Emotion The feelings, or passions, of audience members.

Encoding The process of constructing a message.

Entertain To capture and hold the attention and imagination of the audience.

Ethics Moral principles or values that guide the communicator in choosing and presenting ideas and materials to an audience.

Eulogy A speech of praise that is delivered in honor or commemoration of someone living or dead.

Evidence Materials offered to listeners in support of claims, including examples, testimony, statistics, visual aids, and so forth.

Extemporaneous A speech given with an outline or a few notes.

Eye contact To maintain connection with members of an audience by looking individuals in the eye while delivering a public address.

Facilitator One whose function in a group discussion is primarily to keep the conversation flowing and focused on the announced topic.

Farewell speech Formal remarks given in recognition of one's imminent departure.

Felicitations Remarks designed to create feelings of happiness and goodwill.

Fields of experience In the transactional model of communication, this refers to the sum of personal experiences each communicator brings to the communication exchange that influences the individual's perceptions of, and responses to, the communication process.

Formal review A critique of a book, film, or other artistic endeavor that has been well prepared through clarity of purpose, thorough research, clear organization, and thoughtful language choices.

Forum The exchange of questions and answers between a speaker and an audience.

Fundamentals of preparation See chapters two through five in Unit One.

Genre A kind, or type, as in works of literature, art, and so on.

Genuineness Sincerity.

Gestures Arm and hand movements used to illustrate a spoken message.

Goodwill An attitude reflecting the belief that the speaker is charitable toward the audience; the view that the speaker has the audience's best interests at heart.

Harm In debate, this is the problem which requires the proposed solution.

Homage Showing respect for the worth of another person.

Humor The art or skill of the speaker to evoke laughter in an audience.

Impromptu A speech given with little or no advance preparation.

Incidental motions In parliamentary procedure, these motions are neither privileged nor subsidiary, but may be required in the course of the proceedings. They have no precedence of order as the other categories of motions do.

Inform To instruct; to provide information.

Inherency In debate, this refers to any quality of the present system that prevents or inhibits the problem from being resolved.

Internal summaries Brief restatements of key thoughts covered in significant sections of the speech, usually provided to the audience before moving on to another substantial segment of the speech.

Interview A conversation between two or more people characterized by one party in particular being asked questions by the other(s) for the purposes of gaining information and clarification.

Introduction The beginning of a speech, which should get the audience's attention, give them a reason to listen, and introduce the topic.

Introductory statement An opening statement of a speech that captures the essential purposes of a full introduction: getting the audience's attention, stating your topic and showing enthusiasm for it.

Keynote Usually the first address at a conference, convention, or meeting that identifies key issues participants will address and generates enthusiasm for the work.

Lecture forum An informative speech followed by a period of questions from the audience.

Logic The use of careful reasoning that follows the formulas of standard classical critical thinking patterns such as deduction, induction, and reasoning by analogy.

Manuscript A complete text of a speech that is used as speaking notes.

Messages Meaningful information exchanged between two communicators.

Mood In public speaking, this refers to the emotional environment in a speech setting as well as the emotional context of the topic and the speaker's delivery.

Motion A formal proposal for action or change to be debated by selected speakers or by a group.

Motivated Sequence A five-point strategy of organization developed by Alan Monroe. The steps are Attention, Need, Satisfaction, Visualization, and Action.

Multivoiced Using several voices to communicate a single message; usually refers to radio or television productions.

Need The second step in the Motivated Sequence method of organizing speeches in which the problem, or need for the plan, is fully discussed.

Negative The team or person in a debate who opposes or disagrees with the resolution under discussion.

Noise Interference of any kind that makes a communication transaction unsuccessful.

Nominating speech This speech places the name of a candidate for office before the audience and offers reasons why voters should support that candidate.

Nonverbal communication Any message not involving words such as gestures, tone of voice, facial expressions, or symbols.

Oral book review A critique of a book presented in a speech format.

Oral interpretation A spoken presentation of a written work emphasizing the emotional content of the piece as understood by the speaker.

Order of business The sequence of topics to be addressed by a decision-making body.

Organizational method A general model for coordinating main ideas and supporting materials in a way that can be easily followed or anticipated by an audience.

Outline The main features of a speech usually presented in sentences, phrases, or single words.

Panel discussion A group of people trying to solve a problem through discussion.

Pantomime A performance using only body language to tell a story.

Paraphrasing Taking someone else's thoughts and putting them into your own words as a way of summarizing them.

Parliamentary procedure A recognized procedure for conducting a business meeting in an orderly manner.

Persuasion The process of influencing another to change, modify, or adopt an attitude or behavior.

Pet peeve Something that upsets or disturbs you or causes you to react negatively.

Plagiarize To take someone else's work and represent it as your own.

Plan In debate, this refers to the proposed solution offered by a debate team to resolve the problem being debated.

Poise To maintain a calm, steady, gracious, and assured manner.

Portfolio A collection of works produced by the student, designed to illustrate the student's abilities and show the levels of accomplishment in development of communication skills.

Posture The position of your body.

Precedence of motions The established order of priority of parliamentary motions in relation to other possible motions that may be made.

Preparation The process of planning and rehearsing the speech before the delivery of it in front of an audience.

Preparation time In contest speaking, this is a strictly limited amount of time allowed for the collection and organization of materials into presentation-ready format.

Presentation speech A speech (usually brief) made in honor of a recipient that highlights the purpose of the award, its history and meaning, and the traits of the recipient that qualify that person to receive the award.

Problem-solving The process of discussion, coordination of ideas, and development of agreement on ways to resolve a problematic situation.

Proofreading The careful scrutiny of a written document, paying especially close attention to grammar, spelling, punctuation, and word choice.

Proposition A topic for group discussion, sometime phrased in the form of a question.

Purpose The goal of a presentation, or what the speaker hopes to accomplish by making the presentation.

Rebuttal speech The second speech given by a debater, which responds to the opponent's arguments.

Recapitulation Restating a point or points.

Redundancy The repetition of the same ideas or word choices in the same speech.

Rephrase In a forum, this refers to the occasion when the speaker restates, condenses, or summarizes the meaning of an audience member's question before attempting to answer it.

Sales The use of communication to persuade consumers to purchase goods or services.

Salutation The expression of a courteous greeting in a speech, letter, or ceremony.

Satisfaction The third step in the Motivated Sequence method of organizing speeches in which the solution to the problem presented earlier is discussed.

Self-disclosure The act of revealing personal information about yourself that would otherwise remain unknown to listeners.

Signposts Verbal signals within a speech that indicate a sequence of ideas to the audience. For example, "First, . . ." "Second, . . ." or "Next, . . ." etc.

Simile When two unlike things are compared using such words as *like* or *as* to make the comparison, e.g. "He's as sharp as a tack."

Sources of information Credible, professional, authoritative origins of facts, statistics, examples, quotations, and other materials used to develop a speech, e.g. national news publications or broadcasts, books, and personal interviews with experts on the topic.

Stage fright (speech anxiety) See "Communication Apprehension."

Stock issues The major requirements or issues an affirmative team must include in a constructive speech.

Succinct Using few words; concise.

Summarizing statement A single statement that serves the basic function of putting the speaker's previously spoken ideas in a brief form for review.

Symposium A presentation involving several speakers, each of whom discusses a different aspect of a problem.

Thesis The major idea being discussed in a speech.

Toastmaster The person who presides at a dinner and who is responsible for introducing guests, speakers, and programs.

Transitions A connecting statement between two main ideas or sections of a speech, usually created by referring to the previously discussed idea and previewing the next idea to be discussed in the same sentence.

Tribute See "Eulogy."

Univocal Using only one voice.

Variety A wide range of different approaches or options.

Verbal communication A message that relies on the use of words, either spoken or written.

Visual aids Photos, objects, models, transparencies, videos, and other means of assisting the audience to literally see what the speaker is talking about.

Visualization The fourth step in the Motivated Sequence method of organizing speeches in which the speaker uses vivid imagery to help an audience imagine what the world would be like if the speaker's proposal is enacted (may also be used to help listeners imagine what could happen if the speaker's proposal is not enacted).

Vocal qualities The various aspects of vocal delivery such as tone, rate, pitch, volume, and attractiveness of the voice.

Index

Credits

Continued